Third Edition

Computers in Education

Paul F. Merrill
Brigham Young University

Kathy Hammons
Saint Mary's College of California

Bret R Vincent
International Business Machines (IBM)

Peter L. Reynolds
Higher Education Library Publishers

Larry Christensen
Brigham Young University

Marvin N. Tolman
Brigham Young University

Allyn and Bacon
Boston • London • Toronto • Sydney • Tokyo • Singapore

Editor-in-Chief, Education: Nancy Forsyth
Editorial Assistant: Kate Wagstaffe
Senior Marketing Manager: Kathy Hunter
Production Administrator: Annette Joseph
Production Coordinator: Susan Freese
Editorial-Production Service: Lynda Griffiths
Composition Buyer: Linda Cox
Manufacturing Buyer: Megan Cochran
Cover Administrator: Linda Knowles
Cover Designer: Suzanne Harbison

Many of the designations used by manufacturers and sellers to distinguish their products are claimed as trademarks. Where those designations appear in this book and Allyn and Bacon was aware of a trademark claim, the designations have been printed in caps or initial caps.

Library of Congress Cataloging-in-Publication Data

Computers in education / Paul F. Merrill... [et al.]. — 3rd ed.
    p. cm.
    Includes bibliographical references and indexes.
    ISBN 0-205-18517-7
    1. Education—Data processing.   2. Computer literacy.
  I. Merrill, Paul F.
LB1028.43.C646 1995 1996
370'.28'5—dc20   95-22603
                                CIP

Printed in the United States of America

10 9 8 7 6 5   00 99

Figure Credits:

Figures 1–1, 2–1d–f, 2–5, 2–8, 2–14—Courtesy of International Business Machines Corporation. Figure 1–2—Courtesy of Hillview Elementary School, Salt Lake City, Utah. Figures 2–1a–c, 2–6, 2–19, 4–2, 7–14, 8–11, 11–3, 11–4—Courtesy of Apple Computer, Inc. Photographers Frank Pryor (2–1a, 2–6) and John Greenleigh (2–1b, 2–1c). Figure 2–1g—Courtesy of Cray Research, Inc.

(Figure Credits continued on p. 386)

Contents

Preface

The purpose of the third edition of this book remains essentially the same as that of the first and second editions: to help teachers use computer technology to increase the efficiency and effectiveness of the educational process. However, the application of computer technology in the schools has changed dramatically since the publication of the second edition. These changes, along with feedback from those who have adopted the book, have led to many significant revisions in this third edition. The basic framework of the book remains the same, however. We will continue to use the threefold taxonomy proposed by Taylor (1980) of *tutor, tool,* and *tutee* in order to provide some organization to the myriad of possible applications of computers in education. Each of these types of computer applications will be examined in terms of its relationship to specific learning outcomes.

The book is divided into five major sections. The introductory section consists of the first three chapters, which describe the potential impact of computers in education, computer hardware, and the history of computers in education. The first chapter immediately introduces several divergent examples of how computer technology is making a difference in today's classrooms. These examples are followed by a summary of research findings related to the impact of computer technology on learning outcomes. The chapter concludes by providing an explanation of the tutor, tool, and tutee organizational framework for understanding the many types of applications that will be discussed in detail in the remainder of the book. Chapter 2 has been updated to include descriptions of many of the new types of computers and peripheral devices that have been introduced since the second edition.

The second section contains three chapters. Chapters 4 and 5 detail the tutor applications of drill and practice, tutorials, problem solving, simulations, and games. These chapters describe the advantages and disadvantages of each application, outline the characteristics of effective versus ineffective programs, and describe how the applications may be integrated into the classroom. Each of these chapters has been updated to reflect examples of new software programs. Chapter 6 presents several criteria and techniques for evaluating tutor software programs.

The third section includes four chapters, Chapters 7 through 10, that outline the applications of the computer as a tool. These chapters support the much greater emphasis placed on tool applications in the schools since the previous editions. Chapter 7 discusses a broad range of tool applications—such as word processing, database management, spreadsheets, graphics, desktop publishing, and desktop presentations—that are used to help administrators, teachers, and students organize and share information and ideas with others. This chapter has been substantially revised to place greater focus on the use of integrated tool programs such as *ClarisWorks* and *Microsoft Works*. Chapters 8 and 9 are completely new chapters that have been added to this edition to emphasize the exciting applications of multimedia/hypermedia and networks and telecommunication in the schools. Chapter 10 introduces computer-managed instruction applications. Computer tools can ease the administrative and clerical burdens of principals and teachers. However, this section emphasizes the use of computer tools by students to help them develop higher-order thinking and problem-solving skills.

The fourth section, Chapter 11, focuses on the application of the computer as a tutee. Here, the computer takes the role of learner while the student assumes the role of teacher. Through the use of computer programming languages, the student is able to teach the computer how to perform complex tasks. This chapter has been substantially revised from the second edition. It presents a rationale for teaching programming in the schools and then introduces the main constructs or ideas found in almost all programming languages, using examples from Logo, BASIC, and Pascal. The final part of this chapter, which is totally new, presents an extensive introduction to multimedia/hypermedia authoring systems. It is recommended that this chapter be supplemented with other materials related to a specific high-level language or authoring system to help students gain actual programming or authoring skills.

The final section includes five chapters, Chapters 12 through 16, designed to help teachers and administrators integrate computer hardware and software into the school and curriculum. Chapter 12 is devoted to integration in the reading and language arts curriculum, and Chapter 13 focuses on integration in the social science, science, and mathematics curricula. Chapter 14 is totally new to this edition and reflects the importance of integrating computer applications into the curriculum of the classroom to help meet the diverse needs of all students. Chapter 15 focuses on many of the current and future issues in educational computing. The final chapter presents a rich array of additional resources that educators may draw upon to further increase their knowledge and skills related to the integration of computers in education.

The authors would like to acknowledge the suggestions of the reviewers of the second edition: Robert L. Friedli, Boise State University; Cathy Gunn, Northern Arizona University; and Paul Jones, Townson State University. We would also like to thank the many instructors who have used the previous editions to help preservice teachers learn how to use this exciting technology in the schools. Finally, we gratefully acknowledge the help of Tim Smith, who reviewed many of the chapters in this edition and provided many valuable insights.

Reference

Taylor, R. P. (Ed.). (1980). *The computer in the school: Tutor, tool, tutee.* New York: Teachers College Press.

Chapter 1

The Impact of Computers in Education

Computer technology has a significant impact on almost every aspect of our lives. It is hard to imagine an organization, whether large or small, that does not or could not advantageously use a computer in its operations. What would it be like to call a travel agent and try to get an airline reservation without a computer-based reservation system? Where would the banks and credit card systems be without computers? (Some of us might not be so far in debt!) Advertisers love computers. They send us personalized form letters telling us how much money we can win, or they have the computer call us on the telephone during dinner time and try to sell us the latest gadget. Just think of all the mail we would miss without computer-based mailing lists. We can even use a computer to place our own order at our favorite fast-food restaurant. At the grocery store, bar-code scanners attached to computers allow us to move through the checkout stands more rapidly, our receipt contains an itemized list of our purchases, errors are reduced, and the store manager has greater inventory control. When we go to a football game, a computer is used to control the animated scoreboard. At a rock concert, we are entertained by computer-synthesized music. The ignition system and instrument panel in our cars are controlled by computers. The microwave oven and dishwasher in our homes contain computer chips. Many of us own personal computers to balance our checkbooks, keep Christmas card address lists, type personal letters, send E-mail messages to our senators, write school reports, and even play arcade games. Not even our churches are exempt. The minister keeps track of the parish membership, searches for a verse in the Bible, and writes next week's sermon—all using a personal computer.

But what about the schools? Some educators are making fairly extravagant claims that computers are the solution to many of our educational problems. Others feel that they are a fad and will have no more impact than other technologies such as radio, film, or television. This book will introduce you to a wide variety of ways in which computers are being used in the schools. It will then be up to you to judge whether they are a solution or a fad. Admittedly, the presentation will be biased toward the benefits of using computers in the schools. However, computers are not a panacea for all the problems of education, nor will they replace teachers. Nonetheless, computers are here to stay and they will play a significant role in the classrooms of today and tomorrow.

The next section of this chapter will present several specific examples of innovative applications of computer technology in the schools. These examples will demonstrate the potential applications of computer technology in the schools and provide the motivation for a more in-depth study. Also, the results of some research studies that indicate the impact of computer-based instruction on student learning are discussed. Finally, a classification framework is introduced to help you organize the many different possible applications of computers in the schools. This framework will serve as the basis for a more detailed discussion of each type of application in subsequent chapters.

Example Applications

Writing to Read

The Kettering City Schools in Ohio (Leahy, 1989) have significantly increased the writing and reading skills of their primary-grade students through the implementation of a computer-based program called *Writing to Read*. The *Writing to Read* system is based on the idea that children should learn to write before they learn to read by using a phonemic spelling system to encode the sounds and words that they say into written letters and words. Children are taught to write what they can speak and to read what they write.

Each elementary school participating in the program has converted a classroom into a Writing to Read Center (see Figure 1–1). Kindergarten and first-grade students and their teachers spend an hour a day in the center. The center consists of six learning stations: the computer station, the writing/typing station, the listening library station, the work journal station, the multisensory materials station, and the "make-words" station.

1. *The computer station* contains three or four microcomputers with audio capability where students spend 12 to 15 minutes each day listening to words and sounds and then speaking the words and sounds and typing the letters that make up the sounds and words. The instruction provided by the microcomputers is divided into 10 units, or cycles. Each cycle covers one group of phonemes and is divided into five lessons. After completing a session at the computer station, students may move to one of the other stations to use and practice what they have learned.

2. At the *writing/typing station,* made up of six to eight typewriters or microcomputers with a word-processing program, students type the words they have learned from today's or previous computer lessons. In the beginning, they type one word per line. Soon, they use their own words and write simple sentences. In due time, they write longer sentences and short stories (Martin & Friedberg, 1986).

FIGURE 1–1   Writing to Read Center

3. At the *listening library station,* children put on earphones to listen to cassette recordings of their favorite stories. As they listen, they use their fingers to follow along the printed words of the story in a book. They love to listen to the stories repeatedly. In time, they begin to match the spoken word with the written word.

4. Using soft-lead pencils, children practice writing letters and words they have learned at the *work journal station.* They record their work in notebooks or journals guided by instructions provided through headphones and cassette tape recordings.

5. The *multisensory materials station* provides additional opportunities to use the sense of touch to reinforce the relationship between sounds and letters. Here, the children make words and letters using strings of clay, magnetic letters, chalk, and slates, or they trace letters in sand.

6. At the *"make-words" station,* the students use wooden block letters, letter cards, and the like to play word games. The children work in pairs at this and each of the other stations.

Back in the regular classroom, teachers reinforce the activities of the Writing to Read Center by reading to the children, allowing them to share their stories with each other, encouraging them to read books, and scheduling time for writing activities. Parental involvement is also fostered.

Currently, more than 100,000 children are learning to write and read using the *Writing to Read* system. Many studies (Brierley, 1987; Leahy, 1989; Levinson & Lalor, 1989; Spillman & Lutz, 1986; Stevenson, 1988) have been conducted to validate the effectiveness of the program. Between 1982 and 1984, the Educational Testing Service (ETS) tested the program in 105 schools across the country. They found that on the average, *Writing to Read* kindergarten students scored 15 percentile points higher on standardized reading tests than did control-group students (Martin & Friedberg, 1986).

However, the *Writing to Read* program is not without its detractors. Slavin (1990) summarized several multiyear studies that show that even though *Writing to Read* seems to have positive effects in kindergarten, those effects appear to drop out by the end of the first and second grades. He also suggested that the positive effects in kindergarten may be explained by the fact that the control groups used in the validation studies received no reading or writing instruction at all.

Nevertheless, subsequent studies continue to obtain positive results. For example, a follow-up study of a three-year implementation of *Writing to Read* in 55 rural Appalachian schools (serving approximately 7,000 kindergarten and first-grade students) showed that students who had participated in *Writing to Read* performed significantly better on writing and spelling than students who had not (Childers & Leopold, 1993). Similar positive results were found in a study involving 29 kindergarten and first-grade classrooms from 6 California school districts (Casey, 1994). Unfortunately, neither of these studies provides detailed information about the alternate instruction received by the control groups. Further research needs to be conducted comparing *Writing to Read* to other early intervention alternatives.

Computers and Digital Model Trains

At Hill View Elementary School of the Granite School District in Salt Lake City, Utah, 20 microcomputers are connected in a network to an electronically controlled model train set. The train track has been mounted on a large 8' × 16' piece of plywood in a scaled model layout of a proposed light-rail transportation system for the Salt Lake Valley. The realism of the layout has been enhanced through the use of scale models of the state capitol, office buildings, trees, streets, and automobiles (see Figure 1–2).

Up to 80 trains moving in different directions and speeds can be controlled by several students at the same time on a common track. A large number of accessory devices, such as lights, signals, track switches, and car uncoupling devices, can also be controlled. The students control the trains and accessory devices by instructing the computers to send numeric commands to the train set. Each command is composed of two

FIGURE 1–2   Computer-Controlled Digital-Train Layout

numbers separated by a comma. The first number specifies which locomotive or device is to receive the command, and the second number specifies the action to be taken. For example, the number sequence 8,6 would instruct the eighth locomotive to move at a medium speed. Because the trains are controlled by numbers, or digits, they are referred to as *digital* trains. Embedded track sensors also send digital information back to the computers, indicating the position and direction of each locomotive (Catherall, 1988).

This digital model train layout provides a realistic and concrete setting in which students of all ages can see the relevance of the subjects they are learning in school. Math students can use the train as a concrete model for story problems related to distance and speed; science students can conduct experiments on acceleration and centrifugal force; history students can see the relationship between the growth of cities and train routes. Teachers of kindergarten through second grade can use the train set to teach about transportation systems and community building. Writing computer programs to control the trains brings a new excitement and relevance for computer science students. After a field trip to a modern factory where computer-controlled robots are used on the assembly line, students can learn how to solve problems related to robotic devices using their own robotic trains (Catherall, 1990).

Computer-controlled digital trains are also being used in electrical engineering and computer science curriculums at several universities, including the University of

Colorado, Georgia Institute of Technology, and the United States Military Academy. The model trains are used to help teach real-time control systems, stack operations, and collision avoidance. The trains provide a physical model for otherwise abstract concepts and introduce an element of fun and excitement into the classroom (Goda, Wise, McConkey, & Loy, 1994).

Computer-Based Manipulatives

Many teachers have found that the use of physical objects that children can touch and feel, pick up, hold in their hands, turn, arrange in different patterns, or otherwise manipulate are a valuable aid in helping children move from concrete to abstract ideas. These physical objects are often referred to as *manipulatives* and include children's blocks of various sizes, shapes, and colors, Erector sets, LEGO snap-together blocks, measuring cups, coins, Cuisenaire rods, base-10 blocks, algebra tiles, geoboards, and the like. Several research studies have shown that manipulatives are especially valuable in learning mathematics. In summarizing the research, Suydam (1985) concluded, "The use of manipulative materials in mathematics instruction results in increased achievement across a variety of topics at every grade level from kindergarten through grade 8, at every achievement level, and at every ability level" (p. 2).

Perl (1990) reported that computer software that simulates the use of manipulatives can provide a valuable link, or transition, from concrete, physical manipulatives to the abstract or symbolic representation of an idea. For example, in the classroom, children can play games using attribute blocks of four different shapes, each shape containing blocks in two different sizes and three different colors. In one game, the children can be asked to assemble a "train" of blocks such that adjacent blocks differ by only one attribute. A large yellow circle can be placed next to a large yellow square or a small yellow circle, but it cannot be placed next to a small yellow square that differs on two characteristics. Unfortunately, the teacher may have difficulty providing timely help for all those who may have difficulty building their train according to the rules.

The children can play the same game on a computer using a program called *Gertrude's Secrets.* The computer can provide immediate feedback for those who make errors in playing the game. The children are able to relate quickly to the computer software because it displays colored graphic objects that look very similar to the physical attribute blocks and are used in the same way. The computer game adds to the learning process by providing an extra level of abstraction, immediate feedback that minimizes the likelihood of a child's forming misconceptions, and positive reinforcement. The computer software can also provide an unlimited number of pieces and even allow the children to create new shapes. With the use of a device to project the computer display onto a large screen in the front of the classroom, the teacher can demonstrate concepts to the whole class by using the computer-based manipulatives.

Other computer programs such as *Moptown Parade* and *Moptown Hotel* allow children to transfer the concepts they learned with the attribute blocks to other settings. With these software programs, the manipulatives are "blocks" in the shape of people with varying characteristics.

Many other computer programs are available that mirror other physical manipulatives used in the classroom. *Elastic Lines* simulates the geoboard on which students may explore geometric concepts. *Puzzle Tanks* provides representations of containers of many different sizes that students can use to solve problems related to volume by filling and emptying containers of specified volume. A wide assortment of math manipulatives is also represented in *Math Concepts; Exploring Measurement, Time, and Money*; and *Hands-On Math*. Simulated manipulatives are also available for more advanced mathematics in programs such as *Algebra Concepts, Geometry,* and *Calculus.*

Science Simulations

Students from elementary through high school are learning concepts and problem-solving skills in the earth, life, and physical sciences with the aid of a computer-based integrated learning system developed by Wasatch Education Systems Corporation. Six units of instruction are provided in each of the three science areas. The microcomputers in each classroom are all connected by cables to a central computer station called a *file server.* By connecting the computers in a network, all the computer-based instruction software and student performance data can be stored in the central file server. This configuration eliminates problems related to software checkout and distribution and facilitates the generation of a variety of individual, class, and school progress reports.

Each unit is designed around a simulation of some phenomenon in science. These simulations allow students to observe the phenomenon under study, decide which type of information to observe, take measurements, collect and record data, analyze the data, generate and test hypotheses, and write a summary of their observations.

For example, in the Weather unit, students use simulated instruments to take weather readings in eight major cities across the United States. Two thermometers are provided to measure air temperature in Fahrenheit and Celsius. An anemometer is used to measure wind speed, a weather vane to measure wind direction, a hygrometer to measure relative humidity, a rain gauge to measure precipitation, and a barometer to measure air pressure. Computer-based lessons teach students what each instrument is for and how to read it and gather data. The simulation provides weather readings from each of the simulated instruments four times each day for the month of March from eight different cities. Students select a city, day, and time of day to see the desired instrument readings. A teacher's guide suggests a wide variety of questions and exploration activities students can do to look for patterns in the weather data, compare pressure before and after a storm, determine how wind changes affect other readings, and so on. Many noncomputer discussions and activities are also suggested.

To aid students in their data-gathering and -analysis activities, several computer-based tools are provided: an electronic database in which to record observations, an electronic notebook for making notes, a calculator, a glossary, and a graphing utility. An electronic mail facility is also provided so that students can write notes to each other and to the teacher. This tool encourages the exchange of information and ideas.

The National Geographic Kids Network

Upper-elementary students from more than 1,250 classrooms in the United States, Canada, and other countries are participating in several cooperative science projects sponsored by the National Geographic Society and the Technical Education Research Centers with matching funds from the National Science Foundation. The overall project has come to be known as the National Geographic Kids Network (1989). Students participating in these projects do the work of actual scientists in exploring "real and engaging scientific problems that have an important social context." Curriculum units have been developed to help students study issues such as acid rain and water quality. One of the units is described as follows:

> *Acid Rain helps students examine this timely issue by learning to take pH measurements of rain water and by sharing their results with others across the country. Students also examine the effects of acids on various materials, calculate the weekly amount of nitrogen oxides emitted through their families' car use, make predictions about pH measurements at other sites (on the basis of maps of emissions and wind patterns), and discuss the societal consequences of different approaches for dealing with the acid rain problem. (p. 3)*

Students share their results with others by entering their data into a computer database and instructing the computer to send the database over telephone lines to a central computer. The data from each school are pooled by the central computer, and the combined results are then sent back to each school. Each class then searches for patterns and trends in the combined data and examines how its local results fit into the broader picture. Students also use the computer telecommunications network to send messages back and forth to students in other schools to discuss their findings and conclusions. Computer-based tools are also used to "display data as tables, maps, bar charts, line graphs, and pie diagrams" (National Geographic Kids Network, 1989, p. 4). An evaluation of the Acid Rain unit revealed that more than 90 percent of the teachers wanted to use the unit again and that students' interest in science was significantly increased.

The original Kids Network units were so successful that additional units have been added. Units for grades 4 through 6 include "Solar Energy," "What Are We Eating?" "Too Much Trash?" and "Weather in Action." In 1995, the network was extended into the middle school, grades 6 through 9, with units on such topics as soil use, noise pollution, passive cigarette smoke, and surface water pollution.

Montevidisco

The *Montevidisco* system is designed to teach Spanish by taking students on simulated visits to a Mexican village. As students interact with the program, they are presented with a series of lifelike video situations, with natives of Mexico speaking to them in Spanish at a normal rate of speed. Each scene or situation is concluded by the native asking a question that requires a response by the student.

The video sequences are recorded on a videodisc (a 12-inch platter similar in appearance to a 78 rpm audio phonograph record) and reproduced and displayed on a television set through the use of a videodisc player (see Chapter 2) connected to a microcomputer. A computer program sends commands to the videodisc player that specify which video sequence should be played next.

After a video sequence is displayed, the student is presented with four response options on the computer screen. One of the response options allows the student to ask the Mexican speaker to repeat the question. When students select one of the other options, they will be taken to some other location in the village, based on their response. *Montevidisco* contains 28 different situations that place students in a hospital, jail, bullfight, beach, market, and the like, where they can enter into appropriate conversations. Since each situation has at least four options, there are over 1,100 different options or branches in the program. Two versions (male and female) of *Montevidisco* were produced to reflect the appropriate use of gender in the simulated conversations (Gale, 1983). Several computer-based aids have been added in the latest version to help students understand the conversations. Students can look up a word they do not understand by using an electronic Spanish dictionary; they can request that a friend explain what the speaker said, using slower and more carefully pronounced Spanish; or they can request a written transcription of a conversation in either Spanish or English (Bush, 1994).

Music: An Appreciation

The book publishing industry is beginning to provide computer-based multimedia materials (see Chapter 8, Multimedia/Hypermedia) to supplement their traditional text books. *Music: An Appreciation,* Second Brief Edition is an introductory college text that "provides an approach to perceptive listening and an introduction to musical elements, forms, and stylistic periods" (Kamien, 1994, p. xxi). Accompanying the text are three compact discs and computer software. The compact discs contain almost four hours of music compositions or movements that are discussed in the text. Marginal notes in the text indicate where each piece may be found on the compact disc. The computer software, *Maestro* (Kaufman, 1994), provides a simple mechanism for selecting and playing the musical selections by controlling a CD-ROM player (see Chapter 2, Computer Hardware). The software also provides *listening outlines*, as shown in Figure 1–3, that describe and focus the students' attention on the various characteristics of the music as it is being played.

Research Results on the Effects of Computer-Based Instruction

Numerous research studies have been conducted to determine the effects of computer-based instruction on student learning, student attitudes, and instructional time. They have been conducted across all levels of education: elementary, secondary, postsecondary, and adult. Several reviews of these studies have been published in recent years (Bangert-Downs, Kulik, & Kulik, 1985; Chambers & Spreecher, 1980; Kulik & Kulik, 1986; Kulik, Kulik, & Bangert-Downs, 1985; Kulik, Kulik, & Shwalb, 1986; Niemiec & Walberg, 1987; Roblyer, 1988). Most of the reviewers used a sophisticated analysis technique referred to as *meta-analysis,* which allowed them to equate the results from many different studies and determine an average effect size across all the studies reviewed. This effect size is generally reported in terms of standard deviation and percentile changes.

FIGURE 1–3   Vivaldi Listening Outline from *Maestro*

Source: From *Music: An Appreciation* (2nd ed.) by R. Kamien, 1994, New York: McGraw-Hill. Copyright 1994, by McGraw-Hill, Inc. Reprinted by permission of McGraw-Hill, Inc.

Kulik and Kulik (1987) combined the data from several of the reviews cited in the previous paragraph in an analysis of 199 comparative studies: 32 of these studies were conducted in elementary schools, 42 in high schools, 101 in institutions of higher education, and 24 in adult education settings. The results of their meta-analyses showed that computer-based instruction, when compared to conventional instruction, raised examination scores by 0.31 standard deviations, or from the 50th to the 61st percentile. Some 28 of the studies reported that computer-based instruction reduced instructional time by an average of 32 percent, and 17 studies indicated that students' attitudes toward instruction were raised 0.28 standard deviations.

The other reviews came to very similar conclusions: The use of computer-based instruction, when compared to conventional instruction, has a moderate positive effect on student achievement and attitudes toward computers and instruction, and it substantially reduces instructional time. These results indicate that computer-based instruction can have positive benefits, although certainly it is not a panacea. You are reminded to use caution in the interpretation and application of such research results. Considerable tender loving care and other resources go into the development of computer-based instruction. If the same resources were put into the development of conventional instruction, similar positive benefits might be obtained. These results are based on an average across numerous studies. Just as some books and films are very good, and others are very poor, there is a wide variance in the quality of computer-based instruction software. There are also differences in the quality of conventional instruction. An advantage of computer-based instruction is that it is visible, replicable, and transportable. It can be examined, tested, revised, and improved.

One of the purposes of this book is to enable you to determine the difference between good and poor educational software and to integrate its use into your many other classroom activities. You will also be introduced to a wide variety of other applications of computers in the schools, in addition to computer-based instruction. The next section provides a framework for examining these different types of applications.

Types of Educational Applications

As you saw from the examples described earlier in the chapter, computers are being used in the schools in many exciting ways. Taylor (1980) has suggested that all educational applications of computers can be placed into one of three major classifications: tutor, tool, or tutee. In this categorization scheme, which is used throughout this book, the computer takes on three different roles. It serves either as a tutor (i.e., teacher), as a handy tool, or as a tutee (i.e., student). This section expands Taylor's scheme by defining several subcategories within each classification and identifying where specific applications might be placed.

Tutor Applications

In tutor applications, the computer acts as a tutor by performing a teaching role. In effect, the student is tutored by the computer. These types of applications are often referred to by several different labels such as computer-based instruction (CBI), computer-assisted instruction (CAI), or computer-assisted learning (CAL). The general process is as follows:

1. The computer presents some information.
2. The student is asked to respond to a question or problem related to the information.
3. The computer evaluates the student's response according to specified criteria.
4. The computer determines what to do next on the basis of its evaluation of the response.

Tutor applications can be further classified into five categories: drill-and-practice applications, tutorial applications, simulations, problem-solving applications, and games.

Drill-and-Practice Applications
In drill-and-practice applications, the computer is used to help the student memorize the appropriate response to some stimulus. The most common applications include drills on math facts, spelling words, shapes, and colors. For example, in math drills, the computer might display the problem: $5 + 2 = ?$, and the student would be asked to enter the correct response. The computer would evaluate the response and give the student

appropriate feedback. If the student entered the incorrect response, the computer would display the correct answer on the screen and then present the next problem. In a sense, the computer serves as a sophisticated flashcard presenter. However, by keeping track of how each student responds to each item, the computer can tailor the drill-and-practice sessions to the needs of each individual student. Such strategies are described in detail in Chapter 4, Drill-and-Practice and Tutorial Applications.

Tutorial Applications

The primary purpose of tutorial applications is to teach new information. For example, in a tutorial program dealing with the concept of a noun, the computer presents the definition of a noun, shows several examples of nouns in sentences, and then asks the student to practice identifying nouns in new sentences. Tutorial applications are similar to a programmed textbook. Some relatively small piece of information is presented, the student is asked to respond to a question about the information, and the computer provides feedback concerning the accuracy of the student's response. Then the cycle is repeated: more information, question, feedback. Ideal tutorial programs are able to tailor the material to the needs of individual students. If a particular student is having difficulty, the computer can present remedial material. Students who are doing well may skip over elaborations, extra examples, or practice items. Tutorial applications are discussed in detail in Chapter 4, Drill-and-Practice and Tutorial Applications.

Simulations

Simulations are representations or models of real systems or phenomena. They allow students to experience certain phenomena vicariously with less risk and cost. For example, medical students can interact with a computer-simulated patient in order to practice their diagnostic and prescriptive problem-solving skills. If the computer patient's condition worsens, the medical student will learn the consequences of improper diagnosis and treatment, but no human suffering will occur. Simulations can also allow students to experience phenomena that would otherwise be too expensive or time consuming. A computer simulation of the stock market enables students to buy and sell stocks without investing real money, and they can see the results of their decisions immediately. Simulations are discussed further in Chapter 5, Problem Solving, Simulations, and Games.

Problem-Solving Applications

Problem-solving applications provide settings in which students can learn and improve their problem-solving skills. These settings may or may not simulate some real-world phenomenon. In any case, the students are given a variety of problem situations in which they must use logical reasoning skills. Such applications are examined in Chapter 5, Problem Solving, Simulations, and Games.

Game Applications

Game applications are used to bring interest and motivation to the learning situation. Computer programs of this type involve competitive play between a student and one or more opponents. Elements of gaming can be added to each of the tutor applications already described. Characteristics and examples of effective educational games are given in Chapter 5, Problem Solving, Simulations, and Games.

Tool Applications

In tool applications, the computer is an instructional tool similar to a pencil, typewriter, microscope, slide rule, piano, or drafting table. With the computer, students can calculate numbers with great speed and accuracy. They can type and edit papers, reports, and themes using a word-processing computer program. The computer can even be used as a tool to assist the student composer and artist. Computer-based tools are also helpful to teachers and school administrators. Tool applications are beginning to invade our work, our play, our schools, and even our homes. Chapters 7 through 10 focus on several applications of the computer as a tool.

Tutee Applications

In tutee applications, the computer becomes the tutee, or student, and the user becomes the teacher. The user has to teach the computer to do some task. To do this, the user has to learn how to communicate with the computer in a language that the computer understands. In essence, the learner must learn how to write computer programs. A computer program is a set of commands that tell the computer how to accomplish a particular task or solve a problem. Before students can program the computer to solve a problem, they must first understand how to solve the problem themselves. This requires the development and use of thinking skills and problem-solving skills. Most educators would agree that the development of such skills is one of the major goals of education. Thus, the computer as tutee may well "constitute a new and fundamental intellectual resource" (Luehrmann, 1980). These exciting applications of the computer in education are described in Chapter 11, The Computer as Tutee.

Categories of Learning Outcomes

With so many different applications to choose from, how can you tell which to use? Is a particular application better in one subject area than another? When should you use the computer as a tutee instead of as a tool?

The answers to these important and difficult questions can be found by first identifying the learning outcomes you want for your students and then determining which applications are best suited to help students obtain those specified objectives. To use such an approach, you must first establish categories of learning outcomes.

Gagné (1985) has proposed five major domains of learned capabilities, or outcomes: (1) intellectual skills, (2) cognitive strategies, (3) verbal information, (4) motor skills, and (5) attitudes. The term *problem solving* is used to refer to the domain of cognitive strategies because of its greater familiarity. This section briefly describes each of these categories of learning outcomes and outlines which computer applications facilitate the achievement of each outcome. These relationships between learning outcomes and the various applications in computers in education are discussed in greater detail in the specific chapters that deal with each particular application.

Intellectual Skills

The domain of intellectual skills has been further divided into the categories of discriminations, concepts, and rules.

Discriminations

Discrimination learning enables students to distinguish one object, event, or symbol from another. The most commonly observable student behavior that serves as an indicator of discrimination learning is the stating of the name of the item being discriminated. Other indicators of discrimination learning are pointing to or circling the discriminated object. Discrimination learning is required for a student to be able to name specific letters of the alphabet, label the parts of a camera, give the names of the buildings on a college campus, or identify symbols on a topographical map.

Discrimination learning is involved in most paired-associate tasks on which the learner is required to associate two items (stimulus and response) together. In learning math facts, the student has to associate the problem with its corresponding answer; for example, $5 + 6 = 11$. In learning to discriminate spelling words, the student has to associate the oral pronunciation of the word with its correct spelling. These associations must be memorized. Computer applications that emphasize drill and practice can significantly facilitate the learning of such discrimination tasks.

Concepts

Learning concepts enables students to classify previously unencountered objects, events, or symbols as members of a given class. For example, if students have learned the concept of *verb,* they should be able to pick out the verbs in an unfamiliar sentence. Other outcomes of concept learning include the ability to classify examples of insects, adjectives, integers, operant conditioning, democratic societies, or any other class of items that are grouped together on the basis of common characteristics. Research has shown that the best instructional strategy for teaching concepts includes an initial presentation of definitions, examples, and nonexamples, followed by practice in classifying unfamiliar examples. Such a strategy can be implemented through the use of tutorial computer applications.

Rules

In general, a rule is a procedure or series of steps used to solve a problem or accomplish a task. The stimulus, or input, is operated upon, manipulated, transformed, or changed by the procedure to finally produce the desired solution, output, outcome, or performance. Most how-to tasks are rules or procedures. Outcomes that use rules include the tasks of using proper grammar, performing mathematical operations, and diagramming sentences. Rules are also involved in many motor skills, such as sewing a dress, dissecting a frog, and performing an experiment. Merrill and Bunderson (1981) have proposed the following instructional strategy for teaching rules:

1. Present a verbal statement or other representation of the rule.
2. Demonstrate the rule by applying it to several divergent example problems.
3. Provide several opportunities for students to practice using the rule to solve previously unencountered problems.
4. Provide corrective feedback. When an error occurs, show the student how the problems can be solved using the rule.

Drill-and-practice exercises do not satisfy the first two parts of the instructional strategy just listed. However, such a strategy could be effectively implemented by using a tutorial application. For certain complex rules, a simulation could be combined with a tutorial approach to provide more realistic situations.

Problem Solving

Problem solving enables students to generate solutions to novel problems. There is more to problem solving than the simple application of a previously learned rule to a set of problems known to be within its domain. The solution of the novel problem requires the discovery of a new higher-order rule (which can be a combination of previously learned rules). Problem solving is essentially a creative process. It is required in such tasks as writing a poem, composing a musical score, or inventing a product. To learn problem-solving skills, students must have a variety of problem-solving opportunities. These situations should not have been previously encountered. In the early stages of teaching problem-solving skills, it is often necessary to guide the students, helping them to channel their thinking in the right direction.

Several different computer applications can be used to help students develop problem-solving skills: simulation, problem solving, game, and tutee applications. Simulations and problem-solving applications can present a wide variety of problem situations to students within a short period. The total complexity of real-life problems can be simplified. In this way, beginning students can focus on the relevant aspects of the problem. Gaming elements can be added to provide competition and increase interest. Tutee applications require students to solve a problem themselves before they can teach the computer how to do it.

Verbal Information

Verbal information enables students to state, explain, or verbalize a fact or idea in the form of a proposition. Generally, it is preferable for students to state the proposition in their own words rather than quoting it verbatim. Verbal information is involved in such tasks as listing the names of the original 13 colonies, describing the events that led up to World War II, and giving the date Columbus discovered America. Computers are not necessarily the most effective devices for presenting verbal information. In many instances, printed materials are more flexible, less expensive, and more efficient in presenting information. Tutorial computer applications are often used for this purpose but are generally little more than expensive electronic page turners. However, the computer can be used as a tool to help students search through large databases of information for the specific items that are relevant to their immediate needs.

Motor Skills

Motor skills enable students to execute physical movements with appropriate timing and precision. Motor skills are involved in tying a shoelace, writing cursive letters, throwing a ball, operating a wood lathe, tuning an engine, adjusting a microscope, dissecting a frog, and performing surgery. Performing a motor skill generally involves the execution of a series of coordinated movements. The coordination and sequencing of these movements is governed by an executive routine or rule (Gagné, 1985). The cognitive rule outlining the order in which the movements should be performed can be taught independently of the actual motor components. Locker-room "chalk talks" and playbooks are used in athletic programs to teach executive routines. However, it is difficult to learn the actual movements of a motor skill solely from textual or verbal information. The movements must be shown to the students through a live demonstration or some pictorial representation.

For some skills, a live demonstration may not be adequate. Under some circumstances, the human model is unable to perform the movements slowly enough for students to see the critical aspects of the skill. The tennis serve is difficult to demonstrate for this reason. A series of still pictures might be more useful in showing these critical aspects. However, there can be a problem here as well, inasmuch as still pictures do not reveal the continuity of the movements required in performing the skill. A slow-motion representation would be ideal for slowing down the action so that the critical aspects could be perceived while maintaining the continuity of movements. The learning of subskills, extensive practice, and individual feedback are also critical elements in training for motor skills.

Tutorial and simulation computer applications would be most appropriate for teaching motor skills. The executive routines associated with a motor skill could be taught with tutorial lessons. High-quality computer graphics could be used as a series of still pictures to demonstrate the movements one step at a time, in slow motion or in normal motion. A computer-controlled video playback device (videodisc player or CD-ROM player) could also demonstrate the skill from several visual angles. The student could be given the opportunity to watch parts of the demonstration at different speeds as often as desired. Certain aspects of some skills could actually be practiced using a computer simulation, especially if the motor skill involves the operation of a piece of equipment.

Attitudes

Attitudes are associated with almost every learning activity. An *attitude* is an internal state that affects our tendency to respond in a certain way (Gagné, 1985). People generally have a positive or negative emotional reaction to any learning situation. That emotional reaction influences our attitudes about what we have learned. Our attitudes influence how we respond with respect to our knowledge and skills. Attitudes are involved in choices made about smoking cigarettes, attending an opera, studying, following safety procedures, and obeying traffic laws. Attitudes can be influenced and changed through the use of classical conditioning, reinforcement, and human modeling (Gagné, 1985).

Any computer application will have some influence on student attitudes. If the program is designed to adapt to individual needs, then the student will experience success and have a positive emotional reaction. If the program is too easy or too difficult, the student will become bored or frustrated, which leads to negative attitudes. If appropriate gaming elements are incorporated into the application, then students will be motivated to continue to interact with the program. When students have a choice, they will engage in those learning activities that are enjoyable and relevant to their interests. Computer-based videodisc applications can be used to demonstrate or model appropriate choice behaviors.

Summary

This chapter introduced you to several exciting applications of computers in the schools and summarized research findings on the impact of computer-based instruction applications. An overview of a conceptual framework for the remainder of the book was also presented. Most educational applications of the computer can be placed in three major classifications: tutor, tool, and tutee. Tutor and tool applications may be further divided into categories. Some applications are appropriate for certain learning outcomes but not for others. To provide a basis for relating the various computer applications to different outcomes, Gagné's (1985) domains of learning outcomes were discussed: intellectual skills, cognitive strategies or problem solving, verbal information, motor skills, and attitudes. In future chapters, each of the computer applications will be discussed in depth and more examples of how each application can be used to help students achieve specific types of learning outcomes will be given.

Exercises

1. Give several examples of how computer technology has affected your daily life.
2. Summarize the conclusions from research on the effects of computer-based instruction.
3. Compare and contrast the categories of educational computer applications: tutor, tool, and tutee.
4. Compare and contrast Gagné's categories of learning outcomes.
5. Outline which computer applications are most appropriate for each category of learning outcome.

References

Algebra Concepts. [Computer Program]. Ventura, CA: Ventura Educational Systems.

Bangert-Downs, R. L., Kulik, J. A., & Kulik, C-L. C. (1985). Effectiveness of computer-based education in secondary schools. *Journal of Computer-Based Instruction, 12*(3), 59–68.

Brierley, M. (1987). *Writing to Read and full day kindergarten evaluation.* Columbus: Columbus Public Schools, Ohio Department of Evaluation Services. (ERIC ED 289 626).

Bush, C. D. (November, 1994). Three visits to Montevidisco: Spanish enrichment with interactive videodisc. *ReCall, 6*(2), 14–18.

Calculus. [Computer Program]. San Rafael, CA: Broderbund Software.

Casey, J. M. (1994). Literacy instruction in an integrated curriculum. *The Computing Teacher, 21*(5), 33–36.

Catherall, T. S. (1988). *Users' guide to the Marklin Digital System.* New Berlin, WI: Marklin.

Catherall, T. S. (1990). Interfacing computers with electric trains in schools. *Computers in Education, 14*(3), 227–230.

Chambers, J. A., & Spreecher, J. W. (1980). Computer-assisted instruction: Current trends and critical issues. *Communications of the Association of Computing Machinery, 23,* 332–342.

Childers, R. D., & Leopold, G. D. (1993). *A follow-up study of the ARC/IBM Writing to Read Project in Kentucky, Virginia, and West Virginia, final report.* Charleston, WV: Appalachia Educational Lab.

Elastic Lines. [Computer Program]. Pleasantville, NY: Sunburst.

Exploring Measurement, Time, and Money. [Computer Program]. Dayton, NJ: IBM Educational Software.

Gagné, R. M. (1985). *Conditions of learning* (4th ed.). New York: Holt, Rinehart & Winston.

Gale, L. E. (1983, June). Montevidisco: The anecdotal history of an interactive videodisc. *Calico Journal,* pp. 42–46.

Geometry. [Computer Program]. San Rafael, CA: Broderbund Software.

Gertrude's Secrets. [Computer Program]. Fremont, CA: The Learning Company.

Goda, B. S., Wise, J. H., McConkey, M. S., & Loy, J. R. (1994). *HO scale model trains provide a vehicle for curriculum fusion between electrical engineering and computer science.* Paper presented at the Frontiers in Education Conference, San Jose, CA.

Harris, B., Arntsen, M. K., Thurman, R., & Merrill, P. F. (1987). Computers, gifted students and the development of an elementary school newspaper. *The Computing Teacher, 15*(2), 11–13.

Kamien, R. (1994). *Music: An appreciation, second brief edition.* New York: McGraw-Hill.

Kaufman, R. (1994). Maestro. [Computer Software]. New York: McGraw-Hill.

Kulik, C-L. C., & Kulik, J. A. (1986). Effectiveness of computer-based education in colleges. *AEDS Journal, 19*(2–3), 81–108.

Kulik, C-L. C., Kulik, J. A., & Shwalb, B. J. (1986). The effectiveness of computer-based adult education: A meta analysis. *Journal of Educational Computing Research, 2*(2), 235–262.

Kulik, J. A., Bangert, R. L., & Williams, G. W. (1983). Effects of computer-based teaching on secondary school students. *Journal of Educational Psychology, 75,* 19–26.

Kulik, J. A., & Kulik, C-L. C. (1987). Review of recent literature on computer-based instruction. *Contemporary Educational Psychology, 12*(3), 222–230.

Kulik, J. A., Kulik, C-L. C., & Bangert-Downs, R. L. (1985). Effectiveness of computer-based education in elementary schools. *Computers in Human Behavior, 1,* 59–74.

Leahy, P. (1989). *Summary of the report on the review of the "Writing to Read" programs implemented in the Kettering City School during the 1988–1989 school year.* ERIC ED 307 638.

LEGO Bricks. [Set of Toy Construction Blocks]. Enfield, CT: LEGO Systems.

Levinson, J., & Lalor, I. (March, 1989). *Computer-assisted writing/reading instruction of young children: A 2-year evaluation of "Writing to*

Read." Paper presented at the annual meeting of the American Educational Research Association, San Francisco.

Luehrmann, A. (1980). Should the computer teach the student, or vice-versa? In R. P. Taylor (Ed.), *The computer in school: Tutor, tool, tutee.* New York: Teachers College Press.

Martin, J. H. (1986). *Writing to read: Teacher's manual* (2nd ed.). Boca Raton, FL: IBM.

Martin, J. H., & Friedberg, A. (1986). *Writing to read.* New York: Warner Books.

Math Concepts. [Computer Program]. Dayton, NJ: IBM Educational Software.

Merrill, M. D., & Tennyson, R. D. (1977). *Teaching concepts: An instructional design guide.* Englewood Cliffs, NJ: Educational Technology Publications.

Merrill, P. F., & Bunderson, C. V. (1981). Preliminary guidelines for employing graphics in instruction. *Journal of Instructional Development, 4*(4), 2–9.

Moptown Hotel. [Computer Program]. Fremont, CA: The Learning Company.

Moptown Parade. [Computer Program]. Fremont, CA: The Learning Company.

National Geographic Kids Network: Year 3 Annual Report. (1989). Cambridge, MA: Technical Education Research Centers.

Niemiec, R., & Walberg, H. J. (1987). Comparative effects of computer-assisted instruction: A synthesis of reviews. *Journal of Educational Computing Research, 3*(1), 19–37.

Perl, T. (1990). Manipulatives, and the computer: A powerful partnership for learners of all ages. *Classroom Computer Learning, 10*(6), 20–29.

Puzzle Tanks. [Computer Program]. Pleasantville, NY: Sunburst.

Roblyer, M. D. (1988, September). The effectiveness of microcomputers in education: A review of the research from 1980–1987. *T.H.E. Journal,* pp. 85–89.

Slavin, R. E. (1990, November). IBM's Writing to Read: Is it right for reading? *Phi Delta Kappan,* pp. 214–216.

Spillman C. V., & Lutz, J. P. (1986). A Writing to Read philosophy. *Childhood Education, 62*(4), 265–268.

Stevenson, Z. (1988). *Achievement in the "Writing to Read" program: A comparative evaluation study.* Washington, DC: District of Columbia Public Schools, Division of Quality Assurance and Management Planning. ERIC ED 293 147.

Suydam, M. (1985). *Research on instructional materials for mathematics.* ERIC/SMEAC Special Digest No. 3.

Taylor, R. P. (Ed.). (1980). *The computer in the school: Tutor, tool, tutee.* New York: Teachers College Press.

Weather. [Computer Program]. Salt Lake City: Wasatch Education Systems.

Chapter 2

Computer Hardware

The purpose of this chapter is to introduce you to computers and related devices. After reading this chapter, you should be familiar with the technical terminology associated with computers in education.

A computer is a machine that processes information, or data. Information may be in the form of graphics, text, video, or audio; it may be searched, sorted, modified, calculated, or manipulated. The computer may manipulate the data but it does not understand the data. A computer can only do what people instruct it to do. Other types of machines, such as kitchen appliances or engines, receive a single instruction (such as on/off, higher/lower) and perform the related function. A computer, on the other hand, can store many instructions. This permits the computer to solve problems quickly, because all the necessary instructions or rules are available to be processed.

The computer uses two forms of information: data and rules. The data are entered, or inputted, into the computer where they can be processed. Rules or algorithms are the instructions used to manipulate the data. For example, the following math problem needs to be solved by the computer: $3 + 4 = ?$ The data, 3 and 4, are processed by the computer using an addition rule. A solution, the number 7, is then produced. The rules are stored in the computer in the form of a computer program; this program is written in a computer language. Computer programs and computer languages are explained in more detail in Chapter 11, The Computer as Tutee. In this chapter, we will discuss the devices used to input the data and rules into the computer, the components of the computer that processes the data, and the devices used to output the results of those processes.

Three categories of products are needed to use computers in education: hardware, software, and courseware. *Hardware* consists of all of the equipment attached to the computer, including the computer. Hardware is the tangible, physical components of a computer or computer system. Some examples of hardware are color monitors, disk drives, central processors, and printers. *Software* refers to computer programs used to direct the computer's input, processing, and output. Software is a general term for both computer languages (BASIC, C, Pascal) and applications written in computer languages, such as spreadsheet, word processing, and database management systems. *Courseware* is a more specific term for software that has been designed for instructional use in either education or training.

Hardware comes in many shapes and sizes. Each of the various types of computers is suited for a particular task. Computers can be categorized as shown in Table 2–1.

The ability to categorize computers is getting more difficult as the power and capabilities of the smaller (physically) computers increase. The power of mainframe com-

TABLE 2–1   Types of Computers

Concept	Definition	Examples
Personal digital assistant (PDA)	A very lightweight hand-held computer	Apple Newton, Sharp Wizard, HP
Laptop and portable computer	A lightweight, portable computer designed for use by a single individual	IBM Thinkpad, Apple Powerbook, Toshiba T4800
Personal computer (PC)	A computer designed for use by a single individual; sometimes referred to as a *microcomputer*	Compaq ProLinea, IBM Valuepoint, Apple Macintosh, Gateway 2000, HP Vectra, AST Bravo
Personal workstation	A computer designed for a single individual that has exceptional capabilities, such as high-resolution graphics	Silicon Graphics, Sun, IBM RS/6000
Minicomputer	A computer designed for multiple users; typically a small- to medium-sized department or work group	IBM AS/400, DEC VAX, HP 3000
Mainframe computer	The largest of the general-purpose computers; typically supports a large institution with many people using the same computer at once; requires a controlled environment and a large support staff	IBM ES/9000, Amdahl, Tandem, UNISYS, Fujitsu
Supercomputer	The fastest computer available; typically used to process extremely large amounts of data (e.g., weather patterns, aircraft and submarine modeling)	CRAY 3, IBM SP2

puters just a few years ago is available in personal computers today. Typical primary and secondary education applications use personal computers, personal workstations, and possibly minicomputers. Students will most often work with a personal computer that is inexpensive and can be used for a wide variety of applications. Personal workstations are used for more advanced applications, such as simulations, or they are used as file servers (central places to store programs and data) when personal computers are linked together in a network (see Chapter 9, Networks and Telecommunication). When large amounts of information must be accessed by many people, a minicomputer is most likely used. For example, a school may use a minicomputer to keep student records. In sophisticated learning environments, minicomputers have been used to facilitate all aspects of computer-managed instruction (see Chapter 10, Computer-Managed Instruction), from providing the courseware to performance and psychological testing. Examples of several types of computers are shown in Figure 2–1.

All of the computers we have been discussing may be used in a *client/server relationship*. A *client* is usually one of the computers designed for a single individual (laptop, personal computer, or workstation). A *server* is usually a larger system, ranging from a very well equipped personal computer to a mainframe. With clients connected to servers, both having computing capability, each can handle the computational and storage tasks most appropriate for their respective type of computer. A server, having more computing power and storage, is able to store and process large amounts of data (e.g., an entire school's courseware or student records). Clients handle the processing associated with an individual's computer, manipulating the information that is received from the server or utilizing software that resides on the client computer. Commonly used client/server application include on-line information services such as Prodigy, America Online, and Compuserve (see Chapter 9, Networks and Telecommunication).

The Computer System

As discussed earlier, the computer is actually only one component of a computer system. Most computer systems consist of at least three components. As shown in Figure 2–2, these components are (1) input devices, (2) the computer with its central processing unit (CPU) and internal memory, and (3) output devices. Input and output devices are generally referred to as *peripherals*.

Input

Input devices allow the user to enter information into the computer. The type of information entered may vary from text or numbers entered via a keyboard to graphics entered via a mouse or a graphics tablet. Input devices may also be used to select items on the screen and to move the cursor or other objects around the screen. The value of one of these input devices is dependent on its compatibility with a particular computer, software support for the device, and ease of use for a specific application. Three major types of input are typically used in education: alphanumeric, graphic/spatial, and audio/voice.

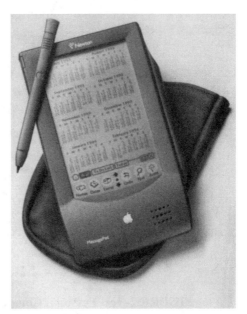

FIGURE 2–1a   Personal Digital Assistant (PDA)

FIGURE 2–1b   Laptop and Portable Computer

FIGURE 2–1c   Personal Computer

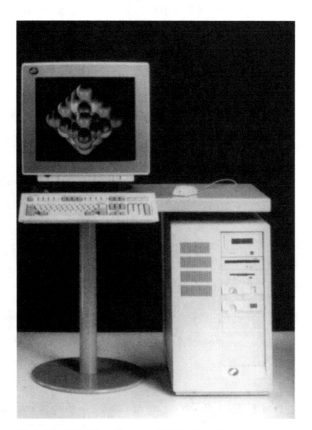

FIGURE 2–1d   Personal Workstation

FIGURE 2–1e   Minicomputer

FIGURE 2–1f   Mainframe Computer

FIGURE 2–1g   Supercomputer

Alphanumeric Input

Alpha-numeric input refers to the input of letters (a, b, c) and numbers (0, 1, 2) into the computer. The most common method of alphanumeric entry is via a keyboard. A faster, more expensive alternative to input existing text is the use of an optical scanner.

Keyboards.   The primary input device for most educational applications is the keyboard. The quality of the keyboard can significantly affect the efficiency of entering information into the computer. Computer keyboards are very similar to standard typewriter keyboards with respect to the layout of the alphabetic and numeric keys. However, most computer keyboards have several additional keys not found on typewriter keyboards, such as the CONTROL, ESCAPE, and RETURN keys. The CONTROL and ESCAPE keys are usually used in conjunction with other keys to send special messages to the computer. For example, a computer program may be interrupted by pressing the CONTROL key and the letter C at the same time. The RETURN key is used to signal the end of a user's entry. Some keyboards have additional sets of keys, including function keys, cursor-control keys, and numeric keypad keys (see Figure 2–3).

The keyboard is standard equipment on almost all computers. Unfortunately, the importance of a high-quality keyboard is often overlooked by computer manufacturers and

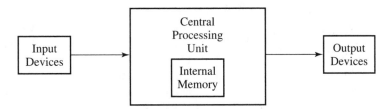

FIGURE 2–2   Components of a Computer System

users alike. The keyboard is used extensively when interacting with the computer, and its quality can significantly affect the efficiency of that interaction. The shape, placement, and touch of the keys are very important. The keys of good keyboards are contoured to keep the fingers from sliding off, and there is an appropriate amount of separation between the keys to avoid interference. The tension on the keys should be neither too soft nor too tight. Special keys—such as the RETURN, DELETE, CONTROL, and SHIFT keys—should be placed in a natural position within easy reach. Many manufacturers have received considerable criticism because of the poor quality of their keyboards. In some cases, a poor-quality keyboard has significantly reduced sales of a particular model of computer. It is sometimes possible to replace an inferior keyboard with a better keyboard from another supplier; however, this increases the cost to the user.

Generally, a *cursor* is a vertical or horizontal bar that is displayed to show the user where typed information will be placed. Cursor-control keys are important for many tool applications, such as word processing and spreadsheets, that require frequent

FIGURE 2–3   Computer Keyboard

movement of the cursor around the screen. Ideally, there should be at least four cursor-control keys arranged in a diamond shape. The up-arrow key should be on top, the down-arrow key on the bottom, and the left- and right-arrow keys on the sides of the diamond. On some computers, the cursor keys may be replaced or supplemented by other cursor movement devices such as a mouse, light pen, or touch screen. When a pointing device is used, two points on the screen are active: the cursor and the symbol used by the pointing device (typically an arrow). Once again, when information is typed on the keyboard, it will appear at the cursor. The pointing device may be used for positioning the cursor or for other functions such as selecting an option from a menu.

Numeric keypads are another important part of the keyboard. They look just like keypads on phones or calculators. Numeric keypads are an important feature if you plan to be doing significant amounts of numeric data entry.

Function keys are designed to save keystrokes. They are used by many application programs to perform commonly used functions with one key press, such as clearing the screen, moving to the beginning or end of a file or document, deleting selected information, requesting help, and saving information to an external diskette. Function keys are usually placed along the top of the keyboard or on the left side. If function keys are not available, function commands must be executed by pressing a series of keys such as CONTROL-K-D. Another alternative would be to use some pointing device, such as a mouse or touch screen, to select the desired function from a menu on the screen.

Experts and users disagree as to the value of cursor-control keys, function keys, and other pointing and selecting devices. Although these items do save keystrokes, some users prefer to use a CONTROL key in conjunction with other standard keys to execute special function commands so they do not have to move their fingers off the "home row" keys.

Optical Scanners.   Two types of optical scanners are in general use today: the optical mark reader (OMR) and the optical character recognition reader (OCR). Both scanners read information from a piece of paper and convert it to a format that a computer can process. The OCR is used to convert text on paper to text in a word processor. The special software used with the scanner tries to interpret the letters on a page of paper and creates a representation of them in the computer that can then be edited. This can save a lot of time when printed material needs to be input into the computer. The OCR is about 95 to 99 percent accurate, so some editing of the scanned material is almost always required. When the scanner does not recognize a word or letter, it places a unique symbol in its place. When the document is edited with a word processor, a spell-checker can be used to find those unique characters and replace them with the appropriate letters or numbers. The desktop models are able to scan an 8½" × 11" page in less than 10 seconds. Although the cost of these devices is decreasing, they are still rather expensive for school and home use.

The OMR is most often used in testing environments. These scanners read little bubbles on a page that are usually colored in by students with a number 2 pencil. OMRs use little black boxes called *timing marks* and *skunk marks* on the form to locate the bubbles. Many testing centers use this method to process tests that require multiple-choice answers.

Graphic/Spatial Input

Another type of input to a computer is of a graphic/spatial nature. The need to select an option from a computer screen by touching or pointing to it is spatial input. This type of input has proved to be a very easy way to interface with a computer because commands need not be typed but merely selected from a palette of options. Because commands are not typed, it is impossible to misspell or forget a command. Sometimes an entire graphic is needed as input. In this case, the spatial devices can be used to draw the graphic on the computer screen, or a scanner can be used to enter an existing drawing or image into the computer. Following is a brief discussion about input devices used for graphic/spatial input.

Mouse. A *mouse* is a small handheld device with a rotating ball underneath it (see Figure 2–4). As the mouse is moved across the flat surface of a desktop, the cursor or pointer moves on the screen in the same direction. The mouse usually has from one to three buttons on top. Menu items or objects on the screen may be selected by moving the mouse until the cursor points to the desired item and then pressing a mouse button. The mouse may also be used to draw graphic figures by pointing to the beginning and end of a line, the upper-left and lower-right corners of a rectangle, the center and radius of a circle, and so on. The mouse can be an effective replacement for function and cursor-control keys; however, it is not a very effective device for freehand sketching. From 6 to 10 square inches of desk space are required for its operation.

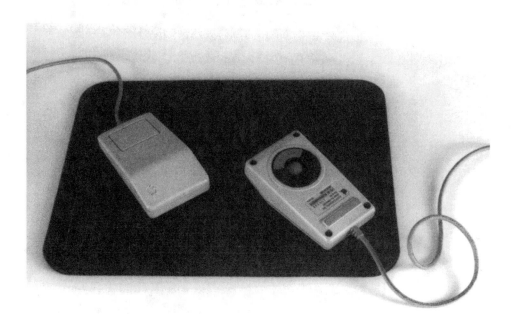

FIGURE 2–4   Top and Bottom Views of a Mouse

Touch Panel.   A touch panel allows users to move the cursor, select menu items, and draw graphic figures by touching the appropriate place on the screen with a finger or some pointed object, as shown in Figure 2–5. Some touch panels are implemented by using a transparent, touch-sensitive cover placed in front of the screen. Inexpensive panels can distort or diminish the clarity of the screen. The intuitive nature of using the touch panel makes it especially effective with young children. Due to various sizes of fingers and the gross sensitivity of the device, the touch panel is not adequate for detailed graphic input.

Pen.   A technology that is growing rapidly is pen-based input. Traditionally, pen input has been used to select or draw on a screen or tablet (see next heading, Graphics Tablet). Pen input is now frequently used with handheld computers called *personal digital assistants (PDAs)*. Current technology not only records the input as an image but also interprets that image; for example, a rough circle drawn by hand can be interpreted and redrawn as a true circle. Handwriting recognition technology is now used to interpret pen-drawn letters and convert these to letters that a computer can use in a word processor (see Figure 2–6). The pen-based computer uses a liquid-crystal display (LCD) with either a grid of wires embedded in the screen or a metallic coating on the display. The computer knows where the pen is by the change in voltage as the pen is moved away from the sides of the display.

FIGURE 2–5   Touch Panel

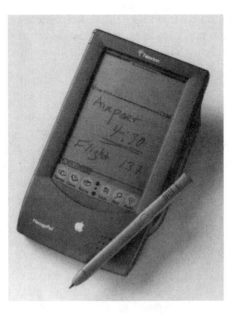

FIGURE 2–6   Pen Input on a
Personal Digital
Assistant (PDA)

Graphics Tablet.   A graphics tablet consists of two major components: a flat drawing surface of 6 to 20 square inches and a special electronic pen, or puck, as shown in Figure 2–7. The computer is able to detect where the pen touches the surface of the tablet. The tablet and pen can be used in much the same way as the mouse. However, it is most often used for the creation of very detailed graphic designs. It also can be used

FIGURE 2–7   Graphics Tablet

for tracing printed drawings. The newer tablets are able to interpret variable pressure placed on the tablet (as opposed to just on or off the pad). This makes it possible for artists to apply both light and heavy brush or pencil strokes to the "electronic canvas."

Sophisticated graphics tablets are fairly expensive. However, there is also an inexpensive device similar to a graphics tablet, called a *graphics pad,* which is sensitive to the touch of a finger or any pointed object. The graphics pad can be used as a pointing device with sensitivity equivalent to that of a touch panel. Graphics pads have been very successful in helping people with physical impairments use a computer. Because all areas of the tablet can be "mapped," the pad can be turned into a very large or specialized keyboard for those who do not have sufficient finger control to use a standard keyboard.

Track-Ball, Track-Pointer, and Track-Pad.   Track-balls are most frequently used to control the movement of video game characters and objects. However, they can also be substituted for the mouse. The device holding the ball is kept stationary while the ball is moved with the fingers. Small track-balls are often built into laptop computers. Track-pointers and track-pads are also used on laptop computers as mouse substitutes. The track-pointer is a little button that looks like an eraser located below the G and H keys (see Figure 2–8). Pushing the button up is the equivalent of moving a mouse up. The track-pad moves the cursor in response to moving your finger across the surface of the pad.

Graphic Scanner.   Graphic scanners are used to convert images—such as photographs, slides, drawings, and paintings—that were originally produced on some other

FIGURE 2–8   Trackpoint II

medium into a digital form represented by a series of binary numbers or digits that can be manipulated by a computer (see Chapter 8, Multimedia/Hypermedia). These digitized images may be displayed on a computer screen, stored in a computer database, merged with text in a school newspaper using a desktop publishing program, edited with a graphics program (see Chapter 7, Tool Applications), or printed. *Flatbed scanners* and *handheld scanners* are used to scan or digitize flat documents, such as a photographs or drawings. *Slide scanners* are used to digitize 35 mm slides, and *video digitizers* are used to convert video frames from camcorders, video cassette recorders (VCRs), and videodisc players into digital form. With appropriate software, the flatbed and handheld scanners can also be used for OCR, as described previously in this chapter. Figure 2–9 shows a handheld scanner.

Audio/Voice Input

Another form of input is an audio signal. Two basic functions are performed on an audio signal: recognition and recording. Audio signals are recorded through the use of an *audio digitizer,* as shown in Figure 2–10. This device takes an audio signal from a microphone, tape recorder, compact disc (CD), or other audio source and converts it to

FIGURE 2–9   Handheld Scanner

FIGURE 2–10   Audio Digitizer

numerical or digital codes (see Chapter 8, Multimedia/Hypermedia) that can be stored, played, and edited by the computer.

Audio recognition not only "listens" to the audio message but also interprets it. The most common application of this is voice recognition. *Voice recognition* systems permit the user to speak to the computer. Because people speak with such a wide range of accents, speed, intonation, and clarity, the computer has a very difficult time interpreting the message. Most voice recognition systems today require the user to "train" the computer to recognize what is being said. Voice recognition is now finding its way into average personal computers to perform simple commands. Personal dictation systems with vocabularies of up to 10,000 words are available on personal workstations. As these systems become more efficient and less expensive, they present great potential for applications in education.

Processing

Processing takes place primarily between two parts of the computer: the central processing unit (CPU) and primary (or internal) memory. Most of the other components involved in processing are in support of the aforementioned functions.

Central Processing Unit

The central processing unit (CPU) is the "brain" of the computer. The CPU is typically composed of two separate units: the control unit and the arithmetic/logic unit. The *control unit* reads instructions, directs the flow of information, and tells the other computer components what to do. The *arithmetic/logic unit* performs all arithmetic and logic operations. In microcomputers, all of the circuitry of these units is located on a single chip called a *microprocessor* (see Figure 2–11).

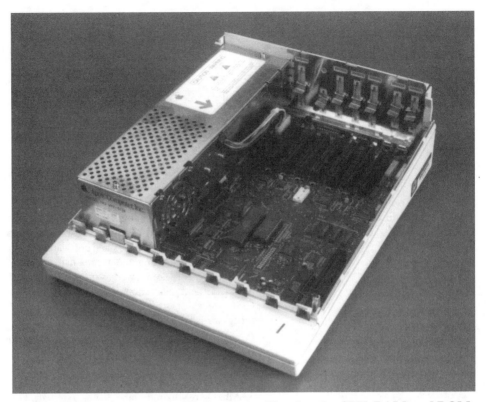

FIGURE 2–11 Inside View of a Computer Showing the CPU, RAM, and ROM

The CPU, or microprocessor, determines, in part, the overall power of the computer. The power of the CPU can be expressed in terms of (1) the type of commands or processes it can execute, (2) the speed with which it executes various commands, (3) the amount of information it can directly access in internal memory, (4) the amount of information it can process at one time, and (5) the amount of information it can transfer from the CPU to a given storage location in memory at one time.

Because most of these power factors deal with either speed or amounts of information, CPUs are usually classified according to these two factors. The *speed* of a CPU is expressed in terms of the number of processing cycles it can perform each second. Most microprocessors run at a speed of 25 to over 100 megahertz (Mhz).

The *amount of information* a CPU processes or transfers at one time is expressed in terms of bits. A *bit* is one binary unit of information, such as 1 or 0. It takes eight bits, commonly referred to as one *byte*, of information to represent one alphabetic character. Therefore, most CPUs are designed to process and transfer some multiple of eight bits of information at one time. Current microprocessors are classified as either 8-, 16-, or 32-bit CPUs: 8-bit CPUs process and transfer 8 bits at one time, 32-bit CPUs process and transfer 32 bits, and so on. Today, 64-bit CPUs are being used in workstations and will soon find their way into the average personal computer as their price decreases.

Several other attributes of processors are important when buying computer hardware. These are somewhat complex and may require some consultation with a computer specialist (typically not the person from whom you are buying the computer). Some of these attributes are included in Table 2–2.

TABLE 2–2   Other Processor Attributes

Attribute	Description
Complex Instruction Set Computer (CISC) vs. Reduced Instruction Set Computer (RISC)	Two types of processor technology are found in microcomputers: complex instruction set computer (CISC) and reduced instruction set computer (RISC). Traditionally, most processors are CISC and most software supports these processors. RISC processors and software that supports them are just beginning to enter mainstream computing. RISC processors are viewed as more efficient and will power the next generation of computers. An example of a CISC processor is the Intel 80486. An example of a RISC processor is the IBM PowerPC 604.
Processor speed	Processors work in cycles. The faster the cycle, the more work can be done. Processor cycles are measured in megahertz (Mhz). Sometimes a processor will work internally at a different rate than with the rest of the computer (e.g., 66/33 Mhz—66 Mhz internal, 33 Mhz external). For example, a Pentium 90/60 Mhz is 50 percent faster than a Pentium 60 MHz.
Processor models	When buying a car, there is a significant difference between SX, DX, LX, and EX models. The same is true for processors. Models differ by more than just clock speed, and this results in a significant difference in performance. For example, an Intel 80486 DX2 (66/33 Mhz) is 70 percent faster than a 80486 SX (33 Mhz). Check with your computer specialist before buying.
Bus architectures	In computing, a *bus* is the vehicle by which other parts of the computer communicate with the CPU (e.g., memory, external devices, video). Bus architectures are important to you in that they will determine what you can add on to a computer and how easy it will be. For example, a device (i.e., CD-ROM) that uses a controller for an EISA bus cannot be used in a computer with a MCA bus. Some buses provide "plug and play" capability that automatically configures the hardware and operating system when new devices are added. Examples of bus architectures are ISA, EISA, MCA, PCMCIA, VL-BUS, NUBUS, and PCI.

As indicated in bus architectures of Table 2–2, computers can be expanded through the addition of adapters, controllers, or cards, either to the *slots* or *ports,* both inside and outside the computer. The most common types of ports are the serial (RS-232) and parallel ports usually located on the back of the computer. The *serial port* is usually used with a mouse or modem. The *parallel port* is usually used to connect printers to the computer. One type of card typically used with laptop computers is PCMCIA, an acronym for Personal Computer Memory Card International Association. These are cards the size of credit cards that can expand memory, add disk space, or even enable communications with a network or phone. PCMCIA cards plug into slots on the side or back of a laptop computer. A controller typically used to control hard disks and tape drives is the SCSI (small computer systems interface; pronounced "scuzzy") controller. This controller permits multiple drives to be "chained" together; in other words, one controller can handle multiple drives.

This ability to expand or update technology may be compared to a camera. You may be able to afford only a base camera and one lens, but over time you then add several new lenses, a flash, and a power advance. Computer technology is improving so rapidly that you want to be able to update and expand with a minimum amount of cost and throwaway.

Primary (or Internal) Memory

The memory of a computer is measured in terms of how much information it can store. An easy way to think of computer memory is to compare it to a mailbox in an apartment building. Each mailbox has an address and a specific capacity to hold mail. The CPU uses each "mailbox" to store and retrieve information with which it is working. Computer memory has a memory address and a memory capacity measured in kilobytes (KB). One kilobyte (1 KB) of memory will store 1,024 bytes, or characters, of information. One megabyte (MB) is 1,000 KB. One page of text containing 500 words, with about seven letters per word, would require 3,500 bytes of storage. Microcomputers typically found in the schools have memories that range from 128,000 (128 KB) to more than 16,000,000 bytes (16 MB). This memory can usually be expanded to well over 32,000,000 bytes (32 MB). Internal memory stores information that the processor (CPU) currently uses, such as what is displayed on the screen or the next instruction in the program.

There are two basic forms of internal memory: read-only memory (ROM) and random-access memory (RAM). Figure 2–11 shows the ROM and RAM chips and CPU of a microcomputer. *Read-only memory* usually contains the fundamental commands needed for the computer to operate. These commands cannot be erased or changed without removing the ROM memory chip from the computer. *Random-access memory* is that storage space that is available for application programs and their data. Each memory location in RAM and ROM is individually addressable by the central processing unit. The information in RAM, unlike ROM, is lost when the computer is turned off. The total amount of internal memory available for processing at one time is dependent on the type of CPU, which can address or access only a certain maximum number of memory locations.

When microcomputers were first introduced, 16 KB of memory was considered to be more than adequate. However, more memory became necessary as computer programmers attempted to implement more sophisticated applications. Modern computer languages such as Logo and Pascal could not be implemented on machines with less than 64 KB. Original versions of Logo included only a subset of the language because of memory restrictions. Even with 64-KB machines, many educational applications were limited because of lack of memory. When microcomputers with 16-bit and 32-bit CPUs were introduced that could access more memory, software producers began developing much more sophisticated programs. Most of the multitasking operating systems now require at least 8 megabytes of memory and recommend 12 to 24 MB. With the fast 32-bit processors and tremendous amounts of memory available, applications that were formerly available only on minicomputers and mainframes can now be used on personal computers and at personal workstations.

One of the slowest tasks in executing a program is to get information from a disk drive. Computers with a large amount of memory can make programs faster by treating the extra memory just like a disk drive. Programs can be copied to this RAM disk in the same fashion as one would copy a program from one diskette to another.

It is possible for a computer to execute programs that are too large to fit in memory all at once by segmenting the program and loading only a few segments at a time from an external storage medium, such as a floppy diskette or a hard disk. When a new segment is needed, previously used segments are overwritten by new ones. However, reading needed segments from a diskette slows down the operation of the program. Some programs may not function properly if partitioned in this way. Larger amounts of internal memory reduce the need for segmentation of a program and thereby allow it to execute more rapidly. More memory not only facilitates the execution of sophisticated programs but it also allows for the manipulation of greater amounts of data. However, additional memory increases the cost of the computer. Again, the amount of memory required depends on how you plan to use the computer. Make sure the computers you purchase contain sufficient memory for intended present applications and that memory can be expanded, if necessary, for possible future applications.

Output

Once information has been processed, the results may be stored, displayed, or even heard. The computer can output information in many ways. The following sections look at external storage, visual display, print devices, and sound and video output.

External Storage

Because the information stored in RAM is lost when the computer is turned off, a more permanent storage medium is needed. Storage devices come in many shapes and sizes. In education, the most common mediums are hard disks, diskettes, and tape—all of which use a magnetic medium. The magnetic material is attached to several bases: a thin Mylar strip for tapes, a plastic disk for floppy disks, or a metal platter for hard disks.

Another technology that is gaining acceptance is optical storage. Rather than having information stored on a magnetic medium, a reflective surface is modified by a solid-state laser beam. The device needed depends on the amount and permanence of the information that is to be stored and the speed with which it needs to be stored and retrieved.

Data can be accessed on a magnetic medium by one of two methods: sequential access and random access. Magnetic tapes provide sequential-access storage. For *sequential access,* the computer must start at the beginning of the tape and read what is stored on the tape until it finds the desired data. Floppy diskettes, hard disks, and optical storage use random-access storage. *Random access* allows information to be accessed directly. Random-access devices are usually used as primary storage devices because of their superior access speed. Devices that access data sequentially are usually used for backup and long-term data storage. As you might suspect, random-access devices are usually more expensive than sequential devices.

Although descriptions of external-storage devices are being presented in this section on output devices, technically they should be classified as both input and output devices since they provide for both the storage and retrieval of information.

Floppy Diskettes. Floppy diskettes can efficiently store from about 360 KB to more than 2 MB of information on each diskette, depending on the quality of the diskette and disk drive, the size of the diskette, and the way information is formatted on the diskette. The size of a diskette ranges from 2.5 to 8 inches, with 3.5 inches being the most popular. These diskettes can be removed from the disk drive and stored or transferred from one computer to another. Floppy disk drives are the most common auxiliary storage devices on microcomputers due to their low cost and portability. Most educational applications require at least one floppy disk drive. Some applications operate more efficiently with two drives. At minimum, each school should have some computers with two floppy drives for making backup copies of diskettes. Figure 2–12 shows examples of floppy disk drives and diskettes.

Hard Disks. Hard disks were first used in mainframe computers as a means to store large amounts of data. Hard disks operate in an environment that is free from contamination and they use a platter that is rigid and hence not affected by the warp and imperfections that are found in diskettes. This medium will store from 20 megabytes (20,000 KB) to several gigabytes (GB) (1 GB = 1,000 MB). Hard-disk drives store and retrieve information up to 20 times faster than floppy disk drives. In the past, hard disk drives used fixed-disk technology that required the disks to be permanently mounted inside the drive housing. Currently, hard disks may be purchased as either a fixed-disk or a removable-disk cartridge. The removable-disk cartridge allows for the storage and transfer of large amounts of data—much more than can be stored on a floppy diskette.

The hard disk is the probably the most worked and hence most likely to fail component of your computer. Hard-disk quality is probably not a good place to look to save money. One attribute you may want to look at when comparing drives is the access rate. This will give you an idea of how fast the hard disk finds information on the disk. Figure 2–13 shows a fixed hard-disk drive and a removable hard-disk drive with cartridge.

In an educational setting, hard disks are also used in conjunction with local area networks (see Chapter 9, Networks and Telecommunication). A *local area network*

FIGURE 2–12   Floppy Disk Drives with 3.5" and 5.25" Diskettes

(*LAN*) allows computers to be connected together to form a system. The server can contain a large hard disk to store data or programs common to users on the network. Students can be given access to various sections of the hard disk via a password. Software that is not copy protected can be loaded on the hard disk where it is accessible by every computer connected to the network. This reduces the need for students to handle fragile floppy diskettes. With a hard-disk-based network, fewer floppy disk drives are necessary. However, some floppy disk drives are needed for storing personal data and programs, backing up important information, and accessing copy-protected programs.

Networks are usually something you want to leave to a computer specialist. The key point to remember is how many users you want on the network and how heavily the network will be used at any given time. This will help the computer specialist determine what networking technology is most appropriate. As usual, the more speed required (more users requiring more data), the higher the price tag for the technology. Some examples of network hardware technologies are Token-Ring, Ethernet, Arcnet, and Applenet. Software, such as *Netware,* has to be used to control the network.

Optical Storage.   Optical storage is one of the newest methods of data storage. Optical storage devices do not use a magnetic medium; they use a reflective surface. The information is stored on the reflective surface by modifying the reflective medium using an optical laser beam. A read-only version of optical storage is the CD-ROM, which holds

FIGURE 2–13a   Internal and External Fixed Hard-Disk Drives

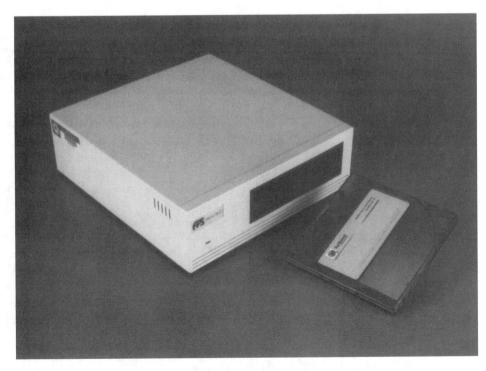

FIGURE 2–13b   Removable Hard-Disk Drive with Cartridge

between 550 and 660 MB of information. The CD-ROM looks exactly like an audio compact disc (CD) that is available at most record stores. CD-ROMs are finding a wide variety of use where large amounts of data need to be distributed to personal computer users. Large databases—such as references for all educational magazines and journal articles or an entire set of encyclopedias—are now stored on a single CD-ROM. Figure 2–14 shows a CD-ROM and player (see Chapter 8, Multimedia/Hypermedia).

New optical storage devices that can be written to and read from many times, similar to hard disks, are now being integrated into personal workstations. These typically hold 128 to 600 MB of information and come in fixed and removable formats.

Tape Drives. Now that hard-disk drives typically store well over 200 MB, backing up your data (so you don't lose the information if the hard disk fails) is not really feasible with diskettes (over 100 diskettes are needed to back up a 200 MB drive). Tape backup provides an inexpensive alternative. Storage tapes used with computers come in a wide variety of formats. They may be either reel to reel or similar to cassettes. Commonly they are used for long-term storage of large amounts of data. The reel-to-reel tapes are used more frequently with mainframe and minicomputers. The two most common types of tape storage use with microcomputers are the quarter-inch cartridge (QIC) and the digital audio tape (DAT). These tapes will hold from 10 MB to over 2 GB (4 GB if data are compressed) of information. A cassette tape and drive are shown in Figure 2–15.

FIGURE 2–14   CD-ROM and Player

FIGURE 2–15   Tape Cassette and Drive

Visual Display

The most common method of looking at computer output is through a visual display. This was not always the case, however; early mainframe computers used only printers to provide output to the user. A wide range of features and capabilities are now available to help the computer communicate information to the user.

Graphics and Color Capabilities.   Almost all microcomputers used in schools have some graphics and sound capabilities. Many can also display graphics and/or text in color. The quality of a computer's graphics is chiefly determined by the resolution, or the number and density of individual dots of light called *pixels* ("picture elements"), that can be displayed on the screen. The greater the number of dots per square inch, the higher the resolution and quality of the graphics. With higher resolution, diagonal lines are less jagged, and drawings and graphic figures can be shown in finer detail.

The resolution of a computer display is usually expressed in terms of the number of dots across the screen and down the screen. Most computers are able to display graphics at several different levels of resolution. Some standard resolutions are SVGA, 1,024 × 800, and VGA, 640 × 480. The number of colors available varies with each resolution. Color capability is usually expressed in terms of the number of colors that can be displayed out of a palette of colors (e.g., 16 colors out of a palette of 4,000).

Black and white computer images are represented in the memory of the computer by binary digits or bits (1 and 0). The numeral 1 is used to represent a dot of light (or pixel) that is turned on; a 0 represents a pixel that is turned off. The higher the resolution of the image, the greater the number of pixels that must be represented in memory. Color images require several bits to represent each pixel. Two bits per pixel will provide for 4 colors, and 4 bits will yield 16 colors; 8 bits for each pixel are required for 256 colors, and 16 bits are needed for more than 65,000 colors. In addition, 24-four bit color provides for over 16 million colors. As the number of colors increases, the quality of the picture and the amount of memory required to represent the picture also increases (see Chapter 8, Multimedia/Hypermedia).

Because color significantly affects the interest and motivation of students, it is used extensively in educational software. Although color may not be essential for learning, some programs that use color to distinguish between objects may not be usable with monochrome (single-color) monitors. Most computers sold in schools today include color monitors.

Visual-Display Devices.   The most common visual-display devices used in microcomputers include *cathode-ray tube (CRT)* screens and *liquid-crystal displays (LCD)*. CRT screens are similar in appearance and technology to television sets. There are several different types of CRT displays to choose from: monochrome monitors, composite-color monitors, and RGB (red, green, blue) monitors. Resolution and color are the most critical features to consider in selecting CRT display screens. The resolution that is required for an application will determine the graphics capability and the monitor needed for the computer system. A high-resolution image will have clearer characters and graphics.

Color monitors are generally twice as expensive as monochrome monitors. A monochrome monitor displays only two colors—a foreground and a background—for instance, green, amber, or white characters on a black background, or black characters on a white background. The ability for a color monitor to display an increasing level of detail is determined by both the monitor and the display adapter. The display adapter may be a card added to the computer or built into the "mother board." Color resolution is determined by the scan rate (measured in hertz), color depth (measured in bits), and video memory (measured in megabytes).

CRT screens come in many different sizes. For use by an individual, 12- to 19-inch screens are preferred. Larger screens may be more useful for group presentations and/or situations where the user needs a lot of detailed information on a single screen (e.g., the blueprints for a house or a two-page layout).

Flat-screen technology is an essential part of portable computers (see Figures 2–1a and b). The most common types of flat-screen technologies in use are liquid-crystal display (LCD) and active matrix (thin film transistor technology). These flat screens offer a very lightweight and compact alternative to the CRT. Their resolution is typically 640 × 480. Flat screens can display either monochrome or color images.

Two technologies have been developed to bring computer use to large audiences. The projection monitor has been improved to accommodate the high resolutions used with computers. Another device, a projection LCD plate (see Figure 2–16), is used in conjunction with an overhead projector to display computer-generated information. In either case, the computer is connected to the projection device so that the image is projected onto a screen, which will enable a group of people to view the computer output simultaneously.

FIGURE 2–16   Projection LCD Plate with Overhead Projector and Computer

A technology currently in development would permit the computer to use high-resolution graphics with a television. This technology, high-definition television (HDTV), would increase the resolution of a television from 525 lines to approximately 1,024 lines (a standard has not been set for the number of lines). This increase in resolution would allow most current personal computer software in existence today to be displayed on a home HDTV monitor.

Print Devices

The output from a computer can be printed on a piece of paper. Print devices come in all shapes and sizes, each with a particular beneficial feature such as speed, low cost, quality print, color print, and so on. All general-purpose print devices connect to computers through one of the ports on the back of computers. These ports come in two varieties: serial and parallel. A majority of computer manufacturers have these ports built into the computer. If a special interface is required, care should be taken to assure that the interface will be compatible with your existing hardware and software.

A *printer* is a device that enables the user to obtain a "hard copy" (i.e., paper copy) of computer programs or data stored in the memory of the computer. The major factors to consider in the evaluation and selection of a printer are cost, speed, and print quality. Printers most common in schools are dot matrix, ink jet, and laser.

Dot-matrix printers use a single-print element or writing head made up of wires or pins. They obtain their name from the fact that the printed characters are made up of a pattern, or matrix, of dots. A specific dot matrix is produced when a corresponding pattern of pins presses the ribbon against the paper. Since the characters are made up of dots, rather than solid lines and curves, the print quality of dot-matrix printers may be noticeably poorer than that of typed documents. However, with the advance of dot-matrix printer technology, this difference in quality is being reduced. Many dot-matrix printers use a high-density print head and overlapping dot patterns to produce characters in which the dots are so close together as not to be evident. Dot-matrix printers print at several different speeds, depending on the quality of print desired. Draft-quality print can be produced at up to 200 characters per second. Several passes of the print head may be required to produce correspondence-quality print, resulting in speeds less than 50 characters per second. Dot-matrix printers can produce graphics and several different type styles and sizes without making any modifications to the printer.

Ink-jet printers usually produce a quality of print between dot matrix and laser. Ink-jet printers use a cartridge that moves across the paper, similar to a typewriter or dot-matrix printer. The cartridge has 50 ink-filled chambers with very small nozzles attached to each chamber. Ink (available in colors) is not sprayed out of these nozzles; rather, it is pushed out. Within several millionths of a second, the back of the nozzles heat to a temperature of more than 900 degrees. This forms a bubble in the chamber, pushing the ink out of the nozzles. The ink droplets then adhere to the paper. Ink-jet printing is an inexpensive alternative to laser printers.

The advent of the inexpensive desktop *laser printer* has begun to replace most other types of printers, especially when high-quality text and graphics are needed. The laser printer is substantially faster than dot-matrix and ink-jet printers. The smaller models print about eight pages per minute. The speed is determined by how much processing has to be performed by the printer. Use of extensive graphics in a document will reduce the number of pages that can be printed per minute. The laser printer is significantly different from other types of printers in that it processes the information sent to it; in other words, it has its own small computer built in.

A laser printer accepts two types of input: text (ASCII) or a page description language (e.g., Postscript). The printer's processor interprets this information and turns on and off a laser that is focused on a cylinder or "drum." Where the laser touches the drum, the spot becomes charged. At the same time, paper is fed into the printer past a charged wire, which gives the paper an opposite charge. The drum rotates past a bin of black powder (toner), leaving powder only where the laser had touched. As the paper comes in contact with the drum, the powder adheres to the paper. The paper is then heated to permanently fuse the powder to the paper. Color laser printers produce very high-resolution color images by following a process similar to that described above, except multicolor plastic or wax film is used in place of powder.

Sound and Video Output

Sound and video output may be created or enhanced through the use of a computer. Only a brief overview of these exciting technologies is presented in this section; a more complete discussion will be presented in Chapter 8, Multimedia/Hypermedia.

Sound Capabilities.   Sound is a valuable medium for gaining attention, enhancing motivation, and presenting certain types of information. Most microcomputers will ring a bell or generate a beep to gain the user's attention. Many computers used in schools can also produce various sound effects and music. Some can even talk.

Sounds can either be *synthesized* by electronic circuits or they can be represented as *digital* information and stored in the memory of the computer or on an external storage device. Synthesized sound circuits may be built into the computer, added as a circuit board, or enclosed in an attached peripheral device. Synthesized sound capabilities of the computer should be evaluated in terms of the number of notes or voices that can be played at one time, the range or number of octaves of musical notes that can be played, and the quality of the sound. The computer may also be interfaced with an external music synthesizer that permits the computer to record the music played on the synthesizer. This recorded information can then be edited or mixed with other sounds and then sent back to the synthesizer to be played. Computers can even generate human speech through the use of a sound synthesizer. However, synthesized speech generally sounds quite mechanical and is often difficult to understand.

Synthesized sounds are generated by issuing appropriate instructions or commands to the computer. Digitized sounds are actually recorded sounds and are usually of much higher quality than synthesized sounds. Digitized human speech is generally of comparable quality to that of telephone transmissions. The quality of digitized sound is determined by the number of binary digits (1 or 0) used to represent the sound. High-quality sound requires considerable memory or external storage. Computers can be used to control the playback of CD-quality sounds by connecting a CD-ROM player to the computer.

In a classroom or laboratory environment, the capability to redirect the sound from an external speaker to private earphones is very important. For classroom presentations, the computer may need to be connected to a sound amplifier and external speakers.

Video Technology. The use of full-motion video under computer control is a fairly new and evolving technology. Full-motion video displays 30 frames, or pictures, per second—the same as that produced by standard videotape players. Full-motion video can be controlled by a computer through the use of videodisc technology or digital video.

The videodisc (see Figure 2–17) is a reflective disk, either 8 or 12 inches in diameter, similar in appearance to a audio phonograph record. Video information is recorded on the disk in circular tracks of microscopic pits, with one picture (frame) per track. A videodisc player (see Figure 2–18) uses a solid-state laser to read the microscopic pits in the reflective surface of the videodisc and reproduce the video images on a television set or video monitor. Each video frame on the disk is preceded by a unique digital frame-number code that can be read by the player. A specific frame may be selected by entering its corresponding number on a built-in or handheld remote control unit. Within a matter of seconds, the player will seek out the specified picture (frame) and display it on the TV screen. This frame may be displayed as a still frame or as the first frame of a normal or slow-motion video sequence. Single still frames may be shown for an indefinite period of time without any wear to the disk or player since the disks are read by a beam of light.

Most videodisc players can be operated as stand-alone units similar to videotape players. However, by attaching a videodisc player to a computer as a peripheral device, a very powerful computer-based instructional system can be created. The computer can

FIGURE 2–17   Videodisc

control the operation of the player and videodisc by sending commands that instruct the player to display a specific still frame, play a sequence of frames in normal or slow motion, or play a particular audio track with or without the corresponding video display. Motion sequences in full color and stereophonic sound can be combined with still slides and computer-generated text and graphics into a sophisticated instructional program under computer control.

Historically, video information has been recorded on videotape or videodiscs in a format analogous to the actual video frequencies. However, recent advancements in video technology have made it possible to convert and store video information in digital form. Unfortunately, digital representations of full-motion color video require great amounts of memory and storage space. However, techniques have been developed to compress video files by a factor of 20 without significant loss of quality. Researchers are continuing to develop techniques for even greater levels of compression. In addition to high-density storage, digital video requires that special software and hardware (circuit boards) be added to a computer to compress and decompress the video information.

Digital video is very exciting for educators because it allows video as well as other forms of information (e.g., text, graphics, speech, sound effects, and music) to be stored in digital format on the same medium such as a CD-ROM. This digital information may be accessed by a computer in any order, duplicated without reduction in quality, transmitted over standard telephone lines, easily edited, mixed in numerous configurations, and easily resequenced. These features provide developers and users great flexibility in the design of and access to the material.

FIGURE 2–18   Videodisc Player

Communication

Computers can communicate with other computers via dedicated networks or through phone lines. In both cases, special hardware is required. A *modem* is required for interfacing between a computer and a telephone. A telephone transmits information in a continuous waveform, referred to as an *analog transmission.* Computers transmit information by digital transmission. To send a message via telephone from one computer to another, the sending computer's signals must first be converted from digital to analog (modulation). On the receiving end, the telephone signals must be converted from analog to digital (demodulation). The term *modem* is derived from MOdulate/DEModulate.

The speed at which information can be transmitted has been measured by *baud* rate, or the number of frequency changes during one second. A more accurate term for today's modems is *bits per second,* since most modems use multiple frequencies to transmit data. Modems usually range between 2,400 to 28,800 bits per second. The higher transmission rates are accomplished through data compression (exchanging shorter codes for frequently repeated messages). *Fax modems,* with the appropriate fax software, permit faxes to be sent and received by a computer.

By connecting individual computers together to form a network, communication between computers, and the sharing of peripherals, are made possible. Networks have different topologies (e.g., Bus, Token-Ring, Star) that manage the information that flows between computers, assuring that the correct information gets to the intended destination. A network adapter card is required for each computer that is connected to the network. For more detailed information on networks in education, see Chapter 9, Networks and Telecommunications.

Operating Systems

An *operating system* is a low-level computer program that handles basic input and output operations of the computer. Without an operating system, each application program would have to invent how to access a disk drive, display information on a monitor screen, and send data to a printer. With an operating system, all of the fundamental communications between computer components are common to all programs. The operating system becomes a standard and platform upon which all other programs are written. An operating system manages disk drive operations, such as storing, retrieving, copying, deleting, and listing disk files. It also manages the allocation of memory to various programs.

The *user interface* for an operating system is the mechanism or view that a user has for interacting with the various functions of the operating system. Most early operating systems—such as *Apple DOS, MS-DOS*, and *UNIX*—provided a command-based user interface. To perform functions such as copying a file, users would have to type in cryptic commands such as copy a:chap2.txt c:chap2b.txt. These commands were often confusing and intimidating for novice users. In the early 1980s, with the advent of the Macintosh computer, *graphical-user interfaces (GUIs)* were introduced to mainstream personal computing. Graphical-user interfaces are based on a desktop metaphor where the computer screen becomes an extension of the user's desktop with folders and papers arranged and organized by the user (see Figure 2–19).

Many operating systems with graphical-user interfaces also provide *multitasking* capabilities that allow more than one task or program to be executed at the same time. Each program can be displayed on the screen simultaneously in its own rectangular area, called a *window*. These windows can be overlapped, resized, and moved so that only the information the user is interested in is visible. Some examples of operating systems with GUI are *Macintosh Operating System, Microsoft Windows,* and *IBM OS/2*.

Hardware Evaluation

The first step in hardware selection is to identify the need for the computer equipment. What problems will be solved or what tasks will be accomplished through its use? Will the computer be used for both instruction and as a tool for the office staff and faculty? Will it be used to teach students how to write computer programs or augment major components of the curriculum? Will it be placed in a computer laboratory where it will be used for many different applications? So often, schools have purchased computer

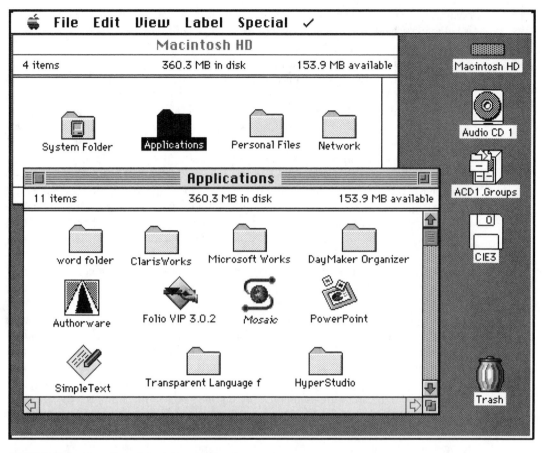

FIGURE 2–19   Graphical-User Interface

hardware and then asked, What shall we do with it? In such cases, the computer equipment will most likely end up unused or misused. It does not make any more sense to buy computer equipment without identifying how it will be used than it does to buy a hammer before determining whether the need is to pound nails or cut boards.

Computer hardware is no better than the software that drives it. Without software, a computer will not function. The quality and quantity of software available for a given computer will greatly determine its utility. A computer may have great specifications, but if there is no good software available to take advantage of its features, those capabilities are of little value. On the other hand, it is difficult for computer software to overcome limitations built into the computer hardware. For instance, if the computer hardware does not contain the necessary electronics to produce sounds, software will not solve the problem.

Remember that software written for one computer may not run on another. This is often the case even for computers produced by the same company. Therefore, before buying computer hardware, make sure compatible computer software is available to meet previously defined needs. Do not place too much reliance on assurances and promises. Seeing is believing. The development of quality software is a difficult and expensive process. In many cases, promised software has been significantly delayed or never completed.

Unfortunately, the state of the art in computer hardware and software is changing so rapidly that hardware selection decisions cannot be made solely on present needs and currently available software and hardware. It is very likely that, shortly after computer hardware and software have been purchased, some totally new computer application will be introduced that would prove very valuable. If the hardware that was purchased has significant limitations, it may not be able to handle the new application.

In making selection decisions for the present and an unknown future, it is important to look at the track record of the company that produces the hardware you are planning to purchase. Is the company financially stable? Does the company provide adequate local technical and maintenance support? How committed is the company to supporting educational application of their hardware? How many schools have already purchased that particular brand and model? How much user support is available in the way of user groups and magazines dedicated to that specific computer? How much educational software is already available? Is the available software competitively priced? How many third-party companies are producing peripherals and software for the computer? Does the computer company encourage and support third-party development? Has the computer company produced new models that will run the software produced for previous models?

The next major factor to consider in selecting a computer system is its compatibility with computer equipment previously purchased by the school or district. On first thought, it might seem wise to purchase several different types of computers. This would minimize the impact of the limitations of a particular model and would not lock the school into the software available only on one specific machine. Notwithstanding these possible advantages, the mixing of several different computers is not recommended—unless it is clearly necessary in order to meet divergent needs. Learning how to operate, maintain, and effectively use the full potential of a given computer is not a trivial investment of time. It is difficult for a single individual or institution to obtain the collective knowledge and experience necessary to effectively use a variety of computers. Computer users often need assistance and support from other users. If nearby users do not have similar equipment, they will be unable to provide the necessary support. Incompatible equipment also makes it difficult, if not impossible, to share peripherals, software, and data files.

Establishing a policy or guideline to purchase a particular model, or models, within a school, district, or state also makes it possible to negotiate favorable volume pricing arrangements with vendors. If a single model will not meet all the computing needs of the school, consider different models from the same manufacturer.

Summary

This chapter reviewed many different types of computers, from laptop computers, which can be held in your hand and carried in a briefcase, to supercomputers, which require large, environmentally controlled rooms. Most computer systems are composed of three major components: input devices, the computer with its central processing unit and internal memory, and output devices. Input devices are used to enter information into the computer; they include keyboards, optical scanners, mouses, touch panels, pens, graphic tablets, joysticks, graphic scanners, and audio digitizers. When the information is entered into the computer, it is stored in internal memory and processed by the central processing unit. After the processing is complete, the results may be stored or communicated to the user by being sent to an output device, such as floppy diskettes, hard disks, optical disks, tapes, visual displays, printers, speakers, and modems. Selecting the appropriate computer and peripheral input and output devices requires careful consideration of many factors, principal of which are their intended applications.

Exercises

1. What is the difference between computer hardware and software?
2. List and describe three different input devices and identify the purposes for which each would be used.
3. What is the difference between RAM and ROM?
4. What factors are used to classify CPUs?
5. List and describe three different output devices and identify the purposes for which they would be used.
6. What is the difference between videodiscs and digital video?
7. After you have completed Chapters 4 through 11 in this book, prepare a memo to your school principal and describe how you would like to use a computer in your classroom, what benefits would be derived from its use, what software is available to meet your needs, and what type of computer hardware is required for your proposed applications.

Chapter *3*

The History of Computers in Education

The family tree of computers as educational tools has a long history and includes fingers, toes, stones, sticks, slates, lead pencils, quill pens, and the printing press. All these are passive learning tools, providing no opportunity for the learner to interact with the device. Efforts to provide students with a more active role in learning have produced innovations such as programmed instruction and the teaching machine. As Heines (1988) reflected on the history of the development of learning tools, he suggested that the theoretical stage for mechanized learning devices was set by Thorndike in 1912, who wrote, "If, by a miracle of mechanical ingenuity, a book could be so arranged so that only to him who had done what was directed on page one would page two become visible, and so on, much that now requires personal instruction could be accomplished by print." Just a few years later, in 1926, Sidney L. Pressey invented a machine that presented multiple-choice questions on a rotating cylindrical drum. Students responded by pressing one of four keys, each of which represented one of the answer choices. In the drill mode, all keys except the one representing the correct answer were locked; in the test mode, no clues of correctness of the response were given, The machine recorded all responses and was capable of giving the user a piece of candy when a programmable number of correct responses had been made. Other machines followed, including inventions in the 1950s by B. F. Skinner, that allowed students to construct responses rather than simply to select from a series of choices. All these efforts to mechanize the learning process have been overshadowed in recent years by the versatility and power of the computer.

Historical Roots

Although the development of the computer can be traced through centuries to seemingly unrelated devices—such as the music box, the weaving machine, and others—

more obvious evolutionary steps are seen in a host of calculating devices, including the abacus, Babbage's Analytical Engine, Grant's Difference Engine, and the many versions of the long-popular slide rule and mechanical adding machine.

Who Was First?

The general-purpose electronic, digital computer is said to have had its beginning with ENIAC (Electronic Numerical Integrator and Calculator). A huge machine having thousands of vacuum tubes and consuming vast amounts of electrical power, ENIAC was developed at the University of Pennsylvania during World War II and put into full use in 1945. However, the question of who really was first with the electronic computer has not been left unchallenged. In a court decision (Jones, Jones, Bowyer, & Ray, 1983), Dr. John Vincent Atanasoff of Iowa State College was declared to be the first, having constructed a device in 1939 for the purpose of carrying out computations related to physics problems. Contesting both of these is evidence (Mocciola, 1981) that the first electronic digital computer was actually the British COLOSSUS, designed during World War II to break German secret codes.

The seemingly simultaneous development of an idea by several people, sometimes unknown to each other, is not new in the field of scientific invention and discovery. History shows that this has been the case with many significant advances, including the discovery of electricity. Regardless of who is recognized as being first, many early creative minds made their mark on the development of today's electronic computer.

Later Developments

The invention of the transistor in 1948 resulted in the replacement of literally hundreds of vacuum tubes by a single small device. In turn, the development of the integrated circuit in the late 1950s replaced thousands of transistors with a microchip, paving the way for the first microprocessor in the early 1970s and giving birth to a new generation of computers. As computers were miniaturized, their power and efficiency skyrocketed and their prices plummeted, opening new avenues for personal and educational use.

Along with other significant advances came the development of the computer's interactive capability. Programs and data were entered into early computers in a batch (usually via punched cards) and results were returned in a batch (usually via a printer). As systems were developed that allowed the user to enter information at a keyboard and get immediate results on a monitor, potential applications for the classroom were vastly increased. Computer-based education requires equipment to display information to, and receive a response from, the learner. Feedback must be provided regarding correctness of the response, and the subsequent flow of instructional events must be tailored to the needs of the learner. Today's computers are capable of such interaction.

Microcomputers were introduced in kit form in 1975. Soon thereafter, preassembled micros—including the Commodore Pet, Apple, and TRS-80—were available to U.S. schools. This stimulated a market that placed hundreds of thousands of microcomputers into the homes and schools of the United States in a period of a very few years.

Acceptance by Society

One of the best-known success stories associated with the advent of the microcomputer is that of Steven Jobs. As a student at Homestead High School in Los Altos (California) during the early 1970s, he attended lectures at Hewlett-Packard, driven by his fascination with technology. After creating and selling an illegal electronic telephone attachment that allowed the user to make long-distance calls at no cost, Jobs and his friend Stephen Wozniak built and marketed one of the world's first microcomputers. From a business that began in a bedroom and garage of his parents' home, Jobs six years later was chairman of the board of a company with $600 million in sales and growing almost out of control. The Apple computer was named by Jobs in memory of a summer spent working in the orchards of Oregon (Taylor, 1982).

With these developments, the computer's impact on society was so evident in 1982 that *Time Magazine* declared it the newsmaker of the year, breaking the 55-year precedent of awarding this honor to a person. With reference to the cover article of *Time Magazine,* which dedicated the annual "Man of the Year" recognition for 1982 to the computer, publisher Meyers stated, "Several human candidates might have represented 1982, but none symbolized the past year more richly, or will be viewed by history as more significant, than [this] machine" (Meyers, 1983, p. 3).

Size Categories

Computers are available in several size categories, including microcomputers, minicomputers, and mainframes. A major difference among them is their capacity to store and process information. With continued advances of the microcomputer, the differences are becoming less obvious. Some large school systems have acquired minicomputers, but for most schools, the desktop microcomputer is adequate. With the added advantage of relatively low cost, most schools can participate in computer-based education. Desktops are affordable for individuals, and laptops and handheld computers are affordable as well as portable and practical for persons on the go.

Major Computer-Based Education Efforts

With the current influx of microcomputers into the schools, many people do not realize that the earliest computer-based education (CBE) applications were developed on mainframe and minicomputers. Two of the best-known systems continue to have an impact on education: PLATO (a mainframe system) and the Time-shared, Interactive, Computer-Controlled Information Television (TICCIT) (a minicomputer system). These and other major projects and events in the development of computers in education are discussed in the following pages.

PLATO

In 1959, engineers, physicists, psychologists, and educators at the University of Illinois, under the leadership of Donald Bitzer, began developing a system to automate individualized instruction. The system, known as PLATO, was initially funded by the

University of Illinois and the Department of Defense, and it evolved into a powerful CBE system. Developments included a computer-assisted instruction (CAI) authoring language called TUTOR (a language designed to simplify the development of CAI programs) and specially designed computer terminals (Rahmlow, Fratini, & Ghesquiere, 1980). These terminals consisted of a plasma panel display, microfiche projector, touch panel, and keyboard. The plasma panel display was made up of 512 horizontal and 512 vertical wires sandwiched with neon gas between two flat plates of glass. Sending an electrical signal to a horizontal and a vertical wire made the intersection glow as a small dot. Patterns of these dots were used to display high-resolution graphics, animated characters, and text in many different sizes and fonts. Since the screen was transparent, color slides could be projected onto the screen from the rear by using a computer-controlled, random-access microfiche projector. Unfortunately, production costs were prohibitive, and these innovative terminals were replaced by high-resolution cathode-ray tube (CRT) terminals.

During the first seven years, the system grew from 1 terminal to 71, 20 of which were operable simultaneously. Nearly 200 lessons were written to demonstrate the teaching flexibility of the system. In 1967, the University of Illinois established the Computer-based Education Research Laboratory (CERL) and moved the PLATO project into the new facility. Efforts there emphasized efficient use of the system, courseware development for a large-scale CBE system, and hardware development.

Control Data Corporation (CDC) obtained the rights to market PLATO and installed a second system at CDC headquarters in Minneapolis in the spring of 1974 and a third at Florida State University in the fall of the same year. Sites were set up at the University of Delaware as well as in other countries, including Canada, England, Belgium, South Africa, and Korea. During the late 1980s and early 1990s, CDC sold their PLATO rights to the Roach Organization and to University On-Line, and CDC is no longer involved with the operation and marketing of this system.

The PLATO system at the University of Illinois supported over 4,000 terminals at 100 to 200 locations. In 1977, PLATO took advantage of microcomputer technology by developing a new system called Micro-PLATO, which added flexible disk drives to the standard PLATO terminal to deliver courseware independently of the central host computer, thus avoiding the expense of telephone communications. Micro-PLATO is no longer in use in the United States, but it is being used and further developed in Japan by TDK.

Over the years, funding for the development of the PLATO system has amounted to hundreds of millions of dollars and has come from a wide variety of sources in addition to CDC, including the joint departments of the Army, Navy, and Air Force; the National Science Foundation; the U.S. Office of Education; the National Institute of Education; and the University of Illinois.

The PLATO system is probably the best-known CAI project in the world and has been the object of considerable research. The system has been shown to be effective and cost efficient. Positive results in both achievement and attitude of users have been reported.

A successor system to PLATO, called NovaNET (a registered trademark of University Communications, Inc.), provides higher-quality graphics and greater efficiency. With this system, cost is reduced in three ways:

1. It operates on a cluster of DEC Alpha computers, capable of running several thousand NovaNET terminals simultaneously.
2. This service is available for personal systems, including DOS, Windows, Macintosh, and UNIX X-11 computers.
3. The system is available by dial-up leased line and on Internet.

All operations, marketing, and further development are currently being shifted to the private sector under University Communications, Inc. (Sinder, 1995).

TICCIT

The TICCIT system began in 1971 with the combined efforts of the engineers from MITRE Corporation in McLean, Virginia, and educators at the CAI Laboratory at the University of Texas. They were later joined by the Institute for Computer Uses in Education at Brigham Young University. With funding from the National Science Foundation, and under the guidance of C. Victor Bunderson, the group set out to develop complete courses in math and English at the college freshman level. The courses were developed using minicomputers, color TV, graphics, a special authoring system, and the expertise of both content specialists and psychologists who were well versed in instructional design. The TICCIT system was typically housed in a learning center and was capable of handling up to 128 terminals.

Instructional strategies of TICCIT differ from previous computer-based learning in several ways—most importantly was that the selection of which lesson was to be studied next and which displays were to be viewed within a lesson were controlled by the learner rather than by the system.

Enthusiasts of CAI have often dreamed of a system that could assess a student's learning style, past achievement, and readiness, and then present to the student the information and strategy most appropriate for him or her. The designers of TICCIT felt that such an effort could be counterproductive by making students totally dependent on the system. Subsequent learning could become more difficult because the real world is not so adaptive to specific needs of individuals. A major objective of TICCIT was to help students become independent learners. When a student learns to select the next display on the TICCIT system, he or she also learned something about selecting the next learning step in noncomputer-based situations.

The TICCIT system was initially designed to provide instruction in English and mathematics for students in junior college. Its actual use was mostly with military personnel and with the instruction of foreign language, English, and algebra at the university level. TICCIT was phased out in 1995 (Hendricks, 1995).

WICAT

In 1977, the nonprofit World Institute for Computer-Assisted Teaching, Inc. (WICAT) was formed. Its principal founder, Dustin H. Heuston, was formerly headmaster of the Spence School, a private school for girls in Manhattan, where he became heavily involved in research in and implementation of CAI applications to education. Other founders of WICAT included educators, instructional designers, and computer scientists who were dedicated to finding ways in which technology could be used to improve training and education (Burn, 1989). WICAT's purposes included developing exemplary software—particularly in basic skill areas such as English, mathematics, and reading—and conducting research in learning and teaching through use of capabilities generated by the new technologies.

In 1992, WICAT was purchased by Jostens, Inc. WICAT Systems, headquartered in Orem, Utah, formerly a developer of educational software, now produces software only for the aviation industry. Educational software is now produced and marketed by Jostens Learning, headquartered in San Diego, California.

MECC

The Minnesota Educational Computing Corporation (MECC) was founded by the state of Minnesota in 1973 to provide mainframe computer time-sharing service to Minnesota schools and to promote the use of computers in education. After identifying the need for schools to obtain high-quality software at cost-effective prices, MECC designed the first software membership program in 1980. As a result, schools nationwide began buying MECC products and services. In 1985, MECC became a public corporation, wholly owned by the state of Minnesota. As the next step in the plan to make MECC a fully independent entity, the company was purchased in January 1991 by North American Fund II, a specialty acquisition fund committed to the growth of companies with high potential. In March 1994, MECC became a public corporation and is identified by the symbol MECC on the Nasdaq National Market.

Today, MECC remains a leading producer of high-quality educational software for all age groups. MECC software is available in Macintosh, Windows, MS-DOS, and CD-ROM formats. MECC's impressive list of over 100 award-winning products includes such popular titles as *The Oregon Trail, Storybook Weaver,* and *Number Munchers* (MECC Communications Dept., April 1995).

CONDUIT

With headquarters at the University of Iowa, CONDUIT began as a consortium effort of the Universities of Oregon, North Carolina, Iowa, and Texas, and Dartmouth College. Established in 1971, its objective was to improve the quality of CAI courseware. This effort was directed by James Johnson and funded by the National Science Foundation and the Fund for the Improvement of Post-Secondary Education. A system was developed for the acquisition, evaluation, and distribution of courseware designed for instructional computing support of university courses. Contrary to the understanding of some people, CONDUIT was not a clearinghouse. Nonetheless, all submissions were subjected to a rigorous review process involving content consultants and in-house technical staff. CONDUIT was phased out by June 1, 1995.

Other Computer-Based Education Efforts

Many other projects have influenced the development of computer-based education. Representative efforts are discussed in this section.

Patrick Suppes, Stanford University

Patrick Suppes began a program of CAI research and development at Stanford University in 1963. Initiated by a grant from the Carnegie Corporation, the project was eventually funded by the National Science Foundation and the U.S. Office of Education. Suppes's work has been well received by educators and has been used extensively in major school projects throughout the United States. The early work at Stanford emphasized the development of materials for individualizing mathematics and language arts for elementary school students, primarily the disadvantaged. Suppes went on to develop CAI materials for gifted elementary students and later turned his attention to the development of materials for use at the university level, including the areas of Russian, philosophy, mathematics, and music. The evaluation of Suppes's CAI materials at both the elementary and university levels has consistently yielded positive results (Chambers & Sprecher, 1983).

In 1967, Suppes's effort developed into the Computer Curriculum Corporation (CCC), which provides an instructional computer system with a large body of courseware. Its objectives are synchronized with local and state objectives in basic skills. The corporation has designed a learning model of mastery that continually analyzes student performance and adapts instruction for each learner that is based on this information. The courses help to provide efficient acquisition of basic skills, problem-solving skills, and higher-order thinking skills. In all courses, current performance levels and student gains are provided on diagnostic reports.

Harold E. Mitzel, Pennsylvania State University

Research, development, and implementation in CBE were initiated at Pennsylvania State University when the Computer-Assisted Instruction Laboratory was established in 1964 under the leadership of Harold E. Mitzel. In December 1967, an IBM 1500 Instructional System, one of the first computer systems designed and built specifically for instructional purposes, was installed at Pennsylvania State. The system included a computer language called Coursewriter designed for the development of CAI materials. This system used a televisionlike screen, a light pen and keyboard for student responses, an optional image projector, and audio playback equipment. Student terminals had to be located within 2,500 feet of the computer. To compensate for this geographic limitation, three mobile vans were each equipped with a complete computer system and 16 student stations. They were used for transporting the CBE programs around the state and eventually around the nation. The vans and the IBM 1500 have been surpassed by microcomputer technology, but they served well in their time.

Seymour Papert, Massachusetts Institute of Technology

Seymour Papert worked in Switzerland with Jean Piaget for five years. From his study of the development of thinking patterns in humans, Papert turned his thoughts toward possible ways of making machines "think" and began research in artificial intelligence at the Massachusetts Institute of Technology (MIT). He started conceptualizing Logo in 1967. The work of Papert and his colleagues at MIT has had a historical impact on CBE. Their development of Logo, which is based on research in artificial intelligence, allows and encourages the learner to instruct (or program) the computer. The claim of the Logo group is that with too many CBE materials the learner is programmed by the computer and that the best learning takes place when these roles are reversed.

Steven Hunka, University of Alberta

The Division of Educational Research Services, under the direction of Steven Hunka at the University of Alberta, has been active in CBE since 1968, when it installed an IBM 1500 Instructional System. The group has been promoting research, production, and demonstration of CBE materials, using them to provide instruction to regularly enrolled students at the university. In some courses, CBE has been used as the primary source of instruction. In others, it provides backup for regular teaching sessions.

Alfred Bork, University of California

With funding from the National Science Foundation, Alfred Bork began the development of computer-based materials for instruction in undergraduate physics at the University of California at Irvine in 1969. These materials emphasized graphics and included simulations that enriched and supplemented basic physics courses. Bork's work has been expanded to other subject areas and today includes microcomputer-based materials. His products have been used extensively throughout the world. Bork has also provided training seminars on the design of CAI courseware that have become popular in the education and business worlds.

Dartmouth College

It was at Dartmouth College that the computer language BASIC was invented by John G. Kemeny and Thomas E. Kurtz (Kemeny, 1984). Modern-structured versions of this language emerged in the 1980s, but the 1970 vintage was used for many years. Dartmouth was also the home base of Arthur Luehrmann, another of the nation's leaders in educational computing.

Chicago Title I Schools

The city of Chicago began a CBE drill and practice program in 1971 using 105 CRT terminals and seven printers equally divided among seven Elementary and Secondary Education Act (ESEA) Title I schools. This effort was expanded to 54 elementary schools with similar equipment configurations and to six special education schools. Each CBE lab served at least 150 students a day, with each student being involved with one session each day in reading and one session in either language arts or math. Evaluations showed that students who used CBE achieved significantly better than those who did not, and that increased achievement was obtained at relatively low cost.

Ohio State University

One of the largest bodies of health-related CBE materials in the world was developed at the Ohio State University (OSU) College of Medicine by the Division of Computing Services for Medical Education and Research. Approximately 480 hours of courseware were developed for this program during the 1970s. During the 1979–1980 fiscal year, more than 26,000 hours of use were logged by OSU College of Medicine and students and health practitioners from 50 other institutions in the United States.

The Military

Since the early 1970s, the Army, Air Force, and Navy have been extensively involved in the development, evaluation, and use of CBE applications. Large numbers of military personnel have received specialized training on computers. In addition, marginal basic skills in areas such as mathematics and reading have been effectively improved, even with decreased instructor involvement.

Level of Use in the Schools

The trend toward miniaturization of the computer opened the doors to a vast new technological world for the schools. As effective as the large mainframe systems and minicomputers are, their costs are usually prohibitive to the average school system. With the microcomputer, however, even small school systems can enjoy the benefits of current technology. Instead of a huge initial outlay for a computer system, the school can, if necessary, start with a single desktop unit with a relatively small capital investment, and then grow as it is able within budgetary constraints.

Today, virtually all secondary schools and most elementary schools in the United States are using some type of computer system for administrative and instructional purposes (Tolman & Allred, 1991). Surveys continue to indicate greater and greater involvement of schools with the new technology (Roblyer, Castine, & King, 1988). The total numbers of computers in the schools is now in the millions. Vast amounts of money are spent annually for software and for teacher training. The employment of computer specialists by state departments of education and by school districts is now common.

Summary

Widespread use of technological advances has historically altered society and, with it, the schools. This was true of the printing press, the automobile, the airplane, and the telephone. It is true of the computer today.

The school system is in a period of transition. Reactions of educators and of the public to the computer and its role as an educational tool cover a broad spectrum. Some people are excited, some are passive, and some are annoyed. Others are intimidated by the technology and apprehensive about the vast unknowns in the future of society and education. The availability and use of computers in the schools brings new hope to some, whereas to others they are still threatening and alienating.

The optimist sees the computer slowly bringing some long-hoped-for capabilities to the classroom: managerial systems that are less tedious and time consuming, freeing more teacher time for preparation and instruction; effective personalized tutorials; a tool with which children can think and learn in new and exciting ways, developing inquiry and problem-solving skills; and a chance to meet more adequately the needs of students who have disabilities and those who are gifted. The optimist finds new hope for the possibilities of effectively meeting the instructional needs of all individuals.

Some of the factors considered by the skeptic are programs that stop working if the user presses the wrong key; programs designed for one machine that will not run on another; limitations of student use on available machines; the staggering cost of supplying school systems with an adequate number of machines; difficulty in getting competent service for computers that need repair; and the expense and inadequacy of much of the available software.

Many educators watch with interest and enthusiasm as each new branch and twig grows on the computer's family tree. History is being made in this area today, perhaps more rapidly than ever before. Methods of teaching in tomorrow's classroom are being molded by today's educators as they accept the challenges of applying technological advances to effective learning techniques.

Exercises

1. Describe the effect of early calculating devices on the development of the computer.
2. How would you settle the question of who really did have the first electronic computer?
3. What is PLATO? Where was it developed? What is its status today as an educational system?
4. What is TICCIT? How did it compare with earlier efforts in computer-based education?
5. Summarize the progress of U.S. public schools in the acquisition of computers.
6. What, to you, are significant arguments for or against full use of the computer in the classroom of the elementary or secondary school of today? In which subject areas do you think the computer can have the greatest benefit?
7. Considering the computer training given to today's students of elementary and secondary age, what do you think the needs will be during the next five years?

References

Burn, Dick. (1989). Telephone conversation, May 1989. (WICAT)

Chambers, J. A., & Sprecher, J. W. (1983). *Computer assisted instruction: Its use in the classroom.* Englewood Cliffs, NJ: Prentice-Hall.

Heines, Jesse M. (1988, 4th quarter). Milestones in early learning devices. *Course Of Action,* 24–29.

Hendricks, Harold. (1995). Personal visit, Brigham Young University, Provo, Utah, April 1995. (TICCIT—BYU Humanities Research Center)

Jones, W., Jones, B., Bowyer, K., & Ray, M. (1983). *Computer literacy: Problem-solving projects on the Apple.* Reston, VA: Reston.

Kemeny, J. G. (1984, November). Personal computers invade the classroom. *Creative Computing,* 173–175.

Merrill, M. D., Schneider, E. W., & Fletcher, K. A. (1980). *The instructional design library: TICCIT.* Englewood Cliffs, NJ: Educational Technology Publications.

Meyers, John A. (1983, January 3). A letter from the publisher. *Time Magazine,* p. 3.

Mitzel, H. E. (1982). *Encyclopedia of educational research* (5th ed.). New York: Free Press.

Mocciola, M. (1981). Who was really first to invent the electronic digital computer? *The Computer Teacher,* 8(6), 48–49.

NEA. (1983). *A teacher survey NEA report: Computers in the classroom.* Washington, DC: National Education Association.

Rahmlow, H. F., Fratini, R. C., & Ghesquiere, J. R. (1980). *The instructional design library: PLATO.* Englewood Cliffs, NJ: Educational Technology Publications.

Roblyer, M. D., Castine, W. H., & King, F. J. (1988). Computer applications have "undeniable value," research shows. *Electronic Learning, 38,* 40.

Sindler, D. (1995). Telephone conversation, April 1995. (PLATO)

Taylor, Alexander L., III. (1982, February 15). Striking it rich. *Time Magazine,* pp. 36–41.

Tolman, M. N., & Allred, R. A. (1991). *What research says to the teacher: The computer and education* (2nd ed.). Washington, DC: National Education Association.

Chapter *4*

Drill-and-Practice
and Tutorial Applications

Chapter 1 suggested that educational applications of computer technology can be classified as either tutor, tool, or tutee. Tutor applications were further subdivided into five categories: drill and practice, tutorial, problem solving, simulations, and games. Drill-and-practice and tutorial applications will be discussed in more detail in this chapter, and problem-solving applications, simulations, and games will be discussed in Chapter 5. In tutor applications, the computer takes on some of the functions of a teacher. Tutorial applications attempt to provide most, if not all, of the events of instruction required to help a student learn a particular learning outcome. In contrast, drill-and-practice applications attempt only to provide extensive opportunities for the student to practice a particular learning task.

Drill-and-Practice Applications

One of the most common applications of the computer as a tutor is in drill and practice. Drill and practice involves any exercise, physical or mental, that is performed regularly and with constant repetition. It is often associated with rote-memory learning. Drill-and-practice applications generally do not include instruction on how to do a particular task. Any necessary demonstration or expository instruction usually comes before the drill and practice.

Computer-based drill-and-practice programs are often considered to be trivial and inappropriate uses of the computer. Many educational computer programs are criticized for being mere drill and practice. Admittedly, many of the drill-and-practice

Portions of this chapter were adapted from Merrill, P. F., & Salisbury, D., Research on drill and practice strategies, *Journal of Computer-Based Instruction,* 1984, *11,* 19–21. Copyright 1984 by the Association for Development of Computer-Based Instructional Systems. Used by permission.

programs being produced today are dry and boring. However, these bad examples should not cause us to underestimate the potential value of computer-based drill and practice. There is considerable evidence, arising from recent research in modern cognitive theory, to suggest that drill-and-practice sessions are valuable when used appropriately.

Many of the modern theories about how learners perform complex tasks, such as reading and computing, suggest that for a learner to learn efficiently, performance of lower-level subskills must become automatic (Anderson, 1980; Gagné, 1982). This is generally referred to as *automaticity of subskills*. The more one practices a skill, the more automatic it becomes. As a subskill becomes automatic, it requires less attention and interferes less with other ongoing cognitive processes (Spelke, Hirst, & Neisser, 1976). Consider a musician learning a new piece of music. Once the mechanics of the piece have been mastered, the musician can focus attention on interpretation. The implication of this research is that drill and practice can serve an important role in bringing the learner to a level of automaticity on lower-level subskills that will allow him or her more readily to perform some higher-level complex skill.

Multiple discrimination skills are often prerequisites for more complex tasks involving classification, rule using, or problem solving. For a learner to become proficient in the more complex task, the multiple discrimination subskills must be automatic. Multiple discrimination skills involve distinguishing various stimuli from one another—for example, distinguishing the letters *b, d,* and *p* both from one another and from other letters of the alphabet. The ability to discriminate between stimuli can be demonstrated by pointing to the appropriate item. For humans, the most common behavior indicating discrimination ability is the appropriate naming of the item being discriminated.

Most discrimination tasks can also be thought of as paired-association tasks, wherein the learner is required to associate two things (stimulus and response or the item being discriminated and its corresponding label). In learning math facts, the student has to associate the problems with their corresponding answers. In learning to discriminate foreign language words, the learner must associate the foreign word with its English equivalent. Although these types of tasks are common in elementary school learning, they are also more common than many people think in higher education and technological training. For example, piano students need to learn the position of the keys on the keyboard and to associate a particular key with a particular note on the written music. Chemistry students need to learn the abbreviations of the chemical elements. Medical students are required to learn the names and locations of body parts. For learners to arrive at a point at which they can perform such skills automatically, drill and practice are essential.

Simple Drill-and-Practice Strategy

A simple drill-and-practice strategy can be implemented by using flashcards. The flashcards with the stimulus on the front and the correct response on the back are presented to the learner one at a time. After the learner responds to each stimulus, he or she is shown the correct answer on the back of the card, which provides reinforcement or corrective feedback. The learner continues to go through the set of cards repeatedly until all the items are learned to the desired level of automaticity.

The main advantage of this strategy is its simplicity. The strategy can be learned and executed with few training or logistical difficulties. No expensive equipment or special materials are necessary. The strategy can even be self-administered by the learners.

However, there are several reasons why this simple drill-and-practice strategy may not be as effective or efficient as it could be. First, the learners are presented all the items in one session. Learning to associate one stimulus and response pair is a relatively easy task. However, when students attempt to learn several pairs of items in one learning session, they often become confused as to which stimulus goes with which response. This interference between item pairs increases as the number of items increases (Bower & Hilgard, 1981; Gagné, 1985).

Second, this strategy is inefficient because an equal amount of time is spent on both the learned and the unlearned items. The learners respond to all items each time they go through the list, even if they have already learned some of the items. There is no provision for learners to concentrate their effort on the unlearned items.

A third problem with this strategy is that the items are always presented to the learners in the same sequence. This sets up a serial learning effect that allows the learners to use the item sequence as a cue for responding to an item. The danger in this approach is that the learners may not be able to respond correctly to the item when the sequence is altered.

Sophisticated Drill-and-Practice Strategy

Assume that by combining instructional design theory, results from research in experimental and instructional psychology, and computer technology, you can devise and implement a more efficient and effective strategy for drill and practice. The use of the computer should make it possible to implement a more complex strategy that could be made simple and easy to use from the learners' point of view. On the basis of instructional design theory and research, the flashcard strategy could be improved in several ways.

1. Instead of having learners work on all items during a given practice session, you could provide them with drill on a smaller subset of items. By practicing on a small subset, the amount of interference between items and the short-term memory load is reduced. The subset of items being drilled during a practice session is called the *working pool* (Atkinson, 1974) (see Figure 4–1). The size of this pool is seven items, plus or minus two, depending on the difficulty of the items and the capability of the target audience (Miller, 1956). The most appropriate size of the working pool must be determined empirically for each set of items and for each audience.

2. To avoid unnecessary practice on learned items and to allow concentrated effort on unlearned items, a separate working pool for each student is needed, as well as a mechanism for moving learned items out of the working pool and replacing them with new items. An example of a simple mechanism is to replace the items in the working pool

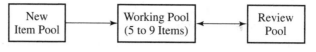

FIGURE 4–1   Item Pools for Sophisticated Drill-and-Practice Strategy

as a block after all the items have been learned by a given student to a specified criterion. A more complex mechanism is to replace each item in the working pool one at a time as soon as it has been learned to the specified criterion. This second mechanism seems to be the most efficient. The criterion is set so that an item is replaced after it has been answered correctly a certain number of times or a certain number of times in a row. The most effective replacement mechanism and criterion level would need to be determined empirically.

3. The sequential learning effect is eliminated by randomly rearranging or shuffling the items within the working pool each time a given student goes through the subset of items.

4. To increase retention, an effective strategy requires a mechanism for reviewing items previously learned. Research (Anderson, 1980; Gay, 1973) indicates that several short-spaced reviews are more effective than a few massed reviews. This pattern is facilitated by setting up a *review pool* (see Figure 4–1). Whenever an item is learned to the criterion level, it is removed from the working pool and placed in the review pool. Each item in the review pool has a date associated with it to indicate when it will next be reviewed. Whenever an item is removed from the working pool and placed in the review pool, the working pool is replenished by the selection of an item from either the *new item pool* or the review pool. The replacement item is selected from the review pool if an item in the review pool has a review date associated with it that is equal to or less than the current date. Otherwise, the replacement item is selected from the new item pool.

5. If it is likely that learners may already know some of the items to be learned in the practice session, it is useful to provide some pretesting mechanism. All the items to be learned are pretested before the first practice session, or each item is pretested whenever it is selected from the new item pool to go into the working pool. This latter mechanism is more appropriate when there are many items to be learned. Items answered correctly on the pretest are skipped.

Example Drill-and-Practice Computer Software

Many of the drill-and-practice programs currently on the market do not include sophisticated strategies similar to the one described in the previous section. In this section, several programs that incorporate such strategies are contrasted with some that do not.

A set of routines, written in the Pascal programming language, has been developed at Brigham Young University (BYU) that incorporates the sophisticated strategies described earlier. These routines have been incorporated into a computer program that selects and presents pictorial stimuli from a videodisc (*The First National Kidisc*). The program is designed to drill students on the names of the flags of more than 90 countries. The stimuli consist of full-color pictures of the flags. If a student responds incorrectly to a flag stimulus, a corrective feedback frame displays a picture of the flag along with the name and map of the country.

Another program developed at BYU uses these same routines to teach children sight words. The sight words are presented on the computer monitor in large letters and paired with the correct pronunciation of the word by using digitized voice output. During the drill-and-practice sequences, a child responds to the visual stimulus by pronouncing the word. The correctness of the child's response is then evaluated using a speech recognition device interfaced to the microcomputer. After each response, appropriate visual and voice feedback are given to the child.

Apple Music Theory contains a set of drill-and-practice lessons on music theory fundamentals. Some of these lessons are little more than electronic flashcards. However, most of them serve as good examples of drills that do not incorporate a sophisticated instructional strategy but that make impressive use of the unique capabilities of the computer. The program contains 18 drill lessons. The learner has complete control over which lesson to study, the number of items to practice within each lesson, and when to review previously learned items.

One of the simple flashcard lessons, called "Name the Note," displays a single note on a music staff and asks the student to enter its letter name. The student selects from one of five levels of difficulty. At the end of a practice session, the program provides corrective feedback and displays the percentage of items answered correctly. However, performance data are not recorded on the diskette nor used to make any strategy decisions. Students may study each note as long as they wish before entering a response. This program could be improved by requiring students to respond within a set time.

One of the more impressive lessons, called "Rhythm," displays a pattern of notes on the screen and asks the student to identify which of three recorded melodies matches the pattern displayed. Students listen to any of the three melodies as often as they wish. After students enter a response, the program provides corrective feedback and allows students to listen to the correct pattern. Another lesson, called "Missing Note," displays four notes on a music staff with a space for a missing note. Students are required to identify the missing note after listening to the melody. Again, students may listen to the melody as many times as necessary. After they enter a response, the correct missing note is displayed on the screen with the other four notes, and students can listen to the melody again. In the lesson called "Rhythm Play," a series of notes is displayed on the screen, and students are required to duplicate the rhythm of the notes by pressing the letter N on the keyboard in the correct rhythm. To establish a standard tempo, the first measure of the rhythm pattern is always four quarter notes. If the rhythm played by the students is incorrect, the program displays the pattern actually entered below the stimulus pattern (see Figure 4–2). At this point, students can request that the correct rhythm pattern be played again.

Whole Brain Spelling is another example of a program that gives learners control over what to study and how long to practice. However, there is no attempt to keep track of student performance or to make strategy decisions based on that performance. The

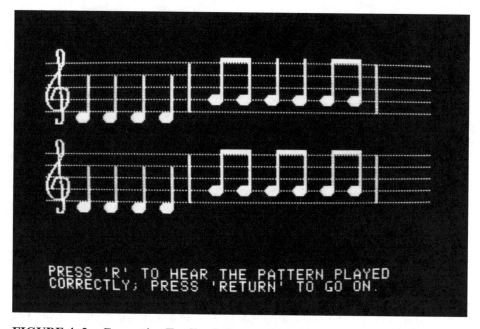

FIGURE 4–2   Corrective Feedback Screen from MECC's *Music Theory*

program contains 200 10-word lists of spelling words that are graded according to spelling difficulty. After selecting a list, students either study or practice spelling the words in the list.

The program is designed to help students to create visual images of the words they are learning to spell. This is done in the *study mode* by allowing the student to see the words displayed in several different ways: in different colors, in lowercase, in upper-case, with the letters displayed one at a time, and with the letters blinking. Students page through these various visual representations of a word by simply pressing the space bar. When they are ready to be tested on the words in a list, students enter the *practice mode*. In this mode, the words are displayed on the screen in random order one at a time. When the students are ready to spell a word, they press the RETURN key and the word is erased. If the word is then entered incorrectly, the computer analyzes the response and indicates the errors. Extra or wrong letters are crossed out, whereas miss-ing letters are indicated by an arrow pointing to their proper location. The correct spell-ing of the word is then presented on the screen. Unfortunately, students' incorrect spelling and the correct spelling of the word are never displayed on the screen simul-taneously for comparison.

Milliken is marketing a 12-diskette package of mathematics programs (*Math Se-quences*) covering addition, subtraction, multiplication, division, laws of arithmetic, integers, fractions, decimals, percentages, equations, and measurement formulas. This is a sophisticated package that keeps track of each student's performance and allows the teacher to print out student progress reports. Figure 4–3 shows a screen from a les-

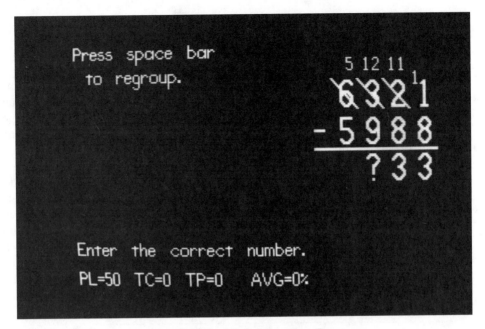

FIGURE 4–3   Screen from Milliken's Subtraction Program

son that instructs the student on each step of the subtraction procedure. If necessary, corrective feedback is given each step of the way.

As can be seen from these brief descriptions, drill-and-practice programs incorporate a variety of strategies and subject matter. Many drill-and-practice programs are on the market, and they vary greatly in quality. Software identification, evaluation, and selection are difficult and frustrating tasks. It may not be easy to find programs that have all the sophisticated strategy characteristics described in this chapter. However, good programs include many of them. Additional guidance on software identification and evaluation is given in Chapter 6.

Using Drill-and-Practice Programs in the Classroom

If computer-based drill-and-practice programs are to be effective in the classroom, they must be consistent with and carefully integrated into the regular classroom curriculum. This seems to be an obvious suggestion, but it is violated repeatedly. It makes no sense to have students use a computer program that drills them on spelling words that are different from those used in the rest of the curriculum. This problem can be avoided by selecting software that allows the teacher to specify the type of problems to be incorporated into a given drill session. For example, the Minnesota Educational Computing Consortium (MECC) has produced a series of spelling programs (*Spelling Workout, Spelling Press,* and *Spellevator*) that include an editor for teachers to enter spelling lists that match their spelling curriculum. *Spell It Plus,* from Davidson, includes an editor and speech capabilities. *Math Blaster Plus* includes an editor to customize math fact drills, and *Word Attack Plus Spanish* allows teachers to add their own Spanish vocabulary words.

Even under the best of circumstances, drill and practice is not very interesting learning activity for students. However, many computer-based drill-and-practice programs include gaming elements (see Chapter 5, Problem Solving, Simulations, and Games) that make them somewhat more interesting. Examples of such programs include *Math Blaster Plus, Spellevator, NumberMaze, Super Solvers OutNumbered, Reader Rabbit, Spell It Plus, Touch Typing for Beginners, Word Attack Plus, States and Traits,* and *Number Munchers.*

The amount of time students spend on the computer doing drill and practice should not exceed their attention span and tolerance for such activities. Several short, spaced drill sessions are better than a few long sessions. Research has shown that even 15 minutes a day of computer-based drill can significantly improve student performance. The logistics of scheduling students on a limited number of computers in the classroom or computer laboratory are discussed in Chapter 9, Networks and Telecommunication.

Tutorial Applications

Most educators would agree that the ideal instructional system is composed of one teacher tutoring one student. However, the use of human tutors in such a system is prohibitively costly. Tutorial computer applications seek to place the computer in the role of a tutor, one that carries the full instructional burden of guiding a student to the achievement of a specified set of objectives. In contrast, other tutor applications—such as drill and practice, simulations, or games—are designed to carry only a small portion of the instructional burden. The remainder of the burden must be borne by a human teacher or by some other medium.

The comprehensive nature of tutorial programs makes them more complex, more difficult to design, and more expensive to develop than other tutor applications. Because of the difficulty of the task, there seem to be more poorly designed tutorial programs than good ones. This section outlines the characteristics that should be considered in the design, evaluation, and selection of effective tutorial programs. Also discussed are when and how such programs may be used in the classroom.

Events of Instruction

If a tutorial program is to carry the full burden of instruction, then it must incorporate most of the events of instruction that are necessary for learning. Gagné, Briggs, and Wager (1992) have outlined nine events of instruction that should be included in most instructional systems:

1. Gaining attention
2. Presenting objectives

3. Recalling prerequisite learning
4. Presenting stimuli
5. Providing guidance
6. Eliciting performance
7. Providing feedback
8. Assessing performance
9. Enhancing retention and transfer

Not every instructional system need contain all these events, nor must the events occur in exactly the order listed. However, a comprehensive instructional system would include most of these events in approximately the order listed.

Gaining Attention

Tutorial programs should be designed to gain and maintain the attention of the learner. Graphics, sound, color, animation, and humor are ways to attract attention. However, care must be used to ensure that events designed to gain attention actually add to, rather than distract from, the task at hand. For motivated learners, attention can be gained by a brief description of the purpose of the lesson and the value of the knowledge or skills to be learned. This description can often be combined with the next event.

Presenting Objectives

At the beginning of a tutorial program, learners need to be informed of the learning outcomes they can expect from participation in the instruction. These objectives can be presented in a fairly informal or conversational manner. It is often useful to present examples of the actual performances that will be required of the learners. For example, learners can be told the objective of a particular math tutorial as follows: "In this lesson, you will learn to convert fractions, such as three-sevenths, into decimal numbers, such as 0.4286."

Recalling Prerequisite Learning

To learn new material, it is often necessary for students to have prerequisite skills highly available in memory at the time the new instruction is given. A good tutorial program should help students to recall these skills at the appropriate time. For example, to learn the concept of *alien* from the definition "a foreign-born resident who has not been naturalized," students have to know and recall the meaning of the subordinate concepts *foreign, resident,* and *naturalized.* A tutorial program can help students to recall these prerequisites through the use of review questions, examples, or definitions such as, "Remember that a resident is a person who lives in a particular place."

Presenting Stimuli and Providing Guidance

Frequently, stimuli and guidance are presented together and comprise the bulk of a tutorial program. The nature of the stimuli and guidance varies according to the subject matter. If the purpose of the tutorial is to teach concepts, the stimuli consist of definitions, examples, and nonexamples. Guidance can include prompts, cues, or directions to facilitate learning. Guidance can also include a carefully designed series of questions to help learners to discover a rule or concept.

Eliciting Performance and Providing Feedback

Performance and feedback are extremely important in most tutorial programs and they must complement each other. Performance is elicited by asking learners to practice the skill to be learned. If the tutorial is teaching a rule, the learners practice applying the rule to previously unencountered problems. The program then analyzes the responses to provide diagnostic feedback indicating the correctness of the response or possible reasons for incorrect responses. Sophisticated tutorials use learners' response histories to determine the most appropriate stimulus to present next. On the basis of their responses, learners can be branched to remedial material or they can bypass additional examples and practice exercises to move on to more difficult material.

Response analysis is not a trivial task for a computer. Simple programs merely check to see if the student's response exactly matches one stored in the computer program. If a match occurs, the computer responds that the answer is correct; otherwise, the computer judges the response to be incorrect. Such a simple analysis does not take into account spelling errors, use of synonyms, different phrases with the same meaning, or alternate correct answers. If a tutorial is to respond to a student's response with some intelligence, it must include sophisticated answer-processing procedures. Such procedures are described in later sections of this chapter.

Assessing Performance

Assessment involves testing learners to determine if they have achieved the objectives of the tutorial lesson. The test can be given and scored with or without the computer. If the test is given by the computer, provisions need to be made for storing, summarizing, and reporting the results. These assessment features of a tutorial program are described in more detail in Chapter 10, Computer-Managed Instruction.

Enhancing Retention and Transfer

Retention and transfer are often ignored by authors of tutorial programs. However, they are of prime importance if optimal learning is to occur. Retention can be facilitated by providing appropriate reviews or practice at spaced intervals. The most powerful way to provide for review is to require the use of previously learned skills in future learning activities. For example, spelling and grammar skills can be reviewed by applying and evaluating their use in future writing assignments. Transfer can be facilitated by providing a wide variety of examples and practice.

Guidelines for the Development and Selection of Tutorial Applications

Tutorial applications hold the promise of automated individualized instruction in which students are allowed to work at their own pace. Instruction is tailored to specific individual needs. Unfortunately, most tutorial programs fall far short of this ideal. Authors of tutorial programs often adapt some previously existing instructional materials from another medium (generally printed materials) to the computer. These programs are generally little more than expensive page turners that require the learner to read through screen after screen of information. Figure 4–4 shows a sequence of frames from the program *Biology: The Cell*. The addition of graphics does not alter the fact that the computer is being used merely to "turn" the pages of the book.

Learners find page-turning computer programs extremely boring. They expect an educational computer program to be different from a book. In fact, a good test of any computer-based instructional program is to ask if it provides instruction that is any better than that which could be provided by a book. It is important to remember that certain characteristics of books make them valuable vehicles of instruction. Books are relatively inexpensive, highly portable, randomly accessible, require no power source, and can easily display text, tables, and high-resolution color graphics. Readers can skip sections in which they are not interested, skim sections of moderate interest, and reread difficult or interesting sections. The book is an extremely versatile medium. If a given tutorial computer program is no better than a book, spend your time, effort, and money somewhere else.

Interactivity and Sensitivity Necessary

For a tutorial computer program to be better than a book, it must be interactive and sensitive to the responses of the learner. It is also important that the interaction required by the program be relevant to the learning outcomes expected from the instruction. One of the most common errors made in eliciting responses is to require students merely to copy information presented earlier. The following is an example of eliciting a copying response:

> An adjective is a word that is used to modify a noun.
> A word that is used to modify a noun is called an _____.

Unless the student is expected to memorize some information, copying responses should be avoided. They require no understanding on the student's part.

Ideally, tutorial programs will elicit responses from students that ask them to perform or apply the skills learned. If the tutorial is teaching a concept, students are required to classify previously unencountered examples and nonexamples of the concept:

> Type the adjective found in the following sentence:
> John has a red bicycle.
> >?

If the purpose of a tutorial program is to enable students to apply a specified rule to solve a set of problems, then the interaction in the tutorial should involve students in applying the rule to previously unencountered problems:

> How many centimeters are equivalent to 25.3 meters?

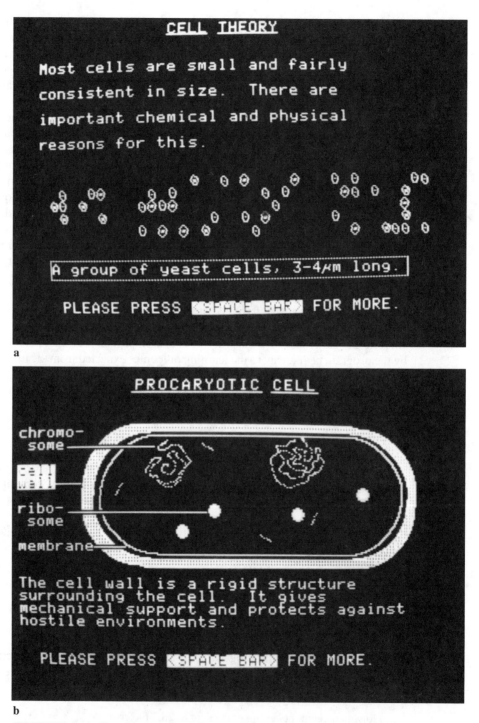

FIGURE 4–4a–b   Sequence of Frames from a Lesson on Cell Theory

Good tutorial programs not only involve student interaction but are also sensitive to the responses made during the interaction. This sensitivity is reflected in the sophistication of the computer feedback and in the way it determines branches to subsequent instructional segments. Response-sensitive feedback communicates more than the correctness or incorrectness of an answer. The feedback also communicates the reasons incorrect answers are wrong and what the correct answer is: For example:

Type the adjective found in the following sentence:
  John has a red bicycle.
>bicycle
Sorry, *bicycle* is a noun. It is a person, place, or thing. *Red* is the adjective because it modifies the noun *bicycle*.

Unfortunately, many tutorials are designed to be so response sensitive that the instructional sequence is totally controlled by the computer. In such programs, students cannot proceed to lesson 6 without first passing through lessons 1 through 5. This sequence control requires a teacher or student to make an all-or-none decision with respect to the use of a tutorial package. This can present a problem. For example, an entire tutorial package of 17 lessons might not correspond to the curriculum of a particular school. However, teachers in that school might find that lessons 3 and 8 meet their specific needs. If the package is programmed so that students must pass the earlier lessons before they can use lessons 3 and 8, the package will be of little use. On the other hand, if the series of lessons is designed modularly, so that each lesson can be used independently of the others, teachers and students can use whatever lessons they need.

The TICCIT Learner-Control System

One of the better models for tutorial lesson design was incorporated into the TICCIT computer-assisted instruction system originally developed during the early 1970s by the University of Texas, Brigham Young University, and the MITRE Corporation under funding from the National Science Foundation. The TICCIT instructional design was based on the philosophy that the learner should have control over the sequence of lessons studied and the sequence of instructional events within a lesson. A recommended lesson sequence is shown to the students in the form of a hierarchical map, or menu. Students can follow the recommended sequence or select an alternate sequence. Within each lesson, students have the choice of accessing several instructional events referred to as *presentation forms:* objective, rule, example, and practice. The desired event, or presentation form, is accessed by pressing special learner-control keys on the right-hand side of the keyboard (Figure 4–5). Students can select as many or as few presentation forms as they desire. They can also select the same form several times within a given lesson.

By pressing the key labeled OBJECTIVE, students access a statement of what they should be able to do on completion of a given lesson. The objective is used by the students as a starting point to determine what to do next. Whether to choose rule, example,

FIGURE 4–5   Close-Up of MicroTICCIT Learner-Control Keys

practice, or map (to exit and go to a different lesson) depends on the students' previous understanding of the skill to be learned and their particular learning strategy.

When the RULE key is pressed, a concise definition, or rule statement, is presented. Pressing the EXAMPLE key accesses an item showing the rule or definition applied to a specific instance. A practice problem is presented on pressing the PRACTICE key. If the students decide they already know the material, they press the MAP key and select another lesson. Examples of these presentation forms from a TICCIT lesson are shown in Figure 4–6.

In addition to the four primary presentation forms already mentioned, four supporting presentation forms are available: help, hard, easy, and advisor. When viewing the rule, students can elect to press HELP for an expanded version of the rule, HARD for a more abstract form of the rule, or EASY for a more simplified version. While the students are studying examples or doing practice problems, the HARD and EASY keys access harder or easier examples or practice items. Pressing the HELP key accesses a detailed description of how a given example relates to the definition or a step-by-step explanation of how a problem is solved. If students are lost or confused, they can press the ADVISOR key to receive a summary of their performance to date and advice on what to do next. Examples of a few supporting presentation forms are shown in Figure 4–7.

Although the learner-control tutorial strategy described here was originally developed for the TICCIT system, the authors have implemented the strategy successfully on Apple IIe, Macintosh, and Windows based microcomputers. Since these microcom-

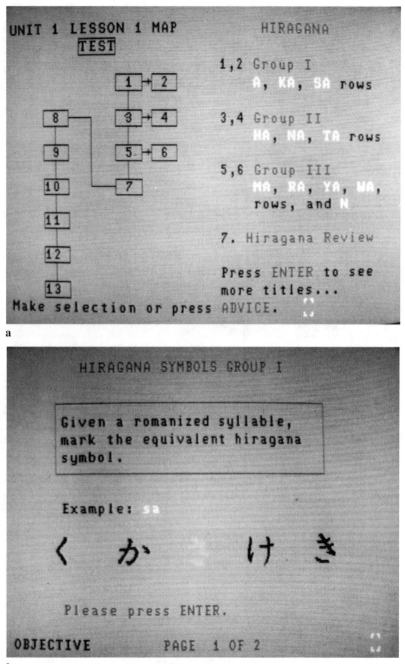

FIGURE 4–6a–d Examples of Presentation Forms from TICCIT Lessons

FIGURE 4–6   (continued)

In the list below the nouns in green are
feminine, and the nouns in blue are
masculine:

  il mare   the sea

  la sete   the thirst

  il sole   the sun

  la nazione   the nation

You should memorize both the article
and the noun together.

EXAMP   ITEM 1   PAGE 1/1

c

MARK the figure which represents a
cabriole, then press ENTER.

d

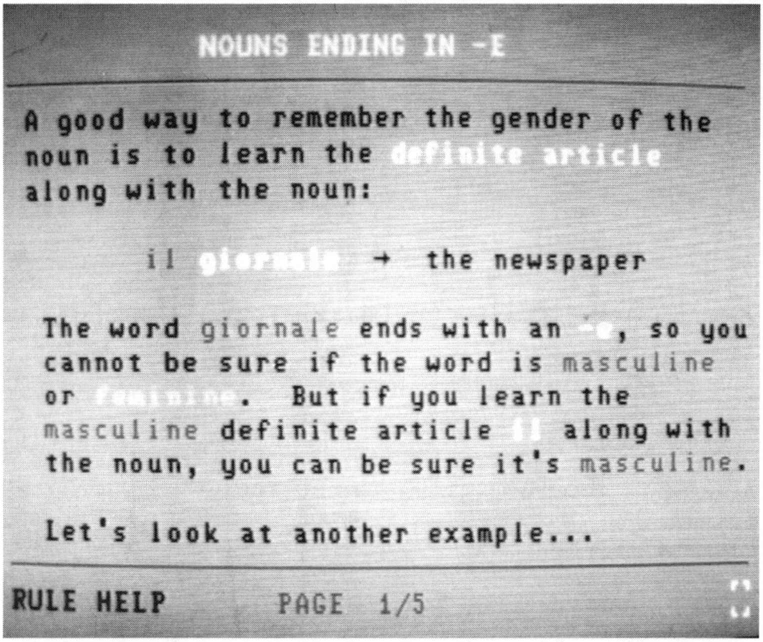

NOUNS ENDING IN -E

A good way to remember the gender of the noun is to learn the definite article along with the noun:

il giornale → the newspaper

The word giornale ends with an -e, so you cannot be sure if the word is masculine or feminine. But if you learn the masculine definite article il along with the noun, you can be sure it's masculine.

Let's look at another example...

RULE HELP   PAGE 1/5

a

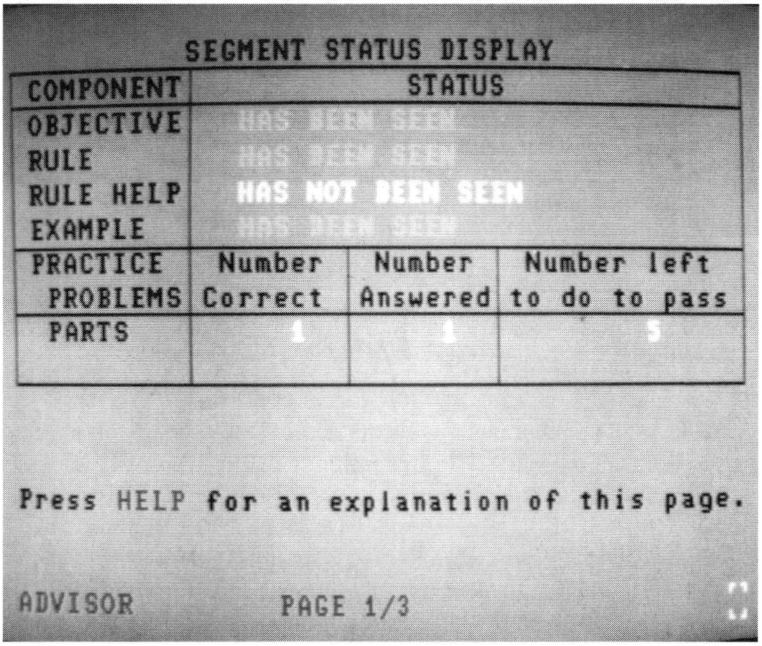

SEGMENT STATUS DISPLAY

COMPONENT	STATUS		
OBJECTIVE	HAS BEEN SEEN		
RULE	HAS BEEN SEEN		
RULE HELP	HAS NOT BEEN SEEN		
EXAMPLE	HAS BEEN SEEN		
PRACTICE PROBLEMS	Number Correct	Number Answered	Number left to do to pass
PARTS	1	1	5

Press HELP for an explanation of this page.

ADVISOR   PAGE 1/3

b

FIGURE 4–7a–b   Examples of Supporting Presentation Forms from TICCIT Lessons

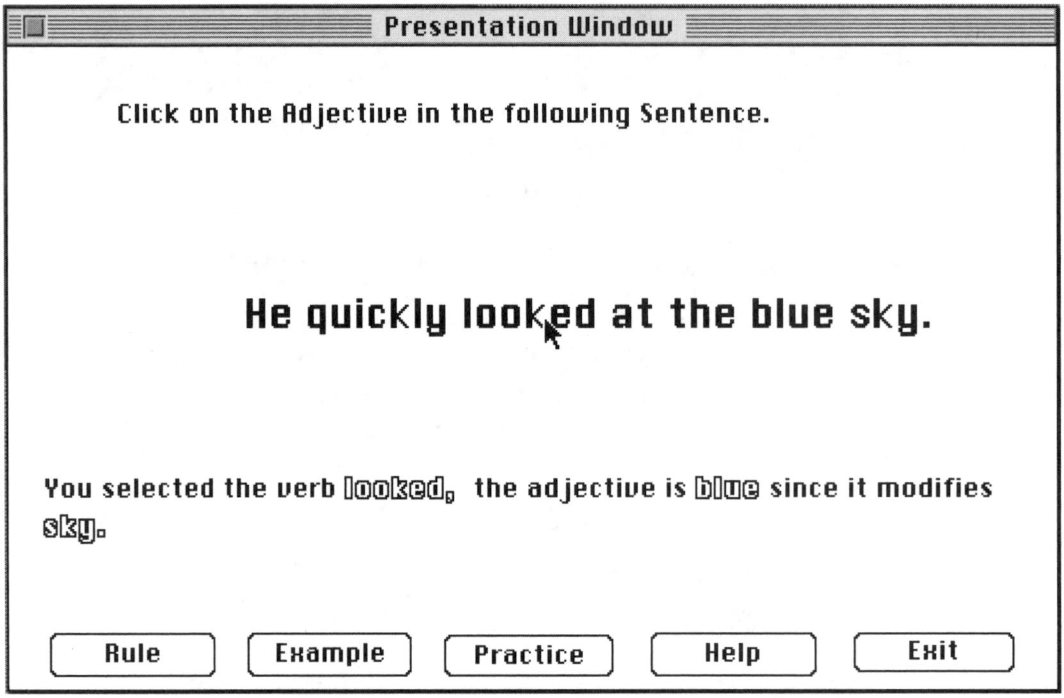

FIGURE 4–8   Practice Item from TICCIT-Like Lesson on the Macintosh

puters do not have the learner-control function keys available on the TICCIT system, the presentation forms are accessed by pressing a single alphanumeric key or by clicking the appropriate button with a mouse. Figure 4–8 shows a sample practice screen from a TICCITlike lesson implemented on the Macintosh using the *AuthorWare Professional* authoring language (see Chapter 11, The Computer as Tutee).

Computer-Controlled Adaptive Systems

One of the major problems with learner-control strategies, such as that used by the TICCIT system, is that many students do not study the lesson long enough to attain a desired level of mastery. In learning new tasks, most students have difficulty in determining their own learning needs. Tennyson and colleagues (Tennyson, Christensen, & Park, 1984) have conducted a series of studies that show that computer-controlled adaptive systems yield superior student performance when compared to simple learner-controlled systems. These computer-controlled systems contain program logic, or "intelligence," to continuously diagnose the instructional needs of each student throughout the learning process and to prescribe successive instructional events adapted to those needs.

Many instructional variables can be adapted to make tutorial programs sensitive to individual students' moment-to-moment learning needs. These include amount of instruction, sequence of instruction, display time interval, and difficulty level. In concept- or rule-learning lessons, the amount of instruction is determined by the number of examples and practice items presented. In a nonadaptive tutorial lesson, the number of examples and practice items given to each student is exactly the same. In an adaptive lesson, the number of examples and practice items given is controlled by a preset mastery criterion level and each individual student's performance on the practice items. One possible adaptive strategy is to continue to present practice items until a given student responds correctly to three practice items in a row. The criterion level used in such strategies needs to be determined so that students have an opportunity, where appropriate, to respond to practice items across several levels of difficulty.

Although computer-controlled adaptive systems produce better student performance than learner-controlled systems, Tennyson and Buttrey (1980) have argued that learner-controlled systems are less effective because students do not have adequate information about their own performance and the nature of the learning task to make moment-by-moment decisions about the best learning strategy. These researchers hypothesized that, if students are provided continuous feedback about their current state of learning performance and are advised on the amount and sequence of instruction that would optimize their performance, they can effectively control their own instruction.

This hypothesis is supported in a study (Tennyson & Buttrey, 1980) where a learner-control-with-advisement group is compared with computer-controlled-adaptive groups and a learner-control group. The students in the learner-control-with-advisement group stayed on task long enough to achieve mastery on the posttest at the criterion level of 80 percent correct. This performance matched that of students in the computer-controlled adaptive groups. However, students in the learner-control group stayed on task 39 percent less than the learner-control-with-advisement group and only scored 58 percent on the posttest. In addition, the learner-control-with-advisement group received 25 percent less instruction and took 22 percent less time than the computer-controlled-adaptive groups.

This research indicates that a learner-control strategy can be as effective and more efficient than a computer-controlled-adaptive strategy if learners are given continual performance information and advice to help them make learning strategy decisions. Furthermore, another study (Johansen & Tennyson, 1984) has indicated that, with continued practice, students gradually improve in their ability to make strategy decisions from advisement information.

Using Tutorial Programs in the Classroom

Tutorials may be very appropriate as the main source of instruction when the number of interested students or the availability of certified teachers in a content area would not justify a normally scheduled class. Well-designed tutorials may enable students in small schools with limited resources to receive instruction in specialized areas that would otherwise be unavailable to them.

Unfortunately, most tutorials currently available are not good enough to serve as the sole means of instruction for a course. Great care should be used in the selection of tutorials that are to be used in this manner. Such tutorials should be designed to help students achieve objectives that are consistent with the course curriculum plan. Each tutorial should be validated on students similar to those who will use it in the classroom. If no published validation data are available, teachers should attempt to validate the tutorial themselves. After students have completed the tutorial, it should be determined how well they have learned the objectives of the program. If student performance is not adequate, another tutorial or means of instruction should be used. If several tutorials are found to be adequate as the sole means of instruction, their use should be interspersed with noncomputer activities.

In most cases, teachers will not want to rely on tutorial programs as the only means of instruction for a course. However, they may find a few excellent tutorials that may be used to teach selected topics. An alternative approach would be to use tutorials to support and reinforce classroom instruction, in much the same way as books are currently used. Students could be asked to go through a tutorial in preparation for a subsequent class discussion or as a review of previous classroom activities. Tutorial programs could also be used by students who may have missed a particular classroom lecture or discussion or who may be homebound for a significant period of time.

In an individualized classroom environment, tutorials might be one of many alternative instructional packages designed to teach a particular objective. A tutorial program can also be used as one component of a more comprehensive instructional system, which may include videotape or videodisc presentations, reading and writing assignments, small-group discussions for guidance and review, and planning or remedial consultations with a human instructor. Because of their comprehensive nature, tutorial programs include many of the elements found in other tutor applications. The practice section of a tutorial lesson includes many of the features and strategies used in drill-and-practice applications. If realistic experience is required to learn a particular skill, the tutorial might include simulation activities. Gaming strategies may also be incorporated into tutorials to help gain and maintain the attention of the learners.

Summary

Drill and practice is an appropriate application of the computer to aid students in learning many discrimination or paired-associate tasks such as math facts, sight words, spelling words, foreign language vocabulary, music notes, names of states and capitals, abbreviations of chemical elements, names of human muscles, and so on. Many of these tasks must be learned to a level of automaticity in order for students to learn and perform higher-level skills effectively. Computer-based drill-and-practice programs can be more effective than flashcard or worksheet approaches if they incorporate sophisticated instructional strategy characteristics. Teachers will need to use care in the selection of programs that are effective and that meet their specific curricular needs.

Tutorial computer-assisted instruction lessons are designed to carry the full burden of instruction. Such lessons should incorporate most of the nine events of instruction: gaining attention, presenting objectives, recalling prerequisites, presenting stimuli, providing guidance, eliciting performance, providing feedback, assessing performance, and enhancing retention and transfer. Tutorial programs are not simply sophisticated page turners. In order for a tutorial lesson to be better than a book, it must be interactive and sensitive to the needs of the learners. The responses elicited need to be directly related to the skills to be learned. Lessons that are sensitive to student responses incorporate sophisticated learner-control or adaptive strategies. Sensitive lessons continuously diagnose the instructional needs of each student and prescribe appropriate instructional events to meet those needs. Admittedly, these lofty guidelines are very difficult to achieve. However, they are goals for tutorial designers to strive for, and they serve as standards for evaluating existing software. Additional research needs to be conducted to increase knowledge regarding the design and development of efficient and effective tutorial programs.

Exercises

1. Describe the characteristics of a simple drill-and-practice strategy.
2. Briefly describe the characteristics of a sophisticated drill-and-practice computer program.
3. Outline how drill-and-practice programs might be used in your own classroom.
4. How are tutorial programs different from other tutor applications?
5. Briefly describe how the nine events of instruction can be included in tutorial lessons.
6. Briefly describe the TICCIT learner-control system.
7. How can tutorials be made adaptive to students' learning needs?
8. Outline how you might use tutorial programs in your own classroom.

References

Anderson, R. (1980) *Cognitive psychology and its implications.* New York: W. H. Freeman.

Apple Music Theory: Music Fundamentals from MECC. [Computer Program]. Cupertino, CA: Apple Computer.

Atkinson, R. C. (1974, March). Teaching children to read using a computer. *American Psychologist,* 169–178.

Authorware Professional. [Computer Program]. San Francisco: Macromedia.

Biology: The Cell. [Computer Program]. Chicago: Encyclopaedia Britannica Educational Corporation.

Bower, G. H., & Hilgard, E. R. (1981). *Theories of learning* (5th ed.). Englewood Cliffs, NJ: Prentice Hall.

First National Kidisc, The. [Videodisc]. New York: Optical Programming Associates.

Gagné, R. M. (1982, June). Developments in learning psychology: Implications for instructional design; and effects of computer technology on instructional design and development. An interview with Robert M. Gagné. *Educational Technology,* 11–15.

Gagné, R. M. (1985). *The conditions of learning* (4th ed.). New York: Holt, Rinehart & Winston.

Gagné, R. M., Briggs, L. J., & Wager, W. W. (1992). *Principles of instructional design* (4th ed.). Fort Worth: Harcourt Brace Jovanovich.

Gay, I. R. (1973). Temporal position of reviews and its effect on the retention of mathematical rules. *Journal of Educational Psychology, 64,* 171–182.

Gilbert, T. F. (1978). *Human competence.* New York: McGraw-Hill.

Johansen, K. J., & Tennyson, R. D. (1984). Effects of adaptive advisement of perception in learner-controlled, computer-based instruction using a rule-learning task. *Educational Communication and Technology Journal, 3*(1), 226–236.

Math Blaster Plus. [Computer Program]. Torrance, CA: Davidson & Associates.

Math Sequences. [Computer Program]. St. Louis: Milliken Computer Courseware.

Miller, G. A. (1956). The magical number seven, plus or minus two: Some limits on our capacity for processing information. *Psychological Review, 63,* 81–97.

Number Munchers. [Computer Program]. St. Paul, MN: MECC.

NumberMaze. [Computer Program]. Scotts Valley, CA: Great Wave Software.

Reader Rabbit. [Computer Program]. Fremont, CA: Learning Company.

Spelke, E., Hirst, W., & Neisser, U. (1976). Skills of divided attention. *Cognition, 4,* 215–230.

Spell It Plus. [Computer Program]. Torrance, CA: Davidson & Associates.

Spellevator. [Computer Program]. St. Paul, MN: MECC.

Spelling Press. [Computer Program]. St. Paul, MN: MECC.

Spelling Workout. [Computer Program]. St. Paul, MN: MECC.

States and Traits. [Computer Program]. San Francisco: DesignWare.

Super Solvers OutNumbered. [Computer Program]. Fremont, CA: Learning Company.

Tennyson, R. D., & Buttrey, T. (1980). Advisement and management strategies as design variables in computer-assisted instruction. *Educational Communication and Technology Journal, 28,* 169–176.

Tennyson, R.D., Christensen, D. L., & Park, S. I. (1984). The Minnesota adaptive instructional system: An intelligent CBI system. *Journal of Computer-Based Instruction, 11,* 2–13.

Touch Typing for Beginners. [Computer Program]. Boca Raton, FL: International Business Machines.

Whole Brain Spelling: A Child's Garden of Words. [Computer Program]. Champaign, IL: Sublogic Communications.

Word Attack Plus. [Computer Program]. Torrance, CA: Davidson & Associates.

Word Attack Plus Spanish. [Computer Program]. Torrance, CA: Davidson & Associates.

C h a p t e r **5**

Problem Solving, Simulations, and Games

This chapter introduces three valuable computer applications: problem-solving exercises, simulations, and educational games. The dynamic, interactive, graphic, and sound capabilities of the computer can often be used to their full potential in these applications.

Problem-solving software presents situations (problems) on the computer that are solved through a process of logical deduction, synthesis, and implementation. Stimulating analytical thinking is one of the primary characteristics of problem-solving software. In contrast, creating an artificial, interactive environment that models a specific real or a specific fantasy environment is the primary characteristic of simulation software. Simulations are never the actual real or fantasy environments but instead are carefully designed representations. The primary characteristic of educational game software is to allow a player or student to interact with instructional materials in a motivationally stimulating game format. The game is usually competitive, uses specific rules, and has an outcome that constitutes winning.

From these brief descriptions, it should be clear that each of these three applications is by no means mutually exclusive of the others. In fact, you'll notice in this chapter that a single software product may include problem-solving situations simulated in an artificial environment and couched in an amusing and enjoyable game. Although characteristics of two or more of these applications may be simultaneously evident, typically the characteristic of one application is instructionally dominant, thus identifying the kind of application the software represents.

With these brief general descriptions understood, let's focus on the applications one at a time. As we do, you'll find three major sections: (1) a definition of the application type, (2) a description of the necessary parts, and (3) further information for classifying various subtypes of the application.

Problem Solving

Many people, on hearing the term *problem solving,* think of math. Although solving math problems is certainly one form of problem solving, it is by no means the only form. Therefore, to get us all on the same wavelength, let's discuss what problem solving is.

Definition

In much of the recent literature, *problem solving* is loosely defined as those skills in critical thinking and/or logic that allow one to arrive at a previously unattained personal solution (Ausubel, Novak, & Hanesian, 1978; Garrison & Macmillan, 1988; Newell & Simon, 1972; Simon, 1978). "Previously unattained personal solution" means that the solution is different from one's earlier concocted solutions because of a difference in the methods used, the circumstances, and so on. Thus, one may say that some original thinking is required in problem solving.

Actually, quite a few things are required for effective problem solving (Palumbo & Vargas, 1988; Sherman, 1988), such as the following:

1. A desire to solve the problem
2. A base of knowledge and experiences
3. A repertoire of possible actions or solutions
4. The ability to take action
5. The resources to monitor and assess the mental and physical actions or solutions as they unfold
6. The controls to effect changes in those actions as the need arises

You will notice that the first requirement is a desire to solve the problem; without that desire, the personal effort required will not be forthcoming. Second, some knowledge and experience are often needed so that the solution may be more effectively discerned. Third, some related actions or solutions to similar problems ought to be understood that will make the new solution easier. Fourth, there is a need to be able to take action when the new solution is obtained; without that ability, the new solution becomes academic, having never been tried. Fifth, the new solution needs to be tested to determine whether, in fact, it is the desired solution to the problem. Finally, some controls are needed to fine-tune the new solution if there is a need to make the solution more efficient and more effective.

Parts and Approaches

Moursund (1985) has suggested that a basic problem-solving path has the following three parts:

1. How something actually is (initial state)
2. How you would like the thing to be (goal state)
3. What you can do about the situation (allowable types of actions or solutions, both mental and physical, to move from the initial state to the goal state)

This three-part path is fairly straightforward. You start where you are, determine where you would like to go, and use allowable actions or solutions to get there. Sounds easy, right? Well, how this translates into the actual approaches for problem solving depends on which approach works best for you.

You are probably wondering which general approach this book recommends. One of the most commonly used has the following steps (Greeno, 1980; Klatsky, 1980; Kahney, 1986; Ludlow, 1989; Polya, 1957, 1968):

1. STATE the problem.
2. STUDY the background factors.
3. LIST the potential solutions.
4. PREEVALUATE the consequences of each potential solution over time.
5. DECIDE on a solution.
6. CARRY OUT the solution.
7. CONFIRM that the solution has indeed solved the problem.

The combination of steps 1 through 4 of this problem-solving approach is often called *brainstorming*. Sometimes, when time is short, steps 1 through 4 seem to merge into a single step. When this happens, the hurried solution usually is not as effective as the one arrived at when each step is clearly explored individually.

This approach is a general-purpose approach to problem solving. It works in a wide variety of circumstances. Almost all other problem-solving approaches are derivatives of this one.

Value of Problem-Solving Software

Problem-solving software is a valuable application resource for at least six major reasons:

1. Evidence shows that experience with problem-solving software increases the user's self-confidence in understanding that other similar problems can be solved (Burton & Magliaro, 1988; Kutz, 1985). This makes sense in light of the need for a base of experiences and a repertoire of possible actions or solutions that may be accessed only through the use of computer software.

2. Problem-solving software seems to create a sense of being self-directed. Since the first requirement in problem solving is that you must desire to solve the problem, it follows that the more you use this self-motivation, the more in control of the situation you seem to feel because the motivation is coming from within. Thus, you feel some sense of personal self-direction.

3. Problem-solving software tends to increase your knowledge and experience base. As mentioned before, this is directly related to the sense of self-confidence that problem solving tends to promote. As you successfully solve problems, the experiences and knowledge you obtain from the exercise will assist you when you are confronted with a new problem that is similar in some way. Thus, the experience and knowledge you gain from the problem-solving software seems to be cumulative.

4. Problem-solving software adds to your repertoire of possible solutions or actions. It is knowing the possibilities, as well as understanding what works and what does not work, that can make problem-solving software so valuable.

5. Problem-solving software enhances your analysis and decision-making skills. Because analysis and decision making are necessary parts of problem solving, it follows that the more practice you have with them, the better you become at them.

6. Problem-solving software seems to increase a person's ability to deal with change. Perhaps the reason for this is that as your confidence with problem-solving skills increases, so does your expectation either to adjust to changes or to alter the circumstances.

Classification of Problem-Solving Software

When Gore and Martin (1986) examined software used to teach and enhance problem-solving skills, they identified the following three categories of problem-solving software:

1. Software designed to teach and reinforce general problem-solving skills
2. Software designed to teach and enhance problem-solving skills within a subject area
3. Software not designed to teach and reinforce problem-solving skills but that is used successfully by teachers for this purpose anyway

Skill-Centered Problem-Solving Software

Many examples are represented by the general problem-solving software category in which the explicit objective of the software is to teach and provide practice in problem-solving skills. One such example is called *The Factory*. This software offers three activity areas: Test a Machine, Build a Factory, and Make a Product. Test a Machine allows students to try the options on three machines: a punch machine, a rotate machine, and a stripe machine. Students may work with each of the three machines individually, making adjustments to the control options and reviewing the corresponding results.

In Build a Factory, students may select from the three machine types to create an assembly line. The settings of the individual machines and the order of the machines along the assembly line determine what the end product will be. Students may edit their creation by changing the settings of the machines and/or the order of the machines along the line. Finally, when they have finished their product, they can challenge a fellow student to set up an assembly line to make a matching product.

In Make a Product, students can choose from three levels of challenge (easy, medium, and hard). In each level, the goal is to duplicate the design of the challenge product. At the easiest level, only two or three machines at certain settings are required on the assembly line to make the product correctly. At the most difficult level, the machines selected, the sequence, and their settings can become very involved. Students may compare their products with the challenge product. If the products do not match, students can try again or move to another challenge.

The Factory software creates an environment in which students can do the following:

1. Develop a base of knowledge and experience by using the Test a Machine section.
2. Acquire a repertoire of possible combined actions and solutions using the Build a Factory section.
3. Brainstorm possible assembly lines that might create a product matching the challenge product.
4. Decide which possible machines, with which settings, and in what order will make the product that matches the challenge product.
5. Act by creating the assembly line.
6. Test the assembly line to see if, in fact, the product matches the challenge product.

Clearly, a variety of problem-solving skills are being learned and practiced when students use this software.

Other software that fits well into this category are *The Pond,* which teaches pattern recognition in the number of hops and turns required by a frog to cross the pond; *Puzzle Tanks,* which requires filling and emptying tanks until the proper quantities are obtained; and *Snooper Troops,* in which a student functions as a sleuth to solve a case. Each of these software programs has the explicit objective to teach and provide practice in problem-solving skills.

Subject-Centered Problem-Solving Software

Many software packages are designed to teach and enhance problem-solving skills within a subject area. One basic assumption of this subject-centered software is that people need a knowledge base before they can successfully solve problems. Software in the subject-centered category can help students to become aware of the necessity to draw from previous experiences and information acquired in the past as part of the problem-solving process.

One good example of subject-centered software is *Flee the Fortress.* In this problem-solving software, students will find they are being held prisoner in the central tower of a fortress designed by Leonardo da Vinci. To escape, they must advance through the fortress's three concentric corridors, collecting clues and unlocking the mysteries hidden within its walls.

This subject-centered problem-solving software is part of a CD-ROM learning system called *Leonardo the Inventor.* In this rather extensive system, students can study the life and times of Leonardo da Vinci—history being the main subject. They can learn why his engineering designs were so important to his benefactors. This multimedia system allows students to see animations, including three-dimensional (3-D) demonstrations using the 3-D glasses that come with the package. *Flee the Fortress* allows students to take the information presented in other parts of the learning system and use it to solve the escape problem. Jt is a fun way to learn, a good way to develop problem-solving skills, and a delightful multimedia presentation.

Another subject-centered problem-solving software is called *Transportation Quest.* The subject in this learning system is the history of travel, from camels to jets. Students are secret operatives from the twenty-fourth century on a mission to collect as much information as possible on the development of transportation through the ages. Students start off in the year 20,000 B.C. and travel to the future, equipped with a chrono-communicator, which is a futuristic personal digital assistant, capable of storing notes, receiving messages, and answering many questions. As students proceed, the quest becomes more difficult. They encounter more challenges and more data that need to be collected. Students learn to deal with the problems of synthesizing data, the important from the useless, much like a real archeologist.

Other software packages that fit into this second category are *Botanical Gardens,* which allows students to experiment with the growth of various plants while varying the environmental conditions; *Teasers by Tobbs,* which teaches problem solving by using addition and multiplication problems that look just like crossword puzzles; *Green Globs,* which addresses algebra; *The Incredible Laboratory,* which focuses on chemistry; *Mind Puzzles,* which deals with general math; *Those Amazing Reading Machines* series, which teach reading and writing skills; *Where in Time Is Carmen San Diego?,* which focuses on world geography during different time periods; and of course, *Where in the World Is Carmen San Diego?,* which addresses world geography in modern times. All these software packages are designed to teach and enhance problem-solving skills within a subject area.

Problem-Solving Software Used by Default

The third and last category of software is used successfully to teach and reinforce problem-solving skills, but it was not specifically developed to do so. This software may or may not be subject centered. Usually, such software was originally designed to function as some other kind of application, such as an educational game. However, teachers have found a way to use the software for the development of problem-solving skills anyway.

An illustration of this category of software package is *Heart of Africa,* an adventure video game that was designed for the home entertainment market. It was not originally designed to be software for enhancing problem-solving skills. However, *Heart of Africa* does challenge players to explore Africa in search of an ancient Egyptian emperor's golden tomb. The computer provides a historically and geographically correct map to this treasure. Students must apply map-reading skills and search strategies to be successful at the game.

Car Builder is simulation software where students discover firsthand what it is like to design cars. It is a simulation, not problem-solving, software. *Car Builder* lets the user design, construct, test, and refine any kind of car. After selecting all the mechanical components and assembling them, students can put together the chassis, suspension system, engine, gear ratios, custom body, and all the other components needed to create the car. The car can then be run through a full diagnostic test, including the wind tunnel and test drive. Just as the major car companies do, students make real choices about style, aerodynamics, power, handling, and fuel economy.

Other software programs that fit into this category are *Lunar Explorer,* a simulation that models the moon for exploration purposes; *Millionaire II,* a simulation of the stock market; *Sargon IV,* a computerized game of chess; and *Wilderness,* a simulation game of wilderness survival.

All three problem-solving categories can contribute to students' self-confidence by helping them to develop skills and strategies they can apply when faced with a problem. Typically, they begin to understand that problem solving is a process in which there is rarely only one right answer. Students may then consciously pay attention to the process of selecting the most appropriate skills and strategies to apply to a problem. In so doing, they will have taken several major steps in developing their own problem-solving skills.

Simulations

A *simulation* is a representation or model of a real or imagined specific object, system, or phenomenon. It is an imitation. Most phenomena can be represented—from galaxies to atoms, from soil erosion to flying a starship. Symbolic representations can be constructed that approximate the look and feel of the real or imagined environment. The understanding of certain aspects of astronomy, chemistry, physics, biology, geography, and so on can often be enhanced through the use of a corresponding representational model.

Fidelity

Because simulations and models are but an imitation of reality, their use requires a certain amount of imagination. The more realistic a simulation is, the less imagination is required. Conversely, the less realistic a simulation is, the more imagination is required. Simulations fall on a continuum of realism. Those that are near duplicates of the actual phenomenon are said to have a high fidelity with reality, whereas those with few characteristics in common with reality are said to have a low fidelity.

The degree of fidelity required in a given simulation depends on the phenomenon being addressed and the purpose of the simulation. The professional flight trainer is common example of a high-fidelity simulation. Through the use of hydraulic arms that move the trainer around, functional "surround cockpits" with mock-up controls and instrument panels, and videographic pictures of the terrain, pilots feel that they are really flying in an airplane or a space shuttle. In reality, the simulator remains on the ground the whole time. The flight trainer is so effective that pilots are not required to spend as much time in a real cockpit to be certified.

Most computer simulations do not provide such a high degree of fidelity. Today's computer simulations are often limited to the use of up to 256 color graphics, simpler animations, and sound effects. There are no hydraulic motions, surround cockpits, or other effects. Although most computer simulations occur only on the computer screen, the trend is that future presentations will increase in fidelity. One of the reasons for this trend is that computers are becoming faster, more powerful, and less expensive. Also, the tools used in the development of simulation software are becoming more powerful and easier to use.

A normal level of simulation fidelity is represented by *Operation Frog*. Three options are available in this software. Students can perform a dissection of a frog, reconstruct the frog as a beginner, or reconstruct the frog as an expert. The graphics portray the frog lying in a dissection tray with four tools—scissors, magnifying glass, forceps, and probe—positioned next to the frog. A ruler scaled in inches and centimeters lies just below the tools. Finally, a display pad is provided for the various organs that are removed from the frog.

Students use the probe to determine where organs are to be clipped. Once they determine those places, they use scissors to clip the organ. Using the forceps, students can grasp the organ, move it next to the ruler and place it on the display pad. After the organ is displayed, students can use the magnifying glass to find out a great deal more about the organ from a larger, more detailed picture. The description that accompanies the larger picture explains the functions and features of the organ being investigated.

Although the students are working on a two-dimensional computer screen, *Operation Frog* uses a rather innovative approach for portraying the important third dimension. Because organs are often layered from front to back, only the uppermost layer of organs is displayed in bright colors; the lower layers are indicated by a shadow. When all the organs in the upper layer have been removed, the next layer becomes highlighted with color. This approach is used until the students have worked through all the layers.

An example of software with a much higher level of simulation fidelity is *Flight Simulator*. In the simulation, students may fly either a Cessna 182 or a WW I Sopwith Camel. Students are provided with a mock-up of the instrument panel as well as a three-dimensional view out the cockpit window, all presented on the screen. The simulation allows the students to master flaps, rudder and ailerons, elevators, throttle, yoke, radar, radio communications, and the like. Students can learn to perform aerobatic stunts like a flying ace or to fly cross-country, practicing landings at some of the major airports in the continental United States. They can even determine the time of day, season, and weather for practicing bad weather landings under full instrument control only.

Older simulation software usually has a lower level of fidelity because the early microcomputers, for which the software was designed, were slower and had less memory, graphics, and audio capabilities. An example of an older, lower-level fidelity computer simulation is the well-known *Lemonade Stand*. Through simple graphics and sound effects, as well as a lot of text, the computer simulates the operation of a curbside lemonade stand, much as what children might set up in front of their home. Three critical variables are controlled by the computer: the day's weather conditions, the cost of making a glass of lemonade, and the cost of making signs for advertising. The computer also controls other events that might affect sales, such as reduced traffic as a result of construction. Variables controlled by the students are the number of glasses of lemonade prepared, how much is charged per glass, and how many advertising signs are made. Because the graphics and sound are quite limited and much of the simulation resorts to a textual description, the students' imaginations must be used fairly extensively.

Component Parts

Every simulation has the following four main components:

1. The presentation system
2. The student (subject)
3. The system controls
4. The system manager

The *presentation system* is anything that stimulates the senses. In the cases of *Operation Frog, Flight Simulator,* and *Lemonade Stand,* the computer and monitor are the presentation system. The simulation is an audiovisual presentation incorporating two- and three-dimensional graphic displays and sound effects. *Operation Frog* and *Lemonade Stand* also use textual description as presentation because part of the simulation is described through text on the monitor. *Supersonic,* which presents multiple instrument panels of six different cockpits and a three-dimensional graphic view from the front of the cockpit while doing a lift-off, is considered to be a partial mock-up. If everything else could be included to make the flight simulation seem real—such as using hydraulic lifters on an enclosed room, cockpit chairs, pedals, and other functional controls—it would be considered a full-scale mock-up presentation system.

The *student (subject),* of course, is the participant in the simulation.

The *system controls* include anything the student manipulates: a joystick, paddle, mouse, roller ball, steering wheel, keyboard, floor pad, microswitch, graphics tablet, light pen, and so on. In *Operation Frog,* a mouse, a joystick, or a keyboard may be used. In *Flight Simulator,* a joystick and a keyboard may be used to "fly" the Sopwith Camel. *Lemonade Stand* permits the use of a keyboard to change numeric variables when "selling" lemonade.

The *system manager* is either a person or a computer. Sometimes, it may even be a combination of both. In the cases of *Lemonade Stand, Flight Simulator,* and *Operation Frog,* a computer is the system manager. The critical requirements are that the system manager must have memory and decision-making capabilities. The manager adjusts the simulation presentation on the basis of manipulation of the system controls by the student.

Value of Simulations

Simulations are valuable tutor applications for at least six major reasons:

1. Simulation involves less risk than reality. If students crash their planes during a computer simulation, they can simply press a button and try again. The potentially fatal mistake causes no harm. Students can learn from the experience and try to do the task correctly the next time.

2. Training costs are reduced. In a real crash situation, an airplane may cost millions of dollars to replace or repair, to say nothing of lives lost. Most companies cannot afford to have their expensive equipment destroyed or used for the training of unskilled students. Although some simulations may have a fairly high initial cost, they usually save money in the long run.

3. Simulations are frequently more convenient than real-life situations. With the use of multiple microcomputers in the classroom or lab, several students can be individually involved in a simulation at the same time. The simulation can be used at any time, regardless of weather conditions, daylight, and other constraints.

4. Simulations minimize the negative effects of time. Some phenomena take place in reality over great periods of time. Through simulations, time can be compressed so that students can experience the critical elements of the phenomenon several times within a short period. Through simulation, landing a plane in several different airports under various weather patterns or managing a stock portfolio under fluctuating economic conditions can be experienced within a single class period. Other phenomena are difficult to perceive adequately because they take place so rapidly. Once again, through simulation, the time factor is adjusted to facilitate understanding. The cycles of a combustion engine, the beating of a human heart, and the flow of data from computer memory to the CPU become open to study through simulation.

5. The ability to focus on specific aspects of a phenomenon is frequently increased. Through the use of color graphics, sound effects, animation, and textual descriptions, useful aspects of the situation can be enhanced, and extraneous aspects can be minimized, thus making it easier for students to learn the critical information.

6. The experiences in a simulation are repeatable. Students can review an experience over and over again until their responses become natural and automatic. Many phenomena occur very infrequently in real life. However, when they do occur, individuals need to be able to react immediately and skillfully. Engine failure when an aircraft is taking off does not happen often, but when it does, a pilot who faced such emergencies in a simulator should know exactly what to do.

Static and Interactive Simulations

Simulations may be classified as either static or interactive. A *static simulation* is usually linear in nature. Students simply watch and/or listen as the phenomenon is demonstrated; they have no impact on the demonstration. Motion pictures, TV programs, and radio dramatizations are typical examples of static simulations of reality.

Interactive simulations allow students to manipulate various factors in the simulation. They may adjust the concentration of the fuel and air mixture, the timing of the distributor, the amount of spark, and the viscosity of the oil, and see the effects of those manipulations in a computer simulation. With interactive simulations, students have the opportunity to form hypotheses, perform experiments, and verify or refute their assumptions. Interactive simulations allow students to gain valuable experience in solving problems.

Rocky's Boots is an example of a very powerful interactive simulation that helps students learn to solve problems in logic circuits. The simulation moves the students through six levels of complexity. In the first level, students are directed to move a colored rectangle through a collection of rooms. Students practice using the appropriate keys on the computer keyboard to move the rectangle up, down, right, or left, and to pick up and put down objects. These manipulatory skills are then used in the next level to control the flow of electricity through circuits. In other levels, students build simple to complex electronic machines and see the effect of various types of logic gates on the operation of the machines.

Examples of Computer Simulations

A wide variety of computer simulations is available for use in schools. A few representative examples are described in this section.

Several programs have been produced that simulate laboratory experiments. For example, *BioSphere* provides an environment in which students can classify a variety of organisms. The students must go into a lake/forest biome and collect organisms. All five biology classification kingdoms are represented in the biome.

After collecting the specimens, students can take them to a laboratory. A vivarium is available for storing "live" organisms. A locker and refrigerator are also available storage locations. The students can dissect the various organisms; observe using a hand lens, a microscope, or a scanner electron microscope; and can even x-ray the specimen. All observations can be recorded on the computerized notebook for later reference.

Finally, the students can try to classify the organism. *BioSphere* will make suggestions in the process that will help the students learn these skills. The program even helps the student to generalize these classification skills by allowing them to classify other similar organisms that have not been encountered in the lake/forest biome. One valuable aspect of this simulation is that when students use *BioSphere,* fewer real organisms are required to develop the students' classification skills. Further, those sample organisms suffer less trauma because the students' skills are already partially developed.

Another outstanding simulation is called *Wilderness.* This program tests the students' mental resources through an adventure that accurately depicts the challenges of surviving in a remote wilderness area. Terrain, climate, wild animals, illness, injury, and so on are all presented as perils. *Wilderness* not only features three-dimensional graphics but it accurately models environments and the human body's response to exposure. Students face everything from toxic plants to life-threatening weather in the Sierra Nevada. The manual, which is part of the materials included in the simulation, contains essential medical and first-aid information, as well as tips on weather, navigation, and traveling. Furthermore, it contains directions on how to start a fire, find food and water, and set up camp under the most inhospitable conditions. Any journey in progress can be saved to disk to complete later. On the other hand, students can take new journeys every time the software is used, as new topographical maps can be generated to explore. The simulation allows students to study geography, ecology, meteorology, and physiology.

Many high-fidelity simulations have been developed by combining computer and videodisc technology (see Chapter 2, Computer Hardware). For example, Great Plains National (GPN) has produced an interactive videodisc program, *Chemistry I,* that allows students to perform titration experiments. Students learn the principles and practice the procedures involved in conducting the experiment in a real lab. The costs of the equipment and chemical solutions are avoided, and students are not required to handle toxic chemicals.

Intelligent Images has produced several videodisc programs that allow students to assess, diagnose, and treat simulated patients with respiratory difficulty, motor vehicle trauma, and abdominal stab wounds. Harvard Law School has produced 18 videodisc simulations of lawyering skills such as negotiations, interviewing, trial objections, and the like.

Games

Flip! Swaashhh! Zap! These sounds have invaded arcades, homes, and schools. During the past decade, computer games have mushroomed into a billion-dollar industry.

Computer-based games are so compelling that children and adults alike spend hours of time and considerable amounts of money playing them. Can the schools somehow harness this power of computer games to motivate students in the pursuit of significant knowledge and skills? Some educational software designers believe that the answer is a resounding yes!

One of the great strengths of educational games is their ability to promote a higher level of student motivation. Curricular areas that have been hard to teach because of low student interest or motivation may be significantly strengthened through the use of a carefully selected and integrated educational computer game. This is especially the case with discrimination or verbal information tasks that require students simply to memorize information.

Many teachers have found that computer games serve as good rewards for students who behave properly in class or do excellent work. Students are motivated to do other assigned activities to earn the opportunity to play computer games, which seems to be a legitimate application of games in the classroom. However, games that build problem-solving skills but have little relevance to the subject matter being taught must be used with discretion. Games that develop these skills and that are congruent with the curriculum have greater educational value than those that are simply amusing. In fact, those games that combine the development of higher-order skills with relevant subject matter not only enhance motivation through the amusement of the game but, at the same time, they present information and reinforce the retention of that information through an easily remembered, challenging experience.

Attributes of Games

Games have certain critical attributes that distinguish them from other types of activities, such as the following:

1. Force or coercion to play is not required.
2. Computer games are fun and they provide recreation.
3. A definite, preestablished set of rules determines how the game is played, what actions are allowed and prohibited, what rewards may be received, and what constitutes winning the game.
4. There are elements of competition or challenge against an opponent or task.

Most students choose to play computer games because they want to, not because the teacher or someone else wants them to. This brings into play the students' own desires, which may make a major difference in the effectiveness of the instruction.

Students should perceive computer games as being fun. This does not mean that no effort is required. On the contrary—a great deal of effort is often required to play computer games successfully. The difference between work and play may not be the difference in the amount of effort but the difference in how the effort is perceived. Does the effort seem to be fun, recreational, and amusing? It all depends on the context and the player.

Computer games have definite, preestablished rules that determine how the games are played. Without these rules, the game will quickly break down and will no longer be fun, recreational, or amusing. Because computer games have been programmed on computers, the rules are built into the program, and the computers have little or no ability to vary those rules.

Finally, most computer games have some elements that are challenging, creating a competitive environment. The competition may be with the computer, with oneself, or with other students. For some students, it is the challenge and the competition that make the games fun and motivational.

Motivational Attributes

Researchers at Stanford University (Lepper & Malone, 1983; Malone, 1980; Malone & Lepper, 1983) have attempted to identify attributes of computer games that optimize their intrinsic motivational power. These attributes suggest useful criteria for selecting educational computer games for the classroom. Malone and Lepper have classified these attributes into two major types: individual motivations and interpersonal motivations.

Individual Motivations

Successful educational computer games generally include one or more of the following individual factors of motivation.

Challenge. For optimal effectiveness, games should provide an intermediate level of challenge for the learners. Different levels of difficulty should be provided to maintain this optimal level of challenge over time and from one student to another. Challenge seems to depend on appropriate goals, uncertain outcomes, performance feedback, and self-esteem.

The games should either present clear, fixed goals or provide an environment in which students can generate goals for themselves. Both short-term and long-term goals should be provided. Uncertain outcomes should be maintained midway between that which is trivially easy and that which is clearly impossible. This can be achieved by using (1) variable difficulty levels, (2) multiple levels of goals, (3) hidden information, and (4) randomness. The games should also provide feedback to the learners concerning their performances. Positive feedback techniques should be used to promote feelings of competence and positive self-esteem. Success can make students feel better about themselves. To promote a more personal feeling of competence, the goals of the activities should be meaningful and have relevance for the students.

The goal of the computer-based game *Master Type* is to shoot down enemy spaceships and satellites before they destroy the mother ship; this is done by accurately typing letters and words displayed on the screen. The challenge of the task can be continually adjusted to match the increasing skill of a specific player or to accommodate the varying levels of skill of different players. The speed at which the words must be typed in order to destroy the attacking spaceships before they hit a player's ship can be adjusted. There are several different levels of goals and difficulty, ranging from typing letters only on the home keys to typing long words with letters from anywhere on the keyboard. The words to be displayed are unknown to the student and are placed on the screen in random order. After typing a word correctly, players are given immediate visual and audio feedback through the destruction of an enemy vessel. At the end of a battle, the student is informed of the number of words typed correctly and the average typing speed. When students demonstrate proficiency at one level, they are advised to advance to the next level.

Curiosity.   A good instructional game should provide a moderate level of content complexity or a discrepancy from the players' current state of knowledge or expectations. Curiosity is generated by activities that are somewhat novel but not totally foreign. Also, curiosity may have sensory as well as cognitive components. Sensory curiosity may be enhanced by variability in audio effects and visual effects (color and animation). Cognitive curiosity is enhanced when activities deal with topics in which students are already interested and that add an element of surprise and intrigue.

Control.   One of the most frequently cited requirements for an effective instructional computer game is that it allows the students a powerful sense of control. Malone and Lepper (1983) recommended three characteristics for enhancing control in educational games: contingency, choice, and power. The outcome of the game should be dependent on the responses of the students. A game should not rely on random events to the exclusion of strategy or skill-dependent outcomes. The level of difficulty of the task will have an effect on students' sense of control. If the task is too difficult, students will feel they have lost control. A sense of control is significantly enhanced when players are given choices and allowed to make decisions. Students can be allowed to choose between things such as alternate goals, levels of difficulty, names and types of character roles to play, and use of sound effects. However, students should not be required to make so many complex choices that they become overwhelmed. As students play the game, their sense of control can be further enhanced if their actions and decisions result in powerful and dramatic effects. This illusion of power is often created in computer-based games through the use of sophisticated graphics and sound effects.

Fantasy.   This final category is clearly important in educational computer games as well as in television programs, novels, and dramatic productions. Malone and Lepper (1983) defined a *fantasy environment* as one that evokes mental images of physical or social situations not actually present. Fantasy is important because it addresses the emotional needs of students and encourages identification with imagined characters or contexts. (Of course, this identification can be dropped easily and at any time.) Fantasy also provides metaphors and analogies that facilitate understanding. Fantasy is most productive when it has an integral relationship to the material being learned. In some games, there is no obvious connection between the fantasy and the subject matter. This is the case in games such as *Yearn 2 Learn—Snoopy* and *Mario Teaches Typing*. In other instructional games, the fantasy has an integral relationship to the task being learned. A good example of this integral relationship is found in *The Icarus Game*. The student uses a design for a human-powered flight created by Leonardo da Vinci. The challenge in the game is for students to keep their contraptions airborne long enough to arrive at various destinations.

Interpersonal Motivations

The second major category of motivation to consider when evaluating computer-based games is interpersonal motivations, which involve interaction with others. Malone and Lepper (1983) have identified three factors that play an important part in interpersonal motivations: cooperation, competition, and recognition.

Cooperation.   The motivational effect of an educational computer game can be enhanced through cooperation with others. Integral cooperative motivation can be produced in segmenting the game activity into interdependent parts. In the game *Microbe,* many different tasks must be performed, including piloting the miniature submarine, repairing broken parts, and providing medical assistance. The game may be played by a group of people. Each member of the group is assigned one or more tasks, or roles, to perform. A team spirit of cooperation can enhance each member's motivation to learn and perform his or her assigned task well in order to promote the success of the group.

Competition.   Interpersonal motivation can be enhanced through healthy competition. Some type of scoring mechanism is usually employed to foster competition between players. In some games, players compete against their previous high scores or the high scores of other players. However, the competition will be more integral to the task if one player's actions affect the status of other players in the game. For example, in *Moptown Hotel,* two players can put guests in 16 different hotel rooms, but each guest must have specific characteristics in order to be compatible with other guests in the room. The goal of each player is to get as many of his or her own guests into rooms as possible. However, the guests placed in a room by one player will limit the options available to the other players.

Recognition.   Interpersonal motivation can be increased through some form of social recognition. Effective educational computer games achieve this motivation through providing natural channels for students' efforts to be appreciated by others. The *Green Globs* game uses a Hall of Fame to enhance recognition motivation. In this game, "globs" are randomly placed on a Cartesian grid, and players enter equations whose graphs intersect as many globs as possible. High-scoring equations are saved in the Hall of Fame for all students to access. Successful players are motivated by the recognition their play receives, and other players learn new techniques and forms of equations from the displayed solutions. However, because the globs are always placed randomly, players are unable simply to copy solutions.

Application of Gaming Attributes

The gaming attributes discussed in the previous sections may be incorporated into each of the other instructional applications. They can be used in drill-and-practice exercises such as *Master Type* and *Spellevator,* in simulations such as *Microbe* and *Lemonade Stand,* or in problem-solving exercises such as *Green Globs, Rocky's Boots,* or *Teasers by Tobbs.* These attributes may be used as a heuristic checklist to guide the design, selection, and evaluation of educational games. However, one should not assume that software that includes more of these attributes may be much more effective simply by virtue of the quantity of attributes.

Powerful educational software is available that not only integrates many gaming attributes but also includes drill and practice, tutorial, simulation, and problem-solving features. One example of such an educational program is an adventure game called *Ambassador Geography.* This game is built around a fantasy that places students in the role of apprentice ambassadors. The apprentices leave a spaceport called Andromidos and are assigned to do their training on a planet called Earth. While orbiting Earth, the apprentice ambassador represents the Inter-Galactic Trade Council (IGTC) by beaming down an android to the planet surface and, through the android, negotiating trade rights with the various countries on the planet. As the apprentice becomes ambassador to various countries, eventually he or she may become the ambassador to a continent. From there, the apprentice will attempt to become ambassador to all the continents.

The first step is to learn the general land masses and oceans on the planet. They can be learned in whatever order and whenever the apprentice chooses. The apprentice then becomes certified (by passing a test). Before he or she can start working with the country or countries that make up a certain continent, the apprentice must be certified for that continent. If the apprentice wants to, he or she can clear as many of the continents as desired, thus obtaining free access to all the various countries.

To receive clearance to beam down an android to a country, the apprentice must learn and then certify he or she knows the name of the country, the country's capital city, and its type of government. Once certified, the apprentice can beam an android down to the capitol. In the capitol building, the android helps the apprentice learn a wide variety of interesting and, in some cases, vital information about the country. Knowing such things as the exchange rates, different kinds of native foods, history, dominant religions, customs, major tourist and industrial sites, natural resources, industrial production, agricultural products, and so on help the apprentice more effectively negotiate the trade rights. It is important to know what the country's ministers have to offer as well as what they need to cement the best deals.

Information is readily available to the apprentice whenever he or she wants to learn it. When the apprentice wants to learn the name of a continent, he or she only needs to move the cursor over the continent and press either the mouse button or the ENTER/RETURN key. The information will then be displayed for that area. The same is the case when looking at the countries that make up a continent.

To take a certification test, the apprentice moves the cursor over the area he or she wants clearance for and either double click the mouse or press the B (for *beam* down) key. If any element of the test is incorrect, the answer is given immediately after the student has attempted to answer the question. (It is typical, at this point, that the apprentice actually wants to know the correct answer.) The apprentice can retake the test as often as it takes to pass all the questions. To certify, the apprentice must answer all the questions correctly.

Once the android has successfully beamed down to the capitol, again the apprentice can determine where and what he or she wants the android to do. Information is available in a wide variety of places and certification quizzes occur before the apprentice can enter a ministry to negotiate a trade. This may mean a few return trips to master the information required to enter a ministry. Finally, negotiating a trade agreement is a real act of problem solving. Many possible approaches may have to be used to negotiate the best trade agreement.

Ambassador Geography presents an element of risk. As the android moves around the capitol, there is a chance that the IGDC may give a pop quiz. It will select a country in the region, pause the game, and test the apprentice on the information about that country. If the test is on a country the apprentice is not an ambassador to, then there are no penalties, no matter how poorly the apprentice may do on the test. Of course, correct answers are presented immediately after a question is answered incorrectly. If the apprentice can pass the test, then he or she will be awarded a substantial number of credits and will be appointed directly to the ambassadorship of that country.

The risk occurs if the computer selects a country to which the student is already an ambassador. If the apprentice does well on the test and passes it, he or she will receive a substantial reward in the form of credits. If the apprentice doesn't pass the test, different penalties occur, depending on how badly he or she did. The worst that can happen is a loss of status as ambassador to that country as well as a sizable loss of credits. In such a case, the apprentice would have to go through the effort of becoming an ambassador all over again. After this happens once or twice to a student, he or she will quickly come up with some way to ensure success on the next pop quizzes. Interestingly enough, such incentives usually lead to an unusually high level of mastery of the information.

The pop quizzes force students to review old information regularly because they never know when a country to which they are an ambassador will be selected for the test. Of course, the further an apprentice gets in the game, the more likely it is that the selected country is one to which he or she is the ambassador. Thus, the difficulty grows or shrinks automatically, depending on where the apprentice actually is at any given moment in the game. The pop quizzes require constant review of old information and thus promote a form of drill and practice. Animated graphics, sound effects, random occurrences, increasing levels of difficulty, integral fantasy setting, and constant feedback generate the necessary motivation to practice, learn, use, and retain a considerable amount of information about the countries of the world.

Many other popular adventure or mystery games are on the market that have significant educational value. Examples are *Deadline, Geo-Race U.S.A., Haunted House, Math Blaster Mystery, Microbe, Mystery at Pine Crest Manor, Return of Zork, Snooper Troops,* and *Wilderness.* There are even videodisc problem-solving adventure games such as *Murder, Anyone?* With this videodisc, the players are challenged to discover the murderer of a rich industrialist. Each player is asked to make decisions at various points in the game. These decisions determine which of many paths on the disk will be followed. The first player to discover the murderer, motive, and method wins the game. However, the game can be played many times because there are 16 totally different plots on the disk. Although this disk was designed principally for entertainment, it provides another model for educational adventure games.

These computer and videodisc games are not only filled with fantasy, challenge, control, and curiosity but they also provide opportunities for students to use logic, reasoning, and organizational skills in solving interesting and compelling problems. Teachers should be aware that such adventure games often require considerable amounts of time and trial and error to discover the most effective way to play the game. Although not always the case, some adventure games provide little guidance as to what move should be made next to progress further in the game. When guidance is sparse, some students may experience a considerable amount of frustration.

Selecting and Using Applications in the Classroom

Problem solving, simulation, and game applications need to be an integral part of other instructional activities in the classroom. For example, let's say that you are a sixth-grade public school teacher with a class of 25 students. Your class has access to a 14-station computer lab for one hour, three times a week. You must divide that lab time between two or three subjects. Furthermore, you have noticed that one subject, world geography, could really use something to spice it up. You have read some reports that many students in the United States are weak in this subject area. Therefore, you have decided that you need something that will quickly get the students interested in world geography and that can be used periodically throughout the year to maintain that interest. What you are looking for is some kind of game—maybe a computer game—that can serve this purpose. The game does not have to cover all possible subjects in world geography, but it should stimulate an interest in world geography and introduce enough information to function as a springboard to other materials you plan to cover. Consulting your lab schedule, it appears that you can spare one hour a week for a computer game if you can just find what you are looking for. However, in talking with the school lab assistant, you find that the lab does not have a game that meets your criteria. What should you do now? Panic and forget the whole idea—right? Wrong!

You decide to keep looking for the world geography game you feel you need. Therefore, after talking with a teacher or two, you realize you could also visit the district media center to search for the needed game. However, when you go to the media center, you find that they do not have the kind of game you are looking for. But the media center director pulls out a file full of software catalogs and brochures and mentions that a salesperson was in the other day who left a brochure on a new game called *Ambassador Geography*. After searching for a moment, the director finds the brochure and suggests that you phone the salesperson whose phone number is on the back. After reading over the description in the brochure, you decide that the game might be what you're looking for. What should you do now? Call the salesperson and arrange for a demonstration—right? Right!

If possible, have the salesperson demonstrate the software on the equipment your class is going to use right at your school. In this way, you will know whether it really works on your equipment. Never purchase any game or other application software and assign your students to use it solely on the basis of a recommendation by a salesperson or another teacher. Take some time and preview the software as you would a film. Assess how well it fits into your curriculum. You may want to ask yourself such questions as the following:

- Is it written for the age level of my students?
- Will my students have the necessary background to benefit from the software?
- Will the attitudes, concepts, principles, and skills learned from the application transfer to real-life situations?
- Is the software easy to use?
- Is the documentation clear, accurate, and complete?
- Will the software gain and maintain the interest of my students?
- Are the benefits students receive worth the required time and expenditure?

After you have looked over the game software and asked these important questions, let's say that you decide *Ambassador Geography* is just what you have been searching for, and so you obtain a copy. Spend some more time playing the game and getting to know the utilities until you are comfortable with it. Think about how you could integrate the game into your geography course. You will probably notice that the game gives you a lot of freedom as to which country to investigate, for how long, and how thoroughly. Since the game allows you easily to address different countries in a region, you could use it as the foundation for a miniature United Nations experience, assigning small groups of students to different parts of a region or to different regions. Within each group you could have a student who specializes in the names of the countries, the names of the capitals, and the types of governments. Another student may cover imports and exports. A third may cover monetary exchange. The list goes on and on. In the class, student groups could represent their assigned countries. During the representation period, you may want your students to address such questions as the following:

- What kind of climate must Ethiopia and Chad have to produce peanuts?
- How can Mali export fresh fish when it is a landlocked country, with no major lakes within its borders and with the Sahara Desert covering almost half of it?
- Is western Africa as heavily industrialized as western Europe?

Is this all the preparation you need to do? Probably not. You will probably want to make decisions about when each region is going to be addressed, what other questions should be asked about the countries and regions, how the game should be introduced to your class, how the information may be customized using the game's Data Editor, and so on. All these issues and more need to be addressed. By addressing the issues before you introduce the game to your class, you will find that it makes all the difference in the ease of use and the effectiveness of the computer application. It is important to spend both time and effort in preparing students for the experience and the debriefing afterward. Avoid the temptation to set up students with a computer game or some other application, leaving it to chance that their initial experience in using it will automatically lead to significant learning. Introductory, intermediate, and follow-up activities will lend a proper perspective to student experiences, thus helping to maximize the value of the application.

Summary

Problem-solving exercises, simulations, and games are exciting applications because they often use the full potential of the computer's dynamic, interactive, graphic, and sound capabilities. Problem-solving exercises are usually designed to teach and reinforce generic problem-solving skills or to teach and enhance problem-solving skills within content areas. Such exercises seem to enhance self-confidence, create a sense of self-direction, increase knowledge and experience, add to the repertoire of possible solutions or actions, improve analysis and decision-making skills, and stimulate greater flexibility in the face of change.

A simulation is an imitation of reality. It is a representation of some real or imagined phenomenon. Simulations may vary in their fidelity to reality. Active simulations allow students to interact dynamically with and manipulate a phenomenon under study. Simulated interactions provide several benefits over real interaction: reduced risk, reduced training costs, more convenience, compression or expansion of time, focus on critical aspects, and repetition.

Games often incorporate problem-solving exercises and simulated fantasy environments. They are a source of amusement, involve elements of competition, and are governed by a set of rules. One of the major uses of games in education is to stimulate motivation. The proper balance of challenge, curiosity, control, fantasy, cooperation, competition, and recognition contributes to a game's effectiveness in motivating students.

Computer games, simulations, and problem-solving exercises need to be an integral part of other instructional activities in the classroom. The teacher should provide the necessary information and background required to enable students to obtain the maximum benefit from participation.

Exercises

1. What is a general problem-solving schema?
2. Name five reasons why problem-solving exercises are valuable forms of instruction.
3. What are the three categories for classifying problem-solving software?
4. What is a simulation?
5. How realistic do simulations have to be?
6. What are the critical components of a simulation?
7. What are the six major reasons simulations are valuable tutor applications?
8. What is the difference between static and interactive simulations?
9. What are the critical attributes of games?
10. What are the major motivational attributes of games?
11. What should be considered when selecting problem-solving software, simulations, or computer games for the classroom?
12. Select a computer problem-solving exercise, simulation, or game that would be appropriate for your own classroom. Describe how you would make it an integral part of your curriculum plan.

References

Ambassador Geography. [Computer Program]. Provo, UT: Higher Education Library Publishers.

Ausubel, D. P., Novak, J. D., & Hanesian, H. (1978). *Educational psychology: A cognitive view.* New York: Holt, Rinehart and Winston.

BioSphere. [Computer Program]. Provo, UT: Waterford Institute.

Botanical Gardens. [Computer Program]. Pleasantville, NY: Sunburst Communications.

Burton, J. K., & Magliaro, S. (1988). Computer programming and generalized problem-solving skills: In search of direction. In W. M. Reed & J. K. Burton (Eds.), *Educational computing and problem solving—Computers in the schools.* (pp. 63–90). New York: Haworth.

Car Builder. [Computer Program]. Middletown, CT: Weekly Reader Family Software.

Chemistry I. [Videodisc]. Lincoln, NE: Great Plains National (GPN).

Deadline. [Computer Program]. Cambridge, MA: Infocom.

Dugdale, S. (1983). Green globs. In D. F. Walker & R. D. Hess (Eds.), *Instructional software.* Belmont, CA: Wadsworth.

Factory, The. [Computer Program]. Pleasantville, NY: Sunburst Communications.

Flee the Fortress. (Leonardo the Inventor CD-ROM) [Computer Program]. New York: InterActive Publishing.

Flight Simulator. [Computer Program]. Redmond, WA: Microsoft.

Garrison, J. W., & Macmillan, C. J. B. (1988). The erotic logic of problem-solving inquiry. In W. M. Reed & J. K. Burton (Eds.), *Educational computing and problem solving—Computers in the schools.* (pp. 29–45). New York: Haworth.

Geo-Race U.S.A. [Computer Program]. Redmond, WA: Mastery Development.

Gore, K., & Martin, N. (1986). *Four methods for using the computer to integrate problem solving into the curriculum.* Proceedings of the Sixth Annual Microcomputers in Education Conference: Ethics and Excellence in Computer education: Choice or Mandate. Rockville, MD: Computer Science Press.

Green Globs and Graphing Equations. [Computer Program]. Pleasantville, NY: Sunburst Communications.

Greeno, J. G. (1980). Some examples of cognitive task analysis with instructional implications. In R. E. Snow, P. Federico, & W. E. Montague (Eds.), *Aptitude, learning and instruction: Cognitive process analyses of learning and problem solving.* (pp. 1–21). Hillsdale, NJ: Erlbaum.

Haunted House (Tales of Mystery Series). [Computer Program]. New York: Scholastic.

Heart of Africa. [Computer Program]. San Mateo, CA: Electronic Arts.

Icarus Game, The (Leonardo the Inventor CD-ROM). [Computer Program]. New York: Interactive Publishing.

Incredible Laboratory. [Computer Program]. Pleasantville, NY: Sunburst Communications.

Kahney, H. (1986). *Problem-solving: A cognitive approach.* Philadelphia: Open University Press.

Klatsky, R. L. (1980). *Human memory: Structures and processes* (2nd ed.). New York: Freeman.

Kutz, R. E. (1985). The computer is a learning tool. In W. M. Reed & J. K. Burton (Eds.), *Humanistic perspectives on computers in the schools—Computers in the schools.* (pp. 19–28). New York: Haworth.

Lemonade Stand. [Computer Program]. Cupertino, CA: Apple Computer and MECC.

Lepper, M. R., & Malone, T. W. (1983). Intrinsic motivation and instructional effectiveness in computer-based education. In R. E. Snow & M. J. Farr (Eds.), *Aptitude, learning, and instruction: III. Cognitive and affective process analysis.* Hilldale, NJ: Erlbaum.

Ludlow, V. L. (1989). *Problem solving.* Unpublished class handout. Provo, UT: Brigham Young University.

Lunar Explorer. [Computer Program]. Electric Transit.

Malone, T. W. (1980). What makes things fun to learn? A study of intrinsically motivating computer games. *Dissertation Abstracts International, 41,* 1955B.

Malone, T. W., & Lepper, M. R. (1983). Making learning fun: A taxonomy of intrinsic motivations for learning. In R. E. Snow & M. J. Farr (Eds.), *Aptitude, learning, and instruction: III. Cognition and affective process analysis.* Hillsdale, NJ: Erlbaum.

Mario Teaches Typing. [Computer Program]. Irvine, CA: MacPlay.

Master Type: The Typing Instruction Game. [Computer Program]. Tarrytown, NY: Scarborough Systems.

Math Blaster Mystery. [Computer Program]. Torrence, CA: Davidson & Associates.

Microbe. [Computer Program]. Renton, WA: Synergistic Software.

Millionaire II. [Computer Program]. San Francisco, CA: Britannica Software.

Mind Puzzles. [Computer Program]. St. Paul, MN: MECC.

Moptown Hotel. [Computer Program]. Menlo Park, CA: The Learning Company.

Moursund, D. (1985). Problem solving: A computer educator's perspective. *Computing Teacher,* 2–5.

Mystery at Pine Crest Manor (Tales of Mystery Series). [Computer Program]. New York: Scholastic.

Newell, A., & Simon, H. A. (1972). *Human problem solving.* Englewood Cliffs, NJ: Prentice Hall.

Operation Frog. [Computer Program]. New York: Scholastic.

Palumbo, D. B., & Vargas, E. A. (1988). Problem solving: A behavioral interpretation. In W. M. Reed & J. K. Burton (Eds.), *Educational computing and problem solving—Computers in the school.* (pp. 17–27). New York: Haworth.

Polya, G. (1957). *How to solve it.* Garden City, NY: Doubleday Anchor.

Polya, G. (1968). *Mathematical discovery: On understanding, learning, and teaching problem solving.* New York: Wiley.

Pond. [Computer Program]. Pleasantville, NY: Sunburst Communications.

Puzzle Tanks. [Computer Program]. Pleasantville, NY: Sunburst Communications.

Return of Zork. [Computer Program]. Cambridge, MA: Infocom.

Rocky's Boots. [Computer Program]. Menlo Park, CA: The Learning Company.

Sargon IV. [Computer Program]. Cambridge, MA: Spinnaker.

Sherman, T. M. (1988). A brief review of developments in problem solving. In W. M. Reed & J. K. Burton (Eds), *Educational computing and problem solving—Computers in the schools.* (pp. 7–15). New York: Haworth.

Simon, H. A. (1978). Information-processing theory of human problem solving. In W. K. Estes (Ed.), *Handbook of learning and cognitive processing: Human information processing.* (pp. 271–295). Hillsdale, NJ: Erlbaum.

Snooper Troops. [Computer Program]. Cambridge, MA: Spinnaker.

Spellevator. [Computer Program]. St. Paul, MN: MECC.

Supersonic. [Computer Program]. New York: Interactive Publishing.

Teasers by Tobbs. [Computer Program]. Pleasantville, NY: Sunburst Communications.

Those Amazing Reading Machine Series. [Computer Program]. St. Paul, MN: MECC.

Transportation Quest. [Computer Program]. New York: Interactive Publishing.

Where in the World Is Carmen San Diego? [Computer Program]. San Rafael, CA: Brøderbund.

Where in Time Is Carmen San Diego? [Computer Program]. San Rafael, CA: Brøderbund.

Wilderness. [Computer Program]. Electric Transit.

Yearn 2 Learn—Snoopy. [Computer Program]. Image Smith.

C h a p t e r **6**

Software Evaluation

It is a common misconception among educators that once teachers learn how to write programs, they will produce their own educational materials. No doubt some teachers will, but for the most part it would be a waste of valuable time. Each hour of computer-assisted instruction developed by a commercial educational software house may take up to 400 hours in development time. How many schoolteachers can afford this amount of time? As competition builds in the educational software market, educational software will become more and more sophisticated and require greater expertise and time in its development. Thus, it is very likely that most teachers will not develop their own software; however, they should be educated evaluators of existing software.

This chapter presents some guidelines for evaluating either commercially produced software or your own software. Two sets of criteria are presented for evaluating educational software: instructional criteria and presentational criteria.

Instructional Criteria

The term *instructional criteria* refers to the pedagogical aspects, teaching techniques, or instructional strategies that should be incorporated into an educational computer program. As outlined in Chapter 1, the appropriate instructional strategy is determined by the type of learning outcome specified by the objective of the instruction. One strategy is appropriate for teaching discrimination skills, another for teaching concepts. We also found in Chapter 1 that certain types of computer applications facilitate certain learning outcomes and not others. Thus, discrimination learning is best taught using an instructional strategy found in sophisticated drill-and-practice applications, whereas concepts are best taught using a strategy consistent with tutorial applications.

Portions of this chapter were adapted from Paul F. Merrill (1982). Displaying text on microcomputers. In David Jonassen (Ed.), *The technology of text.* Englewood Cliffs, NJ: Educational Technology Publications. Used by permission.

Therefore, the first step in evaluating software according to instructional criteria is to identify the objective of the software. What is the learning outcome that students should achieve by using the software?

The second step is to determine if the objective of the software matches any of the objectives in your curriculum plan. Obviously, if the software is not designed to help students to meet objectives found in your curriculum, there is little point in proceeding further. It is possible, however, that a given software package may inspire you to modify your curriculum goals. With creative software, it may be possible to achieve goals that were previously unattainable and that therefore were not included in your current curriculum plans. It is hoped that computer technology will allow students to reach heights not attainable by an earlier generation.

The third step is to determine whether the type of computer application is appropriate for the learning outcome. For example, software designed to help students learn rules should generally be a tutorial or simulation application.

The fourth step is to determine if the software incorporates an instructional strategy appropriate for the application. Is the strategy consistent with current theory and research findings? Does the strategy take advantage of the unique capabilities of the computer or does it only simulate a textbook or flashcards? To review the detailed instructional criteria for each application, see the previous chapters on the various tutor applications (Chapters 4 and 5).

Presentation Criteria

Presentation criteria refers more to the form of the program than to the substance. Instructional criteria are specific to the type of learning outcome and application, whereas presentation criteria are general in nature and cut across all types of applications and learning outcomes. Four major categories of presentation criteria are discussed: screen format, navigation, ease of use, and interaction.

Screen Format

Initially, it would seem that many of the principles relating to the design and layout of print materials would also apply to the design of computer video displays. Although many of these principles are clearly relevant, they cannot all be applied indiscriminately because there are significant differences between the printed page and the videoscreen.

In evaluating software, keep in mind that some software weaknesses are actually imposed by hardware limitations. To make a fair judgment of software, the evaluator must remember that people who develop software for any particular computer are restricted to the capabilities of that machine. For example, the resolution of most videoscreens severely restricts the quality and quantity of the text and graphics that can be displayed as compared to material printed on paper. The quality of text on videoscreens is generally quite poor, owing to the use of a dot matrix to form letters. On some computers, the screen is limited to 40 characters of text per line. Others offer 80 characters or more per line. Most microcomputers have graphics capabilities, but again resolution varies from machine to machine. Higher-quality illustrations and graphics can be produced on machines with higher resolution. See Chapter 2 for further discussion of hardware.

Many elements of software design are limited only by the expertise of the designer. These elements, too, must be considered by the evaluator of software. For example, the format of the screen can significantly affect the readability of the display. Full screens of text are difficult to read and are annoying to the student. Unlike printed material, blank space on the screen costs nothing. Lines, paragraphs, and headings should be spaced for ease of reading. If several textual and graphic elements are combined in the same display, these elements should be organized on the screen in such a way that the viewer's eye moves naturally from one element to the other in the desired order. Usually a top-to-bottom, left-to-right sequence is most desirable. Elements of the display should not require the eyes to jump all around the screen.

Careless programmers often make the mistake of splitting words at the ends of lines, which results in displays that are difficult to read. Errors in spelling and grammar have a similar effect. It has been demonstrated that ragged-right lines are easier to read than right-justified lines (Bork, 1980).

Programmers have various options for highlighting and emphasizing certain parts of the material displayed. When evaluating software, take note of the methods used to see that they are effective and not overdone. Consider, for instance, the use of underlining, boldface type, uppercase letters, varying type styles, inverse video (black letters on white background), flashing text, and color. These techniques are usually most effective if used sparingly. Color and flashing text can be particularly obnoxious if overused. In fact, if any kind of highlighting is overdone, the student can be distracted, annoyed, and confused, and the point of emphasis is lost.

Navigation

When students finish reading a page of printed material, they may proceed to additional material by turning a page. With computer video displays, a variety of techniques may be used for proceeding to additional material. One technique is to clear the screen by erasing all the old material on the screen and then displaying the new frame, or page, of information. Another common technique is to display the new information at the bottom of the screen, one line at a time, while scrolling the old information off the top of the screen. Good software avoids this scrolling technique because it is extremely difficult to read the text while it is being scrolled.

In addition to erasing the entire screen, it is possible to erase only a portion of the screen and display new information in the erased section. For example, a graphic could remain on the screen while several different textual descriptions concerning the graphic are presented sequentially. When using this approach, a slight pause should be placed between erasure and redisplay of the same section of the screen. This pause will allow the viewer to notice that the display has changed and that new information has been displayed that should be read. Visual effects, such as a dissolve or a wipe, could also serve this purpose.

In some applications, additional information to be displayed may also take the form of computer-generated graphics, animated text, or animated special graphic characters. Each of these types of displays involves some movement on the screen. Since movement is very powerful in attracting attention, the software should not require the user to read a textual description and watch an animated display simultaneously. The text should be displayed first; then, when the users have finished reading the text, they can press a key to signal readiness to attend to the animation. In some applications, it may be more appropriate to display the animation first, then the text. In either case, students should not be expected to attend to two things at once.

New information may be presented on the videoscreen by using any of the techniques that have been described under either computer control or student control. Under student control, the viewer is required to take some overt action, such as pressing a key on the keyboard to signal that new information should be presented. Under computer control, a given display remains on the screen for only a fixed period; then the computer automatically presents the next piece of information. This is accomplished by placing a fixed-time delay into the computer program.

In general, the computer program should not control the amount of display time. It is difficult to determine an optimum display time for a broad range of students. Some people read more slowly than others. A display time that is just right for the author of the program may be too short for some students and too fast for others. It is frustrating to have the computer display a new page of information when the student has not finished reading the previous page. A program should display a message at the bottom of the screen to prompt students to press the space bar or some other key when they are ready to proceed.

When new information is presented on the computer screen, it is generally necessary first to erase the old information. This old information is irretrievable unless some mechanism is built into the program for it to be redisplayed. A mechanism should be included to allow students to move both forward and backward through the instruction. If the computer screen is used to present test items, it is critical that the entire test item be displayed on a single screen. If a test item is displayed across two or more screens, then a mechanism for paging back and forth between the different pages of the item is mandatory.

Ease of Use

Historically, ease of use has not been a major issue of concern with respect to print materials. Most print materials, other than reference books, are designed to be read in a linear fashion from front to back. Going from one part to another in such material is relatively simple. Ease of use is of greater concern with respect to materials that are used for reference. Such materials need to be designed so that students can quickly find information in which they are interested. Ease of use is of major concern in the evaluation of computer-based materials because the entire set of materials is not physically visible at one time. It is very easy for students to get lost in a computer program and not know where they are or how to get where they want to go in the materials. Therefore, various mechanisms should be built into computer materials to assist the students in identifying where they are in the materials and how to get from one place to another easily.

The issue of getting from one place to another has been addressed briefly in the last couple of pages. It was mentioned that students should be able to go back and review previous screen pages if they desire. This technique should be expanded to allow students also to go to other sections of the materials without having to access all intervening material. This is often accomplished through the use of menus and/or special commands. A *menu* is simply a screen that lists the various options open to the student, much like a menu in a restaurant. A menu is also similar to the table of contents in a book. However, in computer materials, when students select a given option in the menu, the computer automatically branches to the section of materials corresponding to the selected option. To increase the ease with which students can traverse through a set of material, computer programs should provide several menus organized in a hierarchical fashion. A main menu should list the major sections of the materials. On selecting one of these sections, students should then be presented with a submenu that lists specific options related to the selected topic. Selections from a submenu may lead to a further sub-submenu if necessary.

In addition to the menus just described, computer materials should also include provision for students to enter special commands in order to branch to desired sections of the computer materials. Such commands could be entered by using special-function keys built into the keyboards of some computers, such as the PLATO and TICCIT computer-assisted instructional systems. Although most microcomputers do not have special-function keys, any of the standard alphanumeric keys can be used for the same purpose. If the special command feature is included in computer materials, it is important that the purpose of each command and its corresponding function key are made clear to the students. The name of the function key or the alphanumeric key should be as mnemonic as possible. For example, a function key for the command to return to the menu could be labeled MENU. If function keys are not available, the letter *M* could be used for the same purpose. The letter *D* would not be a good choice because it does not relate mnemonically to the command. If several options are made available to the students as to where to go next, the action required to execute each command should be clear. For example, if the message

PRESS M TO RETURN TO THE MENU

appeared at the bottom of the screen, students might wonder what to do if they do not want to return to the menu. In contrast, the following message would indicate that three options are available and the keys to press to select each alternative:

M)ENU   C)ONTINUE   B)ACK

In some cases, there may be too many commands to place at the bottom of the screen by using these techniques. In such circumstances, students should be allowed to enter one command that will cause a full screen of possible commands to be displayed. After reviewing the available commands, the students should then be able to return to the previous screen where the initial command was given.

When a large number of commands is used, it is very helpful if a printed sheet or card is provided that lists the available commands, their purpose, and the keys that should be pressed to execute each command. An off-line job aid reduces the need for students continually to move to and from the command list on the computer. If the commands are mnemonic, students should be able to memorize the commands after a short period of use and eliminate the need to refer to any command list at all. The commands used should be relatively easy to execute. When possible, students should be required to press only one or two keys to execute a command. The relationship between commands and the action required by students to execute a command should be consistent throughout a given computer program or system of programs. It can be very confusing to students if they are required to press the letter *G* to go to a glossary of terms in one part of a program and the letter *T* in another part of the same program.

Another factor that significantly affects ease of use is the provision of clear, simple, and concise instructions. Instructions should be available both on-line and off-line. The off-line instructions may go into greater detail than the on-line instructions. If a computer program is designed to be used several times, there should be provisions for students to skip the instructions on successive executions of the program. However, students are notorious for not reading instructions carefully. Therefore, it would be very helpful if students could enter a command to return to the instruction page from other points in the program in case they get stuck and do not remember what to do next. The instructions should be broken into sections and placed throughout the program where they would be immediately relevant. Students should be prompted as to what to do next at each critical point in the program. Such a technique reduces the likelihood that students will forget the instructions, and it also reduces the number of response errors.

Some authors like to place fancy title pages at the beginning of their programs. These title pages often include computer-generated graphics and music or special effects, which are relatively slow to produce. If the program is used frequently, this noticeable time delay can turn out to be quite annoying to students.

Many microcomputer programs require data or graphic information to be read off the disk into memory at the beginning or at other points in the program. These disk-reads can cause a noticeable pause in the program. Significant program pauses can also be caused by extensive calculations, sorts, and searches. When such pauses occur, the program should print out a message on the screen to inform students of the delay. Without such a message, students may become quite anxious and think that the program or computer is malfunctioning. If the pause is quite long, students may actually terminate the program or turn off the computer. The pause message can be creative and humorous in nature, thereby reducing students' annoyance at the delay. Another possible approach is a display of some kind of simulated clock that counts down the time till action resumes. Some programs mask time delays by displaying text or graphics just before the delay. Students read or study the information on the screen during the delay.

Interaction

One of the major advantages of the computer as a display device is its interactive capability. Students should not have to be merely passive receivers of presented information. They should be allowed to respond to the information in an interactive fashion. Programs that merely page through several frames of information without requiring some significant response from students have little added value over a book. In fact, a book is probably more flexible and convenient. In general, the more interactive a program is, the more interesting it is. However, the nature of the interaction should be relevant to the purpose of the program. Interaction for interaction's sake has little value. Copy frames (Markle, 1969, 1978) (the repetition of information presented in a frame of instruction) are of no more value in a computer program than they are in a programmed textbook.

When students are required to make a response, the program should display a message that clearly specifies the nature of the response. This can often be done with a very simple prompt:

DO YOU WANT IRREGULAR VERBS INCLUDED (Y/N)?

In this example, students are prompted to enter the letter *Y* for yes or the letter *N* for no. In the following example, students are prompted as to the format expected when entering the date:

PLEASE ENTER TODAY'S DATE (E.G., 08 SEP 96):

Most computer programs require students to press a special key to signal the computer when a response of several characters has been completed. This key is often labeled as the ENTER, RETURN, or NEXT key. Before this ENTER key is pressed, students may make any corrections to their response that they desire. However, it is possible to write computer programs that do not require the pressing of the ENTER key to signal the end of a response. This is often done when only a single-character response is expected. In general, the elimination of the ENTER key requirement is not recommended. Although the ENTER key requires an additional key press in making a response, it also allows students easily to correct any inadvertent mistakes or to change their minds about a choice made.

Even with the best of efforts at prompting the expected response and allowing for typing corrections, students will still make incorrect responses. Therefore, it is necessary for the program to include error traps. An *error trap* is a set of computer program codes that examines a student's response for possible errors. If an error is found, the program then prompts the student to enter an appropriate response. For example, if the computer asks the student to enter the date and the student enters his or her name instead, the program should display an error message and ask the student to enter the date correctly. Without such error traps, the program may terminate abnormally when it tries to process the student's response at a later point in the program.

In educational programs, it is important to give students feedback when they enter an incorrect answer to a question or problem. Practice makes perfect only with feedback. The feedback should do more than simply inform students that their response was correct or incorrect. When an incorrect response is made, the feedback should also provide the correct response. However, research has shown that is not necessary to require the student to copy the correct response before proceeding (Atkinson, 1974).

When students answer a question or problem incorrectly, some authors like to require them to try again. Try-again loops in a computer program are often frustrating for students. This is especially the case when no additional information or hints are provided to help students to determine the correct response. Try-again loops should terminate after students make a mistake several times in a row. If a student makes repeated unrecognizable responses to a free-form (fill-in-the-blank) response question, the computer program should exit the loop and ask the student to choose from several possible alternatives.

The Curriculum Factor

When planning for the purchase of computers and computer software, carefully consider the effect such purchases will have on your school's curriculum. Educational software can range from individual programs that augment classroom instruction to integrated learning systems that entirely replace the need for classroom instruction in a certain subject. In either case, the software should fit into the design of the curriculum, either as it is or with minor modifications.

Suppose you want to use the computers in your school to augment the time you spend on spelling. Some software will not allow you the flexibility of selecting your own spelling lists. In such a case, do you change your curriculum, or do you find a program that is more flexible? This book recommends the latter.

Suppose you want to move remedial math from a classroom situation to computer-assisted instruction. Do you buy several different programs that generally cover what your present curriculum dictates, or do you find a comprehensive software package that covers the entire range of mathematical problems? As you review more and more programs, you will notice that each program has its own idiosyncrasies. Requiring students to go back and forth between each of these vastly different programs slows down the learning process. Also, it is difficult to find independent programmed material that does not overlap in content.

Evaluation Method

The ideal method of evaluating educational software would be to take the actual program into your school and let students try it. The next best thing would be for you, as a teacher, to review each piece of software before implementing it in the school. Current market practices discourage both methods. Because of the widespread practice of software piracy, many of the current educational programs are copy protected (i.e., duplicate copies cannot be made without sophisticated copying programs). Even with this safeguard of copy-protected disks, many pirated copies seem to find their way around the schools. Therefore, software companies are often leery of sending software to schools for review. Because it is not fiscally wise to purchase software simply as a means of evaluating them, the following alternatives are available for evaluating software.

1. *State or district software review.* In each state or district, a committee of trained specialists in educational computers (like yourself) reviews educational software and makes its reports available to each school in the state or district. The software selected for review is selected from those programs that have been rated highly in nationally published magazines and journals of software review.

2. *Published evaluations*

    a. Most educational journals and microcomputer magazines have sections that review various kinds of software. Some of these rank software as to the number of units purchased during the month. Other publishers provide an in-depth analysis and review several software packages each month.

    b. Several publishers provide a yearly review of all the software on the market for a selected computer. These reviews usually include worthwhile information on each software package.

3. *Users' groups.* In many communities, people who own a certain brand of computer have formed users' groups to exchange information about hardware, software, and programming. These groups seem to be very helpful in solving problems with programming and software applications.

4. *Conferences and workshops.* Most college and universities offer continuing-education and special-interest conferences and workshops on various subjects. There are several national conventions and workshops on software and hardware, such as COMDEX, NCC, and SOFTCOM.

5. *Organizations.* Several national organizations—such as Conduit, Microsift, Educational Products Information Exchange (EPIE), National Council of Teachers of English (NCTE), and National Council of Teachers of Mathematics (NCTM)—have developed systematic procedures, guidelines, and criteria for the evaluation of software. Some companies, such as Conduit, review and test programs and then distribute those it feels are worthy of recommendation. Others, such as EPIE, publish regular reports that describe and evaluate educational software.

Summary

Both instructional and presentation criteria should be used in evaluating educational software. The appendix at the end of this chapter not only serves as a summary of these criteria but it may also be used by the teacher as an aid in the evaluation of educational software packages.

Exercises

1. Briefly describe the four steps involved in evaluating software according to instructional criteria.
2. Outline the principal guidelines for evaluating software according to each of the following four categories of presentation criteria: screen format, paging, ease of use, and interaction.

3. Suppose you were asked to identify, evaluate, and select computer software for your school. Describe how you would go about accomplishing this task.

4. Use the software evaluation checklist provided in the appendix to this chapter or one of your own design to evaluate at least one tutor software program. Write a report that describes the software, your evaluation procedure, the results of your evaluation, and your conclusions.

References

Atkinson, R. C. (1974, March). Teaching children to read using a computer. *American Psychologist,* 169–178.

Bork, A. (1980). *Textual taxonomy.* Irvine, CA: Educational Technology Center, University of California, Irvine.

Markle, S. M. (1969). *Good frames and bad: A grammar of framewriting* (2nd ed.). New York: Wiley.

Markle, S. M. (1978). *Designs for instructional designers.* Champaign, IL: Stipes Publishing.

Appendix: Software Evaluation Checklist

Instructional Criteria

A. What are the learning objectives of the software?
B. Does the program fit your current curriculum, or can it be modified to fit your curriculum?
C. Does the program use an instructional strategy appropriate to the application and learning outcome?
D. Are the examples and illustrations appropriate for the intended grade level?
E. Are good-quality tests and quizzes included?

Presentation Criteria

Screen Format

_____ A. Blank space is used liberally.
_____ B. A busy, cluttered screen is avoided.
_____ C. Cryptic abbreviations and codes are minimal (uses another screen if necessary).
_____ D. The screen elements take advantage of natural eye movement.
_____ E. Correct spelling and grammar are used.
_____ F. Flashing text and other forms of highlighting are used sparingly.

Navigation

_____ A. Scrolling is avoided when accessing new material.
_____ B. A visual effect or slight pause is used when erasing and redisplaying the same section of the screen.

____ C. The student does not have to attend to two different things on the screen simultaneously.

____ D. Student responses are required before proceeding to a new screen; time-out displays are avoided.

____ E. The student may proceed forward and backward through the instruction.

Ease of Use

____ A. Menus and/or special commands enable the student to go easily from one part of the program to another.

    ____ 1. Keys used to implement a command are mnemonically related to the purpose of the command.

    ____ 2. All possible alternative commands are made clear.

    ____ 3. A minimum of keystrokes is required to execute any command.

    ____ 4. Keys used to execute commands are consistent throughout the program.

____ B. Instructions are clear, simple, and concise.

    ____ 1. Instructions are available both on-line and off-line.

    ____ 2. The student has the option to skip lengthy instructions.

    ____ 3. The student is prompted what to do next at critical points in the program.

____ C. Minimum time is required to generate title page.

____ D. Messages are provided to inform the student of noticeable pauses in a program.

____ E. Pauses are masked where possible.

Interaction

____ A. Interactive capabilities of the computer have been well used.

____ B. The student is prompted on the nature of the expected response.

____ C. The student is allowed to correct typing mistakes by requiring the pressing of the ENTER key to signal the end of a response.

____ D. Error traps test the appropriateness of the student's response.

____ E. Correct feedback is provided when the student enters an incorrect answer to questions or problems.

____ F. Sarcastic feedback is avoided.

____ G. The number of times the student iterates through try-again loops is minimized.

Chapter 7

Tool Applications

The use of tools is one of the major differences between humans and lower forms of animals. We have invented many tools to extend our physical capabilities. Our hands and feet do not seem to be well designed for digging in the earth, so we use shovels, hoes, plows, and cultivators. Our legs do not move very fast, so we use skates, bicycles, wagons, carts, and automobiles. Even the lack of wings has not deterred us; we have invented tools that allow us to soar faster and higher than the birds of the air. We have machines that wash our clothes, our dishes, our teeth, and even our other tools. We have also developed many tools to facilitate instruction and learning, such as pencils, erasers, chalkboards, slide rules, typewriters, microscopes, drafting tables, rulers, brushes, pianos, and drums.

With the advent of the computer, we now have a tool to extend our mental capabilities. In the past, our abilities to calculate numbers was slow and prone to error. With the computer, we can do millions of calculations in less than a minute with flawless accuracy. We can also manipulate symbols, which are the basic elements of thought. Although we are unable to comprehend the full ramifications of such a tool, it is reaching into every aspect of our lives. If students are to cope with a technological world, they must be prepared to use this extremely versatile tool—the computer.

Because the computer is a tool, all of its applications may be referred to as *tool applications*. However, for the purposes of this book, the term *tool applications* refers to those applications that do not deal directly with either instruction (tutor applications) or computer programming (tutee applications). As tutor, the computer takes the role of teacher; as tutee, the role of learner; as tool, the role of assistant. Many computer tools have been developed to assist school administrators, teachers, and students. This chapter will focus on the following major applications of the computer as tool: word processing, draw and paint graphics, database management, spreadsheets, charts, desktop publishing, and presentations.

Each of these computer tools is available as stand-alone applications. However, these computer tools have become so popular that many software companies have developed integrated software packages that combine several of these tools into one comprehensive program. One of the first integrated programs, *AppleWorks,* combined only three of these tools, whereas two of the most popular programs used in the schools today, *ClarisWorks* and *Microsoft Works,* integrate all of these tools plus communications. Several companies are marketing to the business community a set of separate tool programs, called an *office suite,* that provide some integration capabilities. This chapter will discuss each of these tools and show how they can be used in combination. Communication tools will be discussed in Chapter 9, Networks and Telecommunication, and tools related to multimedia applications will be discussed in Chapter 8, Multimedia/Hypermedia.

Word Processing

Word processing refers to the use of computer software in the writing, editing, formatting, storing, and printing of written documents. A computer program designed for word processing is called a *word processor.* Anyone who has cringed when making an error on a typewriter will greatly appreciate this wonderful tool. Text typed on the computer keyboard is displayed on the computer screen and stored in the computer memory. Deletions, additions, and other modifications are easily made with a few keystrokes. Once a document is perfected, it can be saved on a diskette or hard disk and printed. If more modifications are required, the document can be retrieved from the diskette, changed, and reprinted. There is no need to retype text previously entered correctly. Word processing is such a valuable tool that many people feel this single application is sufficient justification for the purchase of a microcomputer.

Word processing has obvious values for writers, secretaries, and teachers. Teachers can use a word processor to prepare syllabi, lesson plans, handouts, worksheets, examinations, and written reports. It is also highly recommended that students be given access to this tool to facilitate their writing. *Bank Street Writer, pfs:Write, Microsoft Word, MacWrite, MultiScribe, Magic Slate, Wordstar,* and *WordPerfect* are examples of the many word-processing packages designed for microcomputers.

Basic Features of a Word Processor

Typing on a microcomputer keyboard is as easy as typing on a regular typewriter. Differences are minor, but they do exist. The microcomputer always provides a separate key for the numeral one, for instance, whereas some typewriters let the lowercase letter *l* double as a numeral. One of the most noticeable differences between typing on a typewriter and using a microcomputer with a word-processing program is a feature called word wrap. With the word processor, the typist no longer presses the carriage return key at the end of each line of print. When a line is full, the next word is automatically wrapped around to the left margin of the next line. The RETURN key is pressed only at the ends of paragraphs. The main features of word processors can be classified into two areas: editing and formatting.

Editing

As the user types on the keyboard, the text is stored in the memory of the microcomputer and is displayed on the video screen. The editing features allow the user to correct typing errors and make other changes in the text.

Cursor Control.   When editing text that has already been typed, the user needs a way to indicate where deletions or insertions are to be made. This is done by moving a blinking vertical bar, called a *cursor,* around the screen. A good word-processing program provides several different ways to move the cursor. A mechanism should be provided to move the cursor to the left or right one character or one word at a time; to jump to the beginning or end of a line; to move up or down one line, paragraph, or page at a time; or to move immediately to the beginning or end of the document. Such cursor movements are usually performed by pressing special cursor-control keys labeled with arrows and such terms as *page up, page down, home,* and *end.* Older keyboards often required the use of a special key called the CONTROL key in conjunction with certain alphabetic keys. Many computers now use the mouse (see Chapter 2, Computer Hardware) to move the cursor. As the mouse is moved over a smooth surface, such as a desk or a mouse pad, its movements are followed by a pointer on the screen. The cursor is relocated by moving the mouse pointer and clicking the mouse button when the pointer is at the desired insertion point.

Insertion.   Text can be added simply by placing the cursor at the desired insertion point and typing the material to be inserted. Text following the insertion is automatically moved ahead as necessary to make room for the insertion.

Selection.   In order to manipulate blocks or sections of text, a mechanism must be provided to select the desired text. This may be done with the keyboard by moving the cursor to the beginning of the block of text, marking the location by pressing a specified function key or the control key in conjunction with an alphabetic key, then moving the cursor to the end of the block and marking that location. The selected block is usually highlighted through the use of inverse video or a colored background. The mouse may be used to select the text by moving the pointer to the beginning of the block, pressing and holding the mouse button down, moving or dragging the mouse pointer to the end of the block, and then lifting the mouse button. After the text is selected, it may be deleted, moved, copied, or reformatted.

Deleting.   Individual characters are usually deleted simply by moving the cursor immediately after the character and then pressing the BACKSPACE key. To delete words, lines, paragraphs, and larger blocks of material at one time, the desired text is first selected and then the BACKSPACE or DELETE key is pressed. When text is deleted, the remaining text is automatically moved to fill in the gap.

Block Move.   To move a block of text from one location to another, the desired text is selected and then a command is given (by pressing designated keys or selecting an option, such as Cut, from a pull-down menu) to delete the text and temporarily store it in a section of memory called a *buffer* or *clipboard.* The cursor is then moved to the desired location and another command is given to insert, or *paste,* the text.

Block Copy.   Like the block move function, block copy allows a block of text to be placed in another location in the document. However, block copy does it without deleting the material from its first location. The block of material can be placed in several locations within the document, if that is desired, just as several photographic prints can be made from a single negative.

Undo.   This feature provides the option of undoing the last action. For example, if the user deletes a block of material and then determines that the deletion should not have taken place, the user may put it back in. Having replaced the block of material, the user can undo the last action, and the material is again removed. The user can undo actions such as deletions, moves, and insertions. This feature gives a writer the freedom to experiment with different wordings without having to retype an earlier version that may have been deleted.

Search and Replace.   This feature allows the user to search the document, or only part of it, for a word, a phrase, or any combination of characters. Once the computer finds the item, it may be changed, replaced, or left undisturbed. Most word processors allow for automatic replacement of the search object with some other text. For instance, if the word *computer* has been typed as *computor* throughout a document, a student could have the word processor search for all occurrences of *computor* and replace them automatically with *computer.*

Formatting

Format refers to the appearance of a document on paper. Some common formatting features usually provided by word processors are discussed next.

Line Spacing.   Most word processors allow the user a choice between single and double spacing. Some allow the user to specify any desired spacing option.

Margins and Justification.   Left and right margins can be set for a given document or portion of a document. When margin settings are changed, all text or a selected block is automatically adjusted to the new settings. Text can be left-justified (left margins align), right-justified (right margins align), or full-justified (both margins align; the computer may automatically add extra spaces between some words).

Centering.   Words, phrases, or whole lines can be automatically centered between the left and right margins. This is frequently useful for headings, titles, and the like.

Proportional Spacing.   Many typewriters and some word processors use the same amount of space for a wide letter (such as *w*) as for a narrow letter (such as *i*). Proportional spacing allots space according to character size, which results in increased readability.

Tabs.   Tab stops are used for paragraph indentions and tables. Tab alignment options can include left, right, center, or decimal tabs. Decimal tabs line up numbers by decimal points.

Fonts, Size, and Style.   Some word processors allow the user to select the way text will appear on the screen and in print by changing its font, size, and style. The *font* is the overall appearance or design of a set of letters, numbers, and punctuation symbols. Some of the most common fonts include Times Roman, Helvetica, and Courier. *Size* refers to how big the characters are; it is usually measured in units of 72 points per inch. Thus, an 18-point character would be approximately one-quarter (18/72) of an inch high. The type you are reading is 10-point Times Roman. A character, word, or block of text can be highlighted, or made to stand out, by the use of *styles,* such as boldface, underline, italic, outline, and shadow. Some programs also allow for the use of color for highlighting. The font, size, and style of a block of text can be specified before it is typed, or it can be selected and changed later.

Page Breaks.   To most users of word processors, being able to see on the screen where page breaks will occur when the text is printed is a feature that cannot be overlooked. One of its benefits is in caring for widows and orphans. An experienced typist will avoid leaving a lonely first line of a new paragraph (commonly referred to as a *widow*) by itself at the bottom of a page or a lonely last line of a paragraph (commonly referred to as an *orphan*) at the top of the next page. A heading placed on the last line of a page is also considered poor clerical management.

  Problems such as these are easy to avoid if the operator can see on the screen where the page breaks will occur on paper and can adjust the location of the page breaks as desired. Some word processors will even check for widows and orphans automatically. The alternative is to print the document, note the trouble spots, make corrections, and reprint. Sometimes the correction of one widow or orphan will create another further down the document. Several printings may be required to make all necessary corrections. These extra printings are avoided when the word processor shows page breaks on the screen.

Pagination.   Most word processors allow the option to print or not print page numbers. The numbers may be placed at the top or bottom of the page and on the left, right, or center of the page. The type of page numbers themselves can be changed, making it possible to have introductory pages with roman numerals and the remainder with arabic numerals.

Headers and Footers.   At times, the writer wants information to appear at the top or bottom of each page of a document. For instance, a chapter title sometimes appears at the top of each page of the chapter, or the title of a book might appear at the top of each left page of the book. Text that appears at the top of each page is called a *header.* If it appears at the bottom of the page, it is called a *footer.* Many word processors allow several lines of text in headers and footers. Some allow a choice of positioning headers and footers at the left, right, or center of the page. The left and right feature can be adjusted to place the header or footer at the left for even-numbered pages and at the right for odd-numbered pages or vice versa.

Footnotes/Endnotes.   Some word-processing systems provide for use of footnotes and endnotes. With footnotes, the amount of text on the page is automatically adjusted to allow room for the footnote text at the bottom of the page. When a footnote or endnote is inserted or deleted, all footnotes or endnotes following it are automatically renumbered to accommodate the change.

Other Word-Processing Features

Outliner

We all remember our English teachers asking us to prepare and submit an outline of our term papers before we began writing. The preparation of the outlines helped us to think about how the ideas for our papers related to one another and allowed us to better organize our papers. Special programs—such as *Think Tank, MORE,* and *Acta*—have been written to help writers construct such outlines. Recently, outlining tools have been incorporated into word-processing programs. For example, in *Microsoft Word,* the outliner is just another view of your document. Outline entries become headings in your paper. The first-level entries in your outline become main headings in your paper, whereas second- and third-level entries become secondary and tertiary headings. Figure 7–1 shows the outline view of this chapter. The + symbol indicates that there are subordinate entries under this heading, the – symbol indicates that this heading has no subordinate headings.

The outliner automatically indents the various levels of the outline. Tools are provided for demoting a heading to a lower level or promoting one to a higher level. Commands can be given to specify that subordinate headings be collapsed or hidden. In Figure 7–1, the line under a heading indicates that subordinate headings have been collapsed. Body text may be all shown, collapsed to one line under each heading, or completely hidden. A heading can be moved to another location in the outline by selecting it and dragging it to the new location with the mouse. When a heading is moved, all subordinate headings and body text are moved with it. Any changes in the outline are reflected in the document and vice versa. This is a powerful tool for easily reorganizing a document.

Spell-Checker

Some word processors will proofread a document for spelling errors, checking each word against a built-in dictionary. The program will call to the attention of the user any word in the document that is not found in its dictionary and allow the user to determine whether a change is needed. Some programs provide possible spelling suggestions, allowing users to select the appropriate spelling. The computer will then replace the misspelled word with the one selected by the user. If a word processor does not have a spell-checker feature, it is often possible to purchase a separate program for this purpose.

Thesaurus

Word processors with an on-line thesaurus allow the user to select a word and request a list of synonyms and antonyms for that word. A word from the list can be selected to replace the original word or used to identify another list of synonyms based on the new-

```
✛   Word Processing
        ✛   Basic Features of a Word Processor
                ✛   Editing
                        ▭   Cursor Control
                        ▭   Insertion
                        ▭   Selection
                        ▭   Deleting
                        ▭   Block Move
                        ▭   Block Copy
                        ▭   Undo
                        ▭   Search and Replace
                ✛   Formatting
                        ▭   Line Spacing
                        ▭   Margins and Justification
                        ▭   Centering
                        ▭   Proportional Spacing
                        ▭   Tabs
                        ▭   Fonts, Size, and Style
                        ▭   Page Breaks
                        ▭   Pagination
                        ▭   Headers and Footers
                        ▭   Footnotes/Endnotes
        ✛   Other Word-Processing Features
        ✛   Hardware and Software Issues
                ▭   Screen Format
                ▭   Ease of Use
                ▭   Printers
        ▭   Instructional Applications
✛   Database Management
▭   Spreadsheets
✛   Graphics
        ▭   Charting Graphics
        ▭   Drawing Graphics
        ▭   Painting Graphics
▭   Desktop Publishing
```

FIGURE 7–1   Outline View of This Chapter

ly selected word. The value of this tool is highly dependent on the number of entries made available in the program. With rapid access to synonyms, writers can easily broaden the vocabulary used within a document. As with spell-checkers, separate thesaurus programs are available.

Grammar Checker

Several separate programs are now available that will read a document created using a word processor and check it for a wide variety of errors in punctuation, format, grammar, usage and style, as well as spelling. When an error is detected, the problem word, phrase, or sentence will be highlighted within the context of the document, and the nature of the error will be described along with a suggestion on how to solve the problem. If you agree with the solution, you may press a key combination to instruct the program to automatically correct the error in your document. If you do not understand the grammar rule related to the error, some programs provide an on-line tutorial that explains the rule along with examples and nonexamples of correct usage. Of course, the user always has the option to override the grammar checker and leave the text unchanged.

Some of the format and punctuation errors identified by grammar checkers include noncapitalization of the first word of a sentence, noncapitalized proper nouns, nonmatching quotation marks or parentheses, extra spaces between words and punctuation marks, double punctuation marks, wrong format of dates, and misplacement of quotation marks in relationship to periods and commas. Usage and style errors include overuse of jargon, double negatives, repeated words (e.g., *the the*), split infinitives, long sequences of nouns, long sequences of prepositional phrases, redundant expressions such as *past history,* mistaken use of *a* and *an,* informal expressions such as *this here,* and *try and,* overuse of the passive voice, and confusion with *who* and *whom, between* and *among, fewer* and *less.* Grammar errors include mismatched subject and verb, incomplete sentence, and confusion regarding subject and object pronouns (e.g., *he* and *him*), contractions and possessive forms (e.g., *it's* and *its*), and homonyms (e.g., *to* and *too*).

Although a grammar checker may help identify many common errors in a written document, it is no substitute for a human editor. The computer does not know what the writer is trying to communicate. Therefore, it may make inappropriate suggestions or miss errors it is not programmed to find.

Some grammar-checking programs currently available include *Correct Grammar, Grammatik, MacProof/PCProof, RightWriter,* and *Sensible Grammar.* Grammar-checking capabilities are now integrated with many word-processing programs.

Hardware and Software Issues

Word processing involves an interaction between several components of a system, including computer, monitor, software, and printer. Different brands and versions of equipment and software vary considerably in their ability to perform as a part of a word-processing system. If any component is inadequate, the performance of other components can be weakened, and the system will disappoint the user. Some features that should be considered are discussed here.

Screen Format

With some word processors, the way the textual material appears on the screen is very similar to the way it will look on paper when printed. With others, this is not the case. Figure 7–2 shows a comparison of the screen display of two word processors. In the first example, underlining and italics are shown through the use of background highlighting; with the second, these features are shown on the screen the same as they will appear on paper. Some word processors that do not show all features on the editing screen will provide a print preview screen to show what the document will look like when printed. However, editing cannot be done in the preview mode.

Ease of Use

In selecting a word processor, it should be kept in mind that each function is accessed by commands that must be learned by the user. Generally speaking, the more sophisticated programs require more learning time, but this is not always true because some are better designed for ease of use. With some software, commands for bolding text, making footers, using the thesaurus, and so on, are given from the keyboard by pressing a control or command key along with a character key. On other systems, commands are executed by pressing special-function keys on the keyboard, and still others use the

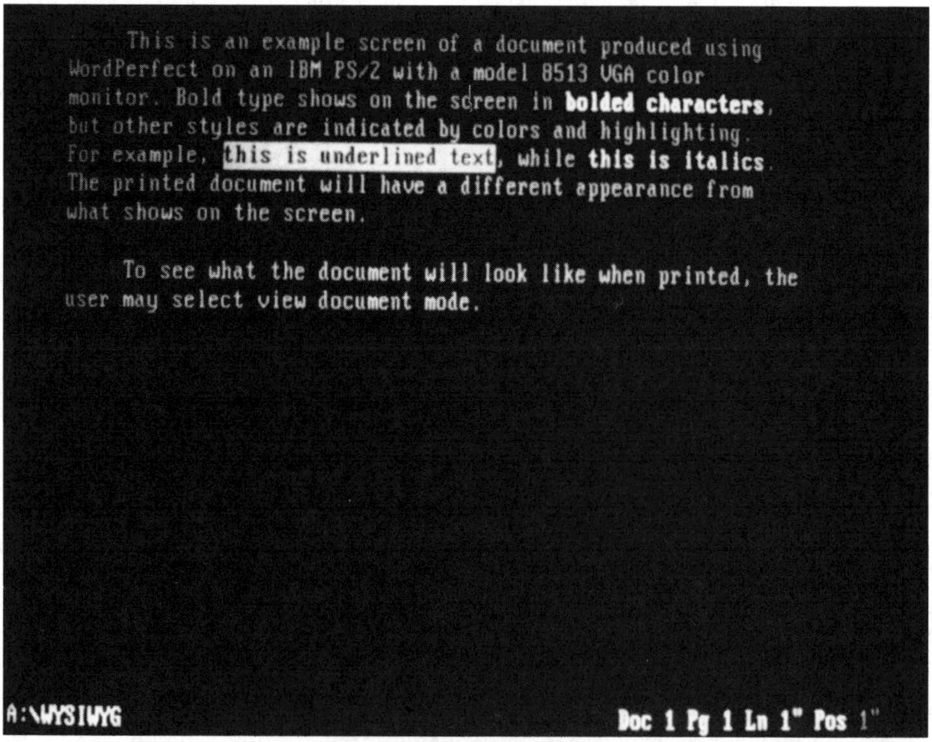

This is an example screen of a document produced using WordPerfect on an IBM PS/2 with a model 8513 VGA color monitor. Bold type shows on the screen in **bolded characters**, but other styles are indicated by colors and highlighting. For example, this is underlined text, while **this is italics**. The printed document will have a different appearance from what shows on the screen.

To see what the document will look like when printed, the user may select view document mode.

A:\WYSIWYG   Doc 1 Pg 1 Ln 1" Pos 1"

a

FIGURE 7–2a–b Comparison of the On-Screen Display of Two Word Processors

mouse to select the command from a pull-down menu. Rulers and tool bars may be added that allow users to select commands by clicking the mouse on an icon (see Figure 7–3). The more sophisticated programs accommodate different user preferences by providing multiple ways for performing the same command.

Another valuable feature of some word processors is the use of multiple windows. Figure 7–4 shows a screen divided horizontally into two windows displaying separate parts of the same document. The user can see any part of the document in either window and even the same part in both windows, if desired. Figure 7–5 shows two windows displaying separate documents. The size of any window can be adjusted as desired. Windows are very convenient for moving text from one part of a document to another or from one document to another. They are also useful any time the user wishes to see a second document or another part of the same document without removing the current work from view.

Printers

Formatting options depend on the capabilities of the printer, as well as the computer and software; therefore, matching a printer to a user's needs should be considered when selecting a word-processing system. Some print high-quality characters, usually preferred for business letters and other formal documents, whereas others print characters

---

☰ File Edit View Insert Format Tools Table Window ✓

WYSIWYG

WYSIWYG

This is an example screen of a document produced using *Microsoft Word.* Double spacing shows on the screen as double spacing. Underlining shows on the screen as <u>underlining</u>, bold type shows as **bold**, and italics shows as *italics.* The printed document will have the same appearance as the document on the screen. In short, with this word processor, what you see is what you get!

-------------------------------- Page Break --------------------------------

The dotted line above indicates where the page will break. This paragraph will be printed on a different page than the paragraph above.

b

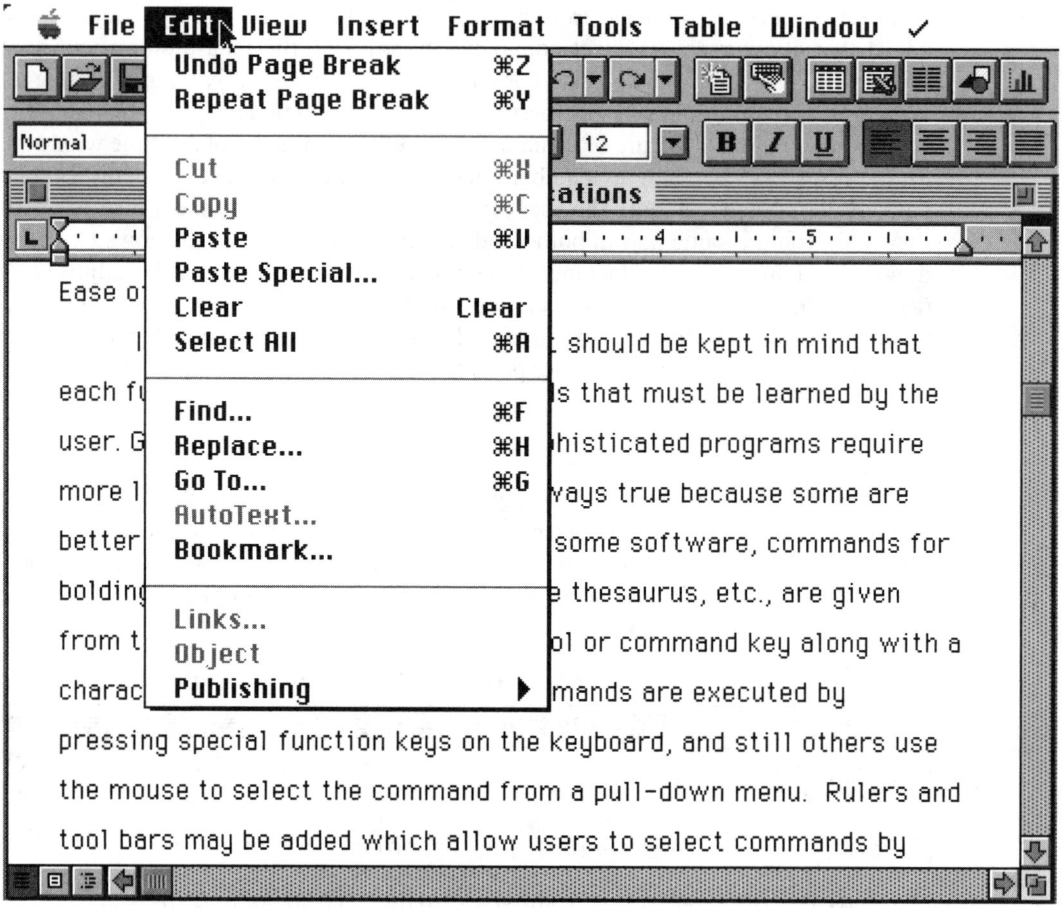

File   **Edit**   View   Insert   Format   Tools   Table   Window   ✓

Undo Page Break   ⌘Z
Repeat Page Break   ⌘Y

Cut   ⌘X
Copy   ⌘C
Paste   ⌘V
Paste Special...
Clear   Clear
Select All   ⌘A

Find...   ⌘F
Replace...   ⌘H
Go To...   ⌘G
AutoText...
Bookmark...

Links...
Object
Publishing   ▶

Normal   12   B I U

ations

Ease of

each fu

user. G

more l

better

bolding

from t

charac

should be kept in mind that

s that must be learned by the

histicated programs require

ways true because some are

some software, commands for

thesaurus, etc., are given

ol or command key along with a

mands are executed by

pressing special function keys on the keyboard, and still others use
the mouse to select the command from a pull-down menu. Rulers and
tool bars may be added which allow users to select commands by

FIGURE 7–3   Pull-Down Menu, Tool Bar, and Ruler Bar

made up of a matrix of tiny dots. Each printer is compatible with certain computers and not with others; and some printers are faster than others. Most quality printers are equipped to provide underlining and boldface type. Laser printers offer a variety of fonts, sizes, and styles. For more detailed information on printers and printing options, refer to Chapter 2, Computer Hardware.

Instructional Applications

Teaching students to write well is one of the important challenges teachers face. Students need to learn the basic rules of good communication. They should be encouraged to spell and punctuate correctly, and creativity should be stressed. Sometimes, these efforts are thwarted because the mechanics of writing and rewriting bring discouragement.

More attention is being given to the value of using word processors with students. Their use encourages students who might otherwise avoid writing. The tasks of plan-

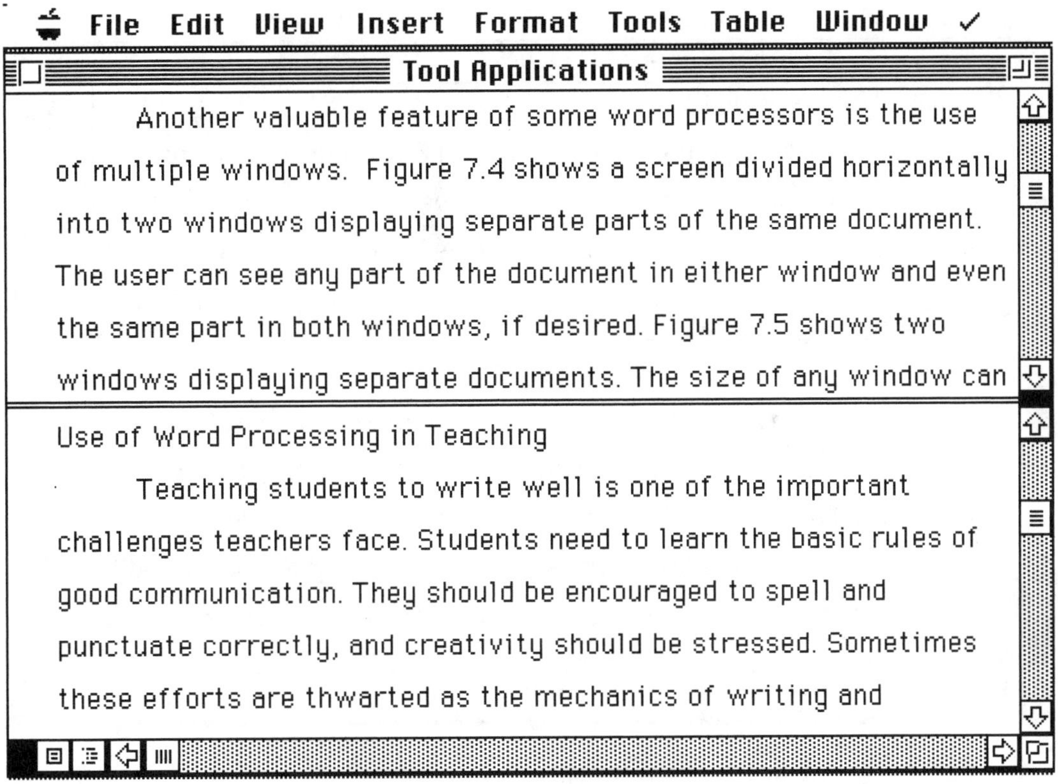

File   Edit   View   Insert   Format   Tools   Table   Window   ✓

═══════════════════ **Tool Applications** ═══════════════════

Another valuable feature of some word processors is the use

of multiple windows. Figure 7.4 shows a screen divided horizontally

into two windows displaying separate parts of the same document.

The user can see any part of the document in either window and even

the same part in both windows, if desired. Figure 7.5 shows two

windows displaying separate documents. The size of any window can

Use of Word Processing in Teaching

Teaching students to write well is one of the important

challenges teachers face. Students need to learn the basic rules of

good communication. They should be encouraged to spell and

punctuate correctly, and creativity should be stressed. Sometimes

these efforts are thwarted as the mechanics of writing and

FIGURE 7–4   Two Windows Showing the Same Document

ning and composing a first draft, editing, rewriting, and proofreading is reduced with the use of a word processor. The writer can easily add, delete, and change the order of items, as needed. Changes can be made and a fresh, corrected copy printed without retyping.

The ability of many word processors to undo any change at the press of a button encourages students to try editing changes. Being able to make the change, examine the work, and quickly change it back if the writer prefers the earlier style provides a psychological freedom that encourages creativity and exploration of ideas.

Teachers must not express the view to their students, explicitly or implicitly, that editing and reediting is a waste of time. Valuable learning comes in the editing and polishing process. This is where tedium usually mounts up and where the word processor shows its strengths. When an entire document is retyped on a typewriter, every word needs to be proofread because new errors might have been made in the retyping. When editing is done on a word processor, proofreading can be limited to the parts of the document that were changed. The user soon gains confidence that all else will remain as it was before.

The question of providing student access to the word processor in the lower grades brings with it the question of how early to teach keyboarding skills. Studies are being

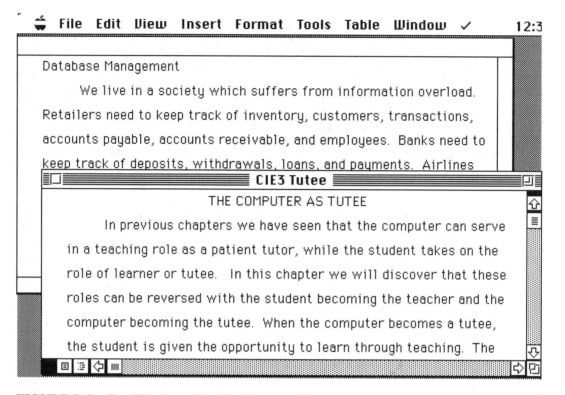

File   Edit   View   Insert   Format   Tools   Table   Window   ✓   12:3

Database Management

We live in a society which suffers from information overload. Retailers need to keep track of inventory, customers, transactions, accounts payable, accounts receivable, and employees. Banks need to keep track of deposits, withdrawals, loans, and payments. Airlines

CIE3 Tutee

THE COMPUTER AS TUTEE

In previous chapters we have seen that the computer can serve in a teaching role as a patient tutor, while the student takes on the role of learner or tutee. In this chapter we will discover that these roles can be reversed with the student becoming the teacher and the computer becoming the tutee. When the computer becomes a tutee, the student is given the opportunity to learn through teaching. The

FIGURE 7–5   Two Windows Showing Separate Documents

done to determine the feasibility of teaching keyboarding skills in the primary grades, perhaps as early as kindergarten. Factors considered include finger dexterity as well as mental readiness. Some are asking, What's the rush?; others are expressing concern that young children are acquiring poor keyboarding skills by being exposed to computer use without proper keyboard training. They are better off to learn correct procedures initially than to develop bad habits that must be overcome later.

A controversial area in using word processors is the use of spell-checkers with young students. Some teachers feel comfortable allowing their students to use spell-checkers, whereas others feel that spell-checkers take the responsibility of being a good speller away from the student. However, spell-checkers still require that students be accountable for determining the appropriate spelling. These features only flag words that are not found in their dictionary and present several alternatives found in the dictionary that are similar to the "misspelled" word. Students must recognize and select the correct alternative. In some cases, the computer may not present the correct spelling of the word as one of the alternatives. So it appears that students are still required to make many spelling decisions, even when using spell-checkers. In fact, spell-checkers might even help students improve their spelling by providing timely feedback concerning their spelling problems. If the word processor comes with this feature, it will usually be on a separate disk or in a separate file. The item can then be removed if a teacher does not want it to be used by students.

Many new software programs are being produced to assist teachers in teaching writing skills. Please consult Chapter 12, Curriculum Integration: Reading and Language Arts, for more detailed information on these tools.

Database Management

We live in a society that suffers from information overload. Retailers need to keep track of inventory, customers, transactions, accounts payable, accounts receivable, and employees. Banks need to keep track of deposits, withdrawals, loans, and payments. Airlines must keep track of flight schedules, reservations, departures, and arrivals. School administrators must manage information about class schedules, bus schedules and routes, faculty and staff, capital equipment, as well as students' names, addresses, phone numbers, and transcripts. Teachers must maintain information on student attendance and achievement, lesson plans, handouts, and other instructional materials. Students must keep information from class lectures, reading assignments, and library research. The computer can be used to help store, organize, and retrieve this mountain of information. Much of what we now do in society would be impossible without this tool application of the computer.

A collection of information or data stored in a computer is called a *database*. Since information stored in the memory of most computers is lost when the power is turned off, the database is usually transferred to an external storage medium such as a diskette or hard disk. A computer program that allows a user to enter, update, organize, and retrieve information in a computer database is generally called a *database management system (DBMS)*.

A computer database is easily understood by comparing it to a manual information management system, such as the card catalog of a school library. A computer database may be divided into files, records, and fields. A *record* is a set of data or information about a single item that is treated as a unit. Each card in a library card catalog could be thought of as a record, since each card contains information about a single item or book. A single piece of information within a record is called a *field*. Thus, the name of the author, the publishing company, and the copyright date would be considered as three separate fields on a library card record. Figure 7–6 shows the fields and records from a computer database. A group of records stored together under a common label or name is referred to as a *file*. All of the author cards stored in a card catalog would be analogous to a file. A database is composed of a group of related files. Thus, a card catalog would be a database consisting of the author, title, and subject card files.

Although a computer database may be similar in organization and content to a manual card catalog, a computer database management system offers many advantages over a manual system. One obvious advantage is the speed with which the computer is able to search the database and retrieve a particular record. This speed advantage is even more pronounced when the computer is used to retrieve several records that are not stored in physical proximity to each other.

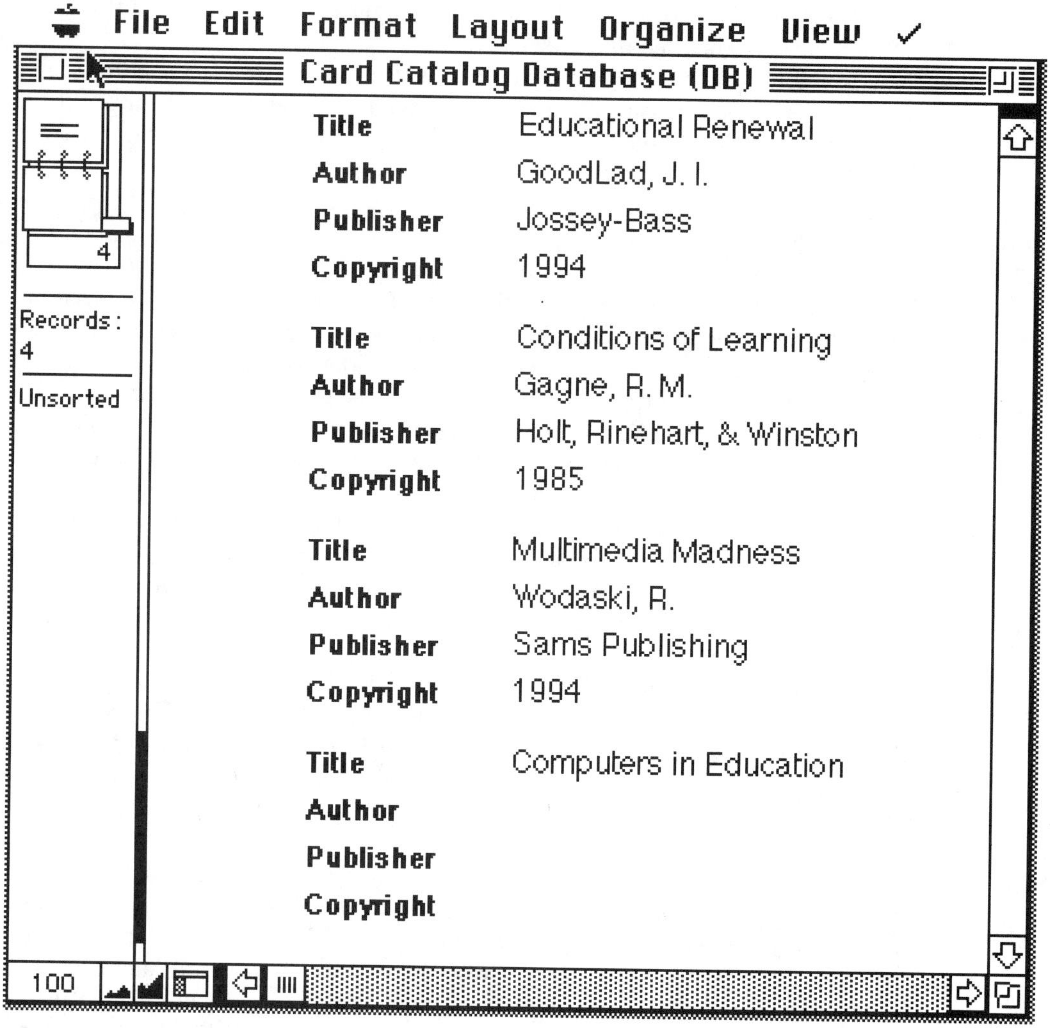

```
☰  File   Edit   Format   Layout   Organize   View   ✓
```

FIGURE 7–6   **Database Records and Fields**

Most database management programs allow rapid retrieval of information independent of the way the records are organized. Library cards organized alphabetically by author may be searched effectively only if the name of the author of the desired book is known. Unfortunately, the name of the author is not always known. In order to solve this problem, libraries must maintain duplicate files that are also organized by title and subject. If you want to retrieve a book based on some other piece of information, such as the copyright date or the name of the publisher, you are out of luck. In contrast, with a computer database, it is only necessary to store one record per book. Records can be retrieved based on any field within the record. If desired, more than one field can be used as the basis of the search. For example, the computer can retrieve all records of books published by John White on operant conditioning since 1984 by examining the author name, subject, and date fields.

Once a set of records that matches specified search criteria has been identified, the computer can be used to organize the records in several different ways. They can be sorted in ascending or descending order based on any field. Thus, the books by John White on operant conditioning, identified by the search described in the previous paragraph, could be sorted alphabetically by title or chronologically by date. Some programs will even allow sorting by two or more fields, such as date and title, simultaneously. In this case, all the books published during 1984 would be listed alphabetically within that year, and all the books published in 1985 would be listed alphabetically under 1985.

After the desired records have been retrieved and sorted, a variety of reports can be printed. The more powerful database management systems allow considerable flexibility in the generation of these reports. Most programs allow users to specify which fields from each record are to be printed. The order in which the fields are printed within each record can also be customized to user needs.

Database management systems may be either special-purpose or general-purpose programs. *Special-purpose programs* are designed to meet the specific needs of a particular application, whereas *general-purpose programs* are designed for a wide variety of applications. These two different types of database management systems are discussed next.

Special-Purpose Database Programs

Every aspect of a special-purpose database program is tailored to the requirements of a specified type of application. The number of fields and the type of data to be entered into each field are predetermined and built into the program. Data entry and modification procedures are tailored to match the demands of the application. The number and type of reports generated by the program are also preset. The user merely selects from a menu any reports desired. Some of the better special-purpose programs may allow for some limited customization of printed reports.

Special-purpose programs are usually easy to learn and use, since the user does not have to define the database structure, the data entry format, or the report formats. They are often programmed to process data in ways that might not be possible with a general-purpose system. The tailored nature of special-purpose programs is both their greatest strength and weakness. Special-purpose programs are very efficient and effective in retrieving information and generating reports to meet specific needs. However, if circumstances change, special-purpose programs may not have the flexibility to accommodate new requirements. New fields or information cannot be added, nor can obsolete fields be removed. The information retrieved and the reports that can be generated are limited to those specifically provided by the program.

In the schools, special-purpose database management programs can be used to generate the payroll each month. The database records would include information on each employee, such as his or her name, address, and salary. The program would be designed to calculate the amount that should be deducted from each employee's salary for federal and state income tax, social security, retirement, and health insurance. After the deductions have been calculated, the program would print out the checks and payroll statements for each employee and a summary report for the school.

Special-purpose programs can also be used by teachers as management tools to keep track of student progress and performance in the classroom. This database application is often referred to as *computer-managed instruction (CMI)*. This tool not only assists in storing and retrieving student performance information but it can also assist in gathering that information. The computer can generate examinations by selecting appropriate items from a database of test items. The selected test items may be printed or administered to students on computer monitors. The computer can score the student responses, summarize the data, store the results, and print the necessary reports. These reports can be made available to teachers, administrators, students, and parents. This type of special-purpose program will be described in greater detail in Chapter 10, Computer-Managed Instruction.

Some special-purpose database programs are designed to keep track of personal finances in the home. Such programs can keep track of checking account transactions and assign expenses into multiple categories, such as food, clothing, housing, medical expenses, and automobile expenses. A running checkbook balance along with monthly and year-to-date totals for each expense category can be obtained. Monthly expense totals can be compared to budget projections through the use of tables or graphs. Most financial programs also help reconcile bank statements at the end of the month and provide data for income tax preparation at the end of the year. Instruction and practice in the use of personal finance programs would be very appropriate in general business courses.

CD-ROM technology (see Chapter 8, Multimedia/Hypermedia) has made it possible for microcomputer users to have access to very large databases that were previously only available on large mainframe computers or in multiple-volume sets of books. A single CD-ROM disc can hold 550–660M (million) characters of textual information. To put such a large number in perspective, consider that an encyclopedia of 25 volumes with 500 pages per volume and 7000 characters per page would only take up 87.5 million characters. Thus it is not too suprising that several encyclopedia companies are producing CD-ROM versions of their sets.

Special-purpose computer programs accompany these CD-ROM databases which allow the user to quickly retrieve any desired article by simple entering key words. Figure 7–7 shows a screen display from the *World Book Information Finder.* The article "Insect" was found by searching for articles that include the words *fossil* and *insect* within the same paragraph. Note that in Figure 7–7 these words are highlighted in boldface type. The icons or small pictures within the outline on the left are buttons that provide access to multimedia elements associated with the article. By clicking with the mouse button on the arrow icons below the fossil picture, other preview pictures related to the article will be displayed. A larger version of the picture in the preview window will be shown by clicking the Show It button. The buttons at the top of the screen provide access to other resources such as an Atlas, Timeline, or Gallery. A dictionary definition of any word can be accessed by simply clicking on the word. The words in all capital letters, such as ANIMAL, and the words at the bottom of the Figure under OTHER INSECTS are hypertext links (see Chapter 8, Multimedia/Hypermedia) to other articles within the encyclopedia.

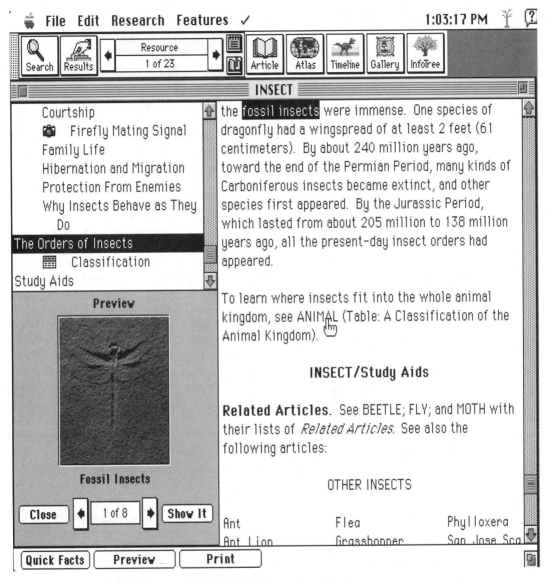

FIGURE 7–7   Screen from *World Book Information Finder*

Many other large reference works are also available on CD-ROM databases such as *Original Oxford English Dictionary, Electronic Whole Earth Catalog, Dissertation Abstracts Ondisc, Wilsondisc Reader's Guide to Periodical Literature,* and the *ERIC* (Educational Resources Information Center) abstracts (*DIALOG Online ERIC*). CD-ROM and videodiscs are also being used to store databases of pictures and video and sound clips. See Chapter 8, Multimedia/Hypermedia, for more information about these applications.

General-Purpose Database Programs

General-purpose database management programs must be flexible enough to accommodate the requirements of many different database applications. A single general-purpose program should be able to handle databases for a videotape library, an inventory for audiovisual equipment, a home economics recipe file, a bibliography, or a music club membership list. General-purpose programs are open ended. The user must specify how many fields will be included in each record, what information will be stored in each field, what search criteria will be used to select a special record or group of records, how the records will be sorted, and the design of any desired printed reports. This flexibility increases the complexity of the program and makes it more difficult to learn and use. However, once a general-purpose program is mastered, it becomes a very valuable tool that may be used in a wide variety of applications.

General-purpose database management programs vary widely in price, capabilities, ease of learning, and ease of use. Care should be used to ensure that a program is selected that will meet both current and future needs. Before you go shopping for a general-purpose database program, take a few minutes to decide what you want from the program. The best place to start is to decide what type of printed reports you would like the program to generate for each application. What information should appear on each report? How should the reports be organized? The nature of your desired reports will determine the type of data your program must store, how the data will need to be processed, and the required report-generation capabilities.

For example, let's suppose you are the school orchestra conductor and would like to keep track of the school's sheet music library and the members of the orchestra. Since these are not common applications, it is doubtful that you would be able to find special-purpose programs for them. Therefore, you need a general-purpose program that will accommodate these applications.

Let's begin by looking at the kind of inquiries you would like to make of these databases. In other words, what information would you like to know about the school's sheet music or its orchestra members? The following is a list of some possible reports you might like generated:

1. An alphabetical list by titles of all the sheet music in the library (this list should also give the location and number of copies available for each title)
2. A list of all the sheet music with a Christmas theme for a woodwind ensemble
3. A list of all the music performed by the band during the last two years
4. A list of all the music composed for bands by John Phillip Sousa

Some information needs related to members of the orchestra might include:

1. An alphabetical list of the names of all members of the orchestra, along with their addresses and phone numbers
2. A list of all those who play in the orchestra, organized by instrument played (for each instrument, the members should be ordered according to their chair positions)
3. A list of all members of the orchestra organized by their year in school (for each year, the names should be listed in alphabetical order)

After you have identified the types of reports you would like to obtain from your database, you are prepared to specify the fields of information you will need for each record within the different files. You cannot retrieve information from your database that has not been properly stored. In order to obtain the reports related to sheet music, you will need to set up a computer file with a record for each sheet music title. Each record would need at least the following fields:

1. Title
2. Name of composer
3. Storage location code
4. Number of copies
5. Theme of music
6. Group (band, orchestra, ensemble, solo, etc.)
7. Instrument (string, woodwind, trumpet, etc.)
8. Date of last performance

The member file would need a record for each student with at least the following fields:

1. Name of student
2. Address
3. Phone number
4. Instrument played
5. Chair position
6. Year in school

Each of these fields would be required in order for the computer to generate the reports listed previously. Now that you know what information needs to be stored in your database files, you can search for a program that will accommodate these requirements.

Most general database management programs available on microcomputers may be classified into three main categories: file-management systems, relational databases, or free-format databases (Krajewski, 1984). File-management systems and relational databases are similar in that they both consist of records that are further divided into fields. They both require that you specify in advance the exact format of the data you will include in the database. The fields that will make up each file and the type of data that will go in each field (numbers, text, dates, etc.) must also be specified. Additionally, some programs require that you specify the maximum number of characters that will be stored in each field. The data entered and stored in the database must conform to your preset format. However, the more powerful programs may allow you to make some modifications in the format at a later date.

File-management (also called *flat-file manager*) programs will allow you to use only one file at a time. You may store more than one file of information but each file is totally independent of the other. You cannot generate reports based on data from more than one file. In contrast, a relational database program allows you to set up a database made up of several related files. The files are related to each other because the records in each file have one field in common. Such relationships allow you to generate reports that draw on data from several related files.

The orchestra member and sheet music files and their corresponding reports (described earlier) could be implemented using a file-management system. However, suppose you want your database program to generate the following report:

> A list of all the solo sheet music that has been checked out by students and is overdue to be returned (this list should give the name, address, and phone number of each student who checked out music and the date it was to have been returned)

You could generate such a report with a file-management system by building another file called Music Checkout. However, such a file would have to contain information that is already stored in the member and sheet music files. This duplication of diskette storage space and data entry time would be wasteful. A better solution would be to use a relational database that would allow you to generate reports based on data from both the member and sheet music files.

In order to implement such a relational database, records in the sheet music file and the member file would need to have a field in common. This common field would serve as a pointer from records in the sheet music file to records in the member file. The name of an orchestra member would be an appropriate common field in this example. Any time a member checked out a piece of music, his or her name would be entered into a member-name field added to the appropriate sheet music record. Another field would also have to be added to the sheet music records in order to store the date when the music should be returned. With these two additional fields, a relational-database program would be able to generate the report desired by retrieving the title of the music, the name of the member who checked it out, and the return date from the sheet music file. The address and phone number of the member would be retrieved from the member file.

Free-format database programs do not require a preset format. You may enter any type of information in any order you like. Totally different formats may be used for each record in the same file. Each record may be of a different length. One record might contain a summary of a telephone conversation, while the next record could be a bibliographic reference and abstract of a journal article. Since the files for such programs contain free-form text, they are often referred to as *text retrieval programs*. Free-format database files often consist of documents originally entered into the computer using a word processor or a scanner and optical-character reader (see Chapter 2, Computer Hardware). The documents may be journal or magazine articles, reports, or the chapters of a book. Each paragraph in the document would be considered a record.

Information is retrieved simply by instructing the computer to find any record that contains a particular word or phrase. To speed up the search process, such programs often create a master index of every unique word in the file with a cross-reference to where each occurrence of that word might be found in the file. From the user's point of view, the search process is very similar to using the find or search command in a word processor. However, free-format database programs are optimized for searching and retrieval and are much faster in retrieving information from large documents. They also allow for more sophisticated search strategies. For example, you can specify that the program find any record or paragraph that contains two different words that may not be adjacent to one another. Or you can request the retrieval of a record that contains one word or phrase but not another. Figure 7–8 shows the results of searching for all verses from a free-format database of the Bible that contain the words *faith* and *hope* but do not contain the word *charity*.

Free-format database programs would not be ideal for the music or orchestra member files described earlier. However, they could be used by students to store class lecture notes and bibliographic references and abstracts, by a literature teacher to analyze the works of Shakespeare, by a history teacher to store essay questions, or by a principal to search a telephone log for a record of an important phone conversation.

Several file-management programs have been developed for classroom and student use, such as *pfs:file, Bank Street School Filer, DCH Notebook Filer,* and *Friendly Filer.* Examples of more sophisticated, professional-quality, file-management programs include: *DB Master, ProFILER, Filemaker, Panorama, Reflex, Q & A,* and *Professional File.* The integrated programs mentioned at the beginning of the chapter also

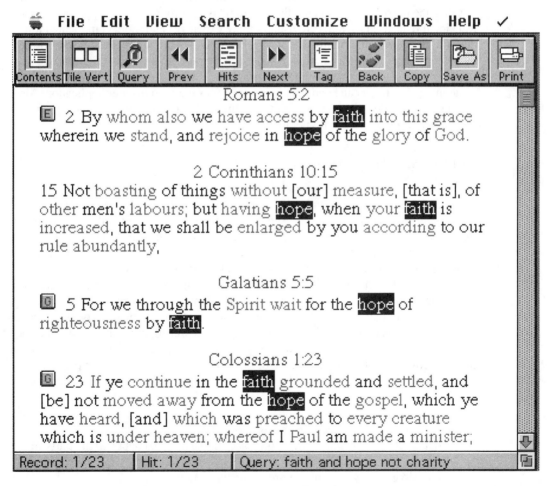

FIGURE 7–8   Results of Free-Format Database Search

contain file-management features. Some of the more popular relational-database programs include *dBase IV, Data Ease, R-Base, SuperBase4, Paradox, FoxPro, Omnis 5, Double Helix,* and *4th Dimension.* Free-format database programs include *Word-Cruncher, Folio,* and *Sonar.* Some programs contain features that cut across the categories listed earlier. For example, *Filemaker,* which is generally considered a file-management program, allows for free-format text fields of up to 32 KB in length and can also retrieve data from multiple files.

Because of the many different types of general-database programs and the large number of commercial programs available for each type, it is difficult for a novice to decide which program to purchase. It is advisable to talk to several knowledgeable people before making a purchase decision. Read reviews of recommended programs in computer magazines. Some reviews compare and contrast the various features of several of the more popular programs. Compare these features with your needs. Will the program handle the number of records you will need to store? Will the maximum number of fields available in each record be sufficient? Will you have any fields that require more characters than the maximum allowed by the program? Is the program of the appropriate type? Relational-database programs are usually more expensive and more complicated to use than file-management systems. If your applications do not require several related files, then you may be able to save money and effort by purchasing a good file-management system rather than a relational-database program. If you purchase a relational-database program, make sure it can handle the number of files required by your application. Also, be sensitive to the speed of the program in sorting and retrieving records. Some programs are much faster than others. Remember—your time is valuable.

Instructional Applications

In addition to using database programs to store and retrieve classroom management information, teachers are finding many instructional applications for these powerful tools. Electronic databases can be used to store and organize large collections of information about many topics studied in the schools. With the help of the computer, this wealth of information can be sorted, searched, examined, and analyzed by students in many different ways in an effort to discover relationships in the data.

For example, a database about the presidents of the United States could contain the following fields of information about each presidential term: name of president, date of inauguration, date at end of term, age at inauguration, political party, home state, cause for end of term (expired, death, assassinated, resigned, impeached), previous political office, occupation before entering politics, amount of increase in national debt during term, amount of increase in federal budget during term, war or peace during term, and so forth. Students could be asked to search this database to discover answers to questions such as the following:

Which state has produced the most presidents?
What is the relationship between increases in the national debt and the party of the president?
What is the average age of the presidents on inauguration?

By using a database to find the answers to such questions, students become actively involved with the subject matter and also increase their inquiry, analytical, and problem-solving skills. More advanced students can generate their own questions and write reports describing their questions, their analytical procedure, the data they find related to the questions, and their conclusions.

Many commercial products are available to assist teachers in the use of databases for instruction (Wheeler, 1987). Several companies market special-purpose databases that include the software program as well as the data in one package: *MECC Dataquest: The Presidents, MECC Dataquest: The Fifty States, USA Profile,* and *One World Countries Database.* These products usually do not allow modifications to the data or field categories. Other companies provide complete or partial data files that can be accessed, searched, added to, and modified using a separate general file-management system. Some of these products include several related files as well as database forms. The forms provide records with field labels, but include no data. With partial data files or database forms, students would be required to locate and add the appropriate data from some other sources. Examples include *Heath Social Studies,* which can be used with DCH *Notebook Filer; Science and Nature Facts,* which can be accessed with *Friendly Filer; Life Science, Poetry and Mythology,* and *World Geography, Cultures and Economics,* which can be used with *pfs:file;* and *Endangered Species* and *Astronomy,* which can be accessed with *Bank Street School Filer.*

Students can also be asked to work together in groups to identify appropriate database fields, collect data from various sources, create relevant questions, analyze the data, and prepare written reports. Such projects can be very exciting, especially if local sources of information are used, such as city and county records, local newspaper files, cemetery headstones, student constructed and administered questionnaires, interviews with business and government leaders, and so forth.

Spreadsheets

Calculating is an obvious tool application of the computer. Students are required to carry out many calculations in mathematics, science, statistics, and other classes. By using a computer, they are able to make such calculations with much greater speed and accuracy. In the past, many problems that students were asked to solve were necessarily contrived and simplified in order to reduce the difficulties of the required calculations. If students have access to computer calculation tools, they should be able to solve much more realistic and challenging problems. By using a computer to perform routine and arduous calculations, students will be able to concentrate on the application and theory of what they are learning rather than on the calculation procedures. Very sophisticated calculating tools, such as statistical packages and electronic spreadsheet programs, are now readily available on microcomputers.

Electronic spreadsheets are general-purpose programs for processing numerical data, much as word-processing programs are general-purpose programs for processing words. Electronic spreadsheets are electronic versions of the familiar manual spreadsheets, sometimes referred to as *worksheets* or *accountant's pads.* A manual spreadsheet is simply a piece of paper marked off in rows and columns that intersect, forming a grid. Each column is labeled at the top by a letter (A, B, C, . . .) and each row is labeled along the left side by a number (1, 2, 3, . . .). The intersection of a specific row and specific column is called a *cell*. A given cell can be specified by its row and column labels. Thus, cell F3 would be the cell intersected by column F and row 3.

A class roll book is an example of a manual spreadsheet. There are rows for each student's name and columns for each day of school. If a student (Jan) attends class on a specific day (October 10), the teacher enters the number one (1) in the cell intersected by the row containing Jan's name and the column for October 10. If Sue is absent, then the number zero (0) is placed in the cell across from her name in the same column. The final row in the roll book may be labeled Total Daily Attendance. This row would contain the sum (or count) of the 1s in each corresponding column.

An electronic spreadsheet serves the same purpose as a manual spreadsheet, but it allows you to take advantage of the calculation speed and accuracy of the computer to perform mathematical calculations and other data-manipulation procedures. An electronic spreadsheet implementation of the roll book just described could be designed to automatically determine the Total Daily Attendance at the end of each day and to calculate the Average Daily Attendance at the end of a term.

Teachers may also use electronic spreadsheets in place of the standard gradebooks. The electronic spreadsheet shown in Figure 7–9 was implemented using the spreadsheet tool in the integrated program, *Microsoft Works*. The students' names and the last three characters of their social security numbers are listed in columns A and B. Columns C, D, and E contain scores for three class assignments. The midterm and final exam scores are entered in columns F and G. The totals and grades in columns H and I were not entered by the teacher, but were automatically generated by the electronic spreadsheet program.

Rather than figure and enter the total score for Jan Brown in cell H2, the teacher entered the formula for determining the score as shown at the top of the spreadsheet. Do not let this complicated-looking formula scare you; it is actually quite simple. The formula differentially weights the assignments and midterm and final exam scores in determining the total score. The first part of the formula, =AVERAGE (C2:E2), calculates the average of the three assignment scores found in the cells C2 through E2. The averaged assignment scores are then multiplied (an asterisk [*] is the symbol used for multiplication) by their corresponding weight, 0.3. This value is then added to the weighted midterm and final exam scores; 50 percent of the student's grade is determined by the final exam, 20 percent by the midterm, and 30 percent by the assignments. The formula is duplicated in the remaining cells under column H with corresponding row specifications. After scores are entered in columns C through G, the computer uses the formula to automatically generate the total scores. The letter grades in column I were automatically determined from the look-up table shown in rows 15 and 16. Total scores between 70 and 74 receive a grade of C+, while those between 90 and 94 receive a grade of A–. Another formula was used to automatically calculate the class averages shown in row 13 for each assignment and exam.

Another powerful advantage of an electronic spreadsheet is its ability to quickly recalculate all the values in the spreadsheet whenever any formulas or relevant values are changed. This allows the user to ask What if? questions and determine the effects

	File	Edit	View	Insert	Format	Tools	Window	✓

H2		=Average(C2:E2)*.3+F2*.2+G2*.5

Grade Spreadsheet (SS)

	A	B	C	D	E	F	G	H	I
1	Name	SSN	First	Second	Third	Mid	Final	Total	Grade
2	Brown, Jan	114	85	79	77	83	80	80.7	B
3	Christiansen, Sue	875	92	93	89	95	96	94.4	A-
4	Eschler, Salley	146	78	80	79	82	84	82.1	B
5	Finn, Norman	797	74	69	65	67	72	70.2	C+
6	Gomez, Ralph	134	88	85	87	80	83	83.5	B
7	Hunt, Trudy	222	91	96	95	93	92	92.8	A-
8	Nelson, Steven	877	83	72	78	85	74	77.3	B
9	Williams, Tracy	385	88	82	85	89	92	89.3	B+
10	Young, Kathy	543	98	93	94	97	95	95.4	A
11									
12									
13	Class Mean		86.3	83.2	83.2	85.7	85.3	85.1	
14									
15			65	70	75	80	85	90	95
16			C	C+	B-	B	B+	A-	A
17									

FIGURE 7–9   Gradebook Spreadsheet

of changing various assumptions or policies. For example, a teacher could easily determine the effects of different weighting schemes on final grades by simply changing the weighting factors in the Total Score formula.

Electronic spreadsheets are such powerful tools and can solve such a wide variety of problems that they have been among the most popular programs for microcomputers. The first spreadsheet program, called *VisiCalc,* was the top-selling program on the Apple II computer every month for several years in a row. Many people purchased Apple II computers just so that they would be able to use this program. Another powerful spreadsheet program, *Lotus 1-2-3,* has been a best-seller on the IBM PC microcomputer. Other popular spreadsheet programs include *Microsoft Excel, Quattro Pro,* and *SuperCalc5.*

Instructional Applications

Spreadsheet programs can be helpful to administrators, teachers, and students. Administrators can use this tool to help in their financial planning and budgeting. The What if? feature can help administrators determine the impact of such things as assumptions regarding inflation rates, wage increase percentages, level of staffing, number of buses, film rentals, and book purchases on budget projections. Spreadsheets can also be used to determine how many computers will be required to service different numbers of students for different periods of time, per day or week. Spreadsheets are obviously valuable tools for students in bookkeeping or accounting classes, for the generation of budgets, profit and loss statements, and so on. In a home economics class, students could easily modify recipes based on different serving requirements. In vocational education classes, spreadsheets could help students understand the relationships between various design decisions and costs. In fact, students can profit from the use of electronic spreadsheets in any class involving numerical calculations. The What if? and automatic calculation features enable users to work with real-world problems and concentrate on the variables and relationships involved rather than the details of the calculations.

Graphics

Recent developments in high-resolution graphics technology have made the computer very appealing as a tool for learning and practicing both creative and commercial art. As a graphic medium, the computer screen can be thought of as a matrix of tiny light bulbs arranged in rows and columns. Each light bulb is independently addressable and can be turned either on or off. When a light bulb is turned on, a dot appears on the screen. Each light bulb is referred to as a *picture element,* or *pixel.* The computer can show any graphic display that can be created by turning on a particular pattern of these tiny pixels. For example, a horizontal straight line can be drawn by turning on all the pixels in a given row. The quality of the graphic display is dependent on the resolution of the screen: The more pixels per square inch, the higher the resolution. On low-resolution screens, diagonal lines and curves will appear somewhat jagged. Finer detail can be shown on high-resolution screens. See Chapter 2, Computer Hardware, for a discussion of the issues related to screen resolution.

Most general-purpose computer languages for microcomputers include commands for displaying graphics on the screen. In Applesoft BASIC the command HPLOT 50, 125 is used to instruct the computer to turn on the dot that is 50 pixels from the left side of the screen and 125 pixels from the top of the screen. The command HPLOT 35, 97 to 146, 28 would draw a line from the point 35 pixels from the left and 97 pixels from the top to the point 146 pixels from the left and 28 pixels from the top. In Logo, the command FORWARD 60 will draw a straight line with a length of 60 pixels. Through the use of these and other graphics commands, computer programs can be written to draw very sophisticated graphics displays on the screen. See Chapter 11, The Computer as Tutee, for a more detailed discussion on the use of the Logo and BASIC computer languages for creating computer graphics.

Fortunately, the user does not have to be a proficient computer programmer in order to use the computer as an art or graphics tool. Many commercial programs have been written that enable us to tap the graphics power of the computer without writing our own computer programs. Graphics programs can be classified into three major categories: charting, drawing, and painting.

Charting Graphics

Computer programs used to convert numeric data into graphs and charts are called *business-graphics* or *charting programs.* Charting programs are frequently integrated with spreadsheet applications. After data are entered into the cells of a spreadsheet, students can request that the charting program draw a graph or chart, based on the spreadsheet data, in one of many possible formats. For example, suppose you wanted a graphic representation of the distribution of student grades for an algebra class. First, you would have to analyze the grades and determine how many students received grades within each category: A, B, C, D, or F. (Additional categories may be used if desired.) After entering the data into a spreadsheet, you could instruct the program to display the appropriate chart. Figure 7–10 shows the numerical data and corresponding bar chart. If you made a mistake in entering the data, you could make the appropriate changes and the computer would automatically redraw the chart to correspond with the new data. The data could also be displayed as a column chart, a line graph, a pie chart, a scatter chart, or an area curve. If you are not quite sure which type of graph would be best, you may experiment by asking the computer to display several different types, one at a time. When the appropriate chart has been selected, the computer can be instructed to make a hard copy of the chart on the printer. These charts can also be

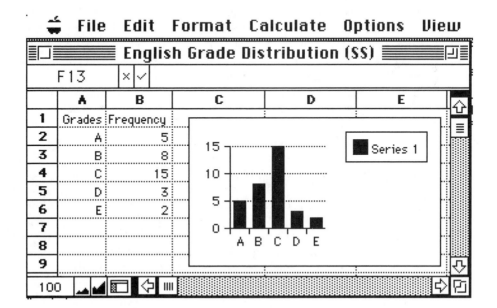

FIGURE 7–10 Numerical Data and Chart Showing Grade Distribution

copied and pasted into word-processing documents or incorporated into classroom presentations using desktop presentation software, as described in later sections of this chapter.

Graphs and charts created by business-graphics programs can be used to show the relationships between numerical data that may otherwise be difficult to see and understand. A school superintendent could create a pie chart to show how much of the school district budget is being allocated to various categories, such as capital equipment, teacher salaries, utilities, and supplies. A teacher could create several column charts to show students the different population distributions for various countries. A student could include a scatter chart in a report showing the relationship between the number of cigarettes smoked per day and incidents of lung cancer.

In addition to the charting programs built into spreadsheet and integrated programs, there are several stand-alone charting programs, including *MECC Graph, Cricket Graph, Harvard Graphics, DeltaGraph, Draw Perfect, Charisma, Graftool, Sigma Plot,* and *KaleidaGraph.* Many desktop presentation programs, which will be described in a later section of this chapter, will also produce business graphs and charts.

Drawing Graphics

Drawing programs are essentially computer-based drafting tables which provide electronic versions of such drafting tools as T squares, scales, compasses, French curves, and templates. The drawing program within *ClarisWorks* uses a mouse as a pointing device to select from a menu of graphic tools and to indicate where various graphic elements should be placed on the screen. Figure 7–11 shows a *ClarisWorks* drawing screen display with the menu of graphic tools on the left. The rectangle drawing tool has been selected by pointing to it with the mouse cursor and clicking the mouse button. Once the tool is selected, the mouse is used to indicate where on the screen the upper-left corner of the rectangle is to appear. The mouse button is then pressed and held down while the mouse pointer is moved to the desired location at the bottom-right corner of the rectangle. When the desired location is reached, the mouse button is released and the completed rectangle is drawn on the screen.

As can be seen from the menu at the left of Figure 7–11, other graphics tools facilitate the drawing of text, straight lines, curves, circles, ovals, polygons, filled geometric figures, and freehand drawings. Each graphic element created is stored as an independent object and can be selected, moved, resized, or erased. Once a drawing is completed, it can be stored on diskette and reproduced on the printer. Figure 7–12 shows a completed drawing created by using a stand-alone drawing program called *MacDraw.* Mechanical drawing programs could be used by a school principal to create a school staff organization chart, by a teacher to produce overhead transparencies, by members of the dance committee to produce posters for the Junior Prom, and by students to produce plan drawings for their woodworking projects. Other stand-alone drawing programs of interest to teachers and students include *ClarisDraw, Cricket Draw, Draw Plus,* and *Canvas. Adobe Illustrator, Aldus Freehand,* and *Coral Draw* are

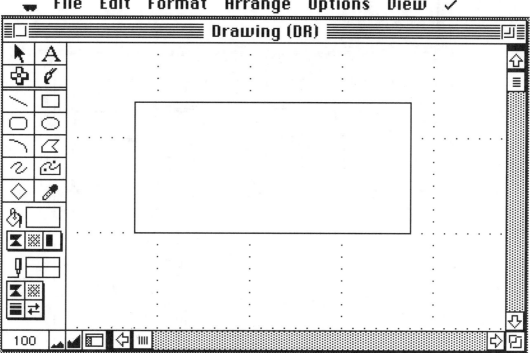

FIGURE 7–11   Palette of Graphic Tools from *ClarisWorks*

packages designed for commercial artists. Examples of professional drafting and computer-aided design (CAD) packages are *AutoCAD, Claris Cad,* and *MiniCad+.*

Painting Graphics

Painting programs turn the computer into a new art medium. Rather than using canvas, paintbrushes, and a palette of oil paints, artists can now use the computer to paint with electronic brushes, pencils, and paints. Examples of creative art programs include *MacPaint, SuperPaint, MousePaint, Dazzle Draw, Paintworks Gold, Deluxe Paint,* and *PC Paintbrush.* Figure 7–13 shows the electronic screen canvas of the painting program within *ClarisWorks.* The menu of tools on the left of the screen is similar to those provided in the drawing program shown in Figure 7–11. For example, there are tools for drawing geometric shapes such as rectangles, ovals, and polygons. However, there are several significant additional tools, such as the paintbrush, paint bucket, pencil, and spray can. Paintbrushes come in different sizes and shapes and can paint in any of several available colors and patterns. The spray can provides a spray effect in any of the available patterns. The program also has a zoom, or magnifying, capability called *fat bits,* which allows the user to enlarge a particular part of a drawing and turn individual pixels on or off.

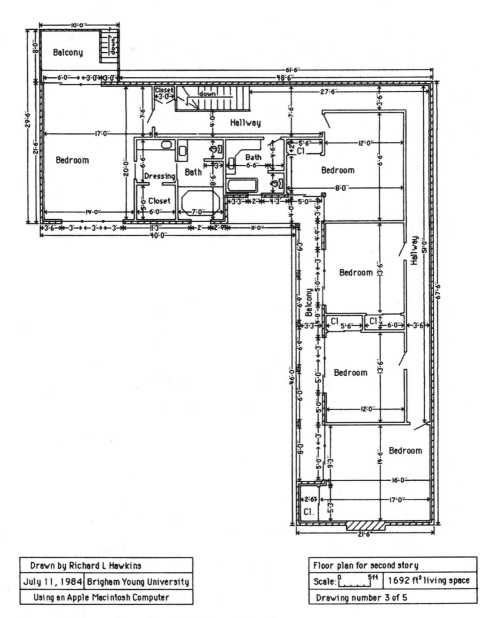

FIGURE 7–12 **Completed *MacDraw* Drawing**

One of the powerful advantages of the computer as an art medium is the ease with which students can experiment with several different versions of the same painting. After one version has been created and saved on a diskette, it can be loaded back into the computer memory and modified. The modified version can then be saved under a different name without destroying the original. Painting programs can be used effectively by students in art classes at all age levels, from kindergarten through college. Figure 7–14 shows a painting created by *MacPaint*.

As can be seen from Figures 7–12, 7–13, and 7–14, drawing and painting programs incorporate many of the same tools. There are many specific graphic applications that could be created with either type of program. However, the distinction is still quite important. Paint programs incorporate several artistic tools that allow for the creation of expressive paintings, whereas drawing programs contain tools for precise mechanical scaled drawings. Technically, the graphics produced by paint programs are bit mapped, and those produced by draw programs are object oriented. As mentioned in the previous section, each graphic element—such as a rectangle, a line, a circle, or a line of text—created in a mechanical drawing program is stored as an independent object that can be moved, resized, or deleted without affecting other objects. Each object is defined and stored in memory according to its mathematical or geometric properties, such as location, number of sides, and length of each side. In contrast, graphic elements in a creative art or

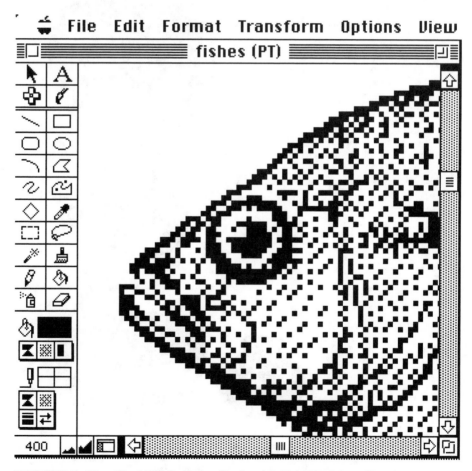

FIGURE 7–13 *ClarisWorks* **Paint Tools with Fat Bits Magnification**

paint program become part of the mosaic of pixel elements that make up the painting. Since each pixel is represented by a single bit (several bits are required for color) in memory, which may be either on or off, the painting is said to be bit mapped. Many graphics programs provide for both bit-mapped and object-oriented graphics in the same drawing.

Although the graphics programs described in this chapter provide many electronic tools for creating charts, drawings, and paintings, artistic talent is still required to produce professional-quality work. Fortunately, for those of us with little talent, professional artists have created and stored on diskettes a large assortment of quality graphics, called *electronic clip art,* that can be purchased and incorporated into our own drawings. Clip-art libraries are available in various categories such as business, school, holidays, famous people, animals, sports, and the like. When purchasing clip

FIGURE 7–14   Painting Created Using
MacPaint

art, remember that a given clip-art library will be compatible only with certain programs. Some graphics programs, such as *Print Shop* and *SuperPrint,* include a minimal library of clip art with the program. These two programs also are very popular for producing posters, signs, and banners.

Desktop Publishing

As mentioned previously, word-processing programs are mainly used in the production of lesson plans, worksheets, exams, reports, memos, articles, essays, poems, and letters. However, early word processors were not able to produce professional-quality documents such as fliers, brochures, programs, newspapers, magazines, manuals, and books. To produce such documents, authors had to prepare the text for the document on a typewriter or word processor, have an artist prepare illustrations or obtain glossy prints of photographs, and then submit the manuscript and photos to a publishing company. The publisher would have the text typeset and then have a pasteup artist lay out the text and graphics for each page. These "camera-ready" pages would then be sent to a printer for printing. Not only was this process very time consuming and costly, but modifications were difficult and very expensive.

Between 1983 and 1985, four significant new technologies were introduced that made it possible for a single individual to produce a professional-quality document at his or her desk using low-cost microcomputers and printers. In 1983, Canon introduced laser printer technology that could print text and graphics at a resolution of 300 dots per inch. Apple launched the Macintosh computer in 1984 with its graphical user interface that allowed high-resolution text and graphics to be easily combined on the same screen. Adobe Systems introduced the text and graphics description computer language Postscript, which made it possible for text fonts and graphic objects to be described using mathematical routines. The next year, Apple followed with the LaserWriter printer, which incorporated the Canon laser printer technology and the Postscript language. Also in 1985, Aldus Corporation introduced the powerful page-layout software program *PageMaker.* With these basic components in place—namely, (1) the Macintosh computer, (2) the LaserWriter printer, (3) Postscript, and (4) *PageMaker*—high-quality publishing came into the hands of the individual for the first time.

The term *desktop publishing (DTP)* was coined in 1985 by the president of Aldus Corporation, Paul Brainerd, to refer to this new computer application. Many people purchased Macintosh computers in order to have desktop publishing capabilities. After 1985, this capability also became available on other computers (Jones, 1988). In addition to *PageMaker,* many other desktop publishing software packages are now available: *QuarkXPress, Ready, Set, Go!, Springboard Publisher, Design Studio, Publish It!, Interleaf Publisher,* and *Ventura Publisher.*

Desktop publishing software such as *PageMaker* provides an electronic pasteboard on the computer screen where text and graphic elements can be layed out. Although most DTP programs provide some minimal word-processing and graphics features, the various text and graphic elements are usually created in separate word-processing and graphics programs and then imported into the DTP program. *PageMaker* provides many powerful tools along with on-screen ruler guides and an underlying grid for positioning these elements on the page easily and precisely. Each element may be repositioned as desired, graphics may be resized or cropped, and the number and width of columns may be adjusted. All elements are displayed in a "what you see is what you get" (WYSIWYG) format that allows the user to see what the page will look like when it is printed.

Figure 7–15 shows a page of a document produced by using *PageMaker* contrasted with a typical page produced by using a word processor. Notice that the *PageMaker* document includes multiple columns of variable widths, embedded graphics with the text flowing around the graphic, multiple typefaces and sizes of text, sidebars (textual elements separate from a main article), multiple articles that continue on other pages, rotated text, and white text on shaded backgrounds. These varied elements give the document a professional and aesthetically pleasing appearance. Other features provided by desktop publishing programs include master pages to give a document a consistent look, automatic hyphenation, kerning (making fine adjustments to the spacing between individual letters), and semi-automatic creation of indexes and tables of contents.

Recently, desktop publishing software has become less expensive, allowing elementary and secondary schools more opportunity to purchase less sophisticated versions. The *Children's Writing and Publishing Center* is a simplified desktop publishing program designed for elementary students. This program is so easy to learn that third- and fourth-graders with keyboarding skills can produce newspapers after a few short training sessions.

Springboard Publisher and *Publish It!* are more sophisticated, include many more options, and are designed for upper-elementary and older students. These packages are effectively used to produce newspapers, graphically illustrate stories and poems, produce novelettes to be placed in the class or school libraries, illustrate cookbooks used for fund raisers, and so on. In addition, many secondary schools are using desktop publishing software and related equipment to produce yearbooks.

The latest versions of some of the more powerful word-processing programs and integrated programs are starting to include many desktop publishing features such as multiple columns, embedded graphics, and different typefaces and sizes of text. Most users are now able to meet their word-processing and desktop publishing needs with a single program.

Desktop Presentations

Other than the textbook, probably the most common technologies used in today's classrooms are the chalkboard and the overhead projector. Even these familiar tools have a computer counterpart. By connecting a microcomputer to large monitors mounted in front of the classroom, or to a large-screen projection monitor, all students in the class can see what is displayed on the teacher's computer screen. Even the overhead projector can be used to project computer images through the use of a liquid crystal display (LCD) panel that is connected to the computer and placed on the projector (see Chapter 2, Computer Hardware). Teachers can face the class and enter information on

PORTRAIT

November/December 1996   *Volume 1, Number 1*

Aldus Manutius— The Original Page Maker

Five hundred years ago, Christopher Columbus was on his knees in throne rooms throughout Europe, scrambling to finance his first voyage to the New World. Meanwhile, his Venetian countryman Aldus Manutius—scholar, printer, and entrepreneur—was establishing what would become the greatest publishing house in Europe, the Aldine Press. Like Columbus, Aldus Manutius was driven by force of intellect and personality to realize a lifelong dream.

Aldus' greatest passion was Greek literature, which was rapidly going up in smoke in the wake of the marauding Turkish army. It seemed obvious to Aldus that the best way to preserve this literature was to publish it—literally, to make it public. The question was, how?

Although it had been forty years since the advent of Gutenberg's press, most books were still being copied by scribes, letter by letter, a penstroke at a time. Because of the intensity of this labor, books were few and costly. They were also unwieldy. Far too large to be held in the hands or in the lap, books sat on lecterns in private libraries and were seen only by princes and the clergy.

One day, as he watched one of his workers laboring under the load of books he was carrying, Aldus had a flash of insight: Could books from the without pulling a muscle? And could he produce the

elegant, lightweight volumes he imagined and still sell them at an attractive price?

The first problem was how to print more legible words per page and thus reduce the number of pages. Aldus needed a smaller typeface that was both readable and pleasing to the eye. The work of the Aldine Press had attracted the notice of the finest typographic artists in Europe, so Aldus was able to enlist the renowned Francesco Griffo da Bologna to design a new one. Under Aldus' direction, Griffo developed a typeface that was comparatively dense and compact and that imitated the calligraphy of courtly correspondence. The result of this Aldus-

A BRIEF HISTORY OF PUBLISHING

400	First known inked impressions on paper.
1440	Johannes Gutenberg develops the movable type printing press in Germany, cutting letters from an alloy of lead, tin, and antimony.
1449	Aldus Manutius is born in Padua.
1501	The Aldine Press publishes Dante's *Divine Comedy*.
1515	Aldus Manutius dies.
1757	In England, William Baskerville publishes Virgil's *Aeneid and Eclogues*, using woven paper and a slender typeface.
1814	The first steam-powered, high-speed printing press is built to print the *London Times*.
1866	The first rotary printing press is brought into production, printing both sides of a continuous web of paper.
1884	Ottmar Mergenthaler invents the Linotype.
1958	Photoelectric methods for controlling color registration and ink density are developed.
1984	The introduction of Aldus PageMaker, the Macintosh computer, and the Apple LaserWriter printer ushers in the era of desktop publishing.

FIGURE 7–15a · **Page Created Using *Pagemaker***

PORTRAIT

November/December 1996   Volume 1, Number 1

Aldus Manutius—The Original Page Maker

Five hundred years ago, Christopher Columbus was on his knees in throne rooms throughout Europe, scrambling to finance his first voyage to the New World. Meanwhile, his Venetian countryman Aldus Manutius—scholar, printer, and entrepreneur—was establishing what would become the greatest publishing house in Europe, the Aldine Press. Like Columbus, Aldus Manutius was driven by force of of intellect and personality to realize a lifelong dream.

Aldus' greatest passion was Greek literature, which was rapidly going up in smoke in the wake of the marauding Turkish army. It seemed obvious to Aldus that the best way to preserve this literature was to publish it—literally, to make it public. The question was, how?

Although it had been forty years since the advent of Gutenberg's perss, most books were still being copied by scribes, letter by letter, a penstroke at a time. Because of the intensity of this labor, books were few and costly. They were also unwieldy. Far too large to be held in the hands or in the lap, books sat on lecterns in private libraries and were seen only by princes and the clergy.

One day, as he watched one of his workers laboring under the load of books he was carrying, Aldus had a flash of insight: Could books from the Aldine Press be made small enough to be carried without pulling a muscle? And could he produce the elegant, lightweight volumes he imagined and still sell them at an attractive price?

The first problem was how to print more legible words per page and thus reduce the number of pages. Aldus needed a smaller typeface that was both readable and pleasing to the eye. The work of the Aldine Press had attracted the notice of the finest typographic artists in Europe, so Aldus was able to enlist the renowned Francesco Griffo da Bologna to design a new one. Under Aldus' direction, Griffo developed a typeface that was comparatively dense and compact and that imitated the calligraphy of courtly correspondence. The result of this Aldus-Griffo collaboration was the ancestor of what we now call *italics*..

The new typeface enabled Aldus to print portable and highly readable books. Besides the first edition of Dante's *Divine Comedy*, Aldus published the essential texts of Greek literature: the histories of Herodotus and Thucydides, the tragedies of Sophocles, the epics of Homer, and the treatises of Aristotle, thus rescuing them from relative oblivion.

The timing was perfect. With the growth of the merchant class in Venice, Florence, Naples, and Rome, a new market ripe for books had recently emerged. This newly prosperous middle class was flush with money and ankshious for intelligent ways to spend it. The new books from the Aldine Press were an immediate success.

FIGURE 7–15b   **Page Created Using Word Processor**

the computer keyboard that they wish displayed to the class. The information typed on the keyboard will be more readable and organized than is usually the case when using chalkboards. When the computer screen or electronic chalkboard is full, teachers do not have to turn their backs to the class to erase the board. Instead, they can press a key on the computer to instruct it to display a blank screen. However, the erased information is not lost, since it is automatically saved in the computer's memory. If a student raises a question about a previous screen, another few keystrokes will tell the computer to retrieve the information from memory and redisplay it.

Information to be displayed to the class also can be prepared beforehand and stored in files on a diskette. A whole new class of software packages, called *desktop presentation programs,* are now available to help teachers prepare and present these electronic displays or transparencies. Example programs include *Persuasion, MORE, PowerPoint, WordPerfect Presentations, Astound,* and *Slide Show. ClarisWorks* and *Microsoft Works,* along with several of the charting programs listed in an earlier section, provide some presentation capabilities.

PowerPoint provides an outline tool, similar to that described in the section on word processing, that you can use to enter and organize the textual information for a series of displays or slides. Several predesigned formats or slide templates are also provided. Once you have created your outline and selected a desired format, the program automatically converts each major heading in the outline with its corresponding subheadings into separate slides using the specified template. The templates contain specifications for background colors; the location, typeface, size, and color of headings and subheadings; and the location and format for added tables, graphics, and charts.

You may also create your own slide template design. Often, the same template is used for all of the slides for a given presentation. However, if desired, different templates may be used for each slide. One of several different chart formats (bar chart, column chart, pie chart, line graph, etc.) may be selected to display data entered into a data sheet or imported from a separate spreadsheet program. Graphics may be created using built-in drawing tools, selected from a library of clip art or imported from other graphics programs. The order of the slides can be changed by moving headings in the outline or moving miniature representations of the slides with the mouse in the on-screen slide sorter. Modifications can be made in the slides themselves or in the outline. Changes made in one are reflected in the other. Once the presentation is completed, it can be shown to a class by using a computer and projection system or it can be printed on overhead-transparency foils or converted into 35 mm slides using a desktop film recorder. *PowerPoint* will also print out teacher notes and class handouts of the presentation slides. Figure 7–16 shows a presentation outline and corresponding slide.

The computer with a large screen projection system can also be used effectively for classroom presentations with many other types of educational software. For example, a simulation program can be used to demonstrate to a class the critical aspects of a chemistry titration experiment. Students can later go to a computer laboratory and use the same software to perform additional simulated titration experiments on an individual basis. These activities might precede student work in an actual chemistry laboratory. In an English writing class, the teacher might use a word-processing program to display the rough draft of a theme or poem for the class to critique and revise together.

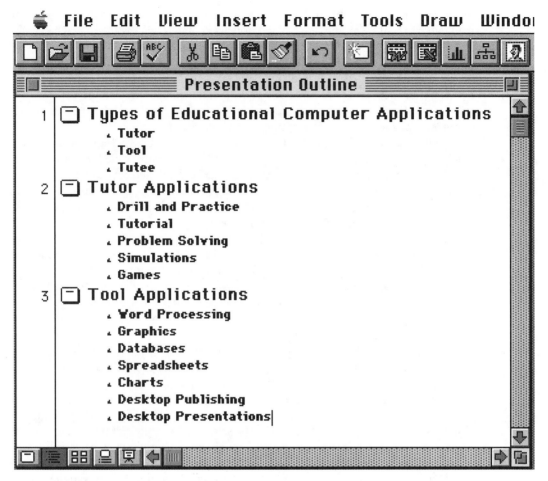

FIGURE 7–16a　*PowerPoint* Presentation Outline

The identification and correction of errors or bugs in computer programs can be demonstrated in a computer programming class. In effect, the creative teacher will find that most programs that are designed for individual use can also be valuable classroom presentation tools. Chapter 8, Multimedia/Hypermedia, discusses how multimedia applications can also be used effectively by the teacher for classroom presentations.

Tool Integration

The concept of *tool integration* includes more than combining several tool applications into one comprehensive program. It also includes the idea of combining data created using different tools into one integrated document or product. For example, while typ-

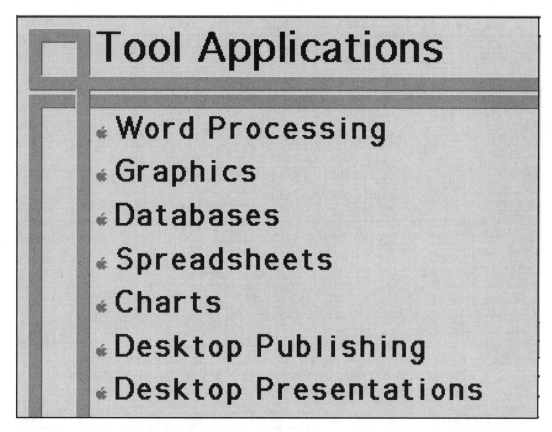

FIGURE 7–16b   *PowerPoint* **Presentation Slide**

ing a report using the *ClarisWorks* word processor, the student may select a spreadsheet tool and imbed a spreadsheet frame within the word-processing document. While still in the word-processing program, the spreadsheet menus and commands are available to enter data and perform calculations in the spreadsheet frame. The spreadsheet data may also be used to create and imbed a chart or graph in the same word-processing document. Draw and paint graphics may also be imbedded in the document by creating graphic frames. Whenever the student attempts to edit the content of one of these graphics or spreadsheet frames, the corresponding graphics or spreadsheet tools become available from within the word processor. Figure 7–17 shows a word-processing document with spreadsheet and graphics frames.

The word processor and database tools in an integrated program can be used together to enhance the relationship between teachers and parents. These tools can by used to create unique, personalized letters for each child's parents to notify them of common problems and solicit their help in the education of their child. They can also be used to let parents know that their child is doing well. (Not all news has to be bad news.) To create these letters, the teacher first creates a database containing records for

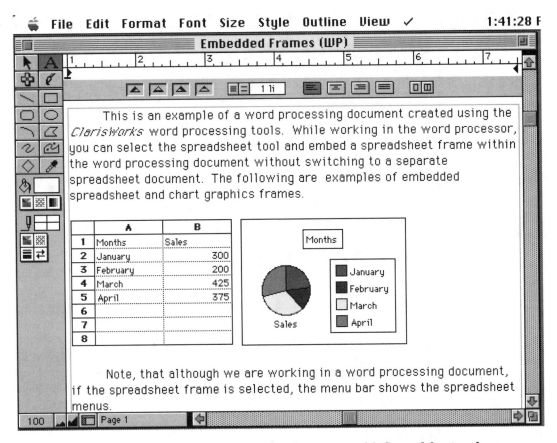

FIGURE 7–17 *ClarisWorks* **Word-Processing Document with Spreadsheet and Graphics Frames**

each child in the class. Each record will contain fields for the the name of the child, names and address of the parents, and any performance information about the child that the teacher would like to insert in the letter. Then the teacher creates a single form letter using the word processor. Special fields are placed in the letter to indicate where personal information about a specific child will be drawn from the fields of the database and inserted or merged into the letter when it is printed. One letter will be automatically printed for each record in the database. Figure 7–18 shows portions of a form letter, database fields, and the resulting merged letter.

ClarisWorks and *Microsoft Works* include several template documents to help teachers and students create frequently used documents. *ClarisWorks* provides templates for business and personal stationery, internal memos, newsletters, mortgage analyzers, presentation outlines, resumés, checkbooks, and mail merge letters and a corresponding name and address database. *Microsoft Works* provides several interactive templates called WorksWizards for creating newsletters, greeting cards and invi-

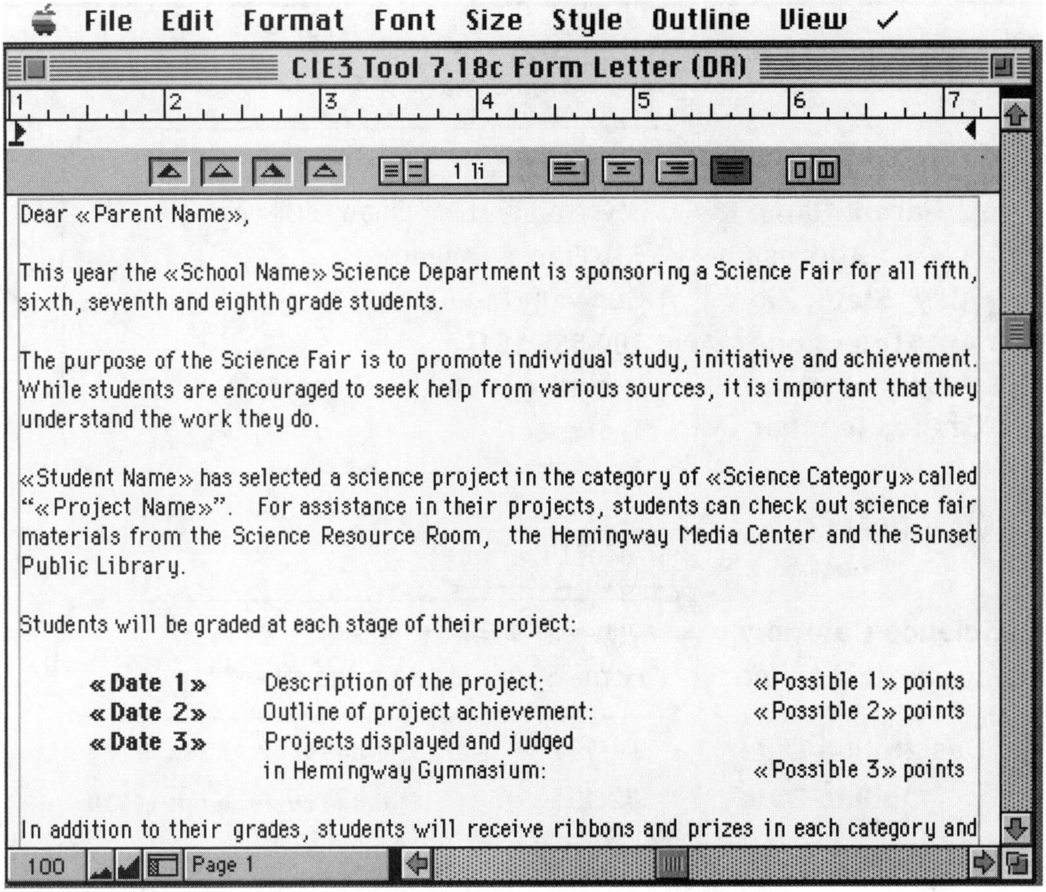

 File Edit Format Font Size Style Outline View ✓

═══ CIE3 Tool 7.18c Form Letter (DR) ═══

Dear «Parent Name»,

This year the «School Name» Science Department is sponsoring a Science Fair for all fifth, sixth, seventh and eighth grade students.

The purpose of the Science Fair is to promote individual study, initiative and achievement. While students are encouraged to seek help from various sources, it is important that they understand the work they do.

«Student Name» has selected a science project in the category of «Science Category» called "«Project Name»". For assistance in their projects, students can check out science fair materials from the Science Resource Room, the Hemingway Media Center and the Sunset Public Library.

Students will be graded at each stage of their project:

«**Date 1**»	Description of the project:	«Possible 1» points
«**Date 2**»	Outline of project achievement:	«Possible 2» points
«**Date 3**»	Projects displayed and judged in Hemingway Gymnasium:	«Possible 3» points

In addition to their grades, students will receive ribbons and prizes in each category and

100   Page 1

FIGURE 7–18a   Form Letter with Fields

tations, certificates, and presentations. After selecting a template, the program asks you to respond to a series of questions to tailor the template to your current needs. Noninteractive templates include personal and business budgets, a gradebook, and a membership roster.

Integrated programs have become so popular that several companion products have been produced to increase their usefulness in the schools. *ClarisWorks 2.0 in the Classroom* (1993) is a project resource guide that provides templates and descriptions of a broad range of projects that can help teachers integrate tool applications across subject areas and grade levels. *Hands-On AppleWorks 3.0* (Luehrmann & Peckham, 1991) is a complete AppleWorks teaching package, including a teacher's guide, student books, blackline masters, a wall chart, and sample files. *In and Out of the Classroom with Microsoft Works: Practical Training for Teachers* (1990) is a handbook that provides a series of lessons and sample computer data files to help teachers use the

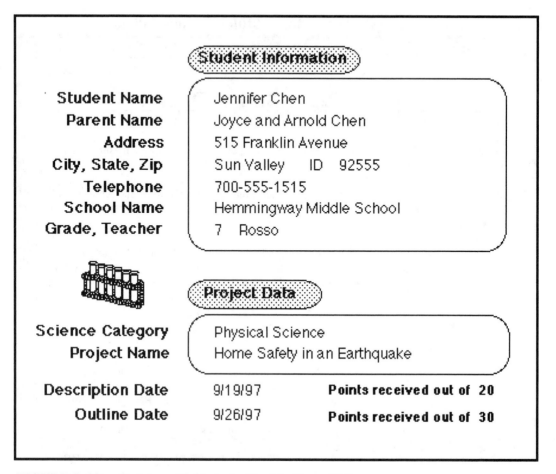

FIGURE 7–18b   Database Fields to be Used in Form Letter

Microsoft Works applications in their classroom. Other printed aids include *Microsoft Works Through Applications—IBM PC Version* (1991), *AppleWorks Resource Guide for Teachers and Parents* (1991), and *ClarisWorks 2.0 for Teachers* (1993). Beagle Bros. has produced a series of AppleWorks software add-on products, such as *Timeout Thesaurus, Timeout Desk Tools,* and *Timeout Superfonts.* Many template files are available from companies such as MECC and K-12 Micro Media.

Summary

The computer is certainly one of humankind's most versatile tools. By simply changing the set of instructions or computer program stored in the memory of the computer, we dramatically change its functions. With one program, it becomes an electronic typewriter or word processor; with another, it is turned into a powerful calculator. By inserting a diskette with still other programs, we can turn the computer into an electronic

---

Dear Joyce and Arnold Chen,

This year the Hemmingway Middle School Science Department is sponsoring a Science Fair for all fifth, sixth, seventh and eighth grade students.

The purpose of the Science Fair is to promote individual study, initiative and achievement. While students are encouraged to seek help from various sources, it is important that they understand the work they do.

Jennifer Chen has selected a science project in the category of Physical Science called "Home Safety in an Earthquake". For assistance in their projects, students can check out science fair materials from the Science Resource Room, the Hemingway Media Center and the Sunset Public Library.

Students will be graded at each stage of their project:

9/19/97	Description of the project:	20 points
9/26/97	Outline of project achievement:	30 points
10/10/97	Projects displayed and judged	
	in Hemingway Gymnasium:	200 points

In addition to their grades, students will receive ribbons and prizes in each category and grade level. Winners in each category and grade level will be

---

FIGURE 7–18c   Merged Letter

filing cabinet, a drafting table, or an artist's easel. It is true that these computer tools are often only new manifestations of other more common tools. However, the computer versions significantly expand their application, speed, accuracy, and power. The computer is a tool that can extend our mental capabilities. Computer tools have potential application in virtually every aspect of the school curriculum. Helping students produce exciting and stimulating written documents and oral and visual presentations can teach them valuable skills for potential employment and motivate them to see new and unique options.

Exercises

1. List and briefly describe those features of a word-processing program that you would consider most important for your own writing.
2. Describe the similarities and differences between word-processing, desktop publishing, and desktop presentation software.
3. Learn how to use a word processor and use it to write your next paper or report.
4. Define and describe the relationships between a database, files, records, and fields.

5. Compare and contrast file-management systems, relational-database programs, and free-format database programs.
6. Describe how you would use a database management system in your own classroom.
7. Design your own database fields, collect and enter appropriate data into a database program, and use the search and sort functions to find significant facts and relationships in your data.
8. How might electronic spreadsheet programs be used in your own classroom?
9. Design your own spreadsheet and make several changes in your data or formulas to find the answers to several What if? questions.
10. Describe the major differences between charting, drawing, and painting graphic programs.
11. What do you consider to be the most valuable computer tool application? Why?

References

AppleWorks. [Computer Program]. Mountain View, CA: Claris.

AppleWorks GS. [Computer Program]. Santa Clara, CA: Claris.

AppleWorks Resource Guide for Teachers and Parents, The. (1991). Santa Clara, CA: Claris.

Astound. [Computer Program]. Mississauga, Ontario, Canada: Gold Disk.

Astronomy. [Database File]. Pleasantville, NY: Sunburst Communications.

AutoCAD. [Computer Program]. Sausalito, CA: Autodesk.

Bank Street School Filer. [Computer Program]. Pleasantville, NY: Sunburst Communications.

Bank Street Writer. [Computer Program]. San Rafael, CA: Broderbund.

BeagleWrite. [Computer Software]. San Diego, CA: Beagle Bros.

CA-Cricket Presents. [Computer Program]. San Jose, CA: Computer Associates International.

Canvas. [Computer Program]. Miami, FL: Deneba Software.

Charisma. [Computer Program]. Richardson, TX: Micrografx.

Children's Writing and Publishing Center. [Computer Program]. San Rafael, CA: Learning Co.

Claris Cad. [Computer Program]. Santa Clara, CA: Claris.

ClarisWorks. [Computer Program]. Santa Clara, CA: Claris.

ClarisWorks 2.0 in the Classroom. (1993). Santa Clara, CA: Claris.

ClarisWorks 2.0 for Teachers. (1993). Santa Clara, CA: Claris.

Correct Grammar. [Computer Program]. San Francisco, CA: Lifetree Software.

Cricket Graph. [Computer Program]. Malvern, PA: Cricket Software.

Data Ease. [Computer Program]. Trumbull, CT: Data Ease.

Dazzle Draw. [Computer Program]. San Rafael, CA: Broderbund.

DB Master. [Computer Program]. Maple Glen, PA: Stone Edge Technologies.

dBase. [Computer Program]. Torrance, CA: Ashton-Tate.

DCH Notebook Filer. [Computer Program]. Lexington, MA: Collamore/D. C. Heath.

Delta Drawing. [Computer Program]. Cambridge, MA: Spinnaker.

DeltaGraph. [Computer Program]. Monterey, CA: Delta Point.

Deluxe Paint. [Computer Program]. San Mateo, CA: Electronic Arts.

DesignStudio. [Computer Program]. Paramus, NJ: Letraset USA.

Dialog. [On-Line Service]. Arlington, VA: Dialog Information Services.

DIALOG Online ERIC. [CD-ROM Database and Software]. Palo Alto, CA: Dialog Information Services.

Dissertation Abstracts Ondisc. [CD-ROM Database and Software]. Ann Arbor, MI: University Microfilms International Electronic Publishing.

Double Helix. [Computer Program]. Northbrook, IL: Odesta.

Draw Plus. [Computer Program]. Gilroy, CA: Activision.

DrawPerfect. [Computer Program]. Orem, UT: WordPerfect.

Electronic Whole Earth Catalog. [CD-ROM, Computer Program]. San Rafael, CA: Broderbund.

Enable. [Computer Program]. Ballston Lake, NY: The Software Group.

Endangered Species. [Database File]. Pleasantville, NY: Sunburst Communications.

Excel. [Computer Program]. Redmond, WA: Microsoft.

Filemaker. [Computer Program]. Santa Clara: Claris.

Folio. [Computer Program]. Provo, UT: Folio.

Foundation. [Computer Program]. Chicago: Foundation.

4th Dimension. [Computer Program]. Cupertino, CA: ACIUS.

FoxPro. [Computer Program]. Perrysburg, OH: Fox Software.

Framework. [Computer Program]. Culver City, CA: Ashton-Tate.

Freelance Plus. [Computer Program]. Cambridge, MA: Lotus Development.

Friendly Filer. [Computer Program]. Danbury, CT: Grolier Electronic Publishing.

Gabel, D. (1984). Sorting out data-base software. *Personal Software, 2*(3), 35, 165.

GEnie. [On-Line Service]. Rockville, MD: General Electric Information Services.

Graftool. [Computer Program]. Redondo Beach, CA: 3-D Visions.

Grammatik. [Computer Program]. San Francisco, CA: Reference Software International.

Harvard Graphics. [Computer Program]. Mountain View, CA: Software Publishing.

Heath Social Studies. [Database File]. Lexington, MA: Collamore/D. C. Heath.

In and Out of the Classroom with Microsoft Works: Practical Training for Teachers (1990). Redmond, WA: Microsoft.

Interleaf Publisher. [Computer Program]. Cambridge, MA: Interleaf.

Jacobson, B. (1984). Choosing and using a data base management program. *Creative Computing, 10*(9), S1–S16.

Jones, R. (1988). *The complete guide to corporate desktop publishing*. Great Britain: Cambridge University Press.

KaleidaGraph. [Computer Program]. Reading PA: Synergy Software.

KidsTime. [Computer Program]. Scotts Valley, CA: Great Wave Software.

Krajewski, R. (1984). Database types. *Byte, 9*(11), 137–142.

Life Science. [Database File]. New York: Scholastic.

LinkWay. [Computer Program]. Atlanta, GA: IBM.

Lotus 1-2-3. [Computer Program]. Cambridge, MA: Lotus Development.

Luehrmann, A., & Peckham, H. (1991). *Hands-on AppleWorks 3.0*. Gilroy, CA: Computer Literacy Press.

MacDraw. [Computer Program]. Cupertino, CA: Apple Computer.

MacPaint. [Computer Program]. Cupertino, CA: Apple Computer.

MacProof/PCProof. [Computer Program]. Salt Lake City, UT: Lexpertise USA.

MacWrite II. [Computer Program]. Mountain View, CA: Claris.

Magic Slate. [Computer Program]. Pleasantville, NY: Sunburst Communications.

MECC Dataquest: The Fifty States. [Computer Program and Database]. St. Paul, MN: MECC.

MECC Dataquest: The Presidents. [Computer Program and Database]. St. Paul, MN: MECC.

MECC Graph. [Computer Program]. St. Paul, MN: MECC.

Microsoft Word. [Computer Program]. Redmond, WA: Microsoft.

Microsoft Works. [Computer Program]. Redmond, WA: Microsoft.

Microsoft Works Through Applications—IBM PC Version. (1991). Gilroy, CA: Computer Literacy Press.

MiniCad+. [Computer Program]. Ellicott City, MD: Graphsoft.

MORE. [Computer Program]. Cupertino, CA: Symantec.

MultiScribe. [Computer Program]. Houston, TX: StyleWare.

Newsroom. [Computer Program]. Minneapolis, MN: Springboard.

Nogales, P. D., & McAllister, C. H. (1987). *Apple-Works for teachers.* Irvine, CA: Franklin, Beedle & Associates.

Omnis 5. [Computer Program]. Foster City, CA: Blyth Software.

One World Countries Database. [Computer Program and Database]. Midland, MI: Active Learning Systems.

Oxford English Dictionary. [CD-ROM]. New York: Oxford University Press.

PageMaker. [Computer Program]. Seattle, WA: Aldus.

Paintworks Gold. [Computer Program]. Gilroy, CA: Activision.

Panorama. [Computer Program]. Huntington Beach, CA: ProVUE Development.

Paradox. [Computer Program]. Scotts Valley, CA: Borland International.

PC Paintbrush. [Computer Program]. Marietta, GA: Z-Soft.

Persuasion. [Computer Program]. Denver: Aldus.

pfs:file. [Computer Program]. Jefferson City, MO: Scholastic Software.

pfs:Write. [Computer Program]. Jefferson City, MO: Scholastic Software.

Poetry and Mythology. [Database File]. New York: Scholastic.

PowerPoint. [Computer Program]. Redmond, WA: Microsoft.

PrintShop. [Computer Program]. San Rafael, CA: Brøderbund.

Professional File. [Computer Program]. Mountain View, CA: Software Publishing.

Professional Write. [Computer Program]. Mountain View, CA: Software Publishing.

ProFILER. [Computer Program]. Emeryville, CA: Pinpoint Publishing.

Publish It! [Computer Program]. Deerfield, IL: Timeworks.

Q & A. [Computer Program]. Cupertino, CA: Symantec.

QuarkXPress. [Computer Program]. Denver, CO: Quark.

R-Base. [Computer Program]. Redmond, WA: Microrim.

Ready, Set, Go! [Computer Program]. Paramus, NJ: Letraset USA.

Reflex. [Computer Program]. Scotts Valley, CA: Borland International.

RightWriter. [Computer Program]. Sarasota, FL: RightSoft.

Science and Nature Facts. [Database File]. Danbury, CT: Grolier Electronic Publishing.

Sensible Grammar. [Computer Program]. Troy, MI: Sensible Software.

Sigma Plot. [Computer Program]. Corte Madera, CA: Jandel Scientific.

Slide Shop. [Computer Program]. Jefferson City, MO: Scholastic.

Sonar. [Computer Program]. Midlothian, VA: Virginia Systems Software Services.

Spinaker Plus. [Computer Software]. Cambridge, MA: Spinaker Software.

Springboard Publisher. [Computer Program]. Minneapolis, MN: Springboard Software.

Stickybear Music. [Computer Software]. Norfolk, CT: Weekly Reader Family Software.

SuperBase4. [Computer Program]. Irving, TX: Precision.

SuperPaint. [Computer Program]. San Diego, CA: Silicon Beach Software.

SuperPrint. [Computer Program]. Jefferson City, MO: Scholastic Software.

Take 1: Animation Graphics. [Computer Program]. Grand Rapids, MI: Baudville.

Timeout Desk Tools. [Computer Program]. San Diego, CA: Beagle Bros.

Timeout Superfonts. [Computer Program]. San Diego, CA: Beagle Bros.

Timeout Thesaurus. [Computer Program]. San Diego, CA: Beagle Bros.

USA Profile. [Computer Program and Database]. Midland, MI: Active Learning Systems.

Ventura Publisher. [Computer Program]. San Diego, CA: Ventura Software.

VisiCalc. [Computer Program]. San Jose, CA: VisiCorp.

VTerm II. [Computer Program]. New York: Coefficient Systems.

Wheeler, F. (1987, March). The new ready-made databases: What they offer your classroom. *Classroom Computer Learning, 7*(6), 28–32.

Wilsondisc Reader's Guide to Periodical Literature. [CD-ROM, Computer Program]. Bronx, NY: H. W. Wilson.

WordCruncher. [Computer Program]. Orem, UT: Electronic Text.

WordPerfect. [Computer Program]. Orem, UT: WordPerfect.

WordPerfect Presentations. [Computer Program]. Orem, UT: Novell.

Wordstar Professional. [Computer Program]. San Rafael, CA: Wordstar International.

World Geography, Cultures and Economics. [Database File]. New York: Scholastic.

Chapter *8*

Multimedia/Hypermedia

The term *multimedia* is probably a buzzword that we are stuck with, even though the prefix *multi* is redundant, since *media* is already plural. Other terms such as *interactive media* and *media integration* are often used as synonyms. Each of these terms usually refers to a combination of several types of media—such as text, graphics, sound, animation, and motion video—into a single computer application. Multimedia applications are distinguished from standard video or film, which may also include all these media forms, by the fact that all these various forms are presented and sequenced under computer control. Placing these media under computer control makes it possible for students to interact with the media in various ways. Rather than passively viewing a predetermined sequential presentation, as with a videotape, students can respond to questions, problems, or situations presented by the media and receive appropriate feedback. They can also combine media elements under computer control to create their own multimedia projects.

The term *hypermedia* is often used as a synonym for *multimedia;* however, the prefix *hyper* adds the connotation of something extra, above, or beyond (Franklin & Kinnell, 1990). Ted Nelson (1965) coined the terms *hypertext* and *hypermedia* to refer to text and media that were multidimensional. He envisioned an electronic information system, which he termed *hypertext,* that would allow the user to jump quickly and easily from one document to another or to another section in the same document. For example, if you were reading a journal article on the computer screen of such a system, and you came across a reference to another research study in a different journal, you would be able to access the text of the referenced study by just clicking the reference with a mouse pointer. Then, with equal ease, you would be able to switch back to the original article or bring up yet a third article that was referenced in the second. With printed materials, following up on cross-references is such a cumbersome process that few readers actually do so. With a hypertext system, following cross-reference links is both simple and immediate. This efficient electronic navigation system frees students to select many different possible paths (or dimensions) through the material rather than following the standard linear path from one page to the next in a printed book.

Hypermedia is an extension of the concepts of hypertext to multimedia. With an electronic hypermedia system, not only can students immediately access related textual material but they can also quickly access other related media elements such as sound, graphics, animations, and motion video. For example, while reading a hypermedia version of *Romeo and Juliet* from *The Shakespeare Quartet,* students can use the mouse pointer to click on any phrase marked in red to display annotations by renowned scholars to help them understand the text. By clicking on special symbols or icons, students can request sound narrations of famous passages or display illustrations and motion video clips of certain scenes. They can also instruct the computer to display a dictionary definition of any word in the play. Teachers and students may even add their own electronic notations in text, graphics, sound, or movies to the text of the play.

This chapter will explore multimedia and hypermedia in depth. To simplify the discussion, the term *hypermedia* will be used throughout the remainder of the chapter to emphasize the use of multimedia under computer control that is interactive and multidimensional with extensive navigation tools that allow for nonlinear and immediate access to any media element at any time. Other sections of the chapter will examine, in turn, how each of the media elements of text, graphics, sound, animation, and motion video are implemented under computer control. However, to understand these discussions, it is important for you to understand how any type of information is represented by a computer. Subsequent sections will describe some of the additional hardware requirements that are necessary to implement hypermedia. Finally, several educational applications of hypermedia that are currently available for use in the schools will be discussed. Chapter 11, The Computer as Tutee, focuses on how both you and your students can use hypermedia authoring systems to create your own hypermedia programs and presentations.

How Information Is Represented by Computers

In an earlier chapter, computers were defined as information processing devices. Computers process, manipulate, modify, change, and transform information. Also, information was defined as data that has meaning. Data include such things as letters, words, digits, numbers, sounds, pictures, and so on. However, it is important to remember that the data or information processed by the computer have no meaning to the computer. Meaning is only given to the data by humans who use the computer as a tool. Data can be given meaning when used as a symbol to represent objects, events, concepts, or ideas. Often, different data or symbols can be used to represent the same thing. For example, the following symbols can all be used to represent a piece of furniture with a flat, smooth surface supported by legs:

TABLE   table   MESA

However, the number of legs possessed by a cow might be represented by any of the following symbols:

Four   4   IIII   IV   ••••   Cuatro

Modern computers are composed of various electronic components that can be in one of two possible states: on or off, open or closed, or positively or negatively charged. The two different states of these components can be used as symbols for two different things. This is not as limiting as it might seem, since these two symbols can represent a different set of two things at different times or under different contexts, as shown in the following list:

Positive Charge	*Negative Charge*
Female	Male
Right	Left
Up	Down
Correct	Wrong
1	0
+	−
Good	Bad
Black	White

As a matter of convenience, rather than referring to these two states or symbols as being on or off or positively or negatively charged, the symbols 1 and 0 are used. These two symbols are called *binary digits. Binary* refers to something consisting of two elements or parts; a *digit* is a symbol used to represent a number. When referring to only one of these symbols, the term *bit* is used. The word *bit* is actually an acronym for BInary digiT.

Unfortunately, there are many sets of things in the world that cannot be represented in pairs. Everything is not just black or white. Life is made up of many shades and hues. How can a computer with only two symbols (bits) be used to represent more than two things at a time? The solution lies in the use of different strings or series of bits, such as

1010   1011   1000   1001

just as different strings of letters of the alphabet are used to represent the names of many different people:

Jill   Jean   Joan   Jane

or strings of the digits 0–9 to represent any quantity:

145   9236   87   308

If a string of two bits is used, the number of unique symbols may be doubled:

00   01   10   11

By using a series of three bits, the number of unique symbols may be doubled again, giving a total of eight:

000   001   010   011   100   101   110   111

Each time another bit is added to the length of the string, the number of unique symbols that can be used to represent several things at the same time is doubled yet again. Remember, the symbols have no meaning in and of themselves. The meaning comes in what humans use the symbols to represent. Thus, in one context the eight unique strings of bits might be used to represent eight different colors, yet in another context they might be used to represent eight different people, and in still another context they might be used to represent eight different decimal numbers:

Bit String Symbols	Colors	Names of People	Decimal Numbers
000	White	John	0
001	Yellow	Bill	1
010	Orange	Sam	2
011	Blue	Mary	3
100	Green	Susan	4
101	Purple	George	5
110	Brown	Paul	6
111	Black	Marvin	7

Clearly, if one wants to represent a larger number of different things in the computer at the same time, a longer string of bits will be needed. However, these strings of bits must be stored in the memory of the computer. As the length of the bit strings increases, so must the size of each memory location. This increases the size and cost of the computer.

If one has to restrict the length of the bit strings in a computer to limit costs, what would be the most appropriate length? To answer this question, computer designers must consider what users are likely to want to represent in computers. Certainly, they would want to represent the digits 0 through 9 of the decimal number system and the 26 letters of the alphabet. How many bits would be required to represent the 10 digits of the decimal number system? We have already seen that 3 bits will provide only 8 unique symbols. Therefore, one would have to go to 4 bits, which would provide 16 unique symbols, in order to handle 10 digits. To accommodate the 26 letters of the alphabet, one would need 5 bits, which gives 32 symbols. However, to include both lower- and uppercase letters, the 10 digits 0–9, and special symbols such as + – ? # $ % & =, most of the 128 different symbols provided by 7 bits would be needed. Because numbers of bits that are multiples, or powers, of 2 are easier to work with, most early microcomputer manufacturers designed each memory location in the computer to store an 8-bit string, which provided 256 different symbols. A string of 8 bits is called a *byte*.

When more than 256 different symbols are needed, several bytes are treated as a single bit string. Two memory locations of one byte each could by used to produce a bit string of 16 bits, which would provide for 65,536 symbols; 4 bytes would produce a bit string of 32 bits, providing for 4,294,967,296 symbols. More recently, microcomputers that can transfer and process multiple bytes simultaneously have been introduced. This significantly increases the power of the computer.

The following sections will show how these binary digits are used to represent different media elements, such as text, graphics, sound, animation, and motion video.

Types of Media Elements

Text

The most frequently used media element in hypermedia applications is text. Text consists mostly of words, numbers, and punctuation symbols. It is normally entered into the computer through the use of a keyboard. When a typist presses a key on the keyboard, a string of eight bits (one byte) is sent from the keyboard to the computer. A unique set of eight bits is used to represent each symbol on the keyboard. The following table shows the bit strings that correspond to the first few capital letters of the alphabet. These particular bit strings have been accepted as a standard representation for the letters of the alphabet and are referred to as ASCII (American Standard Code for Information Interchange) codes. The decimal number (base ten) equivalent for each of these codes is shown in the third column of the table. There are additional codes for the other capital letters, lowercase letters, digits, and punctuation marks. There are even codes to indicate spaces and carriage returns.

Character	ASCII Code Bit String	ASCII Code Decimal Number
A	01000001	65
B	01000010	66
C	01000011	67
D	01000100	68
E	01000101	69
F	01000110	70
G	01000111	71
H	01001000	72
I	01001001	73
J	01001010	74

As these ASCII codes are received from the keyboard, they are stored in the memory of the computer and used by the computer software to determine what letters to display on the screen. After the text is entered into the computer, it may be saved on an external storage device, such as a hard disk, or it may be sent to a printer. It is important to remember that the ASCII code representation of the text is saved and sent to the printer, not the text itself. These codes are used by the printer to determine which letters to print on the paper.

Many hypermedia applications, such as the Shakespeare play mentioned earlier, require the entry of extensive amounts of textual information. In such cases, the text is entered through the use of an optical scanner (see Chapter 2, Computer Hardware) rather than by a keyboard. After the text is scanned, it must be converted into ASCII codes by optical character recognition (OCR) software.

Most hypermedia applications can display text in many different fonts, sizes, styles, and colors. Character styles such as boldface and underlining, along with color, are often used to indicate hyperlinks to other textual or media information.

Graphics

Chapter 7, Tool Applications, discussed several computer tool applications that can be used to produce pictures or graphics in the form of graphs and charts, drawings, and paintings. These graphics can be displayed on the computer monitor, printed on a laser printer, or stored on an external storage medium such as a floppy diskette or a hard disk. You will also remember that computer graphics are drawn on the screen using a pattern of tiny picture elements, or pixels, that are turned either on or off. With black and white painting or bit-mapped graphics, each pixel is represented by a single bit in the memory of the computer—a 1 when the pixel is on and a 0 when the pixel is off. When the picture is stored on a disk, the computer saves a set of binary numbers corresponding to the pattern of on/off pixels. The amount of storage necessary to store the picture is determined by the number of bits or pixels that make up the image. High-resolution pictures require more bits, and therefore more storage, than low-resolution pictures, and small pictures require fewer bits than large pictures.

Color images require additional bits for each pixel to represent the different colors: 8 bits are required for each pixel to represent 256 colors, whereas 16 bits are required for 65,536 different colors, just as 16 bits are required to represent 65,536 levels of sound amplitude. However, 24 bits per pixel are generally considered necessary for high-quality color reproduction—24-bit color would yield over 16 million different colors. A 24-bit color picture requires 24 times as much storage as a black and white picture of the same size and resolution. For example, a standard full-screen black and white picture of 640 by 480 pixels would require 307,200 (640 × 480) bits or 38,400 (307,200/8) bytes of storage (1 byte = 8 bits). The number of bytes is divided by 1,024 to give us kilobytes (KB or K). Thus, 38,400 bytes is equivalent to 37.5 (38,400/1,024) kilobytes (abbreviated 37.5 K). A 24-bit color picture of the same number of pixels would require 24 times as much storage: 37.5 K × 24 = 900 K. Such full-screen color pictures not only require a lot of memory and storage but they also require more time to read from the disk and display on the computer monitor.

Fortunately, techniques have been developed to compress bit-mapped picture storage requirements by a factor of 20 or more without significant loss of quality (Seiter, 1992). Such compression is possible by using coding techniques that take advantage of redundancies in the picture. For example, if there is a large section of the picture with the same shade of blue sky, a few numbers can be stored to indicate the extent of the repetition rather than storing bits for each pixel. One of standard specifications for picture compression is referred to as *JPEG (Joint Photographic Experts Group).* Researchers are continuing to develop new techniques, such as fractal compression, for even greater levels of compression (Gibbs, 1993). However, as the level of compression increases, the quality of the image also decreases.

Drawing or object-oriented graphics generally require less storage than bit-mapped graphics. Each graphic object is defined and stored in memory and on diskette as a set of numbers representing its mathematical or geometrical properties such as location, number of sides, length of sides, color, and so on. These few numbers require much less storage than the pixel pattern of a bit-mapped image. The amount of storage and time required to draw an object-oriented graphic increases as the number and complexity of the objects that make up the image increases.

In addition to creating pictures using graphics programs, there are several other ways to enter your own pictures or graphics into a computer—for example, take your own pictures using a digital camera; use a desktop scanner to digitize photograph prints or pictures found in magazines or books; and digitize TV frames from some video source such as a videotape, videodisc, or single-shot video camera (see Chapter 2, Computer Hardware, for a description of these peripheral devices and Chapter 15, Issues in Educational Computing, for a discussion on issues related to the use of copyright materials). Each of these mechanisms involve the conversion, or *digitization,* of the original picture to a matrix or mosaic of pixels that can be represented by binary digits, as outlined earlier. Once the picture has been *digitized,* the bit pattern can be stored on diskette, read into computer memory, and displayed on a computer monitor.

The bit-mapped picture can also be imported or pasted into a word-processing or desktop publishing document, a hypermedia application, or one of the graphics programs described in Chapter 7, Tool Applications. Once the picture is imported into a graphics program, it can be manipulated and edited in many ways. It may be lightened or darkened, cropped, rotated, and integrated with other pictures or graphics objects; additionally, flaws can be removed, colors can be changed, and so on. Digitized pictures can also be stored on a network file server and accessed by any computer connected to the file server or sent to a remote computer through the use of a modem and standard telephone lines (see Chapter 9, Networks and Telecommunications).

If you do not want to create or scan your own pictures, professionally drawn graphics and professional photographs are available as digital clip art or photo collections from a variety of commercial vendors. Some computer-user groups even offer public-domain graphics collections. These graphics can be read from a floppy diskette, CD-ROM, or Photo CD and used in any of the applications described thus far. Graphics and scanned photos can be stored in several different file formats. Some of the more common formats include PICT, PICT2, TIFF, EPS, BMP, and GIFF. Be careful that the file format of your graphics is compatible with the computer applications into which you plan to import the graphics. Many applications will only import graphics from a few file formats.

Sound

Sounds are produced by vibrations of an object, whether the object is a violin string, a clarinet reed, or your vocal cords. When an object vibrates, it causes the surrounding air to vibrate. These vibrations travel through the air as sound waves. When these sound waves enter your ear, they cause a series of vibrations to travel from your eardrum through the bones of the middle ear to the inner ear. Here, the vibrations are converted to nerve signals that are interpreted as sounds by your brain.

The nature of a given sound is determined by its pitch, loudness, duration, and timbre, or quality (*World Book Encyclopedia,* 1976 & 1994). The *pitch* of a sound, its highness or lowness, is determined by the frequency of the vibrations of the object making the sound. The frequency of vibrations is measured in terms of the number of times an object vibrates per second. Suppose you were to insert one end of a piano wire into a block of wood and then cause the protruding wire to vibrate. Also suppose that you were able to trace the up and down motion of the end of the wire as it vibrates on a rolling scroll of graph paper. Such a tracing would produce a graphical representation of the vibrations and corresponding sound waves, as shown in Figure 8–1.

The upward slope of the curve would be drawn as the wire moved upward, whereas the downward slope of the curve would be drawn as the wire moved back down. Note that the wire and the curve extend downward past the initial point at rest to a distance equal to the movement upward and then returns to the starting point. This back and forth movement continues until the vibration finally comes to a stop. If the paper scrolled at a constant rate, the number of vibrations each second could be graphed. Each movement from the resting point upward, back down past the resting point, and then back up to the resting point is referred to as one *vibration,* or *cycle.* The unit of

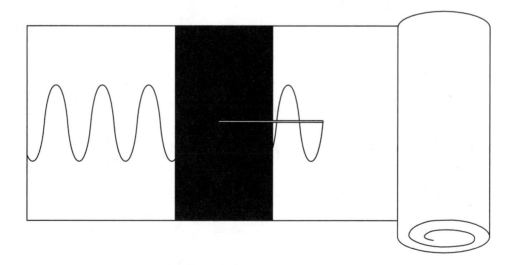

FIGURE 8–1   Tracing of Piano Wire Vibrations Showing Sound Wave Curves

measurement for frequency is the *hertz* (*Hz*). Each vibration or cycle per second is one hertz. A normal person can hear sounds ranging in frequency from 20 Hz to 20,000 Hz (or 20 kilohertz [20 kHz]). An object that vibrates rapidly produces a high-pitched sound or note, whereas one that vibrates more slowly produces a lower-pitched note. For example, a piano string vibrating at 256 hertz will produce the note middle C on the musical scale, whereas a string vibrating twice as fast, at 512 hertz, will produce the C note an octave higher. The length, tightness, and relative mass of a string will affect its vibration frequency. The tighter the string, the higher its frequency. A light string has a higher pitch than a heavy one, and a short string has a higher pitch than a long one. Figure 8–2 shows graphs of four different sound waves. The two on the bottom (c and d) have greater frequencies than those on the top.

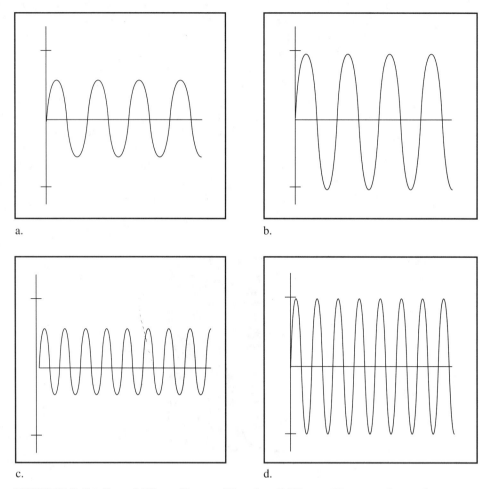

a.

b.

c.

d.

FIGURE 8–2   Sound Wave Curves Showing Different Frequencies and Amplitudes

The perceived *loudness* of a sound is determined by the *amplitude* or distance an object moves as it vibrates. If you caused the wire mentioned earlier to vibrate a greater distance up and down from its resting point, you would increase the loudness of the resulting sound. This could also be shown on the graph paper. In Figure 8–2, the two curves on the right (b and d) have greater amplitudes than those on the left.

The *timbre,* or quality, of a sound allows us to perceive a difference between sounds made by different instruments playing a note of the same pitch and loudness. Most sounds produced by a musical instrument are made up of a combination of frequencies or pitches. The dominant and generally lowest pitch is called the *fundamental.* The higher pitches that make up the sound are referred to as the *overtones.* A vibrating string simultaneously vibrates as a whole, creating the fundamental and in sections producing the overtones. Each instrument produces a different number and pattern of overtones yielding a characteristic sound quality or timbre. Figure 8–3 shows a graph of a musical sound made up of several different frequencies.

Analog Recording

The graph of the sound wave produced by the vibrating piano wire shown in Figure 8–1 is a representation, likeness, or analogy of the original sound. The frequency and amplitude of the original sound has an analogous representation on the curve. If you were to place a microphone in front of a vibrating object, the sound waves produced by the vibration would cause a metal disk or diaphragm inside the microphone to vibrate. The vibrating diaphragm would generate a pattern of electrical current that would correspond to the sound wave pattern just as the graph corresponds to the vibrating piano wire. The pattern of electrical current would be an *analog* of the original sound. If the sound were recorded on a phonograph record, the grooves of the record would consist of jagged waves corresponding to the original sound waves. The phonograph record would be an

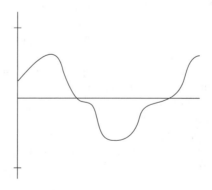

FIGURE 8–3   Complex Sound Wave Curve Made Up of Different Frequencies

analog recording. When you play a phonograph record, the waves in the record grooves cause a phonograph needle to vibrate as the record spins. The vibrations in the needle are converted into an analogous (or similar) electrical signal. This signal is then amplified and used to vibrate the diaphragm of a loud speaker. The vibration of the speaker reproduces corresponding vibrations in the air that are interpreted as sound by your brain.

Synthesized Music

Most microcomputers have the capability to synthesize or generate sounds using electronic circuits that can range from a simple beep to a multiple-instrument musical composition. Computer languages such as BASIC, Logo, and Pascal (see Chapter 11, The Computer as Tutee) often include sound generation commands. For example, the Pascal command

    NOTE (24,96);

instructs the computer to play a note with a pitch or frequency of 24 and a duration of 96. The duration 96 corresponds to the duration of a quarter note, and 24 corresponds to the pitch of middle C. Translating a musical score to such commands is tedious at best.

Fortunately, several music-editing programs such as *Music Construction Set, ConcertWare+, Music Studio, KidsTime,* and *Stickybear Music* are commercially available. These programs graphically display a staff (see Figure 8–4) on the screen and allow the user to select and place notes in the appropriate locations on the staff. Sophisticated editing features allow for the insertion, deletion, and modification of notes. Some editors allow for the composition of pieces with multiple voices and different instrumental sounds. The key and time signatures can be set or changed with a simple command. The composition can be played immediately or stored on diskette for future playback or editing. In some cases, a hard copy of the score can be produced on a printer. Such editors open up totally new musical experiences for schoolchildren. Students with no instrumental skills can now compose, play, and record their own musical selections.

One of the limitations of synthesized music generated by computer programming commands and some music-editing programs is the lack of compatibility across programming languages or editing programs. For example, a Pascal program containing a series of NOTE commands for playing a musical selection cannot be imported into a Logo program or into a music-editing program. Music files created by *KidsTime* cannot be played or edited by *Stickybear Music* nor can they be played by hypermedia programs. Fortunately, standards have been set for storing and transmitting electronically generated music. This standard is described in the next section.

MIDI

MIDI (musical instrument digital interface) is a specification or standard agreed upon by music synthesizer manufacturers to make it possible for electronic musical instruments and associated devices to communicate with one another using a common music language and hardware interface (Yelton, 1989; Rothstein, 1992). The hardware section of

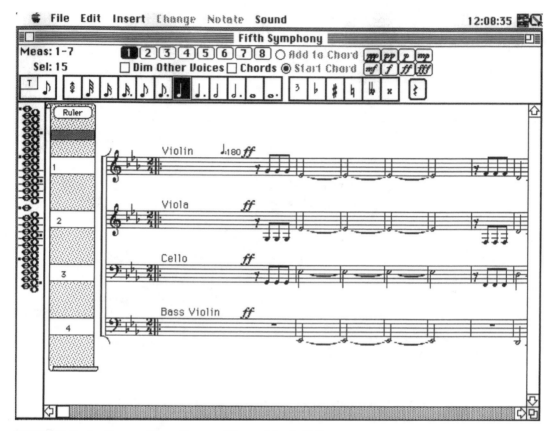

FIGURE 8–4   Screen from *ConcertWare+ Music Editor*

the standard specifies the nature of the cables used to connect two different electronic musical instruments together and the ports or jacks into which the cables are inserted. Figure 8–5 shows a MIDI cable with the five-pin connector that may be plugged into a MIDI port found on an electronic instrument. Most MIDI-compatible instruments or devices provide three MIDI jacks, also shown in Figure 8–5. The In jack receives information from another device, the Out jack sends information to another device, and the Thru jack retransmits incoming information on to another device unchanged.

The common language portion of the MIDI standard specifies the nature of the data or information communicated between devices. MIDI signals consist of bit strings that represent commands or messages for controlling an electronic instrument. These messages might specify which pitch or note is to be played by the instrument and how long and loud the note is to be played. Other messages might instruct a synthesizer to change from a piano sound to a flute sound. MIDI messages can even be used to control stage lights.

Since MIDI messages are simply strings of binary digits, they are amenable to being received, manipulated, and sent by a microcomputer. Some computers have built-

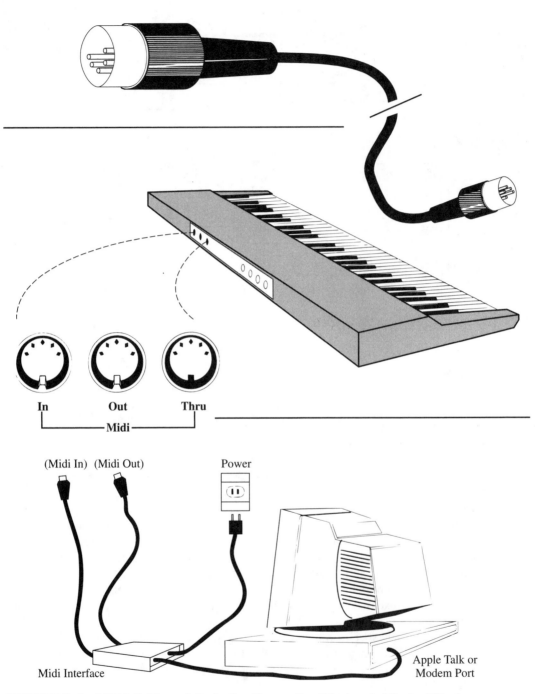

FIGURE 8–5   MIDI Cable and Jacks for Connecting Electronic Musical Devices

in MIDI ports, others may have a MIDI port as part of a sound board, while others require an external MIDI interface connected to one of the computer's serial ports. Several different types of computer programs are available for creating, recording, editing, storing, and playing music based on data in MIDI format. Composition and scoring software such as *Deluxe Music Construction Set* and *ConcertWare+ MIDI* are similar to the music-editing programs described in the previous section, but they also include MIDI capabilities. These programs not only allow you to enter and edit music using standard musical notation but they also allow you to store and transmit the music information in MIDI format. Your composition may be played back using the synthesizer circuits built into the computer, or the composition program may send MIDI messages through MIDI cables to attached external synthesizers that generate the musical sounds specified by the MIDI messages. By attaching an electronic music keyboard to your computer via a MIDI cable, some composition programs, such as *Finale,* will even transcribe, in standard musical notation, what you play on the music keyboard. The resulting musical score may be edited and printed on a laser printer.

Musical compositions stored as MIDI files are a valuable source of sound for hypermedia applications. If you do not have the talent to create your own compositions, there are many professionally produced compositions stored in MIDI format that are available in the public domain or from commercial sources. These MIDI files can be played by many hypermedia programs. One of the main advantages of MIDI compositions is that they do not require the extensive storage required of digital music recordings, which will be described in a later section.

Synthesized Voice

Just as it is possible to generate electronic music using a music synthesizer, it is also possible to have a computer program instruct the sound circuitry of the computer to imitate or synthesize the human voice. Computer-generated voices used to sound quite artificial, but recent advances make it possible for the computer to generate both realistic male, female, child, and adult voices. Voice generation software can take words and sentences saved in standard text files and convert them into synthesized sounds. Although synthesized voice still does not sound as realistic as digital voice recordings, text files require considerable less storage than digital recordings. In hypermedia applications where the computer reads text displayed on the screen, the synthesized voice essentially comes free, since the same text file can be used both to display the text and generate the voice.

Digital Sound Recording

With appropriate sound circuitry or cards installed, a microcomputer can synthesize sounds as well as record your own sounds. Some computers come with a microphone and internal circuitry and software for recording your own sounds. Others require the installation of a sound board or an external digitizer such as MacRecorder (see Figure 2–10 of Chapter 2, Computer Hardware). Recording your own voice is as simple as using the mouse to press the RECORD button on the screen and speaking into the microphone. When you are finished, press the STOP button and then press the

PLAY button to have the computer play back your recorded voice. If you want to preserve your recording, select Save from the menu and give your recording a file name. Your recorded sound will then be saved on a floppy diskette or hard disk. This recorded sound can then be retrieved and played by any software program that has sound playback capability. In addition to recording your own voice or other sounds using the microphone, you can record sounds from a cassette tape or other audio source by attaching a cable from the audio Out jack of the audio player to the audio In jack on the computer or digitizer and following the same recording procedure described earlier.

When the computer is used to record sounds, the analog sound wave pattern produced by the microphone, or sent by an audio player, must be digitized or converted into binary digits that can be interpreted and processed by the computer. Digitizing sound involves *sampling* discrete points along the sound wave curve at regular intervals, as shown in Figure 8–6. The value of the amplitude at each point is then converted to binary digits.

The accuracy or quality of the sound reconstructed from the digital information is determined by two factors: the number of samples and the accuracy of the numbers used to measure the amplitude of the sound at each sample (Pohlmann, 1992). Sounds, as well as most other real-world phenomena, are continuous in nature. Just as air temperatures are not simply hot or cold, and colors are not simply black or white, sounds are not just loud or soft. Each of these phenomena varies over a wide continuum. Essentially, there is an infinite number of levels of loudness, temperature, and color. When you listen to the evening news, the meteorologist reports the high and low temperatures for the day. However, the temperature did not jump from the low to the high. The temperature varied continuously throughout the day. If you want to obtain a more

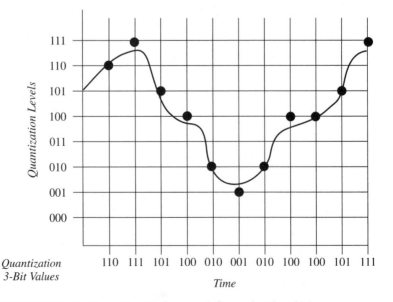

FIGURE 8–6   Sampling Points and Quantization Values

complete and accurate picture of the day's temperature, you would need to take several samples. For example, you could measure the temperature each hour. However, these discrete samples would not tell you how the temperature varied between each hour. To obtain a more accurate record, you would need to obtain more samples. Obviously, the accuracy of your record of the continuously varying temperature throughout the day would increase as you increased the number of samples. Since it would be impossible to take an infinite number of samples, you would have to set some practical limit. This limit could be based on your experience of how much the temperature normally varies over a short period of time.

To reconstruct a continuously varying sound wave accurately, you would also need a large number of samples. The larger the number of samples taken each second, the more accurate the possible reconstruction. The number of samples required is dependent on the frequency range of the original sounds. According to a theorem proposed by Harry Nyquist (1928), a sound wave must be sampled at least twice for each cycle—one sample for the amplitude at the top of the wave cycle and one for the bottom. Thus, if you want to sample a sound of 35 Hz, you would need at least 70 samples per second. Since the normal frequency range audible to human beings is 20 to 20,000 Hz, a sampling frequency greater than 40,000 Hz (40 kHz) would be necessary for adequate reconstruction of frequencies within the audible range. For some applications where the frequency range of the sound is smaller, a lower sampling rate would be acceptable. When lower sampling rates are used, high frequencies will be either distorted or filtered out.

In addition to the sampling rate, the other factor that affects the accuracy and quality of digital sound is the accuracy of amplitude measurement at each sample. This factor becomes an issue because strings of binary digits are used to represent the value of the amplitude measurements. Although real-world sounds are continuous and have an infinite number of levels of loudness, only a limited number of levels can be represented by using binary digits. If you use a string of 4 bits to represent the sound amplitude, you would have only 16 possible levels of loudness. If the actual amplitude of the sound wave curve for a given sample were between 2 of the 16 levels, the digital representation would have a certain degree of error. This error is referred to as *quantization error*. As you increase the number of digits, you increase the number of levels of loudness and more accurately represent the original sound. However, increasing the number of bits used to represent each sample also increases the storage requirement.

Most digitizing software allows you to specify whether to quantitize the amplitude of each sample using 8 bits or 16 bits. The 8-bit strings will yield 256 different levels of loudness, whereas the 16-bit strings will provide 65,536 different levels. You may also choose from several different sampling rates, such as 5 kHz, 7 kHz, 11 kHz, 22 kHz, or 44 kHz. The higher the sampling rate, the greater the frequency range and sound quality. However, higher sampling rates record more information and increase the storage requirements. The lower rates may be acceptable for voice recordings, but the higher rates will be necessary for high-quality music recordings. One minute of sound digitized at at a 44 kHz sampling rate with 16 bits per sample would require 42,240,000 bits (44,000 samples per second × 16 bits per sample × 60 seconds), 5,280,000 bytes (42,240,000 bits/8 bits per byte), 5156.25 kilobytes (5,280,000 bytes/

1,024 bytes per kilobyte), or 5.146 megabytes (5156.25 kilobytes/1,000 kilobytes per megabyte) of storage. At that rate, 60 minutes of sound would require over 300 megabytes of storage. Clearly, high-quality digitized sound requires extensive amounts of storage. Fortunately, such high-volume storage is now available with the common audio compact disc (CD). This exciting technology can be interfaced to and controlled by a computer. Compact disc technology will be discussed in detail in a later section of this chapter.

Several tool programs, such as *Sound Edit 16* and *Wave Turtle Beach,* provide sophisticated sound editing as well as sound recording capabilities (Yelton, 1989; Sydow, 1994). Once you have recorded your sound in *Sound Edit 16,* a graphical representation of your recording will appear in a window on the screen, as shown in Figure 8–7. By clicking and dragging the mouse pointer in this window you can select a portion of the sound (indicated by a black rectangle). The selected portion may then be played back,

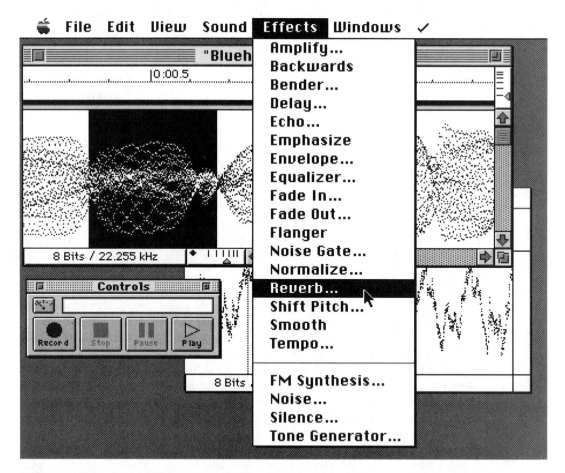

FIGURE 8–7 *Sound Edit 16* **Screen Showing Graphical Representation of Sound Waves and Effects Menu**

cut, copied, or altered using a wide variety of special effects tools such as amplify, bender, echo, filter, reverb, and smooth. A copied sound segment can be inserted anywhere in the same sound file or in a different file by clicking the mouse where you want the sound placed and selecting Paste from the menu. Sounds from several different sound files can also be mixed or combined into a single new sound file. For example, one sound file or track could include a voice narration while another track could provide background music. You may save your sounds in several different formats, such as SoundEdit, SND, AIFF, WAV. The SND format can be used by many Macintosh programs; AIFF is a cross-platform standard format; and WAV is used by many Windows programs. Save the sound in a file format that can be read by the program you are going to use to play back the sound file.

In summary, digital recording uses numbers in the form of binary digits to represent samples of the amplitude of the sound wave at regular intervals of time rather than an analog or likeness of the sound wave itself. On playback, these numbers are used to reconstruct a replica of the original sound wave. The quality of this replication depends on the sampling rate and the number of bits used to represent the amplitude for each sample.

Animation

We have all had experience with animation from the Saturday morning television cartoons (e.g., Bugs Bunny, the Road Runner, etc.), the full-length animated movies (e.g., *Snow White and the Seven Dwarfs, Beauty and the Beast,* etc.), and arcade and computer video games. In the same way, animation can bring hypermedia presentations to life. Animation, like motion picture films and television, is an optical illusion. We actually only see a series of still pictures in rapid succession. Small changes in position of certain objects in successive pictures or frames fool the human eye into perceiving motion. With television, this illusion of motion is achieved by displaying 30 frames every second, whereas film displays 24 frames per second. Adequate hypermedia animations may run from 12 to 16 frames per second.

Three different types of animation may be used in hypermedia applications: frame based, cel based, or object animation (*Concise Guide to Multimedia,* 1994). *Frame-based animations* consist of a series of full-screen images with gradual changes in each image from one frame to the next. Successive frames for this kind of animation can be easily created in a paint or draw graphics program by taking advantage of their many editing features to cut, copy, and paste various common elements from one frame to the next. An animation is created by rapidly showing successive frames.

Cel-based animations are named from the practice of drawing foreground objects that are to be animated on celluloid layers (cels) that are then overlayed on a static background. This type of animation is is more efficient because only the moving objects need to be redrawn for each frame. For example, to create an animation of running cat, several cels are created showing the legs of the cat in various positions, as shown in Figure 8–8. These can be placed over any background and shown in rapid succession to give the appearance of motion. The same set of cels can be shown or recycled many times to give the appearance of continuing motion.

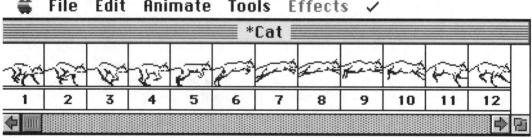

FIGURE 8–8   Animation Cells

Object animation is similar to cel-based animation in that the moving object is overlayed on a static background. However, the object itself is not changed but is moved along a path. With cel animation, the legs of the cat change their position to simulate motion but the cat does not change location. With object animation, the location of the cat is changed but its legs remain motionless.

More interesting animations are often created by combining the cel-based and object animations. With this combination, the cel-based animation is moved to different locations. Thus, the location of the cat moves as well as its legs. Tool software programs, such as *Addmotion* and *Macromedia Director,* are available to allow you to create and edit your own cel-based animations. Once you have created your animation, you can save it as a disk file and import it into a hypermedia authoring systems such as *HyperCard, ToolBook,* or *AuthorWare Professional.* Each of these authoring systems provides tools for combining object and cel-based animations. These and other authoring systems will be discussed in more detail in Chapter 11, The Computer as Tutee.

Motion Video

Through the miracle of television, the wonders of the world can be brought into our living rooms and our classrooms. Surprisingly, television has not had the impact in our schools that many invisioned. However, the advent of videotape players has given teachers greater control over this medium. No longer must the class schedule be made to correspond to an arbitrary broadcast schedule. Although videotape players can be interfaced to and controlled by a computer, this combination is quite expensive and not very satisfactory. The time delay in fast forwarding and rewinding the tape in search for a particular video segment is somewhat frustrating. Fortunately, this problem is solved through the use of videodisc technology and digital video.

Videodisc Technology

The *videodisc player* is an electronic device used to reproduce and display video images on a television set or video monitor. In this way, it is similar to a videotape player. However, rather than playing videotapes, the videodisc player plays a platter or disc of either 8 or 12 inches in diameter, similar in appearance to a phonograph record called a *videodisc* (see Figure 2–19 in Chapter 2, Computer Hardware). The videodisc may contain prerecorded video information such as feature-length movies, television programs, or specially designed educational video material.

Video information is recorded on a glass master disc coated with a light-sensitive or photo-resist material. A video signal is used to modulate or turn on and off a high-power *laser* that focuses a high-intensity narrow beam of light on the photo-resist layer of the disc as it rotates. Wherever the disc is exposed to the laser beam, a tiny oblong spot is formed. The photo-resist layer is then developed and the exposed spots are etched away to form microscopic holes, or pits, in the resist layer of the disc. These *pits,* separated by spaces called *lands,* are arranged in a spiral track running from the center to the edge of the disc. Figure 8–9 shows a magnified view of these pits and lands. The pattern of pits and lands recorded on the disc conform to the pattern of the original video signal. Plastic copies of the master are then replicated through a multi-stage process. The plastic discs are coated with a reflective layer of aluminum followed by a transparent protective layer of lacquer (Pohlmann, 1992).

A videodisc player uses a low-power laser to read the microscopic pits in the reflective surface of the videodisc. As the disc rotates, the laser beam is focused on the track of pits and lands. The light reflected from the disc varies in intensity based on the pattern of pits and lands. This light pattern is used to reproduce the original video images on a television set or video monitor (Elshami, 1990). Since optical devices such as lasers, mirrors, and lenses are used in the recording and reading of videodiscs, they are also often referred to as *optical discs* or *laser discs.*

Videodiscs are manufactured in two different formats: *constant angular velocity* (*CAV*) and *constant linear velocity* (*CLV*). The CAV format provides 30 minutes of full-motion video on each side of the videodisc with one picture or frame per circular track on the disc. Each of the 54,000 tracks or video frames on one side of the disc is preceded by a unique digital frame number code that can be read by the player. Any

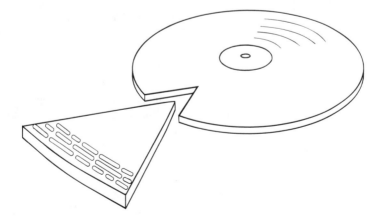

FIGURE 8–9   Magnified View of Videodisc Showing Pits and Lands

frame may be randomly accessed or selected by entering its corresponding number on a built-in or handheld remote control unit. Within a matter of seconds, the player will seek out the specified track and display the corresponding picture or frame on the TV screen. This frame may be displayed as a still picture or as the first frame of a normal or slow-motion video sequence. The laser beam can retrace the same track on the videodisc a specified number of times to produce slow motion or to display a single frame on the screen. Single still frames may be shown for an indefinite period of time without any wear to the disc or player since the discs are read by a beam of light.

The CLV format places more than one picture or frame on the outer tracks of the disc, thereby packing twice as much information on each side. With 60 minutes of video on each side of the disc, it is possible to store most feature-length movies on one videodisc. However, the CLV format sacrifices the unique frame addressing, still-frame, and slow-motion capabilities available with the CAV format. The CLV format is used principally for entertainment applications, whereas the CAV format is best for hypermedia applications. The great value of the videodisc player as a hypermedia storage device stems from the fact that it can quickly access any single picture or sequence of pictures on one side of the videodisc.

In addition to standard film or television programs, many other types of visual or textual material previously recorded on other media such as filmstrips, 35 mm slides, microfilm, transparencies, books, newspapers, and magazines can now be recorded on videodisc. The two discrete audio channels on the videodisc provide stereophonic sound capability or allow the audio to be recorded in two different languages that can be played independently. Still frames, motion sequences, or audio information may be combined and intermixed in any sequence on a given videodisc.

Most videodisc players can be operated as stand-alone units similar to videotape players and can be used effectively by the teacher for classroom presentations. A videodisc player connected to a large screen monitor or projector can give the teacher considerable control over the presentation of still pictures, motion sequences, and sound. With the use of a remote control device, the teacher can instruct the videodisc player to go to a particular frame on the disc and display it as a still picture or show a motion sequence beginning at that point. By pressing the STOP key on the remote, the sequence can be stopped and further frames can be examined one at a time by repeatedly pressing the STEP key. Motion sequences can be shown in slow motion at various speeds, both forward and backward. Any frame on the disc can be accessed in a few seconds. The process can even be simplified further through the use of *bar codes* and a *bar-code reader.* Incorporated into the bar codes are commands that, when read by the reader and sent to the videodisc player, instruct the player to access and play a specified sequence. These bar codes can be prepared in advance and pasted into a lesson plan or script, as shown in Figure 8–10.

Many commercially available videodiscs—such as *Defensive Driving Tactics, Diez Temas, The Heimlich Maneuver, Choices: Learning About AIDS, French in Action,* and *Martin Luther King Jr.*—come with bar-coded teacher's guides. Several publishers (D. C. Heath, Prentice Hall, Glencoe/Merrill, and Holt, Rinehart and Winston) are correlating their high school biology textbooks with the videodisc series, *The Living Textbook,* by providing bar codes with their teachers' editions.

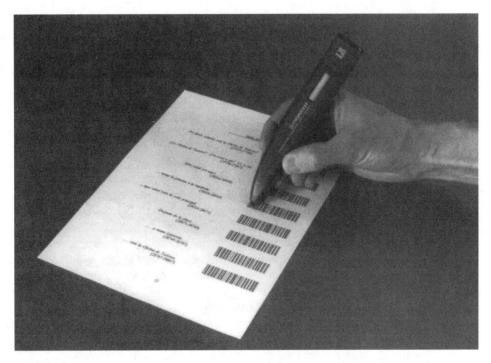

FIGURE 8–10   Lesson Plan with Bar Codes and Bar Code Reader

By attaching a videodisc player to a computer as a peripheral device, a very powerful computer-based hypermedia system can be created. The computer can control the operation of the player and videodisc by sending commands that instruct the player to display a specific still frame, play a sequence of frames in normal or slow motion, or play a particular audio track with or without the corresponding video display. Motion sequences in full color and stereophonic sound can be combined with still slides and computer-generated text and graphics into a sophisticated instructional program under computer control. The computer can be used to present questions or problem situations that allow the student to practice or apply what has been learned. Depending on the student's response, the computer can provide feedback by branching to the appropriate next sequence. A hypermedia program allows the teacher or student to select and play a particular video sequence, sound clip, or full-color still picture at any time.

Generally, computer output is displayed on one screen, whereas videodisc images are displayed on a separate video monitor. However, by adding an appropriate circuit board, called a *video overlay card,* to the computer, both computer output and videodisc images may be displayed on the same computer screen. It is also possible to overlay computer-generated text and graphics on the videodisc images. For example, a lesson on anatomy may display a still picture of a skeleton from a videodisc overlaid with arrows and labels generated by the computer.

Digital Video

The video information stored in the pits and lands of a videodisc is stored in a format analogous to the actual video frequencies. However, recent advances in technology have made it possible to convert and store video information in digital form, just as audio information previously stored on phonograph records in analog form is now stored on compact discs in digital form. The digitization by sampling of video frequencies is similar to the process described above with respect to digital audio.

Unfortunately, digital representations of color full-motion video require even greater amounts of memory and storage space than digital audio or digital pictures. For each second of motion video, 30 frames or pictures are required. Each video frame or picture of normal quality video of 512 by 480 resolution and 24 bits/pixel would require 720 KB. One second of 30 frames/second would require 21,600 KB (30 × 720) or 21.6 MB, and 1 minute would require 1,296 MB (21.6 × 60). Such massive storage requirements make digital video seem next to impossible. However, several compromises are possible: Reduce the resolution of the video pictures, reduce the number of bits per pixel, reduce the number of frames displayed per second, reduce the size of the video window, and use video compression techniques (Luther, 1991).

Since motion video is made up of a series of still pictures, the compression techniques described earlier for digital pictures can also be applied to digital video frames. However, the similarities across a series of video frames makes additional compression possible by coding all the information related to key reference frames and then storing only the differences found in similar adjacent frames (Goldberg, 1993). One of the standard specifications for motion-video compression is called *MPEG (Motion Picture Experts Group)*. If we compress the video information by a factor of 20, reduce the resolution to 256 by 200, and reduce the bits per pixel to 16, we will be able to store 72 minutes of full-motion video on a single compact disc (256 × 200 = 51,200 pixels per frame; 51,200 × 16 bits per pixel = 819,200 bits per frame; 819,200 ÷ 8 bits per byte = 102,400 bytes per frame; 102,400 ÷ 1024 bytes per kilobyte = 100 KB per frame; 100 ÷ 20 compression factor = 5 compressed KB per frame; 5 KB × 30 frames per second = 150 KB per second; 150 × 60 seconds per minute = 9,000 KB per minute; 9,000 ÷ 1,000 KB per megabyte = 9 MB per minute; 9 × 72 minute = 648 MB of storage for 72 minutes).

In addition to high-density storage, digital video requires that special software and hardware (circuit boards) be added to a computer to compress and decompress the video information. The required hardware and software are incorporated into the DVI, CD-I, and CD-TV technologies (described later). By making additional compromises, such as reducing the frame rate and reducing the size of the video window, Apple Computer and Microsoft have been able to implement the playback of digital video on Macintosh- and Windows-compatible computers without additional hardware. These software-only solutions are referred to as *QuickTime* and *Video for Windows*. QuickTime will run on Macintosh- and Windows-compatible computers, whereas Video for Windows is available only under Windows.

QuickTime.   QuickTime is a trademark used by Apple Computer to refer to a whole set of components that make it possible to manipulate by computer dynamic data or information that changes over time such as motion video, sound, or animations (Sydow, 1994). One of the major QuickTime components is a set of computer software routines that are an extension to the Macintosh operating system. QuickTime capabilities can be added to any computer program by calling these software routines. QuickTime also provides a standard file format that allows QuickTime files created by one program to be imported or modified by any other program using QuickTime. This makes it possible to paste QuickTime digital movies into word-processing documents, graphics programs, or presentation programs. QuickTime also provides a standard window format and control bar for displaying and controlling QuickTime movies, as shown in Figure 8–11.

The QuickTime window can be moved, resized, or closed, as any other Macintosh window. The control bar is located at the bottom of the window. By pressing the speaker button on the far left, you can turn the sound on or off. The right arrow button, next to the speaker button, is used to play the movie. The right and left arrow buttons on the far right may be used to step the movie forward or backward one frame at a time. The slider bar in the middle indicates the relative location of the current frame being played and may be moved to rapidly access a particular part of the movie. Some QuickTime programs may provide standard editing commands—such as cut, copy, and paste—to allow you to edit a movie. Portions of the movie may be selected by holding down the SHIFT key and moving the slider bar. The selected portion will be shown in black on the slider bar and may be cut or copied. The selection may then be pasted into another location in the same movie, inserted into another movie, or pasted as a QuickTime movie into another application.

With the introduction of QuickTime, Apple also provided several example utility programs for playing and editing QuickTime movies (*Movie Player*), creating Quick-

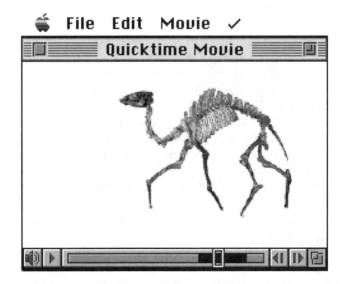

FIGURE 8–11   QuickTime Movie with Control Bar

Time animation movies from a series of still pictures (*Movie Converter*), compressing and decompressing still pictures (*Picture Compressor*), and digitizing or converting analog video from a videotape, videodisc, or camcorder into a compressed, digital QuickTime movie (*Movie Recorder*). The digitizing and compression of analog video into a QuickTime movie requires additional hardware in the form of a video-digitizer circuit board or a computer with built-in digitizing capability. In addition to digitizing motion video, the *Movie Recorder* utility program will also allow you to capture and store single frames from a motion video source. These utility programs are marketed by Apple as part of the *QuickTime Starter Kit.* Once you have digitized your movie, you may want to use a more sophisticated movie editing program than *Movie Player,* such as *Adobe Premier* or *VideoShop,* to edit your movie. These sophisticated editing programs allow you to combine several movie clips and sound files into a single Quick-Time movie; add special effects such as fades, dissolves, and wipes as a transition between clips; apply special filters to alter movie characteristics such as brightness and contrast; and integrate text, graphics, and animation into the movie.

As mentioned earlier, several compromises had to be made to provide a software-only solution for playing digital movies. These compromises included video compression, small window size, and reduced frame rate. These compromises often produce video of a low-grainy quality with jerky motions in a small window of one-quarter the size of the screen. These compromises are especially evident with slow computers. Fortunately, QuickTime has been designed to take advantage of better compression software and faster hardware as they become available. It is anticipated that in the near future, multimedia computers will be powerful enough to provide full-screen, full-motion digital video without additional hardware.

Hypermedia Hardware

The implementation of hypermedia requires more extensive computer resources than most other applications. These additional resources include more internal memory, more external storage, and more processing power or speed. The most important of these is probably more external storage, since the media elements of text, graphics, animations, sound, and motion video all have extensive storage requirements. Because of their high storage capacity, two of the most common peripheral devices used to store media elements are the videodisc and the compact disc. Videodisc technology was discussed at some length in the previous section on motion video, since videodiscs are most often used to store video information. However, because of their still-frame capability, they are also often used to store still pictures. The remainder of this section will focus on the various formats and uses of the compact disc technology.

Compact Discs

Compact discs (CDs) are very similar to videodiscs. They both are optical discs, since laser beams are used to record and play back information stored in circular tracks of microscopic pits on both discs. The same manufacturing facilities are often used to make both kinds of discs, and several players are available that will play either media. The major differences between the media are the size of the discs and the nature of the information stored on them. Videodiscs are usually 12 inches in diameter, whereas most compact discs are about 4.72 inches in diameter. A videodisc recording, like a phonograph record, is an analog recording. The pits and lands on the videodisc are created using a laser beam that is modulated by the original video signal just as the microphone diaphragm and the phonograph record grooves are modulated by the original sound waves. The pattern of pits and lands corresponds to the pattern of the video signal.

In contrast, the compact disc is designed to store information in digital format (McQueen & Boss, 1986). Since information stored on the CD as pits and lands represents numbers or binary digits rather than video or sound waves, the recording is referred to as a *digital* recording. When the CD is played, a laser beam is used to read the pits and lands in a manner similar to that described for reading videodiscs. Each transition between a pit and a land is interpreted as a 1, whereas the length of a pit or land is interpreted as a corresponding series of 0s. In the case of an audio CD, these numbers are used to reconstruct the analog sound wave curve in the form of electrical signals. These analog signals are used to drive loud speakers, which reproduce a replica of the original sound.

Compact discs are manufactured in several different formats: CD-DA, CD-ROM, CD-I, CD-ROM XA, CDTV, DVI, and PHOTO CD. Physically, all of these compact-disc types are exactly the same. Their difference is in the nature of the information stored on the disc and the format or structure of the information on the disc.

CD-DA

This format was designed specifically for the storage of digitized high-fidelity stereo music. It is used for the familiar audio CDs that have become prevalent in our homes and automobiles. Technically, *CD-DA* stands for *compact disc-digital audio.* This format was originally specified by Philips and Sony in a standards document called the *Red Book* (Pohlmann, 1992). The high quality of the sound reproduction from an audio CD is achieved by sampling the original sound waves at 44.1 kHz using 16 bits to quantitize each sample (as explained in the previous section on sound). This sampling rate exceeds that required to adequately reproduce the frequency ranges of human hearing. The high-density storage capacity of the compact disc makes is possible to store up to 74 minutes of stereo music at this sampling rate.

CD-ROM

This format is an extension of CD-DA standard and was designed for the storage of information to be read and manipulated by personal computers. This more general format is specified in the *Yellow Book* standard. The CD-ROM format is used to store computer applications such as *WordPerfect, Excel,* and *ClarisWorks,* computer data files such as word-processing and spreadsheet documents, graphics files created by programs such as *Coral Draw* and *Canvas,* digitized sound files, and digitized video. In essence, a CD-ROM can be used to store any computer file, much as a hard disk or a floppy disk. The *CD-ROM player* is very similar to an audio CD player except that it has an interface that allows the player to connect to and be controlled by a computer, and newer models read and transfer the information on the disk to the computer at higher rates of speed. CD-ROM players access and transfer information to the computer faster than a floppy-disk drive but more slowly than a hard-disk drive. However, the CD-ROM is removable and generally has greater storage capacity than most hard-disk drives.

CD-ROM is an acronym for *Compact Disc-Read Only Memory.* This name can be a little misleading, since a CD-ROM is an external storage medium and should not be confused by the internal read-only memory (ROM) of a computer. The ROM part of the name comes from the fact that the information stored on the disk is read-only and cannot be modified by the user. The CD-ROM is a valuable storage device for hyper-media applications because the disks are removable, and one disk can hold more than 650 MB of information. It would take over 450 high-density floppy diskettes to hold the same amount of information.

The *Yellow Book* CD-ROM standard only addressed the format in which information is physically stored on the disc. A further specification was necessary to define the file and directory structure of the information stored on the disc. A logical file standard was proposed by a group of vendors called the High-Sierra Group and later approved by the International Standards Organization (ISO) and is referred to as the *ISO 9660* standard. CD-ROMs that follow this logical standard can be read by all computer operating systems. By adding their own CD-ROM driver software, each operating system may allow users to access files on the CD-ROM in the same way they normally access files on a hard drive or floppy diskette (Luther, 1991). Since ISO 9660 is a lowest-common-denominator standard, some CD-ROM authors have found it advantageous to use the more sophisticated native file structure used by a specific computer operating system such as the Macintosh hierarchical file system (HFS). However, this practice restricts the use of the CD-ROM to that operating system. Hybrid discs, which store the files under both the HFS and ISO formats, can be used to overcome this problem. Unfortunately, this duplication reduces the amount of unique information that can be stored on a single disc.

Additional CD physical formats have been developed that could be considered as extensions or specific applications of the CD-ROM standard. Principal among these are CD-I, CD-ROM XA, CD-TV, DVI, and PHOTO CD (Pohlmann, 1992).

The *CD-I (compact disc-interactive)* format is specified in the *Green Book* standard. It is designed for a self-contained, mass-market, interactive-multimedia player. . The player can connect directly to a home TV set or monitor. Since the player contains its own microprocessor, it is not necessary to connect it to a computer. To optimize multimedia applications, the CD-I format specifies the physical interleaving of text, audio, and video information. CD-I provides for five different levels of audio quality, ranging from telephone quality to CD audio quality. Lower-quality levels are adequate for speech, whereas higher levels are required for classical music. Three different levels of video resolution are also supported. Since lower-quality audio and video require less storage space than high quality, the use of different quality levels makes it possible to optimize the amount of information that can be stored on the disc. CD-I players can also read CD-ROM and CD-DA discs. However, CD-I discs cannot be read by unmodified CD-ROM or audio CD players.

The *CD-ROM XA (extended architecture)* format is an enhancement of the CD-ROM format. It includes the CD-DA format, and some of the audio and video formats from CD-I. It is considered to be a bridge between CD-ROM and CD-I.

The *CD-TV (Commodore Dynamic-Total Vision)* format was developed by Commodore Electronics for multimedia presentations of text, graphics, animation, audio, and video. A CD-TV player is also a stand-alone system and is similar to and a direct competitor of the CD-I system. CD-TV discs will not play on CD-I or CD-ROM players, but CD-TV players will play CD-DA and CD-ROM discs.

DVI (digital video interactive) was developed by General Electric/RCA to allow for the recording and play back of up to one hour of full-motion, full-screen video from a compact disc played on a standard CD-ROM drive. The specification also allows for text, graphics, and sound to be combined with the video. However, both the recording and playback of video information in DVI format requires that special software and hardware (circuit boards) be added to a computer to compress and decompress the video information. The required hardware and software are currently owned and marketed by IBM and Intel.

The *Photo CD* format was developed by Eastman Kodak Company and Philips to provide for the storage and playback of consumer photographs from compact discs. Consumers may use their existing 35 mm cameras to take the pictures and have them developed in the standard way. They may then take their black and white or color slides or negatives to a local Photo CD processing center. The photographic images are then scanned and recorded on a compact disc. A compact disc can store up to 100 photographs. All 100 images do not have to be stored on the disc at the same time, since additional images may be recorded at a later time. The images are stored on the disc at several levels of resolution or quality. This makes it possible to view the images on a standard TV set, produce high-quality prints, or read the images into a computer for various types of image processing, editing, and display. Photo CD discs can be read by Photo CD players, CD-I players, and compatible CD-ROM players.

Although an expensive mastering and replication facility is required to produce large quantities of compact discs, consumer model compact-disc recording machines are available. These recorders allow schools and businesses to produce single or small quantities of their own compact discs in most of the previously mentioned formats. These recorders are very useful for producing discs for limited distribution or for testing a hypermedia application prior to investing in the replication of a CD in large quantities.

As mentioned earlier, the compact disc is a read-only medium. Once information is recorded on the disc, it cannot be erased or modified. However, related but incompatible technologies have been developed to allow for recordable/erasable optical discs. The most common of these is the *magneto-optical* system. This system records or modifies information on a disc using a laser beam and a magnetic field to change the magnetic orientation of minute spots on the disc. Such discs can be read through the use of a laser beam since the oppositely oriented spots reflect light differently. A lower-intensity laser is used for reading the disc than for writing, so that the reading process does not change the information on the disc.

Sony has introduced another recordable/erasable optical disc format called the *Mini Disc*. This disc is only 2.5 inches in diameter compared to the 4.72-inch diameter of the standard CD. The Mini Disc uses a combination of magneto-optical technology and CD technology. The magneto-optical technology is used to record and erase information, whereas the CD technology is used to read prerecorded, read-only discs. The small size of the Mini Disc makes it more portable than other erasable media.

Videodisc versus CD-ROM

This section has examined the use of the videodisc and compact disc as two of the most common media for storing large quantities of hypermedia information, such as text, still pictures and graphics, animations, sounds, and motion video. The videodisc is mainly used for storing analog motion video, sound, and still pictures. In contrast, the CD-ROM is used to store text, graphics, sounds, and motion video in digital form. Many feel that with the advent of the CD-ROM, the videodisc has become obsolete. Although this may eventually be the case, both media currently have advantages and disadvantages. There is no question that information in digital form has many advantages over the same information in analog form. Digital information may be easily edited and transformed in many different ways through the use of simple computer-based editing tools. Many different types of digital information—such as text, graphics, sounds, and motion video—may be combined into a single document or presentation under computer control. Information in digital form may be easily sent to other locations by standard telephone lines and may be rapidly accessed from network file servers.

The main limitation of digital information is its vast storage requirements. Often, these storage requirements mandate the use of compression techniques and other compromises that can lessen the quality of the information. This is especially the case with digital motion video. In many applications, the lower quality of the information is offset by the advantages of having the information in digital form. However, with those applications where higher-quality video is important, the videodisc may be a more appropriate medium. The videodisc will provide higher-quality video than either CD-ROM or videotape. In addition, the videodisc will provide faster access to a larger library of still pictures than a CD-ROM. With its 54,000-frame capacity, a videodisc can store many more still pictures than a CD-ROM. In most cases, the videodisc player can also access and display the pictures more rapidly.

Multimedia Applications

Now that we have examined the various hardware and software components of hypermedia, text, graphics, sounds, animations, and motion video, let's see how these components are assembled into real applications. Since the number of educational hypermedia applications is much too large for an exhaustive review, only a brief description is given of a few examples from each of the major types of applications. Additional examples are provided in other chapters. Although there is some overlap, the examples are divided into two major categories: those provided on videodisc and those provided on CD-ROM.

Videodisc Applications

With new titles being added daily, any categorization scheme of hypermedia titles will be limited. Nevertheless, some of the current major types of videodisc applications include full-length feature movies, educational films or videos, collections of still slides and short video clips, documentary footage and pictures of current and historical events, second-language acquisition scenarios, and tutor applications for education and training.

Most of the current popular movies shown in movie theaters are also released on videotapes and videodiscs that may be purchased or rented. Although most of the popular movies have little relevance for the classroom, there are some exceptions. Since any segment of a movie can be accessed within a few seconds through the use of a remote-control unit, bar-code reader, or computer program, videodisc versions of these movies are much more convenient than videotapes for classroom use. Short segments of a movie may be shown once or several times as a springboard for lively class discussions. Many educational films, such as the National Geographic films, are also available on videodisc. Again, the simplicity of player operation, the higher quality of the video and sound, and the durability of the videodisc make it a better medium than videotape for school use.

The large capacity of the videodisc makes it an ideal medium for the storage of large collections of still slides and short video clips. Many teachers have small collections of 35 mm slides that they use in the classroom. The main problem with such collections is that they have to be stored in multiple slide trays, and it is often difficult to find a particular slide. Inserting, deleting, or reordering slides can become a daunting task. Building an adequate collection of slides is also difficult. In contrast, it is possible to store up to 54,000 slides on one side of a single videodisc. Any one of these slides may be randomly accessed within seconds by just typing in its frame number and pressing the SEARCH button or scanning the appropriate bar code. With an appropriate computer program, a slide sequence can be created or edited with the ease of editing text in a word processor (see Chapter 11, The Computer as Tutee). It would be too expensive for one teacher to put his or her small slide collection of a few hundred slides on a videodisc. However, it would be feasible and practical for a large school district or consortium of districts to assemble all their slide collections and store them on a single videodisc. This would make it possible for each teacher to easily access his or her own slides and also share collections with one another. Several examples of commercial collections are described here.

The National Gallery of Art videodisc contains a still-frame database of over 1,500 images from the paintings and sculpture collection of the National Gallery of Art located in Washington, DC. The companion *HyperCard* stack (*The National Gallery of Art Laserguide*) includes a card for each work of art containing information concerning the title, artist, nationality, date, style, and medium. Each work is indexed by each of these categories and may be easily accessed through clicking corresponding buttons. The art works of the Louvre Museum in Paris are reproduced in a three-volume videodisc set titled *The Louvre, Vol. 1: Paintings and Drawings; The Louvre, Vol. 2: Sculptures and Objects d'Art;* and *The Louvre, Vol. 3: Antiquities.* These videodiscs contain

35,000 detailed still images of over 5,000 works of art and over 70 motion video commentaries on selected masterpieces narrated in French and English. Corresponding *HyperCard* stacks are also available. Other art videodiscs and stacks include *Van Gogh Revisited, Picasso,* and *Regard for the Planet: 50,000 Photographs by Marc Garanger.*

A *Hypercard* stack (*Bio Sci Laserguide*) is also available for the *Bio Sci Videodisc.* This videodisc contains over 6,000 full-color still images; some motion sequences, maps, charts, and diagrams covering life science topics such as plant and animal histology; vertebrate organ systems; cellular reproduction; molecular biology; ecology; and much more. *Windows on Science* is a series of eight videodiscs divided into three sets: *Earth Science, Life Science,* and *Physical Science.* The *Life Science* set consists of two videodiscs covering 12 units, including cell biology, genetics, plants, animals, and the various systems of the human body. The *Earth Science* and *Physical Science* sets contain three videodiscs each. Topics covered include geology, meteorology, oceanography, astronomy, properties of matter, electricity and magnetism, sound, heat, and light. This videodisc series is designed for upper-elementary and middle school students and includes photographs, diagrams, and movie clips that are narrated in both English and Spanish. The videodiscs are accompanied with a resource binder, a lesson manager binder, and a training videodisc. These materials provide lessons plans, unit summaries, lesson objectives, sample lesson materials, student activity masters, and a listing of every slide and movie clip on the videodiscs. Other science collections include *Chemistry at Work, Physics at Work, Anatomy & Physiology,* and *Evolution: Inquiries into Biology & Earth Science.*

The Apple Multimedia Lab has produced the *Visual Almanac* package consisting of a CD-ROM, a videodisc, and a comprehensive printed user's guide. The CD-ROM contains over 22 megabytes of *HyperCard* stacks along with music, narration, and sound effects. The videodisc contains over 7,000 multimedia objects. Each object may be a single still picture, a video sequence with or without sound, a sequence of related pictures, or a sound sequence. Textual information about each of these objects is included in the corresponding *HyperCard* stacks. The objects are organized into over 10 different collections, such as The Solar System, Everyday Physics, Earth View, Animals and Plants, American History, Historical Portraits, History of Daily Life, Around the World, and Everyday Objects and Studies in Time.

Space Archive Volume 1: Space Shuttle Mission Reports STS 5, 6 & 7 is an example of a documentary videodisc based on current events. It includes a compilation of film segments, excerpts of video transmissions, and over 800 color stills of the first three space shuttle missions. The audio tracks provide actual launch sounds, transmissions of flight and ground crews, and additional explanations and descriptions. An eight-page printed-image directory is packaged with each videodisc. Each motion sequence and color still is identified in the directory by a frame number with a description of the video and audio content.

ABC News has teamed up with videodisc companies to produce several videodiscs based on ABC's huge library of news footage: *The '88 Vote: Campaign for the White House, In the Holy Land, Martin Luther King Jr.,* and *AIDS.* The *Martin Luther King Jr.* videodisc includes video segments of such historical events as the 1956 Montgomery, Alabama, bus boycott and an uncut version of King's "I Have a Dream" speech.

Each videodisc is accompanied by lessons plans with bar codes, printed directories, and *HyperCard* stacks to facilitate navigation through the information provided on the videodisc. The software also allows teachers or students to organize and develop customized presentations

National Geographic, Lucasfilm Learning Systems, and the state of California have collaborated to produce a two, double-sided videodisc set titled *GTV: A Geographic Perspective on American History.* This set contains 40 video segments, 1,600 still pictures, and 200 maps. Themes covered include frontiers, exploration, immigration, settlements, conflict, cultural geography, political geography, communication, technology, and urbanization. A teacher's guide and computer software are also provided. Other historical videodiscs include *American History, Western Civilization, World History,* and *History in Motion.*

Videodiscs have been applied in a variety of ways to facilitate second-language acquisition. You may have noticed that several of the videodiscs mentioned on these pages provide narration for motion sequences in two different languages. This, of course, is made possible because of the videodisc's two audio tracks. The user can switch from one audio track, or language, to another by pressing a button on the remote control, sending a command with a bar code reader or pressing a button with the mouse in a computer program. Chapter 1, The Impact of Computers in Education, described the videodisc, *Montevidisco,* that provides a simulated visit to a Mexican village.

Many classic movies have been produced with two different language tracks and are used to facilitate foreign language learning and English as a second language. The classic Mexican film *Macario* (Merrill & Bennion, 1979) was one of the first used for this purpose. This film was selected because of its difficulty level and its artistic, cultural, and linguistic interest. While viewing the videodisc, a student can press a button to interrupt the movie. After the interruption, several options are presented to the student on a separate computer monitor. The student may choose to have the sequence repeated with English or Spanish dialogue, go to a vocabulary glossary, see a written transcription of the dialogue, respond to comprehension questions related to the sequence, receive historical and cultural information about the sequence, or examine aesthetic aspects of the movie.

English Express is a English-as-a-second-language (ESL) multimedia system consisting of eight double-sided videodiscs, a CD-ROM, teacher lesson guides, and teacher training materials. The CD-ROM contains computer software to provide interaction and practice activities with the text, 300 dramatic storyboard scenes, and 1,500 color visuals from the videodiscs. Dialogues from 67 thematic categories provide a "natural approach" to language acquisition. The teacher training materials offer model lessons, and the teacher's guides provide scripted lesson plans with bar codes.

Videodiscs can be incorporated into each type of tutor application: drill and practice, tutorial, simulations, games, and problem solving (see Chapter 4, Drill-and-Practice and Tutorial Applications, and Chapter 5, Problem Solving, Simulations, and Games). The sophistication and realism of simulations can be greatly increased through the integration of the visual and sound capabilities of the videodisc and the processing and dynamic graphics capabilities of the microcomputer. Such simulations could be used not only in education and training institutions but also on the job to assist both technical workers and professionals. For example, a computer program could lead a technician through a troubleshooting procedure to find and repair a malfunction in a piece of equipment. The computer could instruct the videodisc to display still frames or motion sequences illustrating various possible malfunctions. The technician could then enter data and conclusions into the microcomputer for processing. Once the cause of the malfunction is identified, the microcomputer and videodisc could lead the technician through the appropriate procedure for repairing the problem. A similar program could be developed to assist physicians and dentists in the diagnosis and treatment of patients. When a new medical procedure or piece of equipment is introduced, videodisc and computer programs could be prepared for on-the-job training.

An example of a powerful simulation application is *The CPR Interactive Training System.* This system consists of a videodisc player, a microcomputer, two monitors, and an adult "Resusci-Annie" manikin. The manikin has 14 electronic sensors that can determine correct placement of the hands, proper depth of compression, timing, and so on. The sensors allow the system to provide graphic feedback on the computer monitor of how well the student is performing CPR procedures. A physician on the videodisc provides instruction, verbal and visual feedback, and remediation based on the student's performance.

The Voyage of the Mimi is a simulation of an expedition on board a 72-foot ketch to locate and study whales. It presents a set of integrated concepts in language arts, social studies, math, and science through the use of print materials, computer software, and videodiscs. The videodiscs present 13 dramatic episodes from the expedition, while the computer software provides a variety of investigations for students to work through dealing with expedition themes. Students can also create their own reports using the software.

Math Sleuths simulates real-world situations where students are required to use science and math principles to solve complex problems. The videodisc presents 10 challenging mysteries and provides a variety of resources such as interviews with expert witnesses, photos, lab reports, graphs, maps, a glossary of formulas, and audio tracks in both English and Spanish. Students are encouraged to work in teams and must use planning, research, logical thinking, oral and written communication, and presentation skills in addition to math and science to solve the problems. Student's and teacher's guides with bar codes are provided with the videodisc. A similar package dealing with real-world science mysteries is also available under the title *Science Sleuths.*

CD-ROM Applications

This section examines a few examples of CD-ROM hypermedia applications within the following categories: reference works, electronic books, music commentaries, and tutor applications.

The storage capacity of a CD-ROM is often dramatized by referring to the fact that the complete text of a multivolume encyclopedia can be stored on a single CD-ROM. The *New Grolier Multimedia Encyclopedia* CD-ROM not only includes the text of the 33,000 articles found in all 21 volumes of the *Academic American Encyclopedia* but it also adds over 8,000 photos and illustrations, 325 full-color maps, QuickTime animations, and videos and sounds. In addition to the multimedia components, one of the major advantages of an electronic encyclopedia is the variety of ways to search its vast contents and rapidly access any desired information. Not only can you search by article title but you can also search by sounds, illustrations, movies, and maps. You can also search for all articles containing a particular word or combination of words. While reading an article, you can click the mouse button on hypertext links to follow cross-references included in the text. For example, if you click on Lincoln while reading an article on the Civil War, you will immediately be shown an article on Abraham Lincoln.

The *Microsoft Encarta Multimedia Encyclopedia* includes similar features. Its eight hours of audio include 350 music selections, samples from 45 spoken languages, over 100 readings and speeches, and hundreds of animal sounds. An illustrated time line of world history provides hypertext links to articles related to specific events. *Compton's NewMedia Interactive Encyclopedia* also allows users to pose search requests using natural-language questions such as Who popularized the automobile? Such a question will not only yield information on Henry Ford but will also give a list of articles on automobiles and transportation (Guglielmo, 1994). The *World Book Multimedia Encyclopedia* includes the complete text of the 22-volume print version along with 3,000 pictures, 260 maps, animations, videos, and audio. Dictionary definitions of any word in the encyclopedia are available by links to nearly 225,000 entries in the *World Book Dictionary.*

In addition to encyclopedias, many other types of reference works are provided on CD-ROM. The *Microsoft Bookshelf* CD-ROM includes a collection of reference works: *American Heritage Dictionary of the English Language, Columbia Dictionary of Quotations, Original Roget's Thesaurus, People's Chronology, Concise Columbia Encyclopedia, Hammond World Atlas,* and *World Almanac and Book of Facts.* Other more comprehensive dictionaries available on CD-ROM include the *Random House Unabridged Dictionary* and the *Oxford English Dictionary.* CD-ROM dictionaries often include illustrations and verbal pronunciations of each word entry.

Maps and atlases are also popular CD-ROM reference works. The *World Vista Atlas* contains Rand McNally maps of over 200 countries and 55 cities. Topographical maps, 1,000 color pictures, and music and spoken phrases from each country are also included on the disc. *Small Blue Planet: The Real Picture Atlas* CD-ROM features global and U.S. relief maps using very detailed satellite imagery. Political, historical, statistical, and ecological information is also available. *MapArt Vol. 1: USA & International* offers detailed maps that can be edited or modified in graphics programs (Guglielmo, 1994). *Street Atlas USA* provides street maps of every city and town in the United States. Rural backroads, lakes, rivers, parks, and railroads are included. Maps may be accessed by place name, phone number, or zip code. There is a zoom in and out feature, and maps may be printed at different scales.

Various types of electronic books are available on CD-ROM. Many of these applications not only include the full text of the book but they also include many hypermedia features. Discis Books has produced over 10 children's book titles on CD-ROM, including *Cinderella, Peter Rabbit, Scary Poems,* and *Aesop's Fables.* These CD-ROMs include full-color illustrations from the book, high-quality voice narrations in English or Spanish, and background music and sound effects. Children may click on a word to have it pronounced in both languages or to receive a verbal definition. Printed and verbal labels are presented when a child clicks on various objects in the illustrations. Broderbund has added detailed animations to their *Living Book* series with titles such as *Just Grandma and Me* and *The Tortoise and the Hare*. When a child clicks on objects in the illustrations, they perform some action with sound effects or spoken dialogue.

Electronic books for adults are also available on CD-ROM. *The Shakespeare Quartet,* mentioned earlier, provides the complete text of four plays: *Hamlet, Macbeth, Romeo and Juliet,* and *A Midsummer Night's Dream.* Other titles in the series include works of Mark Twain, Emily Dickinson, and William Wordsworth.

One of the most exciting applications of hypermedia combines a computer program and a standard audio CD of *Beethoven's Symphony No. 9.* The program is divided into five sections: (1) A Pocket Guide provides an outline of the major sections of the symphony that the user can select and hear by pressing the desired button. (2) Beethoven's World examines the historical, social, and political environment in which the symphony was created. Buttons are provided to allow the user to listen to musical examples from the CD. (3) The Art of Listening illustrates many musical concepts with examples from the symphony. (4) A Close Reading gives a continuous real-time commentary for the complete work. (5) The Ninth Game is a question-and-answer game for up to four players. A glossary with musical examples and a find-or-search capability is also provided. Figure 8–12 shows a card from this innovative stack. Other examples of music commentary CD-ROM titles include *Dvorak: Symphony No. 9 From the New World, Mozart: The "Dissonant" Quartet,* and *Stravinsky: Rite of Spring.*

Some of the old popular simulations, such as *The Oregon Trail* and *Where in the World Is Carmen San Diego?,* have now been enhanced and released as CD-ROM editions. With *The Oregon Trail,* students take a simulated journey through the early American wilderness and face the same perils as the pioneers, including snakebites, disease, and death. They must use problem-solving skills to make many crucial decisions that will affect the success of their trek. The storage capacity of the CD-ROM made is possible to add sensational sound effects, digitized speech, original vocal and instrumental music, and realistic graphics.

CD-ROM capabilities have also had a dramatic impact on second-language acquisition tutorials. *Learn to Speak Spanish* provides a complete course of 30 interactive lessons. Students learn to read, write, understand, and speak Spanish using QuickTime movies and digitized recordings of native speakers. Vocabulary instruction and learning is enhanced through spoken words and over 1,300 pictures. With a microphone attached to the computer, students can record their own pronunciation with that of native speakers. Other examples of foreign language titles include *Berlitz Think & Talk German, NihongoWare,* and *The Rosetta Stone.*

Using Hypermedia Applications in the Classroom

The videodisc and CD-ROM database collections described in the previous sections have many applications in the schools. Teachers can use them for classroom presentations to augment their lessons and class discussions. Students can conduct research on many exciting topics and prepare and present hypermedia reports to the class. Chapter 11, The Computer as Tutee, introduces several exciting authoring systems that can be

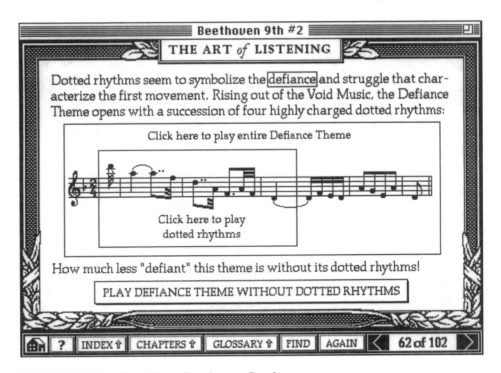

FIGURE 8–12   Card from Beethoven Stack

used by both the teacher and students to construct interactive hypermedia presentations and reports based on these collections. However, it should be remembered that these hypermedia collections only provide access to the information. It is still incumbent on the teacher and the student to determine what questions to ask, what information is relevant to those questions, and what conclusions can be drawn from the information. Some collections, such as *Windows on Science,* provide several teaching and learning aids, whereas others do not. Many are only an instructional resource or tool.

Hypermedia encyclopedias are generally best used in conjunction with their corresponding print versions. The hypermedia versions can be valuable tools in helping students find the appropriate information. However, the print versions are easier to read and include many more photographs. For example, the *World Book Information Finder* contains only 3,000 photographs; the print version contains nearly 30,000.

Although childrens' electronic books bring books to life, the cute animations might distract students from the text of the book. It is recommended that teachers turn off the animation option after students have had an opportunity of exploration. Depending on the age level, students should be encouraged to follow the text as the story is read to them by the computer, read along with the computer voice, or read without the computer voice and click on words they do not know to hear their pronunciation (Steed, 1994). Some of these products can also be used to help students learning a second language, whether it be English, Spanish, or Japanese. As with all computer-based applications, hypermedia should be integrated into the classroom curriculum.

Summary

Multimedia applications combine several types of media—such as text, graphics, sound, animation, and motion video—into a single educational application under computer control. Hypermedia can be thought of as an enhanced version of multimedia. With hypermedia, the user is provided with extensive navigation tools that allow for nonlinear and immediate access to any of the media elements at any time. The user is not locked into a linear or sequential presentation of information. Many of the media elements have extensive storage requirements. New technologies such as videodiscs and CD-ROMs can provide such storage. Videodiscs are mainly used to store motion video and full-color still images in analog format. Any one of the 54,000 video frames located on one side of a CAV videodisc may be randomly accessed within seconds using a remote control unit, a bar code reader, or computer software. CD-ROMs are a type of compact disc that use a format standard designed for the storage of digital information that will be accessed and processed by a microcomputer. In order to store sound and video information in a digital format, a large number of discrete samples of the original wave forms must be converted into a numeric representation. With the information in a numeric or digital form, it can be easily accessed, manipulated, and edited using computer-based tools. A large number of hypermedia applications are now available on both videodisc and CD-ROM. It is now up to educators to identify how they can integrate this exciting technology into their classrooms.

Exercises

1. How is the new multimedia different from the old audiovisual media?
2. What is the difference between multimedia and hypermedia?
3. Describe the difference between information stored in analog form versus digital form.
4. How is sound information converted from an analog to a digital format?
5. Why is it necessary to compress digital video files and what makes video compression possible?
6. What are the advantages and disadvantages of a hypermedia version of an encyclopedia compared to a multivolume print version?
7. Review and evaluate several different hypermedia applications.
8. Describe how you would integrate hypermedia into your own classroom.

References

Addmotion. [Computer Program]. Vancouver: Motion Works International.

Adobe Premier. [Computer Program]. Mountain View, CA: Adobe Systems.

Aesop's Fables. [CD-ROM]. North York, Ontario, Canada: Discis Books.

American History. [Videodisc]. Seattle, WA: Videodiscovery.

Anatomy & Physiology. [Videodisc]. Seattle, WA: Videodiscovery.

AuthorWare Professional. [Computer Program]. San Francisco: Macromedia.

Beauty and the Beast. [Video Cassette]. Burbank, CA: Walt Disney Co., Distributed by Buena Vista Home Video.

Beethoven's Symphony No. 9. [Computer Program and Audio CD]. Santa Monica, CA: Voyager.

Berlitz Think & Talk German. [CD-ROM]. Knoxville: TN: HyperGlot Software.

Bio Sci Laserguide. (1988). [Computer Program]. Santa Monica, CA: Voyager.

Bio Sci Videodisc. [Videodisc]. Seattle, WA: Videodiscovery.

Canvas. [Computer Program]. Miami, FL: Deneba Software.

Chemistry at Work. [Videodisc]. Seattle, WA: Videodiscovery.

Choices: Learning About AIDS. [Videodisc]. Chicago: Encyclopaedia Britannica.

Cinderella. [CD-ROM]. North York, Ontario, Canada: Discis Books.

ClarisWorks. [Computer Program]. Santa Clara, CA: Claris.

Compton's NewMedia Interactive Encyclopedia. [CD-ROM]. Carlsbad, CA: Compton.

ConcertWare+. [Computer Program]. Scotts Valley, CA: Great Wave Software.

ConcertWare+ MIDI. [Computer Program]. Scotts Valley, CA: Great Wave Software.

Concise guide to multimedia, The. (1994). Bellevue, WA: Asymetrix Press.

CoralDraw. [Computer Program]. Ottawa: Corel.

CPR Interactive Training System, The. [Videodisc]. Pittsburg: Actronics.

Defensive Driving Tactics. [Videodisc]. Van Nuys, CA: Aims Media.

Deluxe Music Construction Set. [Computer Program]. San Mateo, CA: Electronic Arts.

Diez Temas. [Videodisc]. Chicago: Encyclopaedia Britannica.

Dvorak: Symphony No. 9 "From the New World." [CD-ROM]. Santa Monica, CA: Voyager.

Earth Science. [Videodisc]. Florham Park, NJ: Optical Data.

'88 Vote, Campaign for the White House. [Videodisc]. Warren, NJ: Optical Data.

Elshami, A. M. (1990). *CD-ROM technology for information managers.* Chicago: American Library Association.

English Express. [Videodisc System]. Torrance, CA: Davidson & Associates.

Evolution: Inquiries into Biology & Earth Science. [Videodisc]. Seattle, WA: Videodiscovery.

Excel. [Computer Program]. Redmond, WA: Microsoft.

Finale. [Computer Program]. Bloomington, MN: Coda Music Technology.

Franklin, C., & Kinnell, S. K. (1990). *Hypertext/Hypermedia in schools.* Santa Barbara, CA: ABC-CLIO.

French in Action. [Videodisc Series]. S. Burlington, VT: The Annenberg/CPB Collection.

Gibbs, W. W. (1993, July). Practical fractal. *Scientific American, 269*:107–108.

Goldberg, R. (1993, November). The big squeeze. *Popular Science, 243*:100–103.

Great Quake of '89, The. [Videodisc]. Santa Monica, CA: Voyager.

GTV: A Geographic Perspective on American History. [Videodisc]. Seattle, WA: Videodiscovery.

Guglielmo, C. (1994). What's happening on CD-ROM? *MacWeek, 8*:31, 44–47.

History in Motion. [Videodisc]. Jefferson City, MO: Scholastic.

Hypercard. (1987). [Computer Program]. Cupertino, CA: Apple Computer.

In the Holy Land. (1989). [Computer Program, Videodisc]. Florham Park, NJ: Optical Data Corp.

Just Grandma and Me. [CD-ROM]. Novato, CA: Broderbund.

KidsTime. [Computer Program]. Scotts Valley, CA: Great Wave Software.

Learn to Speak Spanish. [CD-ROM]. Knoxville: TN: HyperGlot Software.

Living Textbook, The. [Videodisc]. Warren, NJ: Optical Data.

Louvre, The, Vols. I–III. [Videodisc]. Santa Monica, CA: Voyager.

Luther, A. C. (1991). *Digital video in the PC environment* (2nd ed.). New York: Intertext Publications, McGraw-Hill.

Macario. [Videodisc]. Provo, UT: Brigham Young University.

Macromedia Director. [Computer Program]. San Francisco: Macromedia.

MapArt Vol. 1: USA & International. [CD-ROM]. Lambertville, NJ: Cartesia Software.

Martin Luther King Jr. [Videodisc]. Florham Park, NJ: Optical Data.

Math Sleuths. [Videodisc]. Seattle, WA: Videodiscovery.

McQueen, J., & Boss, R. W. (1986). *Videodisc and optical digital disk technologies and their applications in libraries, 1986 update.* Chicago: American Library Association.

Merrill, P. F., & Bennion, J. (1979). Videodisc technology in education: The current scene. *NSPI Journal, 18*(9), 18–26.

Microsoft Bookshelf. [CD-ROM]. Redmond, WA: Microsoft.

Microsoft Encarta Multimedia Encyclopedia. [CD-ROM]. Redmond, WA: Microsoft.

Montevidisco. [Videodisc]. Provo, UT: Brigham Young University.

Mozart: The "Dissonant" Quartet. [CD-ROM]. Redmond, WA: Microsoft.

Movie Converter. [Computer Program]. Cupertino, CA: Apple Computer.

Movie Player. [Computer Program]. Cupertino, CA: Apple Computer.

Movie Recorder. [Computer Program]. Cupertino, CA: Apple Computer.

Music Construction Set. (1984). [Computer Program]. San Mateo, CA: Electronic Arts.

Music Studio. [Computer Program]. Mountain View, CA: Activision.

National Gallery of Art. [Videodisc]. New York: Videodisc Publishing.

National Gallery of Art Laserguide. [Computer Program]. Santa Monica, CA: Voyager.

Nelson, T. H. (1965). *The hypertext.* Proceedings of the World Documentation Federation.

New Grolier Multimedia Encyclopedia. [CD-ROM]. Danbury, CT: Grolier Electronic Publishing.

NihongoWare. [CD-ROM]. Berkeley, CA: Qualitas Trading.

Nyquist, H. (1928, April). Certain topics in telegraph transmission theory. *Transactions of the American Institute of Electrical Engineers 47*(2): 617–644.

Oregon Trail, The. [CD-ROM]. St. Paul, MN: MECC.

Oxford English Dictionary. [CD-ROM]. New York: Oxford University Press.

Peter Rabbit. [CD-ROM]. North York, Ontario, Canada: Discis Books.

Physics at Work. [Videodisc]. Seattle, WA: Videodiscovery.

Picasso. [Videodisc]. Irvington, NY: Voyager.

Pohlmann, K. C. (1992). *The compact disc handbook.* Madison, WI: A-R Editions.

QuickTime. [Computer Program]. Cupertino, CA: Apple Computer.

QuickTime Starter Kit. [Computer Program]. Cupertino, CA: Apple Computer.

Random House Unabridged Dictionary. [CD-ROM]. New York: Random House.

Regard for the Planet: 50,000 Photographs by Marc Garanger. [Videodisc]. Santa Monica, CA: Voyager.

Rosetta Stone, The. [CD-ROM]. Harrisonburg, VA: Fairfield Language Technologies.

Rothstein, J. (1992). *MIDI: A comprehensive introduction.* Madison, WI: A-R Editions.

Scary Poems. [CD-ROM]. North York, Ontario, Canada: Discis Books.

Science Sleuths. [Videodisc]. Seattle, WA: Videodiscovery.

Seiter, C. (1992, March). Image Compression matures. *MacWorld, 9*:146–151.

Shakespeare Quartet, The. [CD-ROM]. Knoxville, TN: BookWorm Electronic Books.

Small Blue Planet:The Real Picture Atlas. [CD-ROM]. San Francisco: Now What Software.

Snow White and the Seven Dwarfs. [Video Cassette]. Burbank, CA: Walt Disney Co., Distributed by Buena Vista Home Video.

Sound Edit 16. [Computer Program]. San Francisco: Macromedia.

Space Archive Volume 1: Space Shuttle Mission Reports STS 5, 6 & 7. [Videodisc]. Madison, NJ: VideoVision.

Steed, R. (1994, November). Personal communication.

Stickybear Music. [Computer Software]. Norfolk, CT: Weekly Reader Family Software.

Stravinsky: The Rite of Spring. [CD-ROM]. Redmond, WA: Microsoft.

Street Atlas USA. [CD-ROM]. Freeport, ME: DeLorme Mapping.

Sydow, D. P. (1994). *QuickTime Macintosh multimedia*. New York: MIS Press.

ToolBook. [Computer Program]. Bellevue, WA: Asymetrix.

Tortoise and the Hare, The. [CD-ROM]. Novato, CA: Broderbund.

Video for Windows. [Computer Program]. Redmond, WA: Microsoft.

VideoShop. [Computer Program]. Tewksbury, MA: Avid Technology.

Vincent: A Portrait in Two Parts. [Videodic]. North American Phillips.

Visual Almanac. (1990). [Computer Program and Videodisc]. San Francisco: Apple Multimedia Lab.

Voyage of the Mimi. [Videodisc and Computer Program]. Pleasantville, NY: Sunburst.

Wave for Windows. [Computer Program]. York, PA: Turtle Beach Systems.

Western Civilization. [Videodisc]. Seattle, WA: Videodiscovery.

Where in the World Is Carmen San Diego? [CD-ROM]. Novato, CA: Broderbund.

Windows on Science. [Videodisc]. Warren, NJ: Optical Data.

WordPerfect. [Computer Program]. Orem, UT: Novell.

World Book Encyclopedia. (1976 and 1994). Chicago: World Book.

World Book Multimedia Encyclopedia. [CD-ROM]. Chicago: World Book.

World History. [Videodisc]. Seattle, WA: Videodiscovery.

World Vista Atlas. [CD-ROM]. West Chester, PA: Applied Optical Media.

Yelton, G. (1989). *Music and the Macintosh*. Atlanta: MIDI America.

C h a p t e r **9**

Networks and Telecommunication

The power and utility of a microcomputer can be significantly enhanced through communication with other computers. A primitive, yet effective, way to communicate information between two computers would be through the use of a common removable storage medium such as a floppy diskette. The information could be saved in a file on a diskette by the first computer; the diskette could be transported in person or by mail to the second computer; and the second computer could read the file of information from the diskette and store it in memory for subsequent processing. Files of information that could be communicated in this manner include computer programs, student attendance and grade records, word-processing documents (e.g., letters and reports), computer graphics, computer databases, and spreadsheet data. Unfortunately, the diskette files saved by one computer may not be readable by a computer of a different model. Although many computers use the same type of diskettes, they store files using incompatible formats. Communication through diskette is also very slow and inconvenient.

A more efficient and effective way to transfer information between computers would be through the use of an electronic communication link, such as a cable, a standard telephone line, or a wireless connection using infrared, microwave, or satellite transmission. With the proper communication software, hardware, and connection lines, a microcomputer can communicate with other microcomputers, minicomputers, or mainframe computers. Direct electronic communication between computers is more rapid and has fewer incompatibility problems than diskette transfer. More dynamic two-way communication is also possible. Linking computers together for the purpose of facilitating communication and transferring information is part of the process called *telecommunication.*

Computers that are located in the same room, in the same building, or within a few thousand feet of each other can be directly interconnected through the use of appropriate cables. In order for such a connection to be made, each computer must have some kind of input/output port or network card. One end of a cable is plugged into the port of one computer, and the other end is plugged into the port of a second computer. Standard telephone lines may also be used for computer communication. However, before telephone lines can be used, the sending computer's digital signals must be converted into modulated audio tones that can travel over the telephone lines. A computer peripheral called a *modem* (see Chapter 2, Computer Hardware) is used for this purpose. A modem is also used by the receiving computer to convert or demodulate the audio tones back into digital signals. (The term *modem* is a contraction of *MOdulator DEModulator.*) The modem is directly connected to the computer via the input/output port and to the telephone line through a standard modular jack.

Special communication computer programs must be loaded into the memory of each computer in order for them to send and receive information. Examples of such programs include *Point-to-Point, MouseTalk, MacTerminal, MicroPhone II, Smartcom II, White Knight,* and *VTerm II.* Such programs are often called *terminal emulation* software, since they also enable a microcomputer to be used as a terminal to communicate with a mini- or mainframe computer. The communication software must be compatible with the modems used and the host computer.

Classroom or Laboratory Networks

When microcomputers were first introduced into the schools, each computer with its peripherals was a stand-alone device. They were totally independent of one another. As additional computers were purchased, it became clear that it was too expensive to purchase a printer for each computer. Thus, a printer would be attached as a peripheral to only one computer within a classroom or computer lab. Students working on other computers would have to copy their work onto a floppy diskette, take their diskette to the computer with the printer, and then print their documents. By adding the appropriate hardware, software, and cables, it became possible to connect each of the computers and the printer together into a *network.* Through such a network, each computer connected to the network could communicate directly with the printer. Students could print their documents from their own computer and were no longer required to transport their documents by diskette.

Computer networks were then expanded to allow the sharing of other expensive peripheral devices such as large-capacity hard-disk drives. By connecting a hard-disk drive to one of the computers on the network and installing special software on the disk drive, called a *network operating system (NOS),* the computer and hard-disk drive became a *network server* that could be shared by all the computers connected to the network. Depending on the services provided to the client computers connected to the network, a network server can become a print server, file server, applications server, or communications server (Madron, 1994). Each of these services may be provided by a single network server, or multiple servers may be required.

Print Server

A *print server* allows for more efficient use of a shared printer connected to the network. When a client computer requests that a document be printed, the document is sent to the server and temporarily stored on the hard drive until it is printed. Since the server controls the printing of the document, the client computer is free to continue other work without having to wait until the printing is completed. This is especially helpful when printing long documents. If two or more users attempt to print documents at the same time, the server will temporarily store the documents on the hard-disk drive and place them in a print queue. When the first print job is completed, the server will automatically begin printing the next.

File Server

A *file server* allows each student using the network to be allocated a certain amount of space on the hard-disk drive to save his or her personal files, such as word-processing documents, spreadsheets, graphics, or computer programs. Each student using the network is given an account on the server with a user name and a password. In order to use the server, the student must *log on,* or connect to the server by executing the appropriate software on their client computer and entering his or her user name and password via the keyboard. The *password* is a secret code, known only to the student user, which prohibits others from accessing a student's private files on the server.

Several students may be given access to the same account. This allows students to have access to common files. Students can be given different *rights,* or privileges, to various accounts. A student can be given read-write privileges to one account and read-only rights to another. *Read-write rights* allows a student to read or view a file as well as to change or write to a file. *Read-only rights* allows a student to view a file but does not allow him or her to delete or modify it. Thus, a teacher can place common files on the server that all students can access and copy to their computer but cannot modify, damage, or delete. Students working on a cooperative project can be given read-write privileges to an account where they can store, access, and modify project files.

Application Server

An *application server* is similar to a file server, but the files stored on the server hard-disk drive are applications or computer programs—such as word processors, spreadsheet programs, graphics programs, or computer-based education programs (drill and practice, tutorial, or simulations)—rather than data files. Students can be given read-only rights to these programs and access them from any computer connected to the network. This service minimizes the need to check out application diskettes that could be lost or damaged. It also minimizes the need to install application programs on the hard-disk drives of each computer connected to the network. When a new version of an application is released, only the single copy on the server needs to be updated. The purchase of a network version of the application is also much less expensive than purchasing separate copies for each individual computer. The server can monitor the number of students who attempt to access an application at the same time and restrict access to the number allowed by the network license agreement.

Communication Server

In a sense, the print, file, and application services could be thought of as communications services, since in each case communication or data transfer is taking place between the client computers connected to the network and the network server. However, this book will use the term *communication server* to refer to the use of a network server to facilitate communication between individuals working on separate client computers connected to the same network or providing access to individuals and services on remote networks. Because of the importance of these communication services, they will be treated in detail in the following sections. Before proceeding, however, you should remember that each of the services just described may be provided by a single network server, or multiple servers may be necessary.

Electronic Mail

An *electronic-mail* communication server provides for the storage and distribution of messages over the network from one individual to another. Electronic mail has the combined advantages of the telephone and the normal postal service. Messages can be transferred at electronic speed to a specific individual, as with the telephone, but the recipient need not be present when the message is delivered, as with regular mail. Messages are stored on the server hard-disk drive until the recipient wishes to read them. However, if a recipient is logged on to the server, he or she will receive immediate notification of the receipt of a mail message. Electronic mail can alleviate the common frustration of "telephone tag," where the caller leaves a message and, when the second party calls back, the original caller is not in.

As mentioned earlier in the discussion of file servers, each student or teacher authorized to use the electronic-mail (e-mail) server must have an account on the server and be assigned a user name. This user name becomes the address where mail can be sent. To send a message, you must log on to the server as explained under file servers. After logging on to the server, you may execute the e-mail program by typing in a command or selecting and opening the e-mail program icon with the mouse pointer. Some e-mail programs will automatically log on to the server for you when they are executed. Next select New Message from the Message menu. The e-mail program will display a form in which you can type your message, similar to that shown in Figure 9–1.

The form provides fields where you can type in the e-mail address of the person you want to receive the message (To:) and your own e-mail address as the sender (From:). There is also a subject field where you can type a brief title or the topic of your message (Subject:). If you want more than one person to receive your message, you may send a copy by including additional e-mail addresses in the field labeled Cc (for carbon copy). After you finish typing your message, click the send button with your

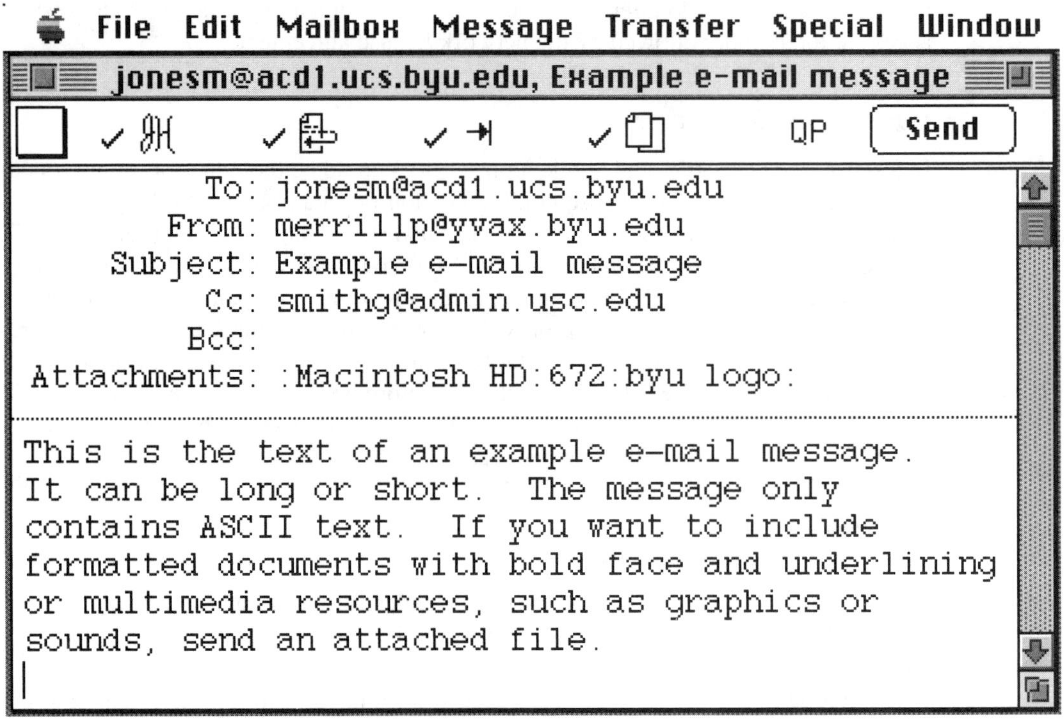

File   Edit   Mailbox   Message   Transfer   Special   Window

jonesm@acd1.ucs.byu.edu, Example e-mail message

☐   ✓ ℋ   ✓ ⊞   ✓ →| ✓ ◻   QP   (Send)

```
         To: jonesm@acd1.ucs.byu.edu
       From: merrillp@yvax.byu.edu
    Subject: Example e-mail message
         Cc: smithg@admin.usc.edu
        Bcc:
Attachments: :Macintosh HD:672:byu logo:
```

This is the text of an example e-mail message.
It can be long or short. The message only
contains ASCII text. If you want to include
formatted documents with bold face and underlining
or multimedia resources, such as graphics or
sounds, send an attached file.

FIGURE 9–1   E-Mail Message Form

mouse pointer. Your message will be sent over the network to the e-mail server and stored on the hard disk in mailboxes or files allocated to the recipients of the mail. When the recipients log on to the server, a message will be sent to them, notifying them that they have received a mail message.

To read your mail messages, log on to the server, execute the e-mail program, and select In from the Mailbox menu. A list of all your mail messages will be displayed. Each item on the list will show the user name or e-mail address of the sender, the subject of the message, and the date and time it was received. Double click the mouse pointer on the message you want to read and it will be displayed on the screen. After messages are read, they may be deleted, stored permanently on disk files, or output to a printer. If you want to reply to a message, select Reply from the Message menu. The e-mail program will display the message form on the screen (see Figure 9–1) with the sender, receiver, and subject fields automatically filled in. The message you received will also be copied into the message field. This allows you to include the original or a modified version of the original message in your reply and makes it easier to respond to specific questions or provide a context for your reply. Each line of the original message is usually proceeded by the > symbol, making it easy to distinguish between the original message and the reply. Your e-mail program may use different commands or menus than the program described here, but it will have similar functions.

Other e-mail functions include forwarding an original or edited message you have received to another person and attaching files created by other application programs with your mail messages. These attached files can include word-processing documents, spreadsheets, databases, and multimedia files (see Chapter 8, Multimedia/Hypermedia), such as graphics, sounds, animations, or digital video. However, you should take into account that the recipient of your e-mail will need to have the appropriate application programs in order to read and use the attached files. Most e-mail programs allow you to save a list of frequently used e-mail addresses. When you want to send a message, you just select an address from the list and it is automatically entered into the recipient field. You can also set up recipient groups. By entering the name of the group in the recipient field, all addresses included in the group will receive the message. This makes it easy for a teacher to send messages to all students in a class at once, or for students to send messages to other students working with them on a particular project.

Remote Networks

Connecting microcomputers in a classroom or computer laboratory together to form a network, as described in the previous section, allows for the sharing of expensive resources and facilitates communication between students and teachers. However, the power of telecommunication can be greatly expanded by extending network connections beyond the classroom or lab to remote sites. These remote sites can range from other classrooms and offices in the same school, to other schools in the same district or state, to other local institutions such as universities, businesses, and government agencies, and even to national and international sites. Each of these remote sites may have its own *local area network (LAN).* By the use of special communication servers, often called *gateways* or *bridges,* and appropriate transmission media (e.g., cables and telephone lines), these local networks can be interconnected to form *wide area networks* (WANs) or even a global network. By interconnecting separate local area networks together, greater resource sharing and communication is made possible. Teachers and students can then communicate with teachers and students from other schools and institutions. Students can work on research projects with students from across the nation and can interact with students from other cultures and backgrounds. A few of the expanding resources made available through linking remote networks are described in the following sections.

Internet

The *Internet* is a worldwide network. It connects LANs, WANs, and regional networks from all over the world together into one global network. Kehoe (1994) referred to the Internet as a "network of networks." It is the beginning of what the media refer to as the "information super highway" or "Cyberspace." The Internet was initiated in 1969 as a network of computers from four universities (called ARPAnet) by the Advanced Research Project Agency (ARPA), an agency of the U.S. Department of Defense. By

1972, ARPAnet had expanded to 50 sites. In 1986, the National Science Foundation (NSF) organized the NSFnet to connect supercomputer research centers. Eventually, the computers connected to ARPAnet and several other networks joined the NSFnet to form the basis of what we now refer to as the Internet.

The Internet has recently been opened to commercial and private usage and has experienced phenomenal growth in the United States and in over 40 countries (Smith & Gibbs, 1994). At the present time, since the Internet is subsidized by government agencies, universities, and corporations, its use is generally free to end users within those organizations. Others may be charged a fee to connect to and obtain an account at a particular site. Many public schools are accessing the Internet through dial-up modem connections or through connections to a local university. Some believe that by the year 2000, most schools in the United States and many homes will have Internet connections (Smith & Gibbs, 1994).

Internet Addressing

In order to communicate with remote computers and networks connected to the Internet, you must be able to refer to any specific computer linked to the network. This is accomplished by assigning each computer on the Internet a unique address, just as your home or apartment has a unique address. Internet addresses consist of a 32-bit binary number that is divided into four 8-bit numbers. For the benefit of humans, these four numbers are usually represented by their decimal equivalents separated by periods, such as

127.140.235.15

These numbers are not arbitrarily assigned. They specify the group, or *domain,* and the subgroups, or *subdomains,* to which the computer belongs.

Fortunately, Internet addresses can also be represented using alphanumeric labels instead of numbers, such as

acd1.ucs.byu.edu

The first subdomain label (acd1) is the name assigned to a particular computer. The next subdomain label (ucs) may refer to a department within the institution where the computer resides, followed by a subdomain (byu) indicating the institution. The domain label (edu) specifies the type of organization or institution. The alphanumeric addresses are automatically converted to their corresponding numeric addresses by an *address server.* To send e-mail to someone connected to the Internet, you must specify his or her user name followed by the "at" symbol (@) and the Internet address of the communication server where the person's e-mail is stored. For example, the Internet e-mail address of a student at Brigham Young University with the name of Mary Jones might be

jonesm@acd1.ucs.byu.edu

Some e-mail addresses may have more or fewer subdomains. For example, the e-mail address of the President of the United States is

president@whitehouse.gov

In addition to *edu* for educational institutions and *gov* for government agencies, examples of other domains include *com* for a commercial business and *mil* for a military institution. Computers outside the United States have domain names that stand for the country in which they are located: *ca* for Canada, *uk* for United Kingdom, and *fr* for France, for instance.

Internet Resources

By linking your computer or local area network to the Internet, you gain access to a wide variety of additional resources, services, and capabilities. You can send e-mail to anyone connected to the Internet, access electronic bulletin boards and news groups, transfer or download computer files (word-processing documents, graphics, spreadsheets, databases, sounds, digital movies, computer programs, etc.) from remote computers, and access an incredible array of information stored in remote databases. All of these resources are made available in the spirit of sharing and cooperation by the good will and generosity of those connected to the network.

Electronic Bulletin Boards and USENET

An electronic bulletin board is analogous to a physical bulletin board found in grocery stores and laundromats. Users are free to read any messages on the board as well as post any of their own messages. Computer bulletin boards are an extension of electronic mail; the communication, however, is many to many rather than one to one. Messages stored on bulletin boards are open to all registered participants, rather than being restricted to specific individuals. Computer bulletin boards may be set up and operated by a single individual on a personal microcomputer, a local computer-user group, a company, a university, a public school, or a commercial information service. A bulletin board may be open to the general public or restricted to members of a particular group or organization. Some bulletin boards contain messages limited to single special-interest topics, such as sports, science, or microcomputers. Commercial information service bulletin boards contain many different special-interest areas. Any bulletin board participant may leave a message, ask a question, or respond to questions posed by other participants. Messages may be completely independent of other entries or may be part of an ongoing dialogue or conference on a particular topic. Conference dialogues may be short lived or may continue indefinitely.

Computer bulletin boards can serve as important sources of information for school administrators, teachers, and students. Administrators can participate in a national computer conference on how to reduce student truancy, and teachers can use a bulletin board to find information on how to use Logo to help teach geometry concepts. Students have found electronic bulletin boards useful for communicating with students in other schools who are working on similar research projects. Bulletin boards have also proven to be valuable as forums for discussing computer programming problems, solutions, and techniques.

One of the most popular bulletin boards on the Internet is called USENET. The USENET bulletin board is a free worldwide information exchange service covering numerous topics in science and everyday life. Topics are organized in news groups, and these groups are open for everybody to post articles on a subject related to the topic of the group. News groups are like minibulletin boards inside the USENET bulletin board. When using USENET, a menu will appear with all the news groups posted. You then choose which news group you want to read. News group topics are usually pretty specific, ranging from modern English poetry to horses.

Before posting anything to a news group, be sure to read the posted messages to make sure the group is focusing on the correct topic and is at the proper level of complexity. Overly simple or off-topic messages many be ignored and will often make other news group users angry. If you cannot find a news group related to a topic of interest, you may request that a new group be formed. Such news groups will allow your students to get input from other students around the world.

File Transfer with FTP
Many remote servers connected to the Internet store a wide variety of computer files containing documents, reports, graphics, sounds, digital movies, and computer programs. These files may be downloaded or transferred from the remote computer to your own computer. To transfer the files, you can use a computer program that uses a standard method for transferring files over the internet called *file transfer protocol (FTP)*. After executing your FTP program, you must log on to the remote computer, where the files you desire to transfer are stored, by entering the address of the computer. The computer will then prompt you to type in a log-on name. If it is a free FTP site, you can type "anonymous." If it is a restricted FTP site, you will have to obtain a log-on account before you can retrieve any files. Once you are logged on to the remote computer, you can browse its directories to find the file you want. Then type "get" and the file name, or type the file name into the appropriate field and click the "get" button with the mouse. A copy of the file will then be transferred to your computer.

To search for files on anonymous/free FTP servers, you can use Archie. *Archie* is a database that contains a listing of free FTP sites and the filenames they contain. Archie uses a key word search to find all anonymous FTP sites that have filenames containing the key words you entered. You can then FTP to those sites to retrieve the files.

Gopher
Servers on the Internet contain a vast amount of information you may desire to view or read but do not necessarily want to transfer and store on your computer. Navigating your way through all this information in order to find what you need can be quite frustrating. Fortunately, there are several tools or services available to help you in your search. One of these services is call *Gopher.* This service provides an intuitive hierarchical menu system for accessing information on Gopher servers across the Internet without having to know the Internet address of each site. Most Internet sites have a lo-

cal Gopher server. When you first execute the Gopher software, it should connect you to your local Gopher server and display the local Gopher menu. The menu will provide a list of several types of information available on the local server as well as links to other Gopher servers around the world. When you select a local menu item, you will either be taken to a submenu or the information you selected will be retrieved and displayed on the screen for you to read. If you select a link to another site, the top-level menu for that Gopher server will be displayed. Now you can retrieve information from the remote server or link to yet another site.

Because of the great number of servers and information available, it can still be frustrating to traverse through many levels of menus to find needed information. A program called *Veronica* is available that allows you to use key word searches to find desired information. After entering your key word expression, *Veronica* will search a database of the menus of Gopher servers on the Internet and display a menu list of all the items it can find that match your expression. You can then select the items you would like to view.

The World Wide Web

The *World Wide Web (WWW),* also called the *Web,* is an Internet navigation system similar to the Gopher system. However, rather than using a hierarchical menu structure, the Web uses hypertext links. Web browsers, such as *Mosaic* or *Netscape,* use a graphical interface rather than a text-based interface. Gopher only displays plain ASCII text. Web browsers can display bolded and underlined text in different sizes. Web documents can also include hypermedia links to graphics, digital video, and sound files.

When you connect to the Web using Mosaic, you will first be shown your home page. While reading the home page, you will see highlighted or underlined words indicating hypertext links. By clicking on these words, you will be taken to another page or article that contains more information on that subject. For example, if you were reading an article about elephants, words such as *ivory tusks, endanger species,* and *zoos* might be highlighted. If you clicked on Ivory Tusks, Mosaic would take you to another article that focuses more on the use of elephant tusks. The article can also contain hypermedia links to full-color pictures, sounds, and digital movie clips, which can be accessed by clicking on a corresponding icon or button. Other hypertext links will take you to documents on remote Web servers or provide access to other Internet services such as Gopher and FTP. The Web also provides a search mechanism, called the *Web Crawler,* which works much like *Veronica* does on Gopher. It uses key word searches to find the articles you want and presents a list with hypertext links to the articles themselves. The Web has been principally used for information retrieval. However, it is quickly evolving into an interactive medium that allows for real-time communication between sites, and with the use of a feature called forms, a medium that allows users to post inquiries, respond to questionnaires, and even order merchandise. With all of these capabilities, the World Wide Web is rapidly becoming the preferred general-purpose interface to the Internet.

The number of resources becoming accessible through the World Wide Web is growing exponentially. The following are just a few examples of the variety of resources that are available:

1. NCSA's Digital Gallery
2. Library of Congress "Scrolls from the Dead Sea" Exhibition
3. College Hockey Computer Ratings
4. White House Interactive Citizen's Handbook
5. Proposed U.S. National Budget
6. North American Free Trade Agreement
7. Museum of Paleontology
8. Images from NASA's Planetary Exploration Program
9. Champaign County, Illinois, U.S.A.
10. Images, Icons, and Flags
11. Fractal Pictures and Animations
12. Rome Reborn: The Vatican Library and Renaissance Culture
13. World Newspaper Headlines
14. World Health Organization Press Releases

If your school or university is connected to the Internet, you can set up your own World Wide Web server and store documents and multimedia resources that you want to make available to other teachers and students in your own school and other Internet sites around the world. Items you might store on your Web server could include a calendar of school events; course descriptions and syllabi; rosters of teachers and students with short biographies and photographs; essays, poems, and songs written by students and teachers; and announcements and descriptions of special events. Figure 9–2 shows the Web home page which has been set up to provide access to such information related to the Instructional Science Department at Brigham Young University. Similar information about many other universities and schools is available through the World Wide Web.

Because of space limitations, only a few of the resources and services available on the Internet have been highlighted here; new resources are added daily. Consult one of the many current books that discuss the Internet in detail (Ellsworth, 1994; Fraase, 1993; Gardner, 1994; Kehoe, 1994; Smith & Gibbs, 1994; Wiggins, 1995). Be warned, however: The Internet is a great resource of information, but the information is not moderated. The Internet can also be a source of offensive and inappropriate information. Teachers need to be aware that giving students free access to the Internet gives them free access to some pornographic and other objectionable material.

Public Information Services

Commercial businesses that provide the general public telecommunication access to a wide variety of information stored on large computers are referred to as *information services* or *utilities.* Anyone may subscribe to these services by paying the current entry fee. Account numbers provide a mechanism for billing subscribers according to the amount of time they are connected to the computer system. Some of the more popular information services include CompuServe, America Online, GEnie, Prodigy, and Dialog. A description of these and other on-line services may be found in Eiser (1990).

FIGURE 9–2   World Wide Web Home Page

These services provide access to such information as the latest news releases, weather forecasts, airline schedules, stock market quotations, latest scores on sporting events, and electronic encyclopedias. Other information services, such as Dialog and Bibliographic Retrieval Services (BRS), offer electronic access to numerous library databases. Entries in these databases include bibliographic citations and abstracts of books, reports, journal articles, and magazine articles. These databases can be searched through the use of keywords. Ready access to such up-to-date information could prove very valuable to students, teachers, and administrators.

Public information utilities also allow users to execute a wide variety of software available on the large computer. Subscribers may even download or transfer public-domain software directly to their microcomputer from the large computer. Electronic mail, bulletin board services, and access to the Internet are also often provided.

Integrated Learning Systems

Microcomputer networks with large-capacity hard-disk drives as file servers have made it possible to implement integrated learning systems (ILS) that combine a computer-managed instruction system (see Chapter 10, Computer-Managed Instruction) with a large set of interrelated computer-based instruction programs stored on the file server. The computer-managed instruction system gathers, stores, and generates reports on the progress of students using the instructional programs. Teachers can set up class rosters and specify which lessons students may study. If a student does not finish a lesson during a particular session, the management system will place an electronic bookmark in the lesson and start the student where he or she left off at the next session. When a student completes a lesson, he or she will automatically be routed to the next lesson in the series or will be allowed to select the next lesson from a menu. Many systems include diagnostic and prescriptive capabilities.

Integrated learning systems may provide hundreds of hours of computer-based instruction covering many subject-matter areas across several grade levels. Companies that provide integrated learning systems include Computer Curriculum Corp. (CCC), Computer Systems Research (CSR), New Century Education Corp., Wasatch Educational Systems, and Jostens/WICAT.

The main advantage of integrated learning systems is their management capabilities. Also, once a school subscribes to such a system, the teachers are generally relieved from the arduous task of continually evaluating and selecting independent software programs. Most integrated learning system companies revise and upgrade their software on a regular basis. Disadvantages include the high cost of the system, a relinquishment of some control of the curriculum by the teachers to the computer system, and the low quality of some of the software. A comprehensive evaluation of integrated learning systems may be obtained from the Educational Products Information Exchange (EPIE, 1990).

Terminal Emulation

A microcomputer may be used as a terminal connected to a mini- or mainframe computer. Through terminal emulation, the microcomputer user can gain access to the sophisticated programs, speed, and extensive databases available on many larger computers. The larger computers may be in the same building or across the country. A school district may store information on students, teachers, and school finances on a mini- or mainframe computer. The principal and other authorized personnel can access and update such information from a microcomputer in their own offices. A teacher can access a database containing descriptions and evaluations of educational software on a large mainframe computer in the State Office of Education. Students can search a computer-based library card catalog from their own home. They can also gain access to sophisticated statistical analysis packages to analyze their research data on a mainframe computer at a local college.

In order to use a microcomputer as a terminal to a mini- or mainframe computer, you will not only need the appropriate communications software and hardware described earlier but you will also need authorization access codes, account numbers, and passwords. These special codes and passwords serve as security devices that limit access to the mainframe and specific databases to those who have authorization.

Location of Computer Resources

The location of computer resources determines, to a great extent, how they are used. The question is usually: Should computers be distributed to individual classrooms, or should they be placed in one or more centralized locations such as the library, media center, or special computer laboratory?

The Classroom

The most popular location for computers in elementary and secondary schools seems to be the individual classrooms. When computers are placed in classrooms, the teachers have control over their use. Additional personnel and space are generally not required. The teacher has immediate access to the computer for clerical applications, such as word processing and computer-managed instruction. The computer can be used for classroom presentations if a large screen or projection device is available. It can also be used by students on a prescheduled or need basis. If a single computer is to be used by both the teacher and students, it is usually helpful to have it on a table or cart with wheels, so it can be easily moved to different parts of the room for presentations, independent student work, and so on. The computer can be fastened to the cart with bolts or other security devices to minimize the danger of theft.

Unfortunately, the number of computers in schools is usually very limited, and those placed in classrooms generally go unused a substantial portion of the time. At certain periods of the day, such as during class lectures and discussions, computers in the classroom are usually idle. Also, with only a few computers in the classroom, students frequently do not have access to a computer when needed. Scheduling of computers must be carefully planned and monitored to ensure that all students in the class have a fair share of access time. It is difficult for all students to get a sufficient amount of time on the computers with only a small number in the classroom. In a class of 32 students, with two computers used four hours per day, students would average only 15 minutes of individual computer time per day. Also, students working at the computers sometimes distract others who are studying at their desks. This is especially the case if two or more students work together at a single computer. The distraction can be minimized by placing the computer behind a visual screen and by having students using earphones when using software that produces sound.

The Computer Laboratory

Placing computers in a centralized location such as the library, media center, or a computer laboratory has several advantages. With carefully coordinated scheduling, the computers can be used throughout the day, and if the lab is equipped with adequate numbers of machines, an entire class can have access to them at the same time. This facilitates scheduling and allows instructions and demonstrations on the use of a particular computer application to be immediately followed by practice on the machines. Time delay between instruction on the use of an application and the actual use of that application obviously increases the need for review of the instructions.

Another advantage of the computer-laboratory approach is that by consolidating computers in a central location, it is possible to share peripheral devices such as printers, graphics input devices, and disk drives. One or two printers would probably be sufficient in a lab with 30 microcomputers. However, if those same 30 computers were distributed to 15 different classrooms, many more printers would be needed.

The breakdown of a single microcomputer has less impact in a laboratory setting than in a classroom. A computer specialist who is assigned to supervise a lab is likely to have more training and skill in the maintenance, troubleshooting, and repair of computers than regular classroom teachers. The computer specialist can also help and advise teachers in the most effective use of the equipment.

Having the computers in a central location instead of in classrooms has its drawbacks. If all computers within a school are placed in a central laboratory, their use by teachers for clerical tasks and classroom demonstrations will be significantly reduced. The effect of this problem can be reduced by allowing teachers to check out computers from the laboratory for classroom use. Several computers could be placed on wheeled carts for this purpose. These computers would be available for student use in the lab when not checked out.

Other objections to the computer laboratory are that the computers seem to be used more frequently by the better-prepared students, the use of the equipment for instructional support tends to take a backseat to the teaching of programming skills, and laboratory computer-based instruction is not well integrated with the classroom curriculum. Some teachers may send students to the computer lab with little interest in or knowledge about what they do when they get there. These problems can be resolved by careful coordination between the computer specialist and the classroom teachers. The computing needs of each class should be assessed and appropriate amounts of computer time should be scheduled to meet those needs. Teachers should ensure that the computer activities are integrated with their classroom curriculum. Some computer time should remain unscheduled to allow interested students to spend extra time on the computers. However, care should be taken to avoid the monopolizing of this time by a few aggressive students at the expense of others who are also interested.

Probably the ideal situation will not be reached until each student has a computer at his or her desk. Second best would be to have a computer laboratory in the school where classes can come for whole-class involvement, plus a few computers in each classroom for access as needed for instructional support. Until such numbers can be acquired, each school will have to weigh the advantages and disadvantages of having one or more computers in the classroom compared to having them in a central location. In either case, it is strongly recommended that all computers in the school, whether in the classroom or laboratory, be connected into a local area network. If possible, the school LAN should be connected to the Internet in order that students, teachers, and administrators may take advantage of the immense resources and services available through international telecommunication.

Summary

Attempting to predict the future of technology is foolhardy. This is especially true when one looks at the changes that have occurred in the last five years. Nevertheless, one can see some broad directions that computer communications may take. First, it appears that a single turn-key hardware unit will be available that encapsulates a computer, television, telephone, modem, fax, and CD-ROM, with an intelligent graphical interface at each application level. Some of these features are appearing on the marketplace today. Second, downsizing the attributes and capabilities of mainframe computing to a wide area network of computers seems evident. The computer is allowing the user to communicate with anyone in the world with a choice of e-mail, fax, voice, or real-time video. This will require rethinking and possibly restructuring the educational system. Technology is truly making education an exciting and changing world.

Exercises

1. What are the benefits of connecting the computers in a computer laboratory or school together into a local area network?
2. Obtain an e-mail account and send a message to someone requesting some information in reply.
3. What is the Internet?
4. List and briefly describe the major services provided to students through the Internet.
5. Access some information you are interested in by using several of the Internet services you listed in the previous item.
6. Use a public information service to access some information according to your interests.
7. What are the advantages and disadvantages of an integrated learning system?
8. What are the advantages and disadvantages of placing computers in a centralized laboratory as opposed to individual classrooms?

References

America Online. [Online Service]. Vienna, VA: America Online.

CompuServe. [Online Service]. Columbus, OH: CompuServe.

Dialog. [Online Service]. Arlington, VA: Dialog Information Services.

DIALOG Online ERIC. [Online Service]. Palo Alto, CA: Dialog Information Services.

Eiser, L. (1990). Keeping in touch: A guide to online telecommunications services. *Technology & Learning, 11*(3), 36–43.

Ellsworth, J. H. (1994). *Education on the Internet.* Indianapolis, IN: Sams Publishers.

EPIE. (1990). *Report of computer-based integrated instructional systems.* Water Mill, NY: Educational Products Information Exchange.

Fraase, M. (1993). *The Mac Internet tour guide: Cruising the Internet the easy way.* Chapel Hill, NC: Ventana Press.

Gardner, J. (1994). *A DOS user's guide to the Internet.* Englewood Cliffs, NJ: Prentice Hall.

GEnie. [On-Line Service]. Rockville, MD: General Electric Information Services.

Kehoe, B. P. (1994). *Zen and the art of the Internet.* Englewood Cliffs, NJ: Prentice Hall.

MacTerminal. [Computer Program]. Cupertino, CA: Apple Computer.

Madron, T. W. (1994). *Local area networks: New technologies, emerging standards* (3rd ed.). New York: John Wiley & Sons.

MicroPhone II. [Computer Program]. Berkeley, CA: Software Ventures.

Microsoft Works. [Computer Program]. Redmond, WA: Microsoft.

Mosaic. [Computer Program]. Champaign, IL: University of Illinois.

MouseTalk. [Computer Program]. Canoga Park, CA: United Software Industries.

Netscape. [Computer Program]. Mountain View, CA: Netscape Communications Corp.

Point-to-Point. [Computer Program]. Emeryville, CA: Pinpoint.

Prodigy. [On-Line Service]. White Plains, NY: Prodigy Services.

Smartcom II. [Computer Program]. Atlanta: Hayes Microcomputer Products.

Smith, R. J., & Gibbs, M. (1994). *Navigating the internet.* Indianapolis, IN: Sams Publishing.

VTerm II. [Computer Program]. New York: Coefficient Systems.

White Knight. [Computer Program]. Beaver Falls, PA: FreeSoft.

Wiggins, R. W. (1995). *The Internet for everyone: A guide for users and providers.* New York: McGraw-Hill.

Wilsondisc Reader's Guide to Periodical Literature. [CD-ROM, Computer Program]. Bronx, NY: H. W. Wilson.

Z-Term: The Professional. [Computer Program]. Los Angeles, CA: United Software Industries.

Chapter *10*

Computer-Managed Instruction

Computer-managed instruction (CMI) is the label for a broad category of computer-based tool applications designed to assist the teacher or school administrator in the management of the instructional process. Good instructional management decisions are based on accurate and up-to-date information on the performance and progress of each student. Applications of CMI can be used to gather, store, update, retrieve, analyze, and report such information. As described in the database management section of Chapter 7, most CMI applications are special-purpose database management tools. Applications of CMI vary from simple gradebook programs to sophisticated diagnostic and prescriptive systems. Each of these applications is discussed in the following sections.

Computer Gradebook

A computer-based gradebook is one of the simplest and most frequently used CMI applications. Chapter 7 discussed how a spreadsheet could be used to record students' scores or grades on assignments and tests. Special-purpose database management programs have also been written for this purpose. Such programs usually provide a menu of options:

1. Begin a new class file.
2. Open an existing file.
3. Add student names to the file.
4. Add assignment and test scores to the file.
5. Retrieve and modify student records.
6. Delete student records from the file.

7. Print student records or class reports.

8. Exit program.

The first time the program is executed, option 1 is selected to begin a new class file. The teacher is prompted by the program to enter the name of the class, the name of the teacher, the number of the assignments or test scores that will be entered in the file, and the method by which each score is to be weighted to determine the final grade. For example, each assignment may count 10 percent toward the grade, each quiz 15 percent, and the final exam 20 percent. After the file has been set up, the teacher selects option 3 to enter the names of all the students in the class. If the names are entered in random order, the program will automatically sort them in alphabetical order if desired. Option 3 may also be used at a later date to add a new student to the file. If any students transfer out of the class, option 6 is used to delete their records. When students complete an assignment or take a test, option 4 is used to enter their scores. If errors have been made or a score is changed, option 5 is used to modify any student's record. Option 5 may also be used to retrieve and examine the record of a particular student.

Option 7 may be selected at any time to generate printed reports for individual students or for the class as a whole. The individual student reports may be given to the students and sent home to their parents. These reports show all assignment and test scores received to date, and they project an expected course grade based on the available information. At the end of the term, the student report shows the actual final grade for each student in the class. The class report includes scores for all the students and some summary information, such as the average score for each assignment or test. The student records can be listed alphabetically or according to the final grade. The student with the highest grade is listed first, and the one with the lowest grade is listed last.

Many good gradebook programs are commercially available. Examples include *MECC Grade Manager, Grade Busters 1–2–3, Gradebook Deluxe, Gradebook Plus, Bradford Class Manager,* and *Report Card.*

Many teachers feel that a computer gradebook is a valuable management tool, whereas others feel that it is just as easy to record grades in the traditional way. The main advantages of the computer gradebook are its ability to automatically compute final grades and average test scores and its ability to generate interim individual reports on student progress. The progress reports can be effectively used in counseling students and soliciting the assistance and support of parents. In using computer gradebooks on a microcomputer, teachers need to keep the data diskettes in a secure, safe place and maintain backup copies to avoid a loss of data. If the grades are kept on a central school computer, then a password security system needs to be used to prohibit unauthorized access to the database.

Test Scoring

Another popular CMI application is the use of the computer to score tests. This application has been used for years to score national standardized tests. Many colleges and universities have established centralized testing centers where students go to take tests that are subsequently scored by minicomputer systems. With the introduction of micro-computers, machine scoring of tests is being introduced into the public schools. Students mark their answers to test items on special answer sheets, which can be read by a mark-sensing or optical-scanning device. In the simplest case, the mark-sensing device reads and scores each test and prints the total number of items correctly answered directly on the answer sheet. By connecting the mark-sensing device to a computer, the responses to each item can be stored for further analysis.

After analyzing the responses to the test items for a whole class or group of students, the computer is able to produce printed reports containing the following information:

1. A list of students with their corresponding test scores is generated. This list can be sorted in ascending order according to test score or alphabetically by student name.

2. A list is produced of test items showing the percentage of students who answered each item correctly, the percentage of students who responded to each response alternative, the percentage that did not respond to an item, and the correlation of each item with the total test. This information can be very useful for improving the quality of the test. Response alternatives that attract few or no responses are poor distractors and should be modified. Items that most students answer correctly or those that most students answer incorrectly do not discriminate between students and serve little purpose on norm-referenced tests. However, such items may be useful for diagnostic purposes on criterion-referenced tests. Low correlations between an item and the total test indicate that students who scored high on the test missed the item and that students who scored low on the test answered the item correctly. Such items are usually misleading and should be modified or replaced.

3. Descriptive statistics are generated on the total test, such as the average or mean score, the most frequent or mode score, the median score (which separates the scores into two equal groups—high and low group), the range of test scores, the standard deviation (which indicates how much the scores vary from the average score), the reliability of the test, and the skewedness of the test (which indicates how much the distribution of the test scores deviates from a normal bell-shaped distribution).

Sophisticated CMI packages may combine test-scoring and gradebook functions into a single system. Once a test has been scored, each student's score is automatically stored in the appropriate gradebook record.

Test Generation

Another very valuable CMI application is the use of the computer to generate the tests themselves. The computer generates a test by randomly selecting items from a file of test items stored on a floppy diskette or hard disk. Most systems of this sort are made up of several different subprograms that are selected from a main menu. One program is used to enter test items into the database, another to modify or delete items, and a third to actually generate the tests. Before items can be entered into the computer database, they must be selected or written and organized into categories. Items may be categorized according to difficulty, topics, objectives, and so on. This organization makes it possible for the generation program to construct a test with items selected from each category.

The data-entry program requires the teacher to enter the name of the test item file, a label for each item category, the actual test items within each category, and the correct answer(s) for each item. After the items have been entered into the database, they should be printed out on paper and reviewed to identify any errors. If errors are found, the database can be updated by using a modification program. When the database of test items is ready, a generation program is used to print out the actual tests. The generation program allows teachers to tailor the test to meet their specific needs by entering the following information:

1. The name of the test item file
2. The number of different parallel test forms that should be generated
3. The number of copies of each test that should be printed
4. The number of items that should be selected from each category for each test form
5. Whether the items selected from one category should be printed together as a group or randomly distributed throughout the test
6. Directions to be printed at the beginning of each test

For example, suppose a teacher wants to generate a test for the second unit of a beginning Spanish class with 33 students. The test should measure the students' knowledge related to five objectives. The students can respond to only about 30 items in the time allocated for the exam. Some of the topics are considered more important than others. Therefore, 8 items should be selected for both objectives 2 and 3, 5 items for objectives 1 and 4, and 4 items for objective 5. To minimize opportunities for cheating, three parallel forms of the test are requested, with 11 copies of each form.

After the appropriate information is entered into the generation program, it randomly selects the requested number of items from each objective category and prints out 11 copies of the first form of the test. Two additional sets of 30 items are selected from the database for the other two forms of the test according to the same specifications. Then, 11 copies of each of these forms are printed. The program also prints a correct-answer key for each form.

Examples of commercially available test generation programs include *Study Guide Teaching Utility Programs for the Apple II, Create-A-Test, Test Generator, Test It! Deluxe, Test Taking Made Easy, Studymate: The Grade Booster,* and *Test Writer.*

The use of a test generation program in a standard classroom setting may not provide many advantages over a manual system. In fact, it may cause more work. The test item file should contain several times more items than will appear on any one test. The writing and selecting of so many items is quite a difficult task. The use of several different forms also makes the grading of the exams somewhat more complicated. With a manual system, the teacher need only prepare the number of items that will appear on the test, type the items on a duplication master, and run off the required number of copies.

However, a computer-based program for constructing tests offers many advantages when it is used in a class structured for instruction in individualized mastery. In such a class, students work at their own pace to achieve clearly specified objectives. To help them achieve the objectives, students have access to several alternate resources such as texts, workbooks, videotapes, computer-assisted instruction, classroom lectures and demonstrations, small-group discussions, and individual tutoring by the teacher or a teacher's aide. When students feel that they have achieved an objective or set of related objectives, they may request a mastery test over those objectives. After demonstrating mastery, they may begin to work on the next objectives in the sequence. However, if they do not pass the mastery test, they go back and do additional work on those objectives. When they are ready, they may take the test again. This cycle continues until mastery is demonstrated.

An individualized mastery instructional strategy clearly creates significant logistic problems for the teacher. How does the teacher keep track of student progress when each student is progressing at a different rate? How does the teacher maintain test security when students may take tests on demand and may repeat a test more than once? Computer-based test generation provides a viable solution to these logistical problems. Whenever a student is ready to demonstrate mastery, the computer can generate a unique parallel form of the appropriate test by randomly selecting items from the test item database. If a student needs to retake a test, the computer can generate a completely different test covering the same objectives. By combining computer test generation, computer test scoring, and computer gradebook applications into one integrated system, the testing, tracking, and reporting of student progress can all be automated.

Terminal-Based CMI

In all three of the applications that have been described, students do not actually interact with the computer. The computer is used by the teacher to generate printed tests, to score mark-sensitive answer sheets, and to record grades. However, CMI systems have been developed that allow students to respond to test items on a microcomputer or terminal connected to a minicomputer. The computer randomly selects items from a database and displays them on the visual display screen. The students respond to the items by typing the answers on the keyboard or using some other input device. The computer scores the students' responses and provides the total score on completion of the exam. The students' responses are also stored on diskettes for subsequent analysis. Some terminal-based CMI systems also provide feedback. After completion of the test, students are shown the items they missed, along with their answers and the correct answers. Correct answers are not given after each item because the answers may serve as cues for subsequent items.

Terminal-based CMI has several advantages and disadvantages in comparison to a print-based system. More microcomputers or terminals are required for a terminal-based system because it takes much less time to print a copy of an exam than for a student to respond to a test on a terminal. If many students must share a limited number of terminals, some students may have to wait a significant amount of time before they can take a test. Some teachers may feel that a limited number of microcomputers would be better used for other computer applications. However, we should not overestimate the number of computers required to implement terminal-based CMI. One computer could administer two 30-minute or four 15-minute tests per week to a class of 30 students. Either system would require some proctoring to ensure test security by verifying that the correct student was taking the appropriate exam. It would be easy for a student to take an exam for a friend on an unproctored system.

The logistics of a terminal-based system are simpler because there is no need to handle and control the printed exams and answer sheets. The constant noise of the printer is also eliminated. It is easier to handle short-answer or fill-in-the-blank questions on a terminal-based system than with a mark-sensitive answer sheet. Essay questions are extremely difficult, if not impossible, to score by computer. Such questions could be generated by either a terminal or print system, but they would have to be graded by a human reader. However, scores on such questions could still be added manually into the students' records stored on the computer.

Sophisticated CMI Systems

A sophisticated CMI system includes test generation, test scoring, storing of student progress data, and generation of reports. However, other features are also possible. A CMI system can be used to provide diagnostic prescriptions. The computer can analyze a student's pattern of responses and determine areas of strength and weakness. The computer can then prescribe what remedial action each student should take to ameliorate problem areas. As students respond to test items during a unit of instruction, they may also be asked to respond to an attitude questionnaire or enter comments concerning their evaluation of specific test items or instructional materials and activities. This evaluation information can be used to improve the quality of the instruction and test items.

Laws (1985) has developed a print CMI system that can generate letters to be sent home to parents. Using form letter techniques, each letter is personalized, describes the student's current performance in school, and suggests several activities the parents can do to encourage or help their child to continue to do well or to improve particular skills.

Many stand-alone drill-and-practice and tutorial programs, such as those described in earlier chapters, include some elements of CMI. A drill-and-practice program designed to help students learn the math facts may keep a record of student responses, provide remedial exercises based on the student's performance, and produce reports showing each student's progress. A tutorial program may include a test at the end of each unit that is presented and scored by the computer.

Several companies have developed integrated learning systems (ILS) that incorporate most of the elements of computer-managed instruction with a large and comprehensive set of interrelated tutor applications, such as drill-and-practice, tutorial, simulation, game, and problem-solving programs. These systems often provide a significant amount of the instruction for several courses, in addition to diagnosis, prescription, record keeping, and other management functions. Chapter 9 described integrated learning systems in more detail.

Considerations and Issues

Computer-managed instruction can be implemented at many different levels. The classroom teacher must decide which, if any, of these applications will increase the effectiveness and efficiency of instruction. When used to manage individualized mastery instruction, CMI is especially effective. Such a system significantly changes the roles of the teacher and the student. Teachers are no longer the focus of attention as presenters of information but are advisors, counselors, and monitors. Students must become active seekers of knowledge rather than passive receivers. Some teachers and students have difficulty adjusting to these new roles. If given too much freedom, many students procrastinate and fall behind in their work. This problem can be resolved through careful monitoring by the computer system and the teacher. The progress reports printed out by the computer can flag those students who are not making continual progress. If a student fails an exam over the same unit several times, the computer can instruct the student to consult with the teacher. The computer does not allow the student to continue until the teacher enters a special code.

Individualized instruction requires considerable investment in the development or purchase of instructional materials that carry the burden of instruction. The development of test item banks, diagnostic rules, and prescriptions are also very time-consuming and difficult tasks. The type of test items that can be most easily scored by computer may not be the type that best measures mastery of particular objectives. In short, the implementation of a sophisticated CMI system is not a simple matter. It requires considerable planning, creative problem solving, and resources. However, many educators have found the benefits to outweigh the costs.

Summary

Computer-managed instruction can be a valuable tool to assist educators in managing the instructional process. Applications of CMI can be used to gather, store, update, retrieve, analyze, and report information concerning the progress of students. A computer-based gradebook can be used to keep track of students' scores on assignments and tests, calculate final grades, and generate progress reports for students, parents, teachers, and administrators. Computer test scoring can significantly reduce one of the teacher's most time-consuming and often unpleasant tasks. In addition, the computer can provide valuable information about student responses to individual test items that can be used to improve the quality of a test. Computer generation of tests makes it possible for a teacher to implement individualized mastery instruction. Students can work at their own pace and take mastery tests on demand. The computer can generate a unique form of the test for every student. The implementation of CMI and individualized mastery instruction requires considerable effort and resources. If desired, a commercial integrated learning system can be used both to present and to manage significant blocks of instruction.

Exercises

1. Define computer-managed instruction (CMI).
2. What are the major advantages of a computer-based gradebook as compared to a manual gradebook?
3. How can computer test scoring benefit the teacher?
4. How is the computer able to generate tests?
5. How does CMI relate to individualized mastery instruction?
6. Describe how you would implement CMI in your own classroom.

References

Bradford Class Manager. [Computer Program]. Acton, MA: William K. Bradford Publishing.

COMsoft. [Computer Program]. Provo, UT: METRA Publishing.

Create-A-Test. [Computer Program]. Elgin, IL: Educational Resources.

Grade Busters 1–2–3. [Computer Program]. Discotech.

Gradebook Deluxe. [Computer Program]. Berkeley, CA: Edusoft.

Gradebook Plus. [Computer Program]. Northbrook, IL: Mindscape/SVE.

Laws, R. D. (1985). *COMsoft.* Provo, UT: METRA Publishing.

MECC Grade Manager. [Computer Program]. St. Paul, MN: MECC.

Report Card. [Computer Program]. Troy, MI: Sensible Soft.

Study Guide Teaching Utility Programs for the Apple II. [Computer Program]. St. Paul, MN: MECC.

Studymate: The Grade Booster. [Computer Program]. New Haven, CT: Compu-Teach.

Test Generator. [Computer Program]. Big Spring, TX: Gamco.

Test It! Deluxe. [Computer Program]. Berkeley, CA: EduSoft.

Test Taking Made Easy. [Computer Program]. Galesburg, MI: Lawrence Productions.

Test Writer. [Computer Program]. Ramsey, NJ: K–12 Micro Media.

Chapter 11

The Computer as Tutee

Previous chapters have discussed how the computer can serve in a teaching role as a patient tutor while the student takes on the role of learner or tutee. This chapter will show how these roles can be reversed, with the student becoming the teacher and the computer becoming the tutee. When the computer becomes a tutee, the student is given the opportunity to learn through teaching. The process of teaching the computer to perform a task requires that the student, as teacher, analyze and understand the task more thoroughly than might otherwise be achieved. Once the task is well understood, the student must provide the computer with an accurate and precise list or set of instructions for performing the task. This set of instructions is called a *computer program,* and the process of identifying and entering the appropriate set of instructions into the computer is called *computer programming.* Unfortunately, computers do not understand instructions written in normal English. Most human languages are too ambiguous and imprecise for computers to understand. Therefore, if you want to teach a computer how to perform a task, you must speak to it by giving it instructions in a computer language. Fortunately, computer languages have a very small vocabulary and their rules of grammar are quite simple compared to those of human languages.

Why should you or your students learn computer programming? You might argue that a person does not need to know how to program in order to use a computer effectively; and you may have no intention of becoming a professional programmer. The authors of this book agree with you. Few teachers or students will become professional programmers, and there are many commercially available programs that allow you to tap the power of the computer without knowing how to program. However, there are many excellent reasons for learning the fundamentals of computer programming that go beyond the obvious and immediate application of the skills.

To many, the computer remains a mystery that works by means of some "black magic." A knowledge of computer programming will help dispel much of this mystery and help you and your students understand what makes the computer work. This deeper understanding will remove much of the fear that is often associated with the use of the computer.

The pervasiveness of computers in our society make an understanding of how computers work an important part of your general education. You may not need to know how an internal combustion engine works in order to drive a car, or how the human digestive system works in order to digest your food, but such knowledge gives you a better understanding and appreciation for the marvels of the world in which we live.

Luehrmann (1980) stated that computer programming skill constitutes a new and fundamental intellectual resource. It is a tool for thinking and problem solving. Just as writing an essay requires that the author clarify and organize thoughts, programming a computer to perform a task requires that the programmer analyze and understand the task at a much deeper level. Papert (1980) has claimed that computer programming is by far the most powerful resource available for teaching children to learn by doing and to think about what they do. The systematic thinking and problem-solving skills learned through computer programming will find application in many other aspects of life.

Writing computer programs provides a new outlook on life's mistakes. Computer programs seldom work perfectly when first written. They often contain errors, or bugs, that need to be found and corrected. This error correction, or debugging process, provides an interesting challenge or puzzle. Even when a program works correctly, it can almost always be enhanced or improved. Students soon learn that bugs in a computer program are not "bad," nor do they make the programmer a "bad" person. Mistakes merely indicate that the program is not yet finished and needs to be fixed or improved. Such an outlook will help students respond positively and constructively to many of life's problems. Their mistakes need not be viewed as failures, but as indications that they have more to learn. This outlook could also help students to have more patience with others and show more tolerance for their mistakes. We all have bugs in our personalities and in our behavior. We all make mistakes—however, bugs can be fixed, problems can be solved, and mistakes can be corrected; we all can improve (Harris, 1969).

Computer programming provides students with a sense that they are in control. Many times, students feel that much of their lives is being controlled by others: their parents, teachers, friends, or circumstances. When they program the computer, they are in complete control. The computer will do exactly what they instruct it to do. They receive a significant sense of accomplishment when they see their "brain child" take its first steps.

Programming skills become very valuable in the use of computer-based tool applications such as spreadsheets, databases, and word processors. The analysis, design, and setting up of a spreadsheet is actually a high-level programming task. The functions entered into various spreadsheet cells are *programming instructions.* When you instruct a database program to sort a set of data or search for a particular group of records, you are issuing programming instructions. Many sophisticated word-processing programs allow the user to set up macros to perform a sequence of instructions that can be executed by issuing a single instruction. Such macros are nothing more nor less than computer programs.

The remainder of this chapter will introduce several types of programming languages and hypermedia authoring systems that can be used to instruct the computer as tutee. How to integrate programming and hypermedia authoring activities into the school curriculum will also be discussed. You will probably find this chapter somewhat more difficult and challenging than the other chapters of this book. However, you will be well rewarded for the extra effort by a deeper understanding of how the computer actually works. Besides, it is not all that difficult and it is fun.

Programming Languages

The computer has built into its CPU circuitry the capability to process information in several different ways. However, each different process the computer is capable of performing is very simple. In order for the computer to perform more complex and sophisticated tasks, it must perform a series of simple processes. This is also the case with human beings. We can perform very complex tasks, such as building a house, by performing a series of simple processes such as pounding a nail, cutting a board, drilling a hole, tightening a screw, and so on.

The modern computer was made possible by the discovery that each simple process it is capable of performing could be represented by a unique bit string, and that a series of processes required to perform a complex task could be represented by a series of bit strings stored in consecutive memory locations in the computer (see Chapter 8, Multimedia/Hypermedia, to review how a computer uses bit strings to represent information). The computer was then designed to consecutively perform the processes specified by the bit strings stored in memory. Each bit string, representing a single process, is referred to as an *instruction*. (The term *instruction* implies that the computer is an able and willing learner, or tutee, that will perform any process it is instructed to do by its human teacher.) A coherent series of instructions designed to perform a given task is called a *computer program*. By changing the bit strings or instructions stored in the memory of the computer, the computer can be reprogrammed to perform many different tasks. Thus, the computer is truly a multipurpose machine.

Machine Language

As already mentioned, every computer has built into its circuitry a small number of simple processes or instructions that it can perform. This set of instructions and the associated rules or syntax for their use are referred to as the language of the machine, or *machine language*. In order to communicate with the computer and tell it what to do, we must use the instructions (vocabulary) and syntax (grammar) that it understands. Before we consider some of these simple instructions, we must understand a little more about the hardware that performs these processes. The following description is based on the Apple IIe computer, because of its simplicity, but the concepts involved also apply to most other computers.

The CPU of the computer contains a special-purpose storage location or register referred to as the *accumulator,* or *A register.* (Some computers have multiple accumulator-type registers.) Nearly all data that are processed by the computer pass through the accumulator. Before data can be stored in the memory of the computer, they are entered into the accumulator through some input device such as a keyboard. Data are then transferred from the accumulator to a specified memory location. To process the data in memory, the data are first retrieved from memory and placed in the accumulator. From there, the data may be transferred to another memory location, sent to some output device such as the screen or printer, or processed in some way. Let's now examine some of the machine language instructions that are used to tell the computer to perform some of these simple processes.

Two of the most basic machine language instructions are the store and load instructions. The *store instruction* is represented by the bit string 10000101. This instruction tells the computer to store or transfer the contents of the accumulator to a specific memory location. This memory location is specified or represented by another bit string given immediately following the instruction. Thus, the syntax of an instruction often requires two consecutive bit strings: the first to specify the instruction and the second to indicate the address where the data are to be stored or from where the data are to be retrieved. The first bit string representing the instruction is referred to as the *operation code,* or *op code,* indicating the operation or process to be performed. The second string is referred to as the *operand,* indicating the memory location being operated upon.

The *load instruction* is represented by the bit string 10101101. This instruction tells the computer to copy or retrieve data from a specified memory location into the accumulator. As with the store instruction, the memory location is specified by an operand bit string found immediately following the instruction. Another version of the load instruction, 10101001, can be used to tell the computer to store the actual value represented by the subsequent operand bit string directly into the accumulator. The following is an example of a machine language program that contains the instructions required to tell the computer to add the numbers 5 and 3 and to store the result in memory location 64. The second column provides an explanation for each instruction but is not part of the actual program.

Instruction: *Operation Codes* *and Operands*	*Explanation*
10101001 00000101	Load accumulator with the following value (5)
01101001 00000011	Add the following value to the contents of the accumulator (3)
10000101	Store the contents of the accumulator in the following memory location
01000000	(64)

Assembly Language

Learning the 120 different bit strings that represent the machine language instructions for the Apple IIe computer (some computers may have more or fewer instructions) would be a very difficult, if not an impossible, task. Fortunately, it is possible to write a computer program using a more meaningful alphabetic representation of the instructions and then have a computer program, called an *assembler,* translate the alphabetic instructions into the machine language bit strings. The alphabetic instructions are referred to as assembly language instructions. For example, the assembly language instruction *STA* is used to refer to the store accumulator instruction (10000101), whereas *LDA* is used to refer to the load accumulator instruction (10101001). In assembly language, the operands may be specified using more meaningful decimal numbers rather than the binary bit strings. The following table shows an assembly language version of a program to add the numbers 5 and 3 shown previously.

Assembly Language	*Machine Language*	*Explanation*
LDA #05	10101001 00000101	Load accumulator with the number 5
ADC #03	01101001 00000011	Add the number 3 to the contents of the accumulator
STA 64	10000101 01000000	Store the contents of the accumulator in memory location 64

Note: A number without a preceding pound sign indicates the address of a memory location, whereas a number preceded by a pound sign refers to an actual value that is to be loaded or added to the accumulator.

Screen Display

The program shown here does not provide any mechanism for us to see the result of the calculation. We need to add some instructions that will tell the computer to transfer the result stored in memory location 64 to some output device, such as the screen or the printer. Most computer monitors or screens will display 24 to 25 lines of text with up to 80 characters per line in standard text mode. Some computers provide other text modes for displaying 40 characters or 132 characters per line. In each case, a certain section of the memory of the computer is set aside for the screen display. One memory location is allocated for each character location on the screen. Thus, 960 memory locations would be required to display 24 lines with 40 characters on each line. On the Apple IIe computer, memory location 1024 corresponds to the first character on the first line, location 1025 corresponds to the second character on the first line, location 1026 corresponds to the third character, and so forth. To display a character on the screen, we merely have to instruct the computer to store the bit string representing the desired character in the appropriate memory location. If we store the bit string 01000011 in memory location 1024, we will see the character *C* in the upper left-hand corner of the screen. The computer circuitry is designed to repeatedly scan the section of memory dedicated to the screen and use the values stored there to determine what to display on the screen. If we change a value stored in one of these memory locations, we will change the character on the screen.

As described previously, there must be a unique bit string for each character that we want to display on the screen. The following table shows the bit strings that correspond to a few of the capital letters of the alphabet. These particular bit strings have been accepted as a standard representation for the letters of the alphabet and are referred to as *ASCII (American Standard Code for Information Interchange) codes.* The decimal number (base ten) equivalent for each of these codes is shown in the third column of the table. There are additional codes for lowercase letters and punctuation marks.

Character	ASCII Code Bit String	ASCII Code Decimal Number
A	01000001	65
B	01000010	66
C	01000011	67
D	01000100	68
...	...	...
H	01001000	72
...	...	...
L	01001100	76
M	01001101	77
N	01001110	78
O	01001111	79
...	...	...
S	01010100	83
...	...	...
Y	01011010	89
Z	01011011	90

The following assembly language program will display the word *SCHOOL* on the first line in the middle of the screen.

Assembly Language	Explanation
LDA #83	Load the accumulator with the ASCII code for the capital letter *S*.
STA 1040	Store the value in the accumulator in memory location 1040, which will cause the letter *S* to appear on the screen.
LDA #67	Load the code for the letter *C*.
STA 1041	Store it in location 1041.
LDA #72	Load the code for the letter *H*.

Assembly Language	*Explanation*
STA 1042	Store it in location 1042.
LDA #79	Load the code for the letter *O*.
STA 1043	Store it in location 1043.
STA 1044	Since storing a value does not remove it from the accumulator, it need not be reloaded. It is just stored again in the next location.
LDA #76	Load the code for the letter *L*.
STA 1045	Store it in location 1045.

Note: On the Apple IIe computer, this program will actually display the word *SCHOOL* in flashing characters. To get normal white characters on a black background, we would add 128 to each of the ASCII codes shown here. (This is one of those cases where the computer designer did something backwards just to drive us all crazy.)

High-Level Languages

As you can see from these examples, programming in assembly language, though easier than machine language, can be quite tedious. It seems to take a great deal of effort to get the computer to do anything. Fortunately, assembly language programming is not quite as bad as the examples selected might indicate. Modern assemblers (programs that translate assembly language programs into machine language) provide many aids that ease the burden of the programmer. Over the years, assembly language programmers found that certain sets of assembly language instructions—those that performed a specific task—could be copied and used in many different programs. This identification of sets of instructions to perform a specific task led to the development of higher-level languages that allowed programmers to tell the computer to perform more complex processes with a single instruction. Through the use of more Englishlike instructions, the higher-level languages also became more meaningful and easier to learn and remember.

Many different higher-level languages have been developed. Like a mechanic's tools, some languages are better suited for one task than for another. Logo, for instance, is an excellent high-level language for teaching the basics of programming and for improving problem-solving skills. FORTRAN is used in scientific computing, COBOL in business applications, and LISP in artificial intelligence research. PILOT is designed to help teachers generate computer-based lessons. BASIC, Pascal, and C are general-purpose languages that are used for a wide variety of applications for business, school, and the home.

BASIC was one of the most popular and pervasive high-level languages. It was usually provided free of charge with the first microcomputers. To better understand the relationship between high-level languages and assembly language, let's look at the BASIC instructions required to tell the computer to display information on the screen and to perform computations. You will recall that it took 11 assembly language instructions to display the word *SCHOOL* on the screen. In BASIC, we can tell the computer to perform the same task using the following single instruction:

PRINT "SCHOOL"

That's it. That's all there is to it. And you thought programming was going to be difficult! Actually, programming is just as easy as telling your little brother to take out the garbage. In fact, it is easier; the computer won't whine or argue with you. It will follow your every instruction without hesitation, as long as you speak to it in a language it understands. The following instruction will add the numbers 5 and 3 and display the results on the screen:

PRINT 5 + 3

Note that in a high-level language, you generally do not have to worry about ASCII codes or memory locations. The instructions are easy to understand and you can use familiar mathematical notation.

Compilers and Interpreters

Actually, computers do not understand high-level languages. Since they can only execute machine language instructions, programs written in other languages must be translated into machine language. We have already seen that a program that translates assembly language programs is called an assembler. There are two different types of programs that translate high-level languages: interpreters and compilers. With an *interpreter,* the high-level instructions are translated into machine language as the program is executing. Each instruction in a program is translated and then executed one at a time. In contrast, a *compiler* translates all of the instructions in a program prior to its execution. This distinction is similar to the difference between having someone translate what an individual is saying as they speak versus translating the entire text of a speech before it is given.

Compiled programs execute faster than interpreted programs because the translation process has already been done. However, when a change is made to a compiled program, the entire program must be recompiled or retranslated before it can be executed again. With an interpreter, the program can be executed immediately after a change has been made without waiting for a recompilation. All else being equal, interpreted programs are easier to develop and modify, whereas compiled programs execute faster. Most versions of FORTRAN, Pascal, and C are compiled, whereas BASIC, Logo, and PILOT are usually interpreted. However, both interpreters and compilers may exist for various versions of the same language.

Major Programming Components

Although there are many different high-level programming languages, there are certain major features, capabilities, and components common to all of them. Each language must provide instructions to obtain information from the outside world through input peripherals that are part of the computer system, such as the keyboard, mouse, paddles, disk drive, or CD-ROM. A language must also provide instructions to store and retrieve information from the memory of the computer and then process that information. Finally, instructions must be available to communicate the results of the information processing to the outside world to output devices such as a monitor or screen, printer, plotter, modem, or disk drive. In other words, a computer language must provide instructions for input, processing, and output.

Let's look at how each of these major capabilities is implemented in three of the high-level languages most commonly used in the schools: BASIC, Pascal, and Logo. Unfortunately, just as there are different dialects of English and Spanish, there are also different dialects of computer languages. Most languages have a minimal standard set of instructions that are the same across different dialects. However, each dialect of a language may have different extensions to the standard that take advantage of the unique characteristics of a particular brand of computer. For purposes of this comparison, the following dialects will be used: *Applesoft BASIC,* available on the Apple IIe computer; *LogoWriter,* available on IBM, Apple, and Commodore computers; and *Think Pascal,* available on the Apple Macintosh computer.

Output

We have already seen the BASIC instruction for outputting textual information on the computer monitor or screen. Similar instructions are available in Pascal and Logo:

Language	*Example*
BASIC	PRINT "It is fun to learn a computer language"
Pascal	WRITELN ('It is fun to learn a computer language');
Logo	PRINT [It is fun to learn a computer language]

Note that each language not only uses different vocabulary for the instruction but also requires different syntax or punctuation. The vocabulary and syntax requirements of a computer language are very specific. If an instruction is misspelled or if the wrong punctuation is used, the compiler or interpreter will not be able to translate the instruction and will give a syntax error message. The programmer must correct the error (bug) before the computer will be able to translate and execute the program.

Most computer languages also have instructions to output graphical information on the screen. To display graphics, the computer screen is divided into rows and columns of tiny dots of light, called *pixels.* Each pixel is like a lightbulb on a football scoreboard or an electronic billboard sign. On the Apple IIe in High Resolution Graphics mode, there are 160 rows with 280 pixels or columns in each row. To draw a graphic figure on the screen, we must specify which pixels are to be turned on and which are to be turned off. Each pixel can be uniquely specified by giving its row and column location, called its *coordinates.* In BASIC, the pixel at the upper-left corner of the screen is considered the origin and has the coordinates 0,0. The number of the horizontal column or coordinate is given first, followed by a comma, and then the number of the vertical row or coordinate. The horizontal coordinates increase in value from left to right and the vertical coordinates increase from top to bottom. The following BASIC instruction will turn on the pixel that intersects the third column and the fifth row:

    HPLOT 2,4

Remember that the columns and rows are numbered beginning with zero.

Turning on and off each individual pixel one at a time would be slow and tedious. Fortunately, BASIC will allow us to draw a line by specifying its beginning and ending points. The following instruction will draw a diagonal line from the upper-left corner of the screen to the bottom-right corner.

    HPLOT 0,0 to 279,159

There is also a instruction to specify the color of the lines or dots. The following instruction sets the color to green:

    HCOLOR = 1

The following BASIC program instructions will draw a square of 50 pixels per side on the screen:

BASIC instructions	Explanation
HGR	Switch to high-resolution graphics.
HCOLOR = 2	Set color to blue.
HPLOT 50,50 to 100,50	Draw the top line of the square.
HPLOT 100,50 to 100,100	Draw the right side of the square.
HPLOT 100,100 to 50,100	Draw the bottom line of the square.
HPLOT 50,100 to 50,50	Draw the left side of the square.

The Logo language uses an approach to graphics called *Turtlegraphics,* devised by Seymour Papert and his colleagues at the Massachusetts Institute of Technology. This unique approach was developed to make it easier for children to learn who might have difficulty with the concepts of coordinates. To make computer programming a concrete experience, a computer controlled robot called a turtle was invented (see Figure 11–1). The turtle robot could be controlled by the instructions of a Logo computer program. The turtle carries a pen that can be placed in the writing position, causing the turtle to leave a trail wherever it goes. With the pen in the raised position, the turtle can be moved around the floor or table top without leaving a trail. The color of the pen can be changed by using appropriate instructions in the computer program. Current versions of Logo simulate the turtle robot with a turtle-shaped icon on the computer monitor or screen (see Figure 11–2).

In Logo, when the computer is placed in graphics mode, the turtle is placed in the center of the screen facing up. Lines are drawn on the screen by moving the turtle a specified distance in a given direction rather than by specifying horizontal and vertical coordinates. The following instruction will move the turtle and draw a line 50 pixels in the direction the turtle is pointing:

FORWARD 50

The BACK instruction would be used to move the turtle in the reverse direction. The turtle may be turned by using the RIGHT or LEFT instructions. The following instruction will turn the turtle 90 degrees to the right:

RIGHT 90

A subsequent FORWARD instruction would draw a line in the new direction beginning from the last position of the turtle. The PD and PU instructions (which stand for pendown and penup, respectively) control whether or not subsequent forward or backward movements of the turtle will draw a line on the screen. The SETPC instruction controls the color of the pen. The following Logo program instructions will draw a square on the screen.

FIGURE 11–1   Logo Robot Turtle

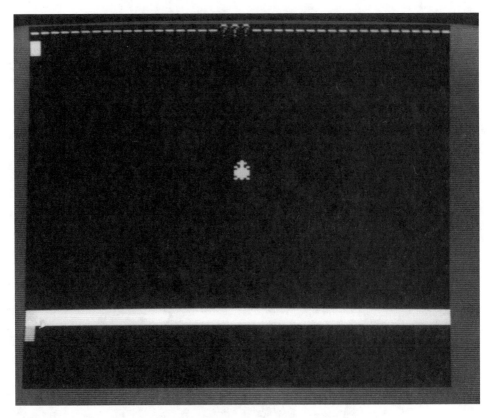

FIGURE 11–2   *LogoWriter* **Screen Turtle**

Logo Instructions	*Explanation*
PD	Place the pen down so that lines will be drawn as the turtle is moved.
SETC 4	Set the color of the pen to orange.
FORWARD 50	Move the turtle and draw a line 50 pixels long in the direction the turtle is facing.
RIGHT 90	Turn the turtle 90 degrees to the right.
FORWARD 50	Draw a line 50 pixels long in the new direction.
RIGHT 90	Turn the turtle 90 degrees to the right.
FORWARD 50	Draw a line 50 pixels long.
RIGHT 90	Turn the turtle to the right.
FORWARD 50	Draw the line.
RIGHT 90	Turn the turtle to the right.
PU	Lift the drawing pen.

Input

The computer instructions listed here are of limited value since every time we ask the computer to execute them we will get exactly the same result. If we want to get a different result, we have to edit or change the program prior to its execution. The programs would be much more useful if they were to request and receive information from the user each time they were executed. This information could then be used or processed to determine different results that could then be output to the user. Every computer language has several instructions that allow the user to input information. This information must be stored in the memory of the computer for subsequent retrieval and processing. In assembly language, we had to specify the exact address of the memory location where we wanted to store the information. Fortunately, with high-level languages, we do not have to be concerned with where the information is stored. Rather than use a number for the memory location address, we can use a meaningful name or label for the storage location. We can later retrieve the information by just referring to its name or label. In computer jargon, the name or label for information stored in the memory of a computer is called a *variable*. The following instructions would allow the user to input information into the computer by way of the computer keyboard:

Language	*Instruction*	*Explanation*
BASIC	INPUT L,W	Input two numbers. Store the first number in memory and give it the variable name or label "L." Store the second number and give it the variable name "W."
Pascal	READLN (L,W)	Input (or read a line of) two numbers. Give them the variable names "L" and "W."
Logo	MAKE "LW READLIST	Input (or read a list of) two numbers. Give (or make) them the variable names "LW." Both numbers are stored under one name.

These instructions are almost always preceded by an output instruction that tells the user to type or enter some specific information into the computer using the keyboard. Thus, in BASIC, the INPUT instruction would be preceded by the PRINT instruction as shown here:

```
. PRINT "PLEASE TYPE THE LENGTH AND WIDTH OF THE RECTANGLE"

INPUT L,W
```

When the computer executes a program and comes to one of the input instructions listed here, it will pause and wait for the user to type the requested information on the keyboard. After the information has been typed, the user must press the RETURN key to signal that the information has been entered and that the program execution may continue. The input instructions may allow the user to enter more than one item of information. These values must be separated by a comma in BASIC and by a space in Pascal and Logo.

Processing

The real power of a computer comes from its ability to manipulate, transform, and process information. High-level languages provide many instructions for this purpose. As we have already seen and as you might expect from its name, computers are able to process numbers by performing computations. The results of these calculations can be stored in the memory of the computer by using variable names or they can be sent to an output device. The following instructions will perform calculations and save the result by assigning it to a variable:

Language	Instruction	Explanation
BASIC	LET A = L * W	Multiply the number stored in the variable "L" times the number stored in "W" and place the result in the variable "A."
Pascal	PERIM:= 4 * SIDE;	Multiply the value stored in the variable "SIDE" by 4 and assign the result to the variable "PERIM."
Logo	MAKE "SUM 3+5+7	Add the numbers 3, 5, and 7 and store (make) the result in the variable "SUM."

Note that the calculations can be performed on actual numbers or constants (such as 3 and 5) or on values stored in the memory of the computer (variables). Most computer languages use the asterisk (*) for the multiplication symbol so that it is not confused with the letter *x*.

The results stored in variables can be retrieved and shown on the screen using the instructions described in the output section. The following BASIC instruction will display on the screen the value stored in the variable A:

PRINT A

Note that the letter *A* will not be printed, but the number that was stored in the memory of the computer and given the label of *A* will be printed. To display the actual letter *A*, we would use the instruction:

PRINT "A"

In addition to even more sophisticated instructions for performing mathematical calculations, high-level languages have other instructions for manipulating words and characters and for making decisions. As humans, we pride ourselves in our ability to think and solve problems. A major factor in these abilities is our capacity to make decisions. When we awake in the morning, we must decide what time to get out of bed. We must decide when to take a shower, what clothes to wear, whether to take an umbrella, where to go to lunch, what TV program to watch, and when to go to bed. We are constantly making decisions. Sometimes we make the wrong decision and must suffer the consequences. If we could not make decisions, our lives would be pretty dull. Computer programs that cannot make decisions are also very dull. Fortunately, all computer languages have instructions that enable a computer program to make decisions. Such instructions do not necessarily give the computer intelligence, but they do make it possible for the computer to solve many problems that previously could be solved only by intelligent humans.

In essence, the computer can only make yes or no decisions. It can decide whether one number is larger than another number, whether the name the user typed is the same as "John," and whether the result of a calculation is equal to zero. In other words, the computer can test a given condition to determine if it is true or false. If the condition is true, the computer will execute one instruction; if the condition is false, it will execute a different instruction. The following Pascal instructions show how this capability could be used in a program:

Pascal Instruction	*Explanation*
WRITELN ('Please enter the verb found');	Write the first line of question on the screen.
WRITELN ('in the following sentence:');	Write the rest of the question on the screen.
WRITELN;	Write or display a blank line on the screen.
WRITELN ('John ran to the store');	Write the sentence on the screen.
WRITELN;	Write a blank line on the screen.
READLN (answer);	Input the student's answer and store it in the variable "answer."
WRITELN;	Write a blank line on the screen.
IF answer = 'ran'	Test the condition (answer = 'ran').
THEN	If the condition is true (the word typed by the student which is stored in the variable "answer" is equal to or the same as the word "ran"), then execute the following instruction.
WRITELN ('Very good')	Write the correct feedback message on the screen.
ELSE	If the condition is false, execute the following.
WRITELN ('Sorry, the verb is ran');	Write the incorrect feedback message.

Conclusion

Three major components included in most high-level programming languages have been examined and examples from three languages frequently used in the schools have been given. Each of these languages provides instructions to allow the user to input information into the computer, instructions to process the information, and instructions to output results on the computer screen. This section has not attempted to teach you how to write computer programs. Only an introduction to a minimum number of instructions was given to help you understand the major components of computer languages. Each language has many additional instructions. As you have seen, the instructions are relatively simple and easy to understand. Hopefully, this introduction will encourage you to learn how to write simple programs in at least one high-level language.

Multimedia/Hypermedia Authoring Systems

With the advent of videodisc and CD-ROM peripherals and digitized video and audio, the computer has become a powerful multimedia/hypermedia device (see Chapter 8, Multimedia/Hypermedia). In order to facilitate the development of hypermedia programs, a wide variety of authoring systems has been developed. An *authoring system* is an integrated set of tools designed to simplify the programming process and make it possible for nonprofessional programmers, such as teachers, to develop computer-based, hypermedia instructional programs. However, claims by some of the vendors of these systems that no programming is necessary is somewhat exaggerated. An understanding of the programming components described in the previous section is still necessary. However, the process by which these components are implemented has been simplified.

For example, rather than requiring you to program an instruction to display text on the screen, a powerful text editor is provided that allows you simply to type the text on the screen where you want it to appear. You can later edit the text and change its size and characteristics, as you would in a word processor. Graphics editors are also provided that allow you to create drawings using the mouse or cursor keys rather than using primitive instructions such as HPLOT and FORWARD. Most authoring systems also permit you to import drawings from other graphic programs such as *MacPaint, MacDraw, PC Paintbrush, Deluxe Paint,* and so on. These systems often include tools for integrating full-motion video sequences from a videodisc into your program by simply specifying the beginning and ending frame numbers of the sequence on the disc. With the appropriate additional hardware, such as a video camera and a scanner, you can create and use your own video clips or drawings and pictures from various print sources. Voice, sound effects, and musical selections can also be included in your program with minimal effort. These audio selections can come from a videodisc, a CD-ROM, or files on a floppy or hard disk. Some systems even provide a microphone and the necessary hardware and software for you to record your own audio selections and incorporate them into your program.

An authoring system may also provide tools for creating animation sequences. You may animate text, graphics, or cartoonlike characters as you see in many video games. This capability allows a program to demonstrate biological processes, such as cell division, or the movements of machine parts, such as the valves and pistons of an automobile engine. Two major types of authoring systems will be discussed in the next sections: card based and icon based.

Card-Based Authoring Systems

One of the first card-based authoring systems, called *HyperCard,* was originally provided free with every Macintosh computer. This system became the prototype for many similar systems, such as *LinkWay* and *ToolBook* for IBM-compatible computers, *AmigaVision* for the Commodore Amiga, and *HyperStudio* for the Apple IIGS. Card-based authoring systems are designed around the metaphor of a stack of three-by-five cards. The cards from the stack are displayed on the screen one at a time. Each card can contain several different types of objects, such as graphics, fields, and buttons (see Figure 11–3).

Graphics can be drawn directly on the electronic cards by using built-in drawing or paint tools similar to those found in many graphics programs (see Chapter 7, Tool Applications). Graphics may also be imported from many other sources, such as scanners, digital cameras, and graphics programs.

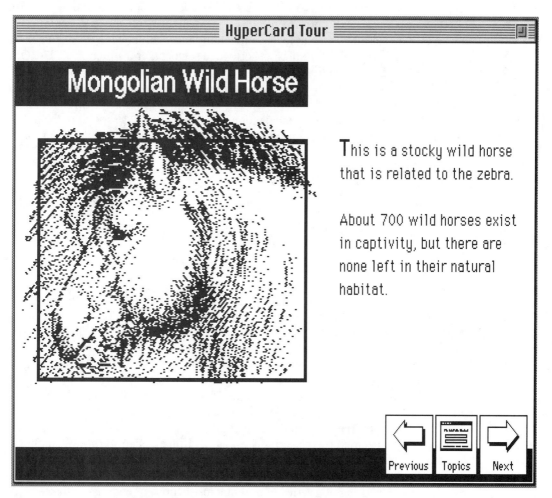

FIGURE 11–3   Card with Graphics, Text Fields, and Buttons

Fields are rectangular areas on the screen for entering and displaying text. The rectangular area can be outlined by different types of borders or may have no border at all. Fields can be of different sizes and placed anywhere on the screen. They can be used to display headings, labels, instructions, or textual information. Text can be entered into the field by the author as easily as entering text into a word processor. The text can be edited using word-processing functions such as insert, delete, cut, copy, and paste. As the text is typed, it word wraps within the field borders. If more text is entered than will fit within the border of the field, scroll bars can be added to the right of the field so that the user can scroll to another section of the text by clicking the mouse pointer in the scroll bar. The text in the field can be of different sizes, fonts, and styles. With some card-based authoring systems, the text can also be of different colors.

Buttons are small areas on the screen indicated by a small picture or icon or by a rectangular box with a textual label. When a user clicks on a button with the mouse pointer, the computer will perform some action, such as displaying a different card, playing a digitized sound, displaying an animation sequence, showing a hidden object, instructing a videodisc player to play a short video segment, or instructing a CD-ROM player to play a CD audio clip. The label or icon on the button generally indicates the action that will be performed when the button is clicked. Which action is performed depends on the set of computer commands or instructions associated with the button. These instructions are essentially small computer programs, as described in the previous section, and are generally referred to as *scripts*. For example, the following *Hypercard* script instructs the computer to show a hidden field containing a correct feedback message and play a short digitized musical tune, when the associated button is clicked with the mouse pointer.

```
on mouseup
    show field "feedback"
    play "happy"
end
```

Programming in card-based authoring systems is quite different from traditional programming. With traditional programming, the program has a definitive beginning and end, and the program controls the sequence of information presentation and user input. In contrast, programs written in card-based authoring systems are *event driven*. Every action taken by the user—such as selecting an item from a menu, typing keys on the keyboard, or pressing the mouse button—is considered an event. With an event-driven program, the user controls the actions of the program rather than the program controlling the actions of the user. Whenever an event occurs, the computer sends a *message* to the appropriate object. If the object has a script for handling that event message, the action specified by the script is executed. If there is no script for handling a particular message, no action is performed. The script for a particular object may have multiple handlers that allow it to respond to different events. A *handler* is part of a program or script consisting of a series of program instructions or commands that specify the response to a specific event message. The following *HyperCard* script contains two handlers:

```
on mouseup
      visual effect dissolve
      go to next card
end
on mousedoubleclick
      visual effect venetian blinds
      go to last card
end
```

The body or series of instructions of each handler is delimited by a header and the word *end.* The first line or header begins with the word *on,* followed by the name of the message to which the handler is to respond. Thus, the first handler above will respond to the "mouseup" message and the second handler will respond to the "mousedoubleclick" message. The "mouseup" message is sent when the user clicks the mouse button once; the "mousedoubleclick" message is sent when the user clicks the mouse button twice in rapid succession. With a single click, the computer will display the next card in the stack, using a *dissolve transition* visual effect, whereas with a double click, the computer will jump to the last card in the stack using a *venetian blinds* visual effect.

Buttons are not the only objects that can receive and respond to event messages. Messages can also be sent to fields, cards, and the stack. For example, the messages "openCard" and "closeCard" allow for specific actions to be performed when a card is displayed or opened and when it is left or closed. The following handler will place the current date in a field, called *day,* when the card is displayed.

```
on openCard
      put the date into field "day"
end openCard
```

Several cards in a stack can share a common background. This common background can also contain graphics, fields, and buttons. Any object placed on the background will appear on all cards that share the background. Backgrounds greatly reduce the work required to create cards that share common features. Backgrounds may also have associated scripts and handlers that respond to event messages such as "openBackground" and "closeBackground." Backgrounds may also contain special fields, often called *record fields,* that are similar to the fields of a database (see Chapter 7). Since these fields are placed on the background, they will appear on each card sharing the background. However, the textual information stored in the field can be different for each card. Each card serves as a separate record in a database. For example, the background could contain three different fields, one for the name, another for the address, and a third for the phone number. Each card would contain the name, address, and phone number for a different person in the corresponding fields. Such stacks could contain buttons and scripts for sorting the card records and searching for a specific persons record (see Figure 11–4).

Card-based authoring systems are very versatile and allow for a great deal of creativity in the creation of stacks. Only a few of the capabilities of such systems have been introduced here. The scripting languages of such authoring systems provide many of the same input, processing, and output functions provided by high-level languages.

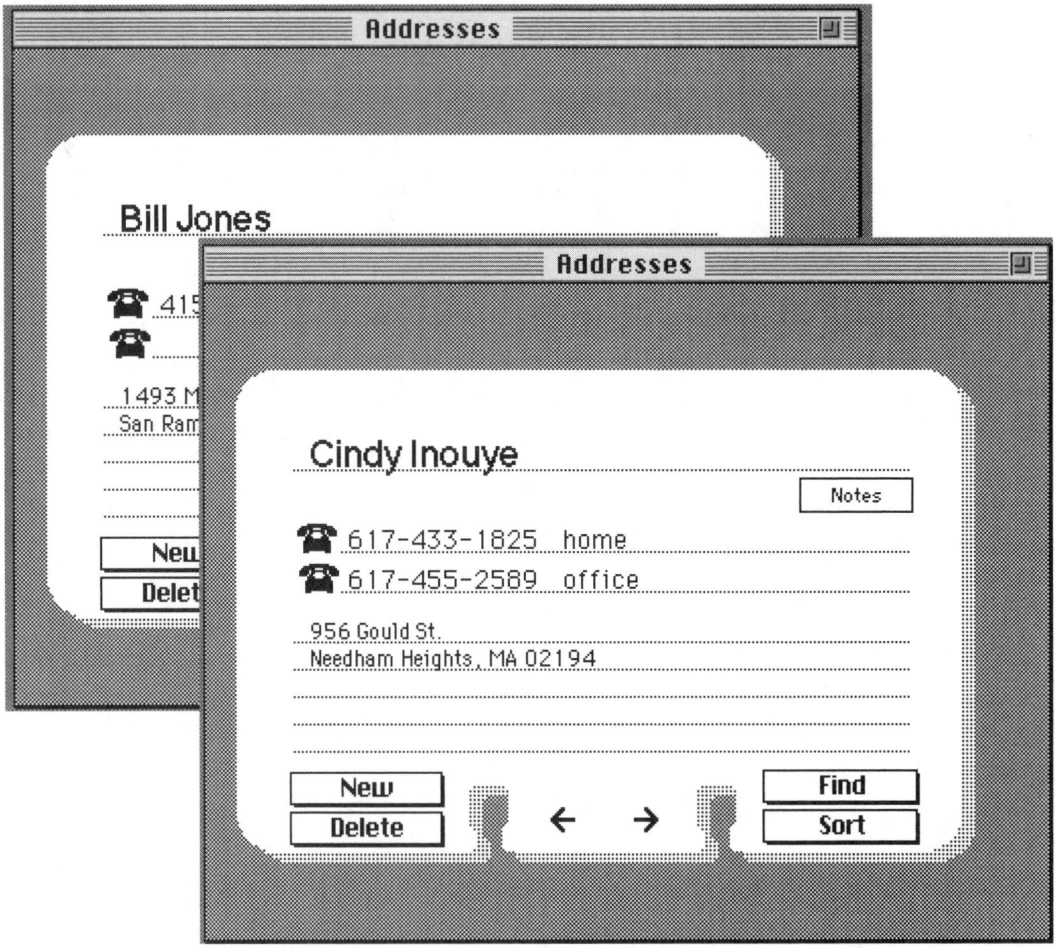

FIGURE 11–4   Cards Showing Two Database Records with the Same Background

HyperStudio is somewhat unique in that it attempts to shield the programmer or author from having to write handlers and scripts. After the author creates a button on the screen, a series of dialog boxes appear that allow the author to select the characteristics or properties of the button and the actions he or she wants the button to perform. Let's walk through the steps required to create a simple hypermedia application using *HyperStudio*.

After starting the *HyperStudio* program, we will first create a new stack by selecting the New Stack menu item from the File menu with the mouse, as shown in Figure 11–5. This will create a new stack with one blank card. We will place a title field, a simple graphic, and a button for going to the next card on the first card. To create a field, we will select Add a Text Item . . . from the objects menu (see Figure 11–6). A dotted rectangle will appear on the screen showing the outline of the field. We may

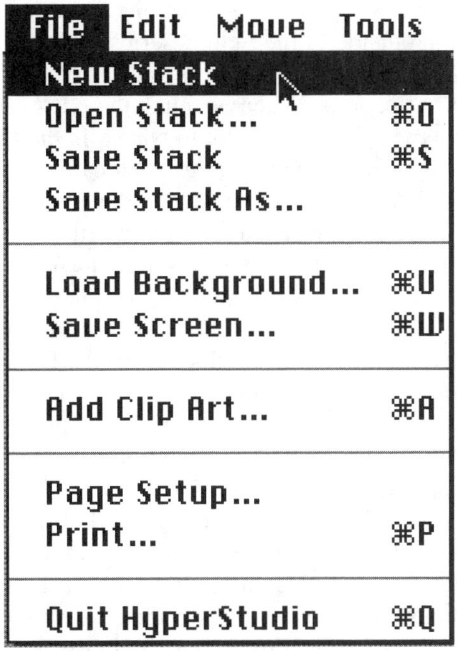

FIGURE 11–5 New Stack Menu Item from File Menu

FIGURE 11–6 Add a Text Item from the Objects Menu

then use the mouse to move or resize the field (see Figure 11–7). When we click the mouse button outside of the field, a series of dialog boxes will appear, allowing us to select the size, style, font, and colors of the text and background of the field. Figure 11–8 shows our selections. When we click the OK button, the dialog box will disappear and we can type the text we want to appear in the field. Next, we will use the graphic tools to draw a small tree on the card. Our card now appears as shown in Figure 11–9.

To add a button to go to the next card, we select Add a button... from the Objects menu. The Button Appearance dialog box will be displayed and we can select the style, color, and other characteristics of our button (see Figure 11–10). By clicking the icon button, we can select an arrow icon for our button to indicate the action it will perform (see Figure 11–11). When we click OK, the button will appear on the screen. After moving the button to the desired location, the Button Actions dialog box will appear (see Figure 11–12). Instead of writing a script to specify the action to be performed when the user clicks the button, all we have to do is select the desired action (Next card) in the dialog box and then click DONE. After selecting a visual effect from the Transitions dialog box (see Figure 11–13), our card will appear as shown in Figure 11–14.

We are now ready to add a second card to the stack by selecting New Card from the Edit Menu. On this card, we will place a button that will allow the user to play a video sequence from a videodisc. First, we create the button as before. However, in the Button Actions dialog box, we select the Play a Movie or Video... action, as shown in Figure 11–15. After selecting Laserdisc, in the next dialog box (see Figure 11–16), a LaserDisc Conrol dialog box, as shown in Figure 11–17, will appear. We can use the buttons in this box to control the videodisc and find the desired sequence. When we

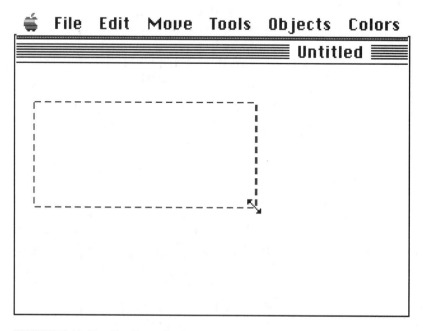

FIGURE 11–7   Outline of a New Field

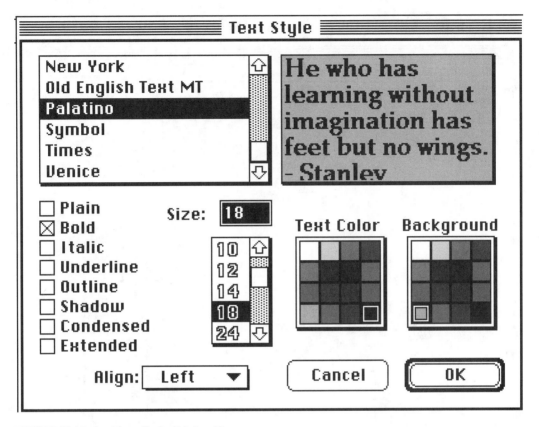

FIGURE 11–8   Text Style Dialog Box

locate the beginning of our sequence, we click on the BEGIN button and the appropriate frame number will appear in the box to the right. We then play to the end of our sequence and click the END button. We can try out our sequence by clicking the TEST button. When we are satisfied with our sequence, we click the KEEP button. After adding a field with some text to describe the videodisc sequence, our sample stack is complete. To save our stack on a diskette, we select Save from the File menu.

When we run our program, the title card will appear on the screen, and we can click the arrow button to go to the next card. By clicking the button on the second card, our videodisc sequence will play on a separate monitor.

As you can see, creating a hypermedia application with the *HyperStudio* authoring system is as simple as "point and click." This simplicity makes it possible for even young children to become hypermedia authors.

Icon-Based Authoring Systems

Rather than using a list of verbal instructions or commands to specify the operations a computer should perform, *icon-based authoring systems* use a visual representation

FIGURE 11–9   Card Showing Text Field, Graphic, and Tools Pallette

consisting of small pictures or icons in a flowchart structure. The icons represent the operations to be performed, and the flowchart represents the sequence in which the operations are performed. Figure 11–18 shows a simple program created in an icon-based authoring system called *AuthorWare Professional.*

On the left-hand side of the screen, you will see a palette of 13 icons; 11 of these are used to indicate the operations to be performed. The two flags, labeled START and STOP, may be placed on the flowchart to indicate where the program should begin and end during a particular test run. This allows for testing a small section of the program without running through the whole thing. The icons are placed on the flowchart to the right by moving the mouse pointer over an icon, pressing and holding the mouse button down, and dragging the icon to the desired location on the flowchart and then lifting

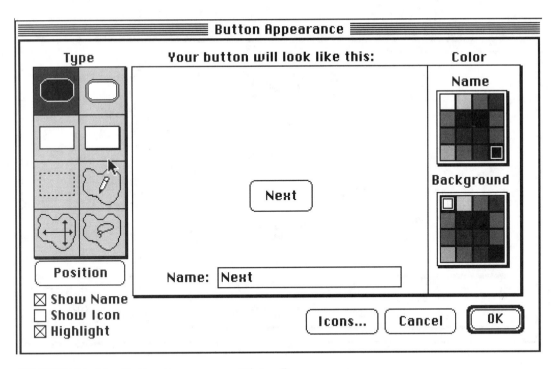

FIGURE 11–10 **Button Appearance Dialog Box**

the mouse button. The flowchart with its icons represent the "skeleton" of the program. The "meat" of the program is added using powerful editors and dialog boxes associated with each icon.

The first icon on the palette is called the *display* icon. It is used whenever the author wishes to present textual or graphical information on the screen. Once a display icon is placed on the flowchart, we can access its associated editor by double-clicking the icon with the mouse pointer. A *presentation window* will be displayed over the top of the flowchart window, as shown in Figure 11–19. In the upper-right corner of the window is a palette of tools, similar to those found in drawing programs (see Chapter 7, Tool Applications) that may be used to place text and graphics on the screen. Graphics may also be imported from other applications. Text may be placed anywhere on the screen just by moving the mouse pointer. Menu items are available for specifying the size, style, color, and font of the text. When the text and graphics associated with the display icon are completed, the author may return to the flowchart window by selecting Jump to Icons from the Try It menu.

The next icon, with an arrow pointing to the upper right corner, is called the *animation* icon. This icon is used to move objects placed on the screen with the immediately preceding display icon. When an author double-clicks the icon to create or edit an animation, the Animation Type dialog box appears, as shown in Figure 11–20.

Here, the author selects one of five different types of animations. The Fixed Destination animation is used to move an object in a straight line from one location to

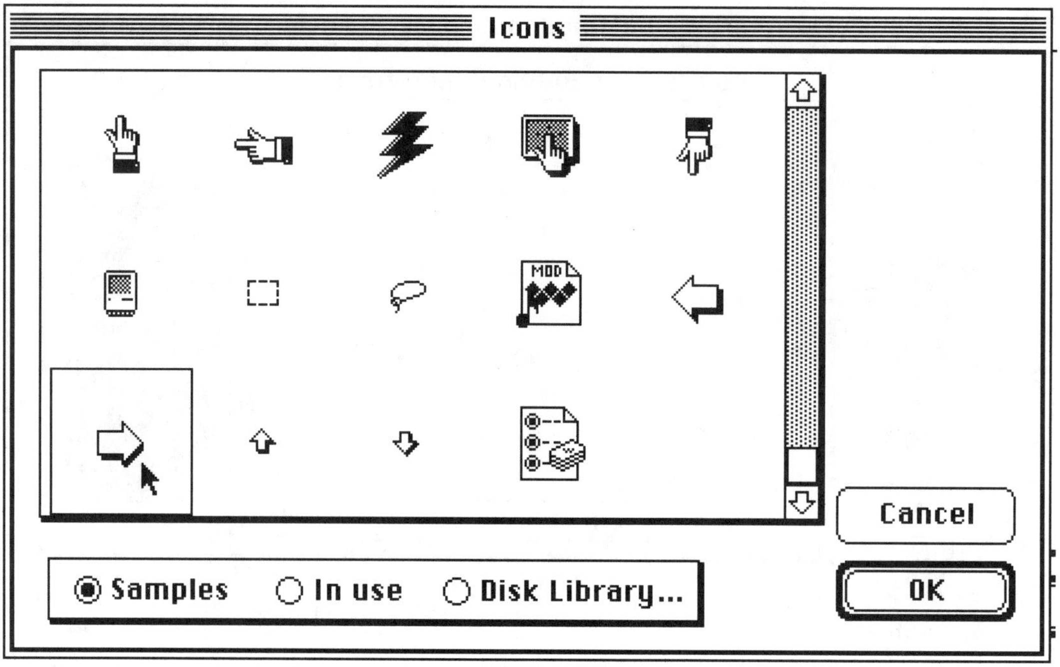

FIGURE 11–11   Icons Dialog Box

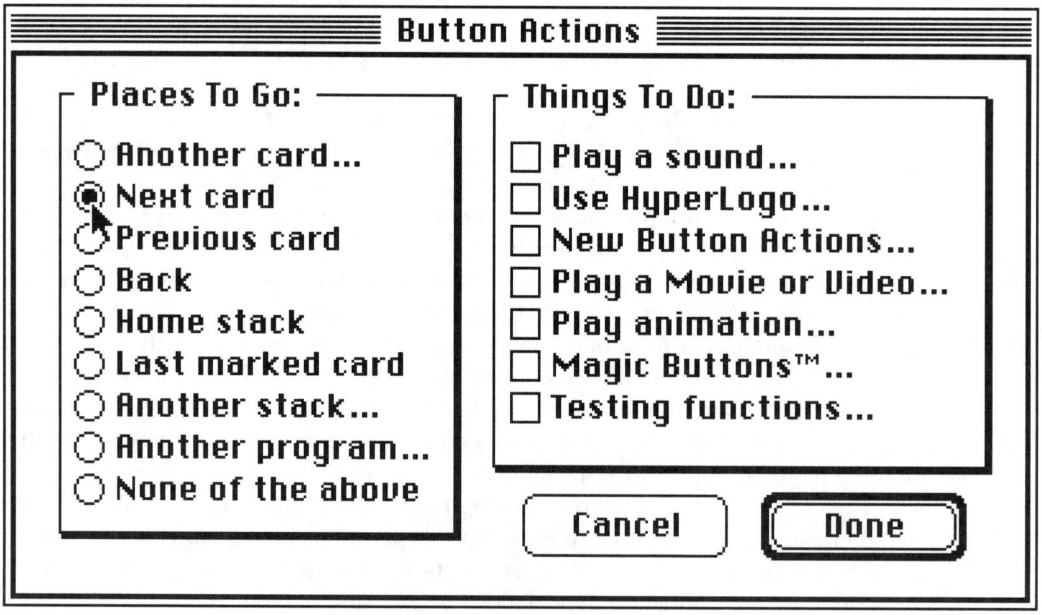

FIGURE 11–12   Button Actions Dialog Box

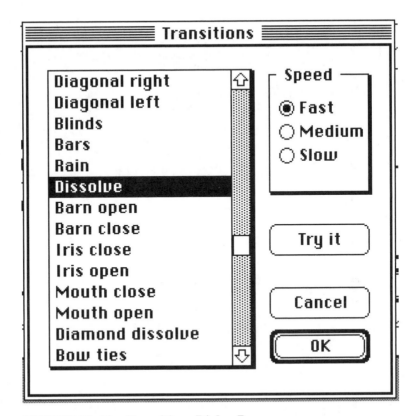

FIGURE 11–13   Transitions Dialog Box

another. The Fixed Path animation is used to move an object along a jagged or curved path specified by several points. The other three animation types allow an object to be moved along a path, or to a point on a line, or within an area according to the value of some variable or expression. For example, the Scaled X-Y animation could be used to move a chess piece to a particular location on the board.

If the author selects the Fixed Path animation, the presentation window of the previous display icon will be displayed on the screen along with the Fixed Path dialog box, as shown in Figure 11–21. When the dialog box first opens, there is a message at the top instructing the author to "Click display to be moved." After clicking the display or object to be moved, the instruction message changes to "Drag display to create the path." After dragging the display to another location on the screen, the instructions change again to "Drag display to extend the path." By clicking and dragging the display object to various locations on the screen, a path is created represented by line segments and triangular points (see Figure 11–21). The path may be edited by deleting, adding, or moving the points. The speed of the animation can be controlled by changing the value in the rate box, and the animation can be viewed and tested by clicking the REPLAY button. The lines and points indicating the path are hidden when the program is executed.

FIGURE 11–14   Card with Text Field, Graphic, and Button

The third icon, called the *Erase* icon, is used to erase all the text and graphics in a particular display icon. The author can select a visual effect to be used during the erasure.

The fourth icon, shaped like a stop sign and called the *Wait* icon, is used to pause the execution of the program for a specified amount of time, or until the user presses a key or the mouse button. The author also has the option to show a clock to indicate the amount of time remaining or to display a button for the user to click to continue.

The *Decision* icon, the fifth on the palette, provides branching and repeat loop capabilities by determining which icon(s) attached to the decision icon should be executed next. The branching or repetition decision parameters are specified by the author using the decision options dialog box, shown in Figure 11–22.

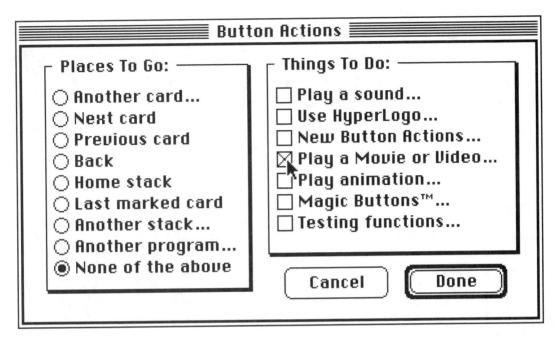

FIGURE 11–15   Button Actions Dialog Box

The *Interaction* icon is the next on the palette, and it provides for student interaction with the program. Based on the student's response to a problem situation, question, or menu choices, the program will branch to the appropriate icons attached to the interaction icon. This icon is used to provide differential feedback to the student based on his or her response. Figure 11–23 shows the types of responses the author can require of the student. Powerful answer-processing capabilities are provided to access the accuracy of the student's responses.

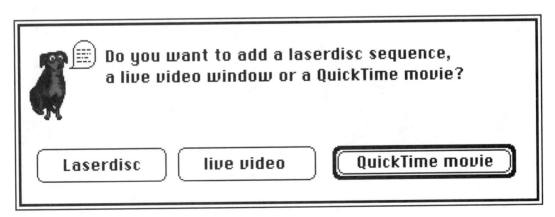

FIGURE 11–16   Video Selection Dialogue Box

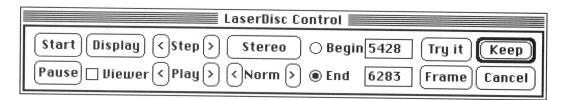

FIGURE 11–17   LaserDisc Control Dialog Box

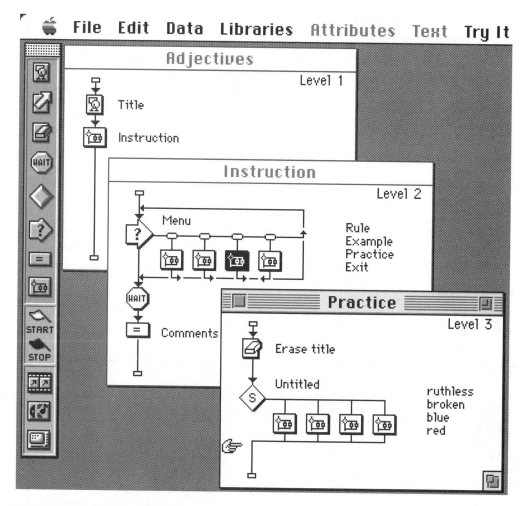

FIGURE 11–18   *AuthorWare Professional* Flowchart

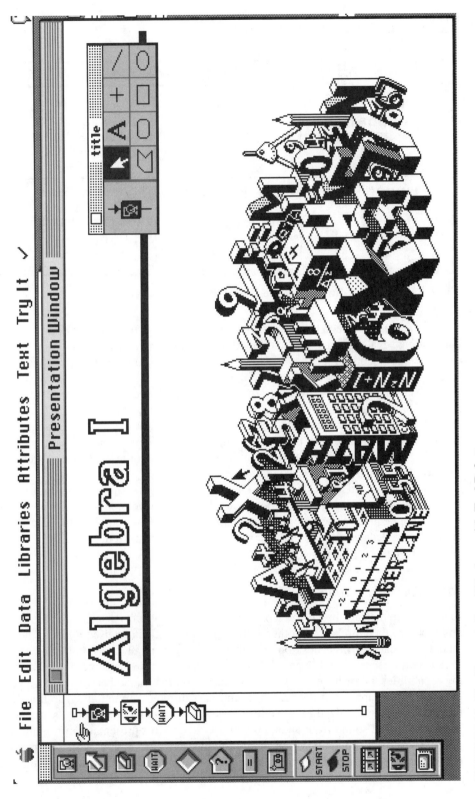

FIGURE 11–19   Presentation Window with Tool Palette

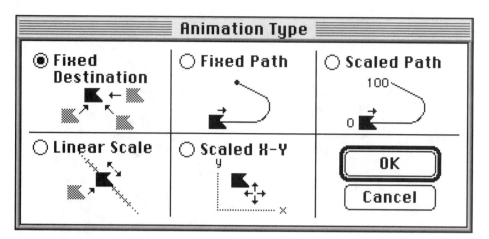

FIGURE 11–20   Animation Type Dialog Box

The *Calculation* icon has an equal sign (=) as a label. This icon is used to perform calculations, evaluate mathematical functions, and assign values to variables.

The eighth icon, called the *Map* icon, may be used to combine several icons into a single group.

The last three icons—called the *Movie, Sound,* and *Video* icons—provide powerful multimedia capabilities. The *Movie* icon presents QuickTime digital movies, the *Sound* icon plays digitized sounds, and the *Video* icon plays still frames or motion sequences from a videodisc player. By double-clicking the *Video* icon, the author can access a powerful videodisc options dialog box to identify and select the videodisc sequence to be played (see Figure 11–24).

AuthorWare and other icon-based authoring systems—such as *CourseBuilder, IconAuthor,* and *Quest*—provide a rich array of tools for developing sophisticated multimedia applications. They are used extensively to develop computer-based training applications. Because of their higher cost, they are not used as frequently in the schools as the card-based authoring systems.

Other Authoring Tools

In addition to the card-based and icon-based authoring systems discussed in the previous sections, there are several other authoring tools that can be used to create hypermedia applications. The desktop presentation programs, such as *PowerPoint* and *Persuasion* (discussed in Chapter 7, Tool Applications) provide some limited authoring capabilities. Some have more hypermedia capabilities than others. They can all display text and graphics on the screen. Some have limited animation capabilities and most will display digitized movie clips. Very few will allow you to access videodisc images or digital sound from an audio compact disc. Most presentation programs are designed for the presentation of linear slide shows and have no or very limited interaction capabilities. However, it is anticipated that future versions of these programs will include more hypermedia features.

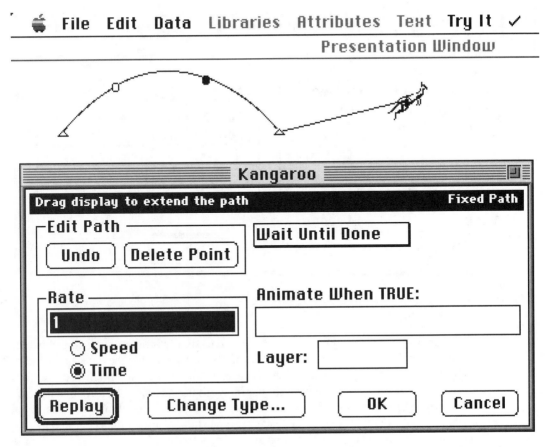

FIGURE 11–21   Fixed Path Dialog Box with Animation Path

Another type of authoring system is represented by *Macromedia Director,* briefly described in Chapter 8, Multimedia/Hypermedia. *Director* uses a theatrical play as a metaphor rather than a metaphor of a stack of cards. The play takes place on an electronic stage and uses a variety of cast members. This program provides very sophisticated tools for synchronizing animation and sound. Because of its complexity, it would probably be used only by quite advanced students.

Integrating Computer Programming and Authoring into the Curriculum

Computer programming is generally first introduced in middle school or high school as an independent subject. However, a few progressive schools are beginning to introduce programming concepts in the elementary grades and are integrating programming activities throughout the curriculum.

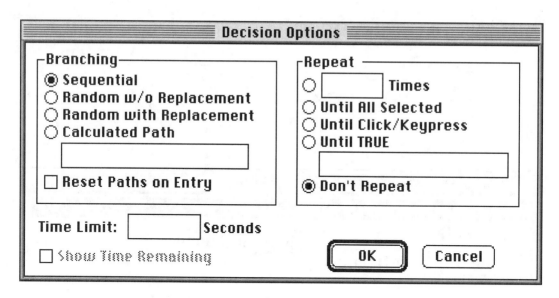

FIGURE 11–22   Decision Options Dialog Box

Even very young children can be introduced to simple programming concepts. For example, you can teach the concept that computers only do what they are instructed to do by comparing computer instructions to those instructions a child might receive from a teacher or parent. The teacher might begin by giving a student instructions to go to the pencil sharpener and sharpen his or her pencil. Another student might be instructed to pick up a book and bring it to the teacher. Some students might then be asked to give some instructions to one of their classmates. This activity can be extended to show the frequent ambiguity of English language instructions. In order to reduce this ambiguity, it becomes necessary to give more detailed and specific instructions. For example, the instruction "Go to the pencil sharpener and sharpen your pencil" is ambiguous because is does not specify which pencil sharpener to use or which pencil is to be sharpened. If a new student comes into the class and doesn't know where the pencil sharpener is located, even more detailed instructions will have to be given, such as "Walk to the end of the row of desks, turn left, then walk to the wall." Computers require even more detailed instructions. This level of detail can be demonstrated by blindfolding students, disorienting them, and then giving the necessary detailed instructions required for them to go pick up a book from one student and deliver it to another. This would require instructions such as "Go forward 10 steps, now turn left a quarter turn, now go forward 15 steps. Oops, that is too far. Go back 3 steps." The concept of a program can be introduced by having students write a set of instructions on a piece of paper rather than giving them orally one at a time. The detailed instructions might describe how to go from the school to a child's home.

The next level of abstraction can be introduced through the use of a Logo robotic Turtle or a *LEGO TC Logo* construction set. With *LEGO TC Logo,* children can con-

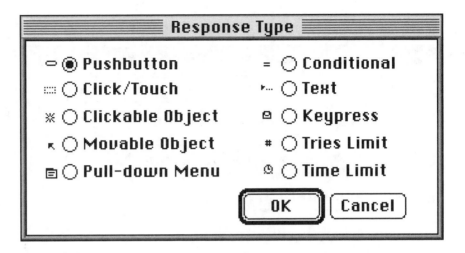

FIGURE 11–23   Response Type Dialog Box

struct many different robotic devices with LEGO blocks (see Figure 11–25). These devices can be connected to a computer and controlled through the use of Logo programming instructions. This combination is very exciting and can provide the vehicle for the integration of programming, mathematics, and science. A recognition of the similarities between LEGO blocks and Logo instructions is enlightening. A programming language is a construction set in its own right, as instructions and procedures are used as building blocks to construct more complex programs. A digital electric train set can also be used to provide a concrete programming experience and integrate programming into the social science curriculum (as previously described in Chapter 1).

After experience with programming a robotic device, children can be introduced to the electronic Logo turtle on the computer screen. This turtle can be programmed to create many exciting graphic figures. Here, programming concepts can be integrated with many mathematical, measurement, geometric, and artistic concepts. Logo programming requires that students clearly understand concepts related to distance, angles, and degrees and learn valuable planning, problem solving, analytical, and critical thinking skills. As they write Logo programs to draw geometric shapes, they should predict the results, preferably sketching on graph paper what they think the turtle will draw on the screen. They then execute their program and compare the result with their predictions. Students will enjoy making modifications in their designs, predicting the effects of the changes, and verifying the results by executing the modified program. Logo can provide many geometric insights that students would be unlikely to otherwise obtain.

LogoWriter integrates Logo with many word-processing features. This combination facilitates the integration of programming into the language arts curriculum. *LogoWriter* can be used by students to write and illustrate their own stories with Logo pictures and animated characters. More advanced students can use Logo's text string

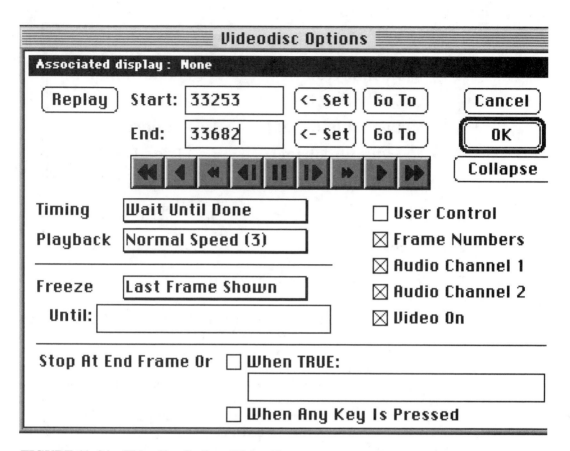

FIGURE 11–24 Videodisc Options Dialog Box

manipulation commands to write programs that will generate sentences based on grammatical rules and words categorized by part of speech. The writing of such programs will help students learn and appreciate the relationships between sentence structure, parts of speech, and grammar rules. As recommended by Papert (1980), students could also write simple drill-and-practice programs that would help them learn math facts or lists of spelling words. The writing of a computer-based tutorial program to teach some topic would force students to consider all possible misunderstandings and mistakes, thus enhancing their ability to analyze a situation and derive solutions. Children become passionately involved when writing programs that teach and critiquing each other's work.

The most obvious place where programming can be integrated into the curriculum is in mathematics, since the computer is clearly a calculating machine. Students will gain a deeper understanding of mathematical procedures and formulas if they teach the computer how to execute the procedure or formula. Students with minimal programming experience can write programs to convert Fahrenheit temperatures to Celsius, to

FIGURE 11–25   Robotic Device Created Using *LEGO TC Logo*

calculate the distance given the rate and time, to determine how many miles a car will go on a gallon of gas, and so on. More advanced students can write programs that will generate graphs of many mathematical functions.

Computer programs can also be written in science classes to demonstrate the relationships between current, voltage, and resistance or between temperature and pressure. Students who develop a simple computer model to simulate the effects of various factors on air pollution gain a greater appreciation for the complexity of ecological systems.

Multimedia/hypermedia authoring systems may also be introduced in the elementary grades. Many fairly sophisticated projects can be implemented in *HyperStudio* without the use of scripting. The integrated text editing and graphics capabilities of authoring systems makes them ideal for language arts and social science projects. Writing activities become very exciting when students can add their own graphics, clip art, or scanned photographs to illustrate their story. Voice annotations and sound effects can be added to further enliven the written word. History classes can go beyond learning names and dates to actually doing history research. Students can compile original documents, transcriptions of personal interviews, scanned photographs, and digital recordings of personal statements and incorporate them into a hypermedia report. Small groups of students or an entire class can collaborate in conducting the research, gathering the data, and preparing the hypermedia report.

More advanced students can use the animation capabilities of authoring systems to demonstrate their understanding of many phenomena, such as the circulation of blood, cell division, the cycles of an internal combustion engine, and the water cycle. Both teachers and students can employ authoring systems to prepare classroom presentations using videodisc still images and motion sequences.

Some educators have questioned whether they should teach their students traditional high-level programming languages, such as *LogoWriter,* or focus on authoring systems, such as *HyperStudio.* The authors of this book feel that both high-level programming languages and authoring systems have an important place in the elementary and secondary curriculums. In addition to all of the benefits outlined at the beginning of the chapter, high-level programming activities also provide a good background of understanding and skill on which students can build as they learn and use authoring systems. Sophisticated applications written in an authoring system require an understanding of each of the programming components described earlier. It is interesting to note, in this context, that the latest version of *HyperStudio* has incorporated a version of Logo as a scripting language, and the creators of *LogoWriter* have introduced a new version of Logo, called *Microworlds,* that includes many of the authoring capabilities found in card-based authoring systems.

Only a few ideas of how computer programming and authoring systems might be integrated into the curriculum have been included here. The possibilities are many. The potential impact is significant. As Luehrmann (1980) suggested, computer programming is indeed a new and fundamental intellectual resource that should be applied across the curriculum.

Summary

The computer has many potential roles to play in the classroom. One of the most significant in its effect on learning is that of tutee. Well-known experts in the field of computer use with children advocate teaching beginning programming skills to the general student population. This effort is not intended to make professional programmers of everyone; rather, it is to broaden students' general education, provide a deeper understanding about how computers work, strengthen problem-solving skills, provide a healthier perspective on making mistakes, provide a sense of control and accomplishment, and enhance skills in using computer-based tools.

Programming the computer should not be relegated solely to computer science classes, any more than reading and writing should be limited to language arts classes. Students who are competent in a computer language have an intellectual resource that can be used in math, science, art, social science, and physical education classes. Students will obtain a better understanding of procedures used in mathematics and science if they have the opportunity to teach a computer how to perform those procedures. Programming a computer to transpose a piece of music provides insight into significant musical relationships. Authoring systems allow students to work together on interdisciplinary projects that combine skills in language, creativity, problem solving, and inquiry. Clearly, the use of the computer as tutee should be infused throughout the school curriculum.

Exercises

1. List and briefly describe several reasons why it is valuable for students to learn how to program a computer.
2. Describe the purpose of the ASCII code.
3. Explain the difference between machine language, assembly language, and high-level languages.
4. Explain the difference between an assembler, a compiler, and an interpreter.
5. Describe the purpose of each of the major programming components and provide a programming instruction to exemplify each component.
6. Read an article from a teaching journal that provides suggestions on how you might integrate computer programming into the curriculum you expect to be teaching.
7. Learn how to write simple computer programs in a high-level language such as Logo, BASIC, or Pascal.
8. Write a simple computer program that would be relevant to your own curriculum.
9. Describe the difference between high-level programming languages, card-based authoring systems, and icon-based authoring systems.
10. Learn an authoring system and develop a hypermedia application.

References

AmigaVision. [Computer Program]. West Chester, PA: Commodore Business Machines.

Applesoft BASIC. [Computer Program]. Cupertino, CA: Apple Computer.

Authorware Professional. [Computer Program]. Bloomington, MN: Authorware.

Course Builder. [Computer Program]. Knoxville, TN: TeleRobotics International.

Greenfield, E. (1990). Authoring systems focus on new structure and users. *T.H.E Journal, 18,* 7–14.

Harris, T. A. (1969). *I'm ok—You're ok.* New York: Avon Books.

HyperCard. [Computer Program]. Cupertino, CA: Apple Computer.

HyperStudio. [Computer Program]. El Cajon, CA: Roger Wagner Publishing.

IconAuthor. [Computer Program]. Nashua, NH: AimTech.

LEGO TC Logo. [Computer Program, Interface Box, Construction Blocks]. Enfield, CT: LEGO Systems.

LinkWay. [Computer Program]. Atlanta, GA: IBM.

LogoWriter. [Computer Software]. New York: Logo Computer Systems.

Luehrmann, A. (1980). Should the computer teach the student, or vice-versa? In R. P. Taylor (Ed.), *The computer in the school: Tutor, tool, tutee.* New York: Teachers College Press.

Macromedia Director. [Computer Program]. San Francisco: Macromedia.

Microworlds. [Computer Software]. New York: Logo Computer Systems.

Papert, S. (1980). Teaching children thinking. In R. P. Taylor (Ed.), *The computer in the school: Tutor, tool, tutee.* New York: Teachers College Press.

Quest Authoring System. [Computer Program]. Salt Lake City, UT: Allen Communication.

Chapter 12

Curriculum Integration

Reading and the Language Arts

Integration refers to the combination of technology and traditional teaching procedures to produce student learning. Integration is an attitude more than anything else. It comes with a willingness to combine technology and teaching into a productive experience that moves the learner to new understanding.

Educators have acknowledged the need for integration of technology into education for many years. Integration of technology into curricula requires a new perspective as well as time and work. The information presented in this chapter will heighten your awareness of the complexity of the issue.

Efficient use of technology requires that teachers understand the goals of the curriculum and know the capabilities of technology in meeting those goals. Teachers must take a fresh look at the curriculum to be taught and ask whether there is a technology application that will "enhance" the achievement of selected goals.

Recently, we have begun to see teachers who have been working with technology for many years. They are comfortable with electronic tools such as databases, spreadsheets, word processing, hypermedia, CD-ROMs, and the like, and have had the opportunity to experiment over years in various settings. We are learning much from these teaching pioneers. This chapter presents an overview of the results of many of their efforts and will refer you to other resources.

Why Integrate Technology into Classroom Curricula?

By looking into the workplace, the need for skilled labor capable of using technology on the job is apparent. Many of our students will use technology in occupations that will require little or no training, such as using scanners in supermarkets. Other students will need to know how to use word processors to meet employer needs. Database management software is used by financial management and engineering personnel to solve problems generated on the job. If our students have an understanding of what this software can accomplish and how its application can save time, energy, and money, they will be able to contribute more than their predecessors.

We are in a transition period in which educators can choose to ignore or to accept the responsibility of teaching with and about technological tools—tools that can be used to increase personal and national productivity. If the decision is to take on this responsibility—if it is appropriate to infuse technology into our classrooms—we have another issue to confront: Do we teach computer literacy only as an independent subject, or do we expect students to learn how to use computer applications as learning tools across the curriculum?

Many educators believe that if we consider computer use in the same way that we think of reading and writing, we will create a population that is more computer literate. By teaching the computer and other technological tools as part of our normal curricula and then asking students to use these tools to complete educational activities, we develop students who are better prepared to use technology in later life. Just as we teach our students how to read and write in the early years, we need also to teach them how to use available technology tools.

Because the computer has such a wide variety of educational uses, the process of learning how to use the computer as a learning and problem-solving tool takes a number of years. Educators and researchers are still learning how and when this can best be done, but there is no doubt that it is necessary.

Using Technology Where It Best Fits

Over time, educators using technology have found where technology applications more easily fit into various subjects commonly taught in elementary and secondary school curricula. Word processing can enhance student writing skills; simulation software can develop student inquiry skills in social studies and science; computers can help capture and analyze scientific data; database management software can help students collect, organize, classify, and retrieve social science information; graphing software can display and assist students in interpreting science and social science information. By incorporating word processing and database management and spreadsheet software tools, teachers can more readily develop higher-level thinking skills in their students.

Organizing Resources to Promote Integration

Another realistic aspect of integration is the amount and kind of hardware and software available for integration at a given site. As a result of limited budgets, many administrators have chosen to cluster their computer resources into lab settings and to hire computer specialists to oversee computer use in their schools. Classes are then scheduled into the lab, frequently without the classroom teacher. This practice often limits the computer curriculum to that of computer literacy development only.

It takes a visionary administrator to create a computerized environment in which integration can flourish with a minimal budget. These administrators know that teacher training is the key. If classroom teachers remain computer illiterate, integration is impossible. Teachers must first be computer literate and then be introduced to specific integrative strategies that enhance what they are already doing in their classrooms. Once this is accomplished, teachers must have ample time and resources to explore and play with integration. Obviously, this takes time and resources to accomplish.

By asking teachers to actively make curricular decisions that include computers, administrators keep the concept of integration alive. If teachers go to the labs with their students or are involved in the decisions of what is done in computer labs, integration can still be achieved. When budgets then allow for computer placement in classrooms, as well as labs, then teachers can choose the equipment configuration that best meets their curricular needs.

Those teachers who have become computer literate and who have access to a computer lab and computers in their classrooms have developed rich educational environments. For example, a teacher may use a single classroom computer, a projection system, and a word processor to accompany a brainstorming session involving discussion by the whole class. As the students make their verbal contributions, the information can be categorized or placed in outline form and displayed on a large screen. After the discussion is complete, this information can be printed out and copies made immediately, or students can directly load the information into other computers to expand and refine the material electronically. Small groups can take responsibility for further discussion and elaboration of a subsection of the outline. They may choose to incorporate graphics designed by students or scanned by scanners. Students may transfer their information into a desktop publishing software program that allows them to create a newsletter format. With the advent of hypermedia, videodisc, and CD-ROM, the possibilities are endless and exciting.

Teachers who can access computer labs can teach electronic tools such as word processing, database management, and spreadsheet applications faster and more effectively. After students master the basics of these applications, they are free to use them in class or lab settings, depending on which is easier and available. They are free, then, to learn by using these electronic tools. Just as we teach the tools of reading and writing and ask students to independently use these tools to further their learning, we can do the same with computerized tools. Then we have moved from computer literacy training into the world of integration.

Organizing for Curriculum Integration

Integrating technology into educational settings is a multifaceted process. Let us look at one example of how teachers can organize for integration of technology into curricula. We will visit a first-grade classroom where the teacher is integrating technology to support her learning objectives. Mrs. Fredericks has 30 first-grade students who have had computer experience in kindergarten.

The kindergarten computer experience consisted of monthly visits to the school computer lab with their sixth-grade "buddies" and a weekly time at the class computer where they interacted with drill-and-practice programs that supported learning objectives such as color, shape, letter, and number recognition. As part of the sixth-grade curriculum, students prepared Logo experiences to share with their kindergartner "buddies" once a month. The goal was to show kindergartners that people are in charge of computers and can make them do remarkable things.

Now that these students have reached first grade, Mrs. Fredericks has several ways to use technology to help meet her objectives. She is fortunate to have three microcomputers in her class and the use of one of the school's four projection systems. She also has two, one-hour sessions reserved weekly for her class in the school computer lab.

After Mrs. Fredericks concludes the morning routines, she starts "reading time" by having all the students join her on the rug in the front of the room. She has borrowed the projection system that projects material displayed on her computer monitor onto the large screen at the front of the room. She begins the language experience reading lesson by asking students about their walk to the park the day before. First, a student responds orally to Mrs. Frederick's question. The teacher orally restates the child's response word by word, simultaneously typing the words using a word-processing program that produces primary type on the large screen on the wall. When Mrs. Fredericks has several sentences dictated by the children, she reads the words aloud as she points to each one. She asks the students to read the words aloud with her. After several repetitions of each sentence, she returns to the computer and saves that version of the sentences on a disk. She is then free to modify the sentences on the screen to meet the learning objective of the day—namely, adjectives are words that describe. After the oral lesson is completed, two copies of the class-generated sentences are printed on the class printer. The teacher places one copy in the file she keeps that will eventually be made into a class book. The other copy is photocopied for a writing activity later in the day.

The advantages of conducting the language experience activity using a computer is the time saved in producing, modifying, and printing the student-generated material in a variety of useful formats. By using a computer program such as *Bank Street Writer III* by Scholastic, Mrs. Fredericks is able to produce the primary print version where letters are printed in the same type size that is universally used with first-grade students.

Students are then asked to return to their seats, where they are subdivided into their reading groups to complete their independent reading assignments for the day. One group of six children is assigned to the computer section in the back of the room. A timer is set for 15 minutes. Two students are working on each computer. The first pair works with an activity designed by the teacher using the program *Bank Street Writer III* to reinforce recognition of descriptive words. Two students use *KidWorks 2* to extend the language experience lesson by cooperatively writing several more sentences that include descriptive words (adjectives). The final two students use the same sentences created by the class earlier in the day and substitute adjectives different from those previously selected.

When the timer rings, the second group of six children come to the computer section and the original group returns to their seats to finish another assignment. During this time, the teacher is working with oral reading groups and the aide monitors the rest of the class at their seats and at the computers. As the aide monitors the computer group, she looks for signs of boredom or frustration and is automatically called over to view student output and reteach concepts if necessary.

When the teacher concludes the reading lesson, the aide removes the reading software from the three machines and loads the appropriate math software indicated on the lesson plan for the day. She also completes the daily checklist of which children accessed the computer software and level of competency.

After the children return from morning recess, they prepare for their math lesson. Today, Mrs. Fredericks is reviewing the concept of *subtraction*. After she has concluded her class lesson at the board, the students are assigned practice pages in their workbooks. On the basis of a pretest taken the day before, five students have been identified as needing extra attention. These students are sent to the computer section, where the aide can easily access the three computers and a table with math manipulatives. Because the computer provides immediate feedback, students are given more opportunity to practice with immediate reinforcement.

The single-digit subtration level of *Math Blaster Plus* has been selected as the math software. Students who complete the series of 20 problems correctly and within time limits are rewarded with an opportunity to play a game.

Three students work independently on the computers while the aide uses manipulatives with the other two. The two subgroups exchange places when appropriate. The aide monitors closely, reteaching the concept with manipulatives if necessary. The students' response rate is noted and is entered in the gradebook in place of the seat assignment the rest of the class is completing.

Computer lab time is scheduled after lunch. Because Mrs. Fredericks has two, one-hour sessions weekly in the computer lab reserved for her class, she has several choices. The lab accommodates only half her class at a time. She can send half the class for a 30-minute session or half her class for the hour, waiting until the second weekly session to send the other half of the class. Depending on what she wants to accomplish with her lab time, she varies the practice.

Today, the class is working on keyboarding skills. Because first-graders have limited attention spans and the keyboarding software is demanding, Mrs. Fredericks sends half the class for 30 minutes and the other half for the second 30 minutes of the hour. Today, the aide will accompany the students to the computer lab and actively monitor students along with the computer lab teacher.

Meanwhile, Mrs. Fredericks takes the opportunity to use the sentences generated by the students that morning and asks the students to create new sentences by substituting different descriptive words. By the end of the hour, both groups have spent 30 minutes practicing their keyboarding skills in the computer lab and have also reinforced reading and writing skills.

During recess, the teacher prepares the computer and projection equipment, loading a popular program by Tom Snyder Productions, *Timeliner.* Today, Mrs. Fredericks is preparing for the celebration of George Washington's birthday. As she tells the students about the major events in Washington's life, she types the year and a brief description of the major event into the computer. The information is displayed on the large screen at the front of the room in the format of a time line. By the time she has completed her story of George Washington, she has constructed a time line that can be saved and printed. The printout is large enough for all students to read across the room. She pins the time line on a bulletin board she has prepared earlier. It also has space for the equivalent time line of Abraham Lincoln's life. Later in the week, Mrs. Fredericks will duplicate this lesson using Lincoln as her subject. By displaying the two time lines on the bulletin board, she can easily draw comparisons between the lives of the two presidents.

Organization of Integration Chapters

The remainder of this chapter, as well as Chapter 13, is organized to help teachers learn how they can use technology to increase student learning. Material in this and the next chapter is divided into the content areas of (1) reading and the language arts, (2) social science, (3) science, and (4) mathematics. In addition, information is given on how technology can support meeting the needs of diverse populations. Elementary and secondary-level examples of software and integration strategies are also provided.

Reading and the Language Arts

Reading and the other language arts have traditionally been clustered—so much so that it is difficult to discuss one without the others. This fact has provided many opportunities for programmers to experiment with integration technology. Whether teachers are using the traditional methods of developing reading, writing, speaking, and listening skills in isolation or are adopting the more holistic approaches that concentrate on processing language, computer software is available.

The remainder of this chapter focuses on how to enhance student writing using word processing and other related software, as well as overviewing how technology can help educators increase student reading capabilities.

Enhancing Writing by Using Word Processing

When overviewing all the software used in these subject areas, one tool stands out as the primary integration program selected by teachers: word processing. Many teachers have selected word processing as their personal entrance into the computer world. After experiencing positive personal benefits, many are motivated to use the tool to enhance student learning, particularly by developing student writing skills.

There are two primary methods for teaching writing in the United States today: those that are process based and those that are skills based.

Word Processing and Process Writing
Many writing development projects such as the Bay Writing Project and the South Coast Writing Project in California have focused on developing student writing capa-

bilities by assisting students while they write rather than evaluating a finished product. This approach is a process approach, focusing on developing process rather than isolated writing skills. Word processing gives students the ability to alter their work easily as they write. Peer and teacher suggestions can be incorporated and updates printed easily. For example, when trying to develop the concept of a sentence, some primary teachers ask their students to write sentences describing likes, dislikes, or special events such as holidays. As children work at computers, teachers, aids, or parent volunteers can monitor students' work and assist them as they write, thus taking advantage of a "teachable moment." Because they can easily move a cursor and add or delete versus the traditional pattern of erasing or starting over again, students more readily accept and use suggestions for change.

Another positive attribute of word processing is that it lends itself to collaborative writing efforts. For example, when upper elementary students are asked to put together a monthly newspaper it generally involves a collaborative effort. Students are much more inclined to make suggestions and alter the product when the software gives them the opportunity. Peer editors can free teachers to assist students in ways that they may not have been able to before. Knowing that students can input and print-out frees teachers and paraprofessionals to assist in helping students edit and revise their own writing by asking questions to better understand student thinking. When trained writers and novice writers have time to discuss writing choices during the composition phase rather than afterwards, students are free to incorporate suggestions with understanding.

Word Processing and Development of Writing Skills

Although many teachers are using the process approach to teach writing, some develop writing skills in isolation. Teachers are frequently frustrated by a lack of reinforcement or extension activities when teaching specific writing concepts such as writing a complete sentence or paragraph. The present practice is to rely on dittoed material taken from supplementary materials. The computer provides an alternative that can be cost effective and allows teachers to easily alter activities to meet specific class and student needs.

Integration strategies of electronically based writing activities include using specific activities to reinforce text-based writing assignments for the whole class. Some teachers use software that is actually a collection of activities that have been developed using selected word-processing software. For instance, writing development experts such as Jon Madian have produced a series of writing activities, *Write On*, to help elementary and secondary students develop their writing skills. These are categorized and marketed on separate disks. Because they are created using the word processor and are merely text files, teachers are free to easily modify and adapt the files to meet individual class or student needs. The advantage of using electronically based reinforcement for writing activities is that teachers can easily tailor the activity to meet an individual need and that a student can more easily modify the text, whether it is during draft, composition, or correction phase.

Many school sites that have limited software budgets develop their own activities using the word processor available for student use such as *Microsoft Works* and *Claris Works*. By storing the activities for future classes, teachers are saving valuable preparation time. Teachers use teacher resource or textbook materials to help them create writing development activities. This is one of the most successful initial integrative techniques chosen by teachers because it is flexible, is inexpensive, and can address immediate specific student needs.

Using Other Software to Develop Writing Skills

Educators are required to teach students to produce various types of written work. Expository writing; creative writing of various genres such as fiction, poetry, and drama; and specific instruction on grammar, punctuation, and spelling are general curricular goals.

One common educational practice when teaching composition is to take students systematically through the phases of writing an essay or paper. This process is commonly called *process writing*. These stages may include (1) generating ideas, (2) organizing ideas, (3) drafting, (4) revising, and (5) formatting. Whether focusing on one phase or all phases, specialized software is available. Those computer programs focusing on all phases are called *composing systems*.

One example is *Writer's Helper*, available on Apple II, Macintosh, IBM, and Windows equipment. This prewriting/postwriting aid lets students explore and organize their writing. Once a draft is created, students may select from 18 revision tools to finalize their product. *Process Writer* is available on IBM and Apple and guides students through brainstorming ideas, developing outlines, creating drafts, revising, and final editing steps. *Writing to Write, Form II* uses graphics, written and audio instruction, and feedback. Students are taken through prewriting, drafting, revising, editing, and publishing stages. Students write papers of description, observation, definition, persuasion, narration, and so on. These products help create independent writers who are comfortable moving through the process approach.

Many secondary English teachers are using these composing system software programs in computer labs as their primary instructional system. Others may be limited to a few machines in classroom settings and use appropriate program sections to meet individual needs or in conjunction with an overhead projection system to demonstrate student problem areas.

Other types of software that teachers are using to support writing development are revision tools such as spell-checkers and grammar-checkers. When using revision tools, it is important that the user understands the limitations of the approach and the programming methods used. For example, a revision tool may flag redundancies that the author has knowingly used to increase impact. Colloquialisms can also be flagged by revision programs. When writing plays, a specific characterization may depend on the use of colloquial expressions. The writer must keep in mind that he or she still makes the final choices and that revision tools are used to assist the writer in uncovering unknowing mistakes.

By using this type of software, students can further develop their individual writing skills without direct teacher assistance. By becoming less dependent on teacher input, students can gain confidence and will risk writing more sophisticated and more in-depth material than they might have using the more traditional writing tools. Using these tools also frees teachers to spend class time working with students on those aspects of writing that are not covered by the software programs.

The products and practices presented so far function primarily with expository writing. Students may also develop their creative writing capacities with computer assistance. The remainder of this writing section will overview the enhancement of genre writing.

Fiction

Creative writing is another major curricular goal found at both the elementary and secondary levels. The search for tools and techniques to help motivate student writers can be time consuming and frustrating. Fortunately, many teachers are beginning to use innovative computer programs to help stimulate students to write interesting fictional works.

Elementary teachers frequently use a pictorial stimulus to help students produce fiction. *Storybook Weaver* combines both graphics and word-processing tools to assist the writer in developing illustrated text. Help is provided in developing characters, settings, and plots, as well as illustrating stories. *Once Upon a Time* is a multivolume set of programs that provides a variety of settings or scenes that students can use to support their personal text as they publish their own illustrated books. Newer versions include digitized speech. *KidWorks 2,* designed for prekindergarten through grade 4, combines a word processor, a paint program, and speech capabilities. Students create, illustrate, and have the computer read their stories aloud to them. This is a highly motivating environment for prewriting students, reluctant writers, and students who speak English as a second language. This is available on CD-ROM for Macintosh and Windows.

Older students may be asked to demonstrate competence regarding a particular aspect of fictional writing. For example, students can be asked to develop written narratives or character sketches of living, historical, or fictional characters that are pertinent to classroom objectives. *The Children's Writing and Publishing Center* (Apple/IBM) and *The Writing Center* (Macintosh) are two popular simplified desktop publishing tools developed by The Learning Company. *The Student Writing Center,* which is the Windows version, also incorporates features such as process writing and grammar tips along with spell-checker, thesaurus, and personal journal area with password security.

High school literature teachers are faced with the task of teaching students not only to appreciate specific writing styles but also how to produce them. Using word processors can help students efficiently explore varied writing styles. For example, some teachers challenge high schoolers by giving them an opportunity to work with opening and closing lines of classic short stories. Students can work to match the original author's writing style, mood, characterization, and so on. Matching a predetermined set of parameters forces the writer to analyze writing style in order to duplicate it (Schwartz & Vockell, 1988). By having students take a beginning and ending from an Edgar Allan Poe story and write a short story that reads like D. H. Lawrence, students are required to compare, contrast, analyze, and synthesize both writers' styles.

Poetry

Poetry is generally introduced in the elementary grades and revisited throughout secondary and postsecondary education. Traditionally, there are two basic goals when students are introduced to writing poetry. One is to study the traditional forms or structures of poetry; the other is to help students explore their own self-expressions through poetic form.

In *MicroWorld's Language Art,* two of the four choices are Poetry and Visual Poetry. A unique prompting device helps students create rhyming couplets, haiku, and cinquains. This Logo-based hypermedia environment provides an exploration palette unlike any other. In Visual Poetry, students are given a prompt and a set of powerful buttons that they can use to produce a visual poem that suggests the chosen concept not only by text but also how the text is placed on the page. Students can select from tools, such as a word processor, drawing tool, minimusic synthesizer, voice input system, and Logo. Students create "scenes" that can range from a simple combination of text and pictures to an elaborate presentation using moving text, images, music, and voice. This provides students with a powerful visual/text toolbox to share their poetic spirits in a visually unique way (Yoder, 1993).

A number of computer programs introduce students to standard poetic formats. For example, *Poetry Palette* introduces 13 forms of poetry, providing help screens, rhyming dictionary of 12,000 words, and a graphics illustrator. *Poetry in Motion,* a collection of great poets performing their works on CD-ROM, is a powerful resource for secondary students. Students can watch a poetry reading as the poem's text scrolls by. The CD-ROM provides teachers and students with the ability to randomly access poems of interest. It could be used as a single learning station, as a catalyst for small group discussion, or as a focus for whole group discussion.

Drama

Drama lends itself to student expression. Even shy students can frequently express their viewpoints through other characters. The format of plays gives student authors an opportunity to shape both situation and solution, using conversation as a primary tool.

Any word processor can assist student writers in developing characters, plotlines, settings, and so forth. Modification of a script in progress is eased through the move and copy functions. Frequent printouts make revision a choice rather than a drudgery. Multiple copies of scripts are easily achieved with a printer. Actors can run through their lines aloud, allowing authors an opportunity to evaluate and make changes easily and quickly.

Another superior tool to assist novice playwrites is the software program *Author! Author!* This highly motivating program can be used with second-graders through adults. The software uses graphics and word processing to help students develop their own plays. One option assists students in outlining a play by asking leading questions about dramatic form, conflict, and character. Once an outline is prepared, it can be expanded by entering dialogue and selecting props, backdrops, and character graphics from the program. After the outline is completed, the results can be viewed on screen or printed out as a script. This motivating and versatile program is a remarkable stimulus to individuals and small groups alike. By providing motivation and structure, it frees the teacher from performing these functions. Students can rely on the computer to lead them through the steps of creating a play.

Multimedia and theater are also finding each other. *The Shakespeare Project* is a multimedia system consisting of a hypercard stack and a two-screen workstation linking Macintosh, videodisc player, and video monitor (Friedlander, 1991). Another successful multimedia/drama venture is the *Twelfth Night* CD-ROM that provides information on the play, as well as Shakespeare himself, the historical setting, and more. Students can view an Elizabethan town, view sketches of the Globe Theater, and access definitions from the glossary, short descriptions of any character, plus information on each scene in which that character appears (Schneider, 1993). This provides students with important contextual material that can increase student comprehension of the substance as well as the times in which the material was written.

Using word processors or specialized software programs, students can create interpretations of historical events, adapt basal reading plots to "play" format, and create new myths or restage old myths with modern characters. Students may use TV characters and demonstrate solutions to common problems or develop political commentaries on current events.

Using Telecommunications to Improve Writing

Telecommunications has proved to be a rich resource for writing development. By giving young authors authentic audiences, many students have benefited. Collaborations using a larger constituency are being developed using E-mail capabilities. Using telecommunications, students from one class are now able to communicate with students in other classes in the same school, in other district schools, across the state or nation, and even at international locations. Furthermore, educators are now designing projects that bring together members of diverse populations who are creating authentic meaningful communities.

One successful collaboration consists of K–12 students, teachers, teacher candidates, and college professors who are developing high-quality teaching units. Teacher candidates accessed teams of elementary students to provide resources and feedback as they developed curricular units (Traw, 1994). Another unique project provides students with an opportunity to "communicate" with a variety of literary characters through telecommunications. Student teachers, master teachers, students, and professors take the roles of characters that students have read about in their literature. After a novel is read in class, students "communicate" through telecommunications with a character of their choice. This project increases student comprehension and understanding of character development (Casey, 1990).

Another noteworthy network project was designed to increase student writing skills specifically tailored to specific California Achievement Proficiency (CAP) areas. Teachers are provided with CAP-aligned writing prompts complete with prewriting suggestions and student writing samples. Assignments are given to the whole class, selected subgroups, or cooperative writing teams. The network enables young authors to send or receive files written by others, thus providing a flexible environment for interaction during brainstorming, draft, editing, and final proofing stages.

Telecommunications is also being used to develop a sense of poetry. In a middle school in Virginia, students use conference system techniques to process each other's poetry development. They post poetry on a poetry conference bulletin board then use item responses to provide constructive feedback and to post poem revisions.

Researchers have noted specific benefits from networking projects. Enjoyment in writing increases when writing for distant audiences. Many students are more careful about spelling, punctuation, grammar, and vocabulary choice, and they are more aware of issues beyond their classroom (Casey, 1990).

Grammar, Spelling, and Punctuation

A major concern of elementary and secondary teachers is the capability of their students to master the mechanics of writing, grammar, spelling, and punctuation. Here again, teachers can choose between a skills or process approach.

Skills Approach

Those educators who are teaching skills in isolation are supported by computer programs that are primarily tutorial, drill and practice, and/or game formats. Some products provide resources for teaching and practicing the use of capitalization, punctuation, usage, and spelling together. *Cornerstone Language Series* spans grades 3 through 8. Each of the 175 lessons has a five-step approach: assessment, individualized review, practice, testing, and gamelike reinforcer. On-line tests and teacher reports are also included.

Grammar. Grammar rules can be taught using tutorials, practiced using drill and practice, and reinforced using a game format. Frequently, teachers become frustrated with student lack of interest in learning and using grammatic structures. Motivation and an increase in time on task is addressed by software that presents grammar rules in game format. *Grammar Mechanics* provides two disks of practice in basic grammar rules offered for grades 2 through 3 and grades 4 through 6. An on-disk rulebook helps students to correct sentences. The *A+ Series* provides practice with English grammar and includes a complete authoring system to produce additional lessons. Tom Snyder's *Group Grammar* provides a flexible and fun exploration of stories, asking students to search for certain elements of grammar. Teachers or students can create their own files. This program is designed to be used with one computer and a whole class, pairs or individual use. A collection of 46 best-selling grammar programs, *Mastering English Grammar,* for grades 6 and higher is available on CD-ROM through Queue.

Spelling. Spelling instruction lends itself to a drill-and-practice format. Rather than having students write words five times each, many teachers are asking students to interact with computer programs that flash the spelling word for a fraction of a second and then require the student to type the correct spelling. These programs can be programmed to drop words that are correctly spelled a specified number of times and keep displaying those that do not. This assures that time is spent on unmastered words and not on those that have already been mastered.

Computer programs that allow teachers to add words increase integration possibilities. Some teachers are using parent volunteers to enter spelling words presented in student spelling books. Poor spellers are scheduled for 10 minutes a week to practice their weekly spelling words by using a software program that provides immediate reinforcement and correct response reports to the teacher. Teachers who have problems finding time to teach spelling of specialized science and social science vocabulary words are also turning to spelling software that allows the addition of words.

Some spelling software is totally based on a drill-and-practice/game format. By increasing student time on task, the software can have a dramatic impact on spelling capability. *Spell It 3* provides over 3,600 words plus the ability to add words. Having the words spoken aloud, even those added by a user, increases its value for students who speak English as a second language or who have limited spelling capabilities. The Learning Company has several products that allow addition of words—namely, *Magic Spells* (Apple) and *Super Solvers Spellbound* (Mac/IBM; also CD-ROM).

For those teachers who elect to supplement their spelling programs with skills-oriented software, there are many programs from which to choose. Primary selection criteria should include (1) ability to add words, (2) record-keeping capability, and (3) more time spent on spelling practice than viewing visual reinforcers or manipulating letters.

Punctuation.   Punctuation, like grammar, is another subject that requires memorizing rules. The combination of tutorial, drill-and-practice, and game formats have provided teachers with a motivating tool to increase student time-on-task with punctuation rules and usage. *Essential Punctuation* includes drill and practice, an arcade-style reward game, and a management system for grades 4 through 10.

Some programs on the market are designed to provide tutorials as well as drill-and-practice time on punctuation rules. Selection of appropriate programs and verification that rules used in the classroom match those used by software are critical. Monitoring student contact time with drill-and-practice programs is also recommended. Due to the repetition in some programs, boredom and overattention to the game portions of some programs are prevalent.

These programs have been designed to help teachers introduce or remediate individual needs. When students need assistance in specific areas, this type of computer software can effectively introduce or reinforce spelling words, grammar, or punctuation rules. Those students who require many repetitions to master a skill can be easily serviced. Students who have missed the introduction of specific rules can use tutorials combined with drill-and-practice programs that provide immediate feedback to students and teachers.

Process Approach

Apart from teaching skills in isolation, the computer can also assist in developing writing mechanics—such as grammar, spelling, and punctuation—by using the process approach. Those teachers who have decided to use the process approach have a number of tools from which to select, such as grammar or style analyzers and spell-checkers. With this approach, students write and select appropriate electronic tools to analyze and further refine their products. If your objective is to create independent learners, then giving students practice in selection and use of these electronic tools seems appropriate.

Probably the most used analyzer is the spell-checker. These electronic spelling analyzers can be purchased separately or can be integral parts of word-processing programs. A popular format is the spell-checker that flags words in the text that do not match directly with the words in the spelling dictionary. Possible correct spellings are presented on the screen to allow the user to select or reject.

Revision software typically includes analysis of grammar and punctuation. *Correct Grammar* checks grammar usage, punctuation, style, capitalization, and spelling errors. *Write This Way* is designed for grades 4 through 12 and highlights spelling and grammar errors. The program is designed to guide students to locate and correct their own mistakes.

No matter how much software is available to help learn spelling, punctuation, grammar, and word usage, the teacher is still a vital component in the learning process. It is important that the teacher not overrely on the use of computer software. The programs are available only to *assist* teachers in their efforts to improve student learning.

Reading

Reading is still this nation's most crucial literacy skill. It is no surprise that software developers continue to explore the potential of using technology to increase reading skills at all levels. Unfortunately, the reading field has proven to be one of the greatest areas of challenge. Traditional reading instruction focuses on the development of word recognition, vocabulary, and comprehension skills in isolation. Tutorial, drill and practice, as well as game formats are commonly used in computer programs based on this skills approach.

On the other hand, more recently developed holistic approaches such as literature based or whole language indicate that readers learn how to read best when they are connected with text that is interesting and meaningful to them personally. Many reading experts believe that students learn to read more readily when they approach reading by focusing on language rather than the traditional symbol/sound phonics approaches that represent the skills orientation.

In this section on reading and technology, the skills approach will be overviewed first, then the process and holistic approaches. A short discussion of multimedia and its contributions to reading instruction will be followed by disclosure of how technology can enhance the study of literature. Finally, information organizers and their part in increasing reading levels will be presented.

Teaching Reading Using the Skills Approach

Many reading programs in the United States are still based on the skills approach. Many textbooks adopted by states for elementary school use are based on the theory that reading is learned best by learning the basic skills of (1) sound/symbol relationship, (2) vocabulary development, and (3) comprehension development. These skills are introduced and practiced primarily in isolation. Many of the computer programs that provide reading instruction are also based on the skills approach.

Prereading.   Research on the benefits of using technology to impact early reading has shown positive effects. In studying kindergarten and first-grade classrooms that use technology, teachers are reporting that more kindergarten students who use technology are ready for formal first-grade reading instruction than before. Fewer retentions and increased scores on reading and writing achievement indicators were noted. Students showed increased motivation and self-confidence. Some researchers are recommending that preschoolers should be introduced to computers so they can see that computers are an information source and a communication tool. Encouragement of exploration and understanding of technology early on can enhance problem-solving skills and build self-confidence and self-esteem (Shaver & Wise, 1991).

Many computer programs focusing on the development of prereading skills are being marketed for both home and school use. Most successful programs make effective use of color graphics as well as animation and sound capabilities of microcomputers. Most young children have limited attention spans that have to be captivated to maintain.

Some of the most successful software designed for preschool-age children are exploratory by nature. *The Playroom* gives children the opportunity to click, discover, and play with numbers, letters, and time. *Bailey's Book House* provides children with animated characters, colorful graphics, and music as they explore prereading concepts such as letter identification, finding and hearing rhyming words, visual discrimination, and memory. The open-ended structure of these programs allow younger children to control the computer by choosing what, how often, and how long they connect with specific concepts. Buckleitner (1994) pointed out that young children respond to novelty effects that accommodate their imaginations. Use of simple icons and speech allow young children to access and manipulate exciting, concept-rich environments. Programs such as *KidWorks 2* reads back everything typed into it, which helps reinforce sound/symbol relationship, decoding skills, and improve sight vocabulary.

Sunburst/Wings markets a variety of programs that can be used with a touch screen or a special keyboard—the Muppet Learning Keys—designed for young children. This keyboard has upper- and lowercase letters organized in alphabetical order. It is an invaluable product to parents and professionals working with students who have special needs. *The Muppet Word Book* program introduces letters, words, and writing using six games dealing with upper- and lowercase letters, word endings, beginning consonants, and vowels.

Letter and Word Recognition.   As children begin to study letter and word recognition, computer applications can provide appropriate repetition and feedback. Speech generation is making an impact on reading software. Now, not only can children see a letter and a graphic of an object that begins with that letter but they can also hear the sound or sounds associated with that letter and hear words that begin with that letter. *A to Zap* uses full-color animation, dynamic children's voices, and letters changing to words to support motivating alphabet play. Programs such as *Stickybear's Early Learning Activities* focus on letter recognition, first letter and picture association, as well as counting, shapes, color recognition, and opposites. Each activity has a free play and a structured mode. Print and spoken instructions can also be set to Spanish to increase accessibility.

Reader Rabbit's Ready for Letters and *Reader Rabbit 1* also provide ample reinforcement of letter and word recognition in colorfully motivating formats.

Vocabulary.   Vocabulary development is frequently taught in isolation. Students have various contacts with preestablished lists of words. *Word Attack 3* provides students four ways to interact with each target word. Words, definitions, and example sentences can be added to personalize word lists, concentrating on specialized vocabulary if needed. Other vocabulary development programs such as *Crossword Magic* and *Crossword Creator* are easily learned by students and teachers alike. Their flexibility provide users with a tool that can be used to quickly develop crossword puzzles and answer keys using any combination of words.

Comprehension.   Reading experts have traditionally developed reading comprehension by exposing readers to short reading selections and posing questions that require an understanding of the material read. Some programs follow the patterns established in many of the textbooks traditionally used in U.S. schools. *Read and Roll* incorporates comprehension reading skills with five sets of activities for grades 3 through 6. American Education Corporation produces a similar product, *Reading Comprehension,* that provides exercises for identification of main ideas, sequencing, details, as well as working with cause and effect, analogies, and comparisons.

A slightly more motivating and innovative series of reading development software that has been very popular with upper elementary and remedial junior high students is from Mindplay. Each program places the user in a different role. *Ace Reporter II* concentrates on developing main idea and details. Students become reporters who must uncover who, what, when, where, and why by using simulated teletypes and conducting simulated telephone interviews to gather facts. A story creator is used to reinforce reading for detail and main idea skills. This is an innovative interactive program using material on the third- to fifth-grade reading level. Other programs in the series focus on fact or opinion (*Ace Inquirer*), drawing conclusions (*Ace Detective*), and sequencing (*Ace Explorer*).

Teaching Reading Using a Holistic Approach

Educational software developers have been challenged by holistic reading approaches. Creating computing environments that require students to intimately approach language in written form has brought surprising results. Programs seeking to support this philosophy generally involve higher-level thinking skills and do not focus on using skills in isolation; rather, they focus on using many skills simultaneously, simulating the reading process more closely.

One traditional holistic reading approach is the *language experience approach.* Beginning students are asked to share their thoughts and feelings about a particular experience orally with the rest of the class. The teacher publically writes the spoken words, normally using pen and paper or chalk and chalkboard. Students see, firsthand, how "reading" is the "spoken word" written down. Students are then asked to orally read what has been written down. Students learn how to read those words that mean the most to them—their own.

Teachers are now using word-processing programs and projection systems to facilitate the process. This gives the teacher greater flexibility to demonstrate variations. Comparisons and word patterns can more readily be produced. Children can enter their own letters, words, and sentences. Printouts are immediate and typewritten. An additional advantage is that immediate multiple copies can be produced via printer. As students progress to writing and reading child-authored material, collections can be easily compiled, reorganized if need be, and printed for class use. Although any word-processing program simplifies reading instruction using the language experience approach, the Teacher Support Software publishing firm markets a product entitled the *Language Experience Recorder Plus.*

Many teachers are using the *Big Book Maker* series to supplement their whole language programs. One version provides background scenes and clip art from almost every fairy tale and nursery rhyme (*Favorite Fairy Tales & Nursery Rhymes*). One teacher of high school students with disabilities reported the high degree of success her students attained when they produced products for an elementary school using this software program. Students can create their own big books after whole group and/or small group reading experiences. These products can be laminated and used for repeated readings. Some teachers use the cloze procedure with these programs to produce individualized big books for students to fill in the blanks (Wepner, 1991). Printout formats include minibook and big book, allowing students to create beautifully illustrated personal books for classroom libraries.

A more recent and more complicated computerized reading approach that seeks to teach reading and writing in conjunction is IBM's *Write to Read* program. This reading development program has been heavily researched and its effectiveness is well documented. This program is based on student-developed written products. The *Write to Read* center comes equipped with voice output, cassettes, work journals, a listening library, and games. Words, sounds, and phonetic spellings are introduced.

The cloze reading procedure is another traditional reading approach designed to improve student reading comprehension. It is a flexible approach where short reading selections are altered by removing letters or words using a specific pattern. Students are asked to fill in the missing words using context, syntax, spelling, and vocabulary clues. *M-ss-ng L-nks* is based somewhat on the cloze procedure. Letters, vowels, or words can be deleted, requiring students to use contextual cues to fill in the blanks.

Multimedia Programs and Literature Exploration

Chapter 8 discussed the exciting CD-ROM electronic books, such as the *Living Book* series, that combine text with rich illustrations, sound effects, music, and animation. Glossaries, dictionaries, second language tracks, along with high-quality speech enable students to gain assistance in reading the text. Students can listen and simultaneously see highlighted text as it is read orally to them, thus assisting beginning readers in making the sound/symbol connection. Students can explore these books as individuals, in small groups, or in whole groups using projection equipment. The format keeps students engaged and on task.

The *Wiggleworks* system includes multiple aids to help students and teachers interact with written material. For example, before students write a sentence, they can first digitally record the sentence in their own voices to be replayed at anytime. As students type in their own sentences, they can have the computer read what they have typed in synthetic speech. Students can continually compare the two sentences for correctness. This form of technology supports independent exploration and experimentation as students produce letter sequences and words, thus giving them an opportunity to be more independent learners (Rose & Meyer, 1994).

Multimedia programs using CD-ROM and videodisc technology also support high school literature classrooms. *Illuminated Books and Manuscripts* combine both formats to assist students in researching and understanding five documents and literary works, including Martin Luther King's *Letter from Birmingham Jail,* Tennyson's *Ulysses, The Declaration of Independence,* and Shakespeare's *Hamlet* and *Black Elk Speaks.* The primary focus is the written word. Options may include dramatic readings by professional actors, experts presenting personal interpretations of passages, and audiotapes of appropriate music. Button selections help students define, provide context, interpret, recognize literary techniques, and link major themes. Reference categories include Author and Times, People, Places, Events, and Themes.

Interactive videodisc programs employ several formats. Several use the California Literature Project format: Into, Through, and Beyond. The *Language Navigator Series* uses this format as it pairs titles such as *The Grapes of Wrath/The Great Gatsby* and *Romeo and Juliet/West Side Story.* Teachers and students can select from Into activities such as viewing preselected video clips. A Through activity may be tracing a character's trip on a map, and a Beyond activity may be selected from strategies such as Venn diagrams and reader's theater (Schneider, 1993).

Information Organizers

Information organizers are tools that help learners learn. A generalized description could be electronic aids that support reading, writing, listening, and speaking, as well as helping students organize for studying content area material. *Reading, Writing, and Computers* (Howie, 1989), provides an exhaustive look into the many ways that electronic study aids such as word processors, outliners, hypertext, and database tools can be used to move and link information in new ways, assisting learners in better understanding and presenting information.

Anderson-Inman and Tenny (1989, May) have discussed how reorganizing information in personalized ways helps individual learners learn. They demonstrated how word processors and outliners help students move information into new relationships, thus creating new understanding, and how these "movers" can enhance studying of content material. By using outlining software, students have a much more flexible medium to arrange information into personally meaningful units. Some outlining software, such as *Inspiration,* can reformat outlines into other formats such as concept maps, semantic maps, or webs. This flexibility can assist students in personalizing their study habits and increasing their understanding of studied material.

Anderson-Inman and Zeitz (1993) explained that by actively creating and modifying concept maps, students have a highly flexible tool to integrate new information with previously learned information. Research suggests that "mapping is most effective when students create their own maps throughout the learning process and that students benefit most from maps that 'show' the connections between concepts using labeled links" (p. 6). By producing electronically based concept maps, students may update them more easily. Products such as *Inspiration* allow users to create concept maps with labeled links and to easily switch the concept map to a traditional outline format. These tools are valuable study aids to students with diverse learning styles; they can also support varied content area learning.

Using outlining software can also assist students in increasing their personal information organizing capabilities and can help them plan and organize reports. Traditionally, when students create a report on a topic using multiple sources, they (1) create an outline or concept map, (2) read and insert information, and (3) organize the information into conceptual units. Outlining programs can facilitate student ease in successfully accomplishing these tasks. Students can insert information into the outline at any point in the process with ease. This differs from the traditional word-processing program and the traditional paper outline. Certain products also have special features that allow the user to hide unwanted detail. This gives students the opportunity to take notes as they develop the outline without cluttering the conceptual flow. The concept mapping option can also assist students as they synthesize and reorganize collected information (Anderson-Inman & Zeitz, 1994).

Furthermore, databases and hypertext aid students in linking information or data in ways that increase understanding. These "linkers" provide students with a powerful tool for exploring vast amounts of information quickly and accurately. For example, exploration of hypertext material gives readers the flexibility of approaching the material in many ways. Students are free to get a general overview first and then go back and explore more detailed options, transforming or reorganizing information in ways that meet their individual learning styles (Anderson-Inman, 1989, June).

These electronic information organizers provide educators with new ways to help students develop information gathering, evaluation, and reporting techniques, and to promote independent research, thinking, and reporting skills.

Summary

This chapter gave an overview of how technology enhances writing and reading development. Word processing, writing development, and revision software are helping beginning and reluctant writers gain motivation, confidence, and skill in written literacy. Telecommunications is providing authentic audience and information to support communication and information exchange. Genre writing—such as fiction, poetry, and drama writing—are being supported by technology. Software developers are increasing student mastery of grammar, spelling, and punctuation using skills and holistic approaches.

Reading development is springing from both skills and whole language philosophies. The traditional prereading, letter and word recognition, vocabulary, and comprehension skills are being presented, practiced, and tested using software. Whole language and literature-based approaches are being supported by multimedia, particularly with the upswing of electronic books and multimedia systems. Information organizers, such as outlining and concept maps, and hypermedia programs are offering educators new formats to support personal idea organization and learning.

Much time and energy is needed to explore the many options available today. Successful educational institutions will recognize this fact and plan accordingly. If we are to continue to improve our educational system and our literacy rate, there is no doubt that electronic tools can help. Only when our teaching force is computer literate can we collectively have integrated technology in our classrooms. As more and more individual teachers explore the options and expose more and more students to computerized learning opportunities, we will eventually converge on total integration.

Exercises

1. Describe how you might use technology to enhance your future writing development lessons.
2. Describe how computers can enhance reading skill development.
3. Explain how computers can support holistic reading programs.
4. List three ways to use computer technology to develop secondary-level reading skills.

References

A to Zap. [Computer Program]. Pleasantville, NY: Sunburst/Wings.

Ace Reporter II. [Computer Program]. Tucson, AZ: Mindplay.

Anderson-Inman, L. (1989, June). Electronic studying: Information organizers to help students study "better" not "harder," Part 2. *The Computing Teacher, 16*(9), 21–53.

Anderson-Inman, L., & Tenny, J. (1989, May). Electronic studying: Information organizers to help students study "better" not "harder," Part 1. *The Computing Teacher, 16*(8), 33–36.

Anderson-Inman, L., & Zeitz, L. (1993, August–September). Computer-based concept mapping: Active studying for active learners. *The Computing Teacher, 21*(1), 6–11.

Anderson-Inman, L., & Zeitz, L. (1994, May). Beyond notecards: Synthesizing information with electronic study tools. *The Computing Teacher, 21*(8), 21–25.

Author! Author! [Computer Program]. Tucson, AZ: Mindplay

Bailey's Book House. [Computer Program]. Redmond, WA: Edmark.

Balajthy, E. (1989). *Computer and reading.* Englewood Cliffs, NJ: Prentice Hall.

Big Book Maker. [Computer Program]. Fairfield, CT: Toucan.

Buckleitner, W. (1994, February) What's hot for the computing-using tot? *Technology & Learning,* 18–19.

Casey, J. (1990). Literature comes alive with KidLink computer conferencing. ERIC: ED320158.

Children's Writing and Publishing Center. [Computer Program]. Fremont, CA: Learning Co.

ClarisWorks. [Computer Program]. Santa Clara, CA: Claris.

Cornerstone Language Series. [Computer Program]. Baltimore, MD: Skills Bank.

Costanzo, W. (1989). *The electronic text: Learning to write, read, and reason with computers.* Englewood Cliffs, NJ: Educational Technology.

Crossword Magic. [Computer Program]. Northbrook, IL: Mindscape.

Electronic Bookshelf, The. [Computer Program]. Jacksonville, IL: Perma-Bound.

Essential Punctuation. [Computer Program]. Big Spring, TX: Gamco.

Franklin, S., & Madian, J. (Eds.). (1987). *Making the literature, writing, word processing connection: The best of the writing notebook 1983–87.* Mendocino, CA: The Writing Notebook.

FrEdWriter. [Computer Program]. Concord, CA: Softswap.

Friedlander, L. (1991, April/May). The Shakespeare Project: Experiments in Multimedia, Writing Notebook.

Grammar Mechanics. [Computer Program]. Northbrook, IL: Mindscape.

Group Grammar. [Computer Program]. Watertown: MA: Tom Snyder Productions.

Howie, S. (1989) *Reading, writing, and computers.* Boston: Allyn and Bacon.

Illuminated Books and Manuscripts. [CD-ROM]. Atlanta, GA: EduQuest.

Inspiration. [Computer Program]. Portland, OR: Inspiration Software.

Intellectual Pursuits. [Computer Program]. Dimondale, MI: Hartley.

KidWorks 2. [Computer Program]. Torrance, CA: Davidson & Associates.

Kidwriter. [Computer Program]. Cambridge, MA: Spinnaker Software.

Language Experience Recorder Series. [Computer Program]. Gainesville, FL: Teacher Support Software.

Language Navigator Series. [Videodisc]. Pleasantville, NY: Sunburst/Wings.

Living Books Series. [CD-ROM]. Novato, CA: Broderbund.

M-ss-ng L-nks. [Computer Program]. Pleasantville, NY: Sunburst/Wings.

Magic Spells. [Computer Program]. Fremont, CA: Learning Co.

Mastering English Grammar. [CD-ROM]. Fairfield, CT: Queue.

Microsoft Works. [Computer Program]. Redmond, WA: Microsoft.

MicroWorlds Language Art. [Computer Program]. Montreal, Quebec, Canada: Logo Computing Systems.

Moore, J. (1988, October) Online help from IBM. *Exceptional Parent,* 56–60.

Muppet Learning Keys Toolkit. [Computer Program]. Pleasantville, NY: Sunburst/Wings.

Muppet Word Book. [Computer Program]. Pleasantville, NY: Sunburst/Wings.

Once Upon a Time. [Computer Program Series]. Compu-Teach.

Playroom, The. [Computer Program]. Novato, CA: Broderbund.

Poetry Palette. [Computer Program]. Northbrook, IL: Mindscape.

Process Writer. [Computer Program]. New York: Scholastic.

Read and Roll. [Computer Program]. Torrance, CA: Davidson & Associates.

Reader Rabbit. [Computer Program]. Fremont, CA: Learning Co.

Reader Rabbit's Ready for Letters. [Computer Program]. Fremont, CA: Learning Co.

Reading Comprehension Program. [Computer Program]. New York: Scholastic.

RightWriter. [Computer Program]. Sarasota, FL: Rightsoft.

Roberts, N., Carter, R., Friel, S., & Miller, N. (1988). *Integrating computers into the elementary and middle school.* Englewood Cliffs, NJ: Prentice Hall.

Rose, D., & Meyer, A. (1994, April). The role of technology in language arts instruction. *Language Arts,* 290–294.

Schneider, R. (1993, April). Multimedia programs for the high school literature classroom. *Technology and Learning,* 24–29.

Schwartz, E., & Vockell, E. (1988). *The computer in the English curriculum.* Santa Cruz, CA: Mitchell Publishing.

Shaver, J., & Wise, B. (1991). Literacy: The impact of technology on early reading. ERIC: ED 340 002.

Spell It 3. [Computer Program]. Torrance, CA: Davidson & Associates.

Stickybear's Early Learning Activities. [Computer Program]. Optimum Resources.

Storybook Weaver. [Computer Program]. St. Paul, MN: MECC.

Student Writing Center, The. [Computer Program]. Fremont, CA: Learning Co.

Success with Reading. [Computer Program]. New York: Scholastic.

Super Solvers Spellbound. [Computer Program]. Fremont, CA: Learning Co.

Traw, R. (1994, March). School/university collaboration via E-mail. *Tech Trends,* 28–31.

Twelfth Night. [CD-ROM]. Santa Barbara, CA: Intellimation.

Wepner, S. (1991, September). Linking technology to genre-based reading. *The Reading Teacher,* 68–70.

Wiggleworks. [Computer Program]. New York: Scholastic.

Word Attack 3. [Computer Program]. Torrance, CA: Davidson & Associates.

Write On! [Computer Program]. Hood River, OR: Humanities Software.

Write This Way. [Computer Program]. East Lansing, MI: Hartley.

Writer's Helper: Stage II. [Computer Program]. Iowa City, IA: Conduit.

Writing Center, The. [Computer Program]. Fremont, CA: Learning Co.

Writing to Write, Form II. [Computer Program]. Atlanta, GA: Eduquest.

Yoder, S. (1993, August/September) MicroWorlds: Logo, hyperCard, and more. *The Computing Teacher,* 26–28.

Chapter *13*

Curriculum Integration

Social Science, Science, and Mathematics

Social Science

For many years, educators have watched the number of pages increase in social science texts and each year teachers complain of their inability to complete all curricular requirements. The microcomputer has given educators a chance to change the focus of social science education from memorization of facts to acquiring and utilizing higher-level functions needed in the inquiry approach. These functions include location of pertinent information, evaluating, judging, making determinations, and evaluating outcomes.

The microcomputer can store, organize, reorganize, and display vast amounts of related information much more rapidly and accurately than most of us can imagine. By focusing social studies educational goals on the manipulation and interpretation of information, we not only promote a greater understanding of historical and social interaction but we also prepare students to make more informed decisions in the field of social science and elsewhere.

By asking our students to use technological tools to gather, manipulate, and report new understanding, we give our students electronic tools that may also be valuable to their future employers and our voting public. Students who have used database management tools or survey or graphing programs can better understand the strengths and weaknesses of conclusions drawn using such tools.

The remainder of this section will present specific computer programs such as (1) word processing and desktop publishing, (2) database management, (3) spreadsheets, (4) graphing, (5) telecommunications, (6) multimedia, (7) simulations, (8) educational games, and (9) specialized software programs that are currently being used to work with and teach social science processes.

Word Processing and Desktop Publishing

Word processing and desktop publishing are logical and welcomed aids to presenting information efficiently and creatively. Desktop publishing software such as *The Children's Writing and Publishing Center* give second-graders and older students the opportunity to construct reports or two-columned formatted materials with little time invested in learning the software. By using software that saves time, provides a more polished end product, and allows easy modification, students can place more energy into learning the nuances of the subject area.

Students respond to writing activities that bring them into the historical time period. For example, elementary students can create journal entries from the perspective of a historical figure on a critical day in his or her life. Student output can be categorized and published as a collection. Comparisons and contrasts drawn through oral discussions using an overhead projection and student work could bring additional insights that may not normally have been uncovered. Or, perhaps during a U.S. history class, half the class could create a small-town newspaper that reflected the life and times of southern prewar conditions. The other half could do the same for the postwar period. The class could then compare, contrast, and draw conclusions from the two documents, ultimately comparing findings with actual reports generated by historical experts.

Furthermore, students could demonstrate their understanding of campaign platforms of presidential candidates during critical historical periods in U.S. history by writing a campaign advertisement for a specific candidate. These advertisements could be produced using desktop publishing software, giving students further exploration of techniques commonly used to persuade the public to adopt specified views. By studying and using these persuasive techniques, students can be more aware of the power of persuasion and respond appropriately. By using more technologically sophisticated tools such as desktop publishing, hypermedia, and others, students are better equipped to evaluate the more sophisticated tools that modern television and print media provide.

The outcomes of these activities, when compared with traditional reading assignments, provide greater opportunity for students to learn and practice higher-level thinking skills that can be directly applied to making decisions when voting in a democratic society.

Database Management

Much of social science is a compilation of information that is organized in ways to help us learn about the past. It is hoped that by being aware of the mistakes and successes of different cultures, we can better understand ourselves and our neighbors and produce a world that can meet the needs of all who share it.

In the past, students have been required to memorize events and dates to prove their contact with presented information. Many educators are now asking students to go further with such information—to analyze it, make judgments about it, and extrapolate from it. By using database management software, students have an opportunity to view large organized lists of information and to manipulate data in ways not possible by earlier elementary and secondary students. Databases allow students the freedom to search and sort textual data in new and interesting ways, thus giving students greater opportunity to explore data and improve their own personalized problem-solving strategies.

Teaching Students Database Management

Database management (see Chapter 7, Tool Applications) is one of the most exciting computerized applications available. It is also one of the most challenging from a teaching standpoint. Students must be taught what a database is, what a database management tool is, the mechanics of interacting with a specific management program, and how to form questions to answer with the aid of the software. This is no easy task.

Because database use and development is a multistep process, many educators are teaching database management skills at several grade levels. A simple database program such as *Friendly Filer* can be used in second or third grade to introduce students to the basics of database usage. Students are given a prepared database and are taught how to arrange, sort, and select data. They are then given a list of questions that can be answered by using the database.

Later, students may be asked to build database files. For example, students may be introduced to a specific American Indian tribe and asked to gather information about it. Once they have assembled all the information on that tribe, the class (in small group formation) is asked to categorize the information and attach meaningful labels. Using the labels determined by the class, each group then takes a different tribe and collects information that will be placed in each of the predetermined categories.

Once the information is collected and compiled by the groups, the class will have created a personalized database on the subject of American Indians. At this point, the teacher may choose from a variety of options. Students may be asked to develop questions for the entire class to answer. Teachers may develop a series of questions and ask for individual student, group, or whole class responses in either oral or written formats.

As students mature and become familiar with using database software, they can be introduced to the concept of designing a database to solve a specific problem. Now, students are challenged to discern which problems lend themselves to database solution. Students must see the ways that textual and numerical information can be organized and adjusted to answer questions and solve problems. Usually, this would occur at the upper-elementary or secondary level.

Students begin by identifying a problem. They then formulate questions related to the problem and research to gather the necessary information. Next, they create a computer database in which to feed the information and enter the data. Finally, they develop and test their hypotheses and draw their conclusions.

Database Activities in Social Science

Obviously, as soon as students can use a database they can start using the tool to solve generated problems. Many primary-level teachers ask their students to provide information about themselves and their tastes that can then be entered into a database and sorted to answer questions about the general tastes or attributes of the class. For example, name, eye color, hair color, age, favorite dessert, favorite movie, and so on. can be used as possible topics. By using a large screen projection device, teachers can lead student discussion and help students generate questions that can be answered by the database. This can be a wonderful ice-breaker at the beginning of the school year.

Many students enjoy the very popular computer program *Where in the World Is Carmen San Diego?* by Broderbund. In order to solve the mystery, students are required to understand clues that involve 30 countries of the world. Two inventive teachers suggested that if students developed a database, it would assist students as they played the game. As a result, students generated a 13-category database as suggested.

A secondary-level project dealt with European countries prior to World War I. Fields such as nation, government type, population, language, and religion were determined. After students researched and entered data, they sorted files and made hypotheses that were then compared with actual historical outcomes. The interpretation of the data became highly valuable during class discussions where students could delve more deeply into the understanding of that time period.

There is no doubt that the process of creating databases to answer specific questions develops higher-level thinking skills. Once students begin to sort information in order to see relationships and draw specific conclusions, they also have to evaluate the importance of categories of information.

Spreadsheets

Some teachers are using spreadsheet software to help students better understand the relationship of numerical information. The spreadsheet tools included in *ClarisWorks* and *Microsoft Works* can be used to run a class simulation of the stock market. Each student can select a stock or stocks to monitor and report on daily using the spreadsheet. Stocks are tracked every day over a period of a few weeks. Students are then asked to make predictions as to the best stock investment.

Another popular application for elementary students is to record expenditures on a trip across the United States or any other given locale. Individual or student teams can keep track of driving time, car expenses, lodging, meals, and so on, and make comparisons and predictions as to who will make the trip in the least amount of time, spend the least amount of money, and so forth.

Secondary students studying U.S. or world history can run comparisons of indices such as industrial growth, agricultural production, and natural resources of a specific era, and then draw conclusions and make predictions of future trends. Another spreadsheet activity that strikes closer to the hearts of many secondary students is centered around their ability to understand the consequences of their personal financial choices. Because spreadsheet programs can calculate the time-adjusted value of money, simulation can show young adults the consequences of financial decisions long before reality does. Allowances, summer job earnings, and college financial aid monies can be motivating data to teach secondary students the value of using spreadsheet programs to make personal financial decisions. From here, teachers can broaden student awareness to more global social issues such as voting trends, population shifts, and international economic indices.

Graphing

Many students get a better grasp of relationships when they can view data graphically. There are several graphing programs that help students develop their own graphs using data of their making. Once students have created their own graphs, they have a more intuitive understanding when reading other graphs.

Software such as *Graph Power* gives elementary students the opportunity to see how placing information in different graphic formats influences its interpretation. Frequently, primary-grade social science curricula centers around the family and community. Students are asked questions about their family, such as number of siblings, pet ownership, favorite colors, and the like. This information can be collected and presented using graphing software and a projection system. The class can compare the number of cat owners with the number of dog owners or bird owners. Viewing similarities and differences of class members' pet choice can help the teacher focus on the similarity and diversity of communities.

Graphing software can also help students better understand which graphic formats are appropriate for different types of information. Secondary students who have access to MS-DOS and Macintosh hardware can choose from many professional spreadsheet products such as *Lotus 1-2-3* and *Excel,* or from integrated packages such as *ClarisWorks* and *Microsoft Works,* which can be used to display data in pie, bar, line, or other appropriate graphic formats.

Telecommunications

Telecommunications (see Chapter 9, Networks and Telecommunication) has entered elementary and secondary classrooms in several forms. Students and teachers are communicating with each other globally, mining and collecting information from bulletin boards, joining in collaborative projects, as well as developing reading, writing, and technology skills.

With the success of Internet, the influx of elementary and secondary students on-line has increased dramatically. Perhaps one of the most valuable applications has been in creating opportunities for students to interact with students from other cultures and countries. One elementary school in Minnesota has become a magnet school specializing in technology and global studies. Telecommunications is an important part of their curricula. The sixth-grade teachers and the Global Specialist have connected with the World School for Adventure Learning through the University of St. Thomas in St. Paul, Minnesota. Through this connection, students go on line via telecommunications to "talk" to other children and teachers who have studied the topic of interest. They eventually become resources themselves. Students can communicate with other people, collecting resources around the world on a topic of choice. Students who attend this school are taught basic skills of reading, writing, and math using technology in the context of global concepts such as interdependence, economics, and cultural change (Kadrmas, 1994).

There are many networks that are being accessed by K–12 educators. Following are several examples. *AT&T Learning Network* places participants into learning circles based on subject, location, and grade level. Students follow provided curricula and share their work regularly with other learning circle classes. The outcome is usually a final product such as a news magazine or journal. Curricular emphasis is geographic and cultural awareness, computer literacy, and team building. Units include government, economics, history, and geography. *FrEd Mail* is a network dedicated to providing low-cost services to K–12 education, helping teachers and students participate in a wide range of learning experiences, including exchange of information and participation in collaborative learning projects. Teachers also share ideas and materials through the network. *K12NET* is a system of more than 500 linked bulletin boards that carry thousands of messages weekly among sites around the world. Project collaboration and subject-specific conferencing are routinely held. This is a free service available to anyone who can access it through a bulletin board.

Several states, such as California (CORE) and Florida (FIRN), have developed telecommunication systems for K–12 and postsecondary institutions. Consult Chapter 16, Resources for Further Study, for more information regarding accessing these networks.

Multimedia and Social Science

One of the most dramatic changes in social studies and technology is the increase in multimedia products (see Chapter 8, Multimedia/Hypermedia). The videodisc and CD-ROM have made it possible to conduct rapid searches and to immediately access information in the form of text, speech, graphics, music, audio clips or video clips.

General Reference Tools

Electronic CD-ROM encyclopedias are a common tool in many school libraries and computer laboratories; their use requires searching skills. Searching using *key words* or *key phrases* produces myriads of possibilities in seconds. Students then must determine how to refine, or further limit, their search to more efficiently access desired information. Learning these processes requires direct instruction and practice, yet this is probably one of the most valuable skills students can learn as they mature into the information age.

Reading maps remains an important aspect of social studies. Electronic versions provide quick, easy access to multiple maps at one sitting. These products may be found in the traditional disk formats or on CD-ROM. Those mounted on CD-ROM take advantage of multimedia possibilities. *World Vista Atlas* and *America Vista Atlas* are based on digitized maps and data from Rand McNally. Each country or state is first seen on a locator map that establishes a regional context. Detailed maps and data are available. Data files are well organized and easily accessed but not searchable. Picture files are extensive, showing as many as 14 photos per state. Sound files include regional music from the selected country or state. The Phrase Book includes a collection of spoken phrases in the language of the country selected. Clearly, multimedia formats provide more motivating, richer information that appeals to students of different learning styles and capacities.

PC Globe, PC USA, MacGlobe, and *MacUSA* are electronic atlases that provide quick, easy access to country or state maps. Each can be viewed in four forms: a base map, a cities map, an elevation map, and a geographic features map. Each state or country has a folder with background information such as historical, political, as well as graphs and statistical data. Regional, thematic, and historical maps are included. Relationships among states and specific categories such as infant mortality or per capita income can easily be obtained. Comparisons may also be made among individual countries or between an individual country and the relationship to regional or world data. Clearly, these tools provide teachers and students with ease of access and flexibility in juxtaposing different types of information quickly. Teachers and students can better spend time posing and answering high-level questions, rather than spending the same amount of time sifting through traditional print texts, atlases, and so on.

Specialized Reference Tools
Software developers are producing products that are large multimedia collections of information on specific topics. This also supports the premise that research skill instruction must emphasize key word searching and the ability to explode or refine searches. Students will be spending less time locating pertinent information and more time evaluating its viability.

For teachers interested in providing students with short multimedia introductions to important events in the last century, *20th Century Video Almanac—The Best of Our Century* is a CD-ROM that provides cultural, political, and technological events of searchable articles, pictures, and video clips. American history teachers and their students may use the *CD Sourcebook of American History* as a powerful research tool. It includes 1,000 primary source documents along with 28 interpretive volumes of text as well as photographs and pictures. These research tools provide teachers with a vast array of historical information in text, audio, and graphic form in easily accessible formats.

Another new exploratory format for electronically stored information centers around the concept of capturing newsworthy events, placing them in a chronological format, and providing searchability, something like an electronically based news magazine. Both *Time Magazine* and *Newsweek* are publishing compendiums of articles published in their weekly magazines. *TIME Almanac 1994* features every article in *Time Magazine* from 1989 through 1993 along with photos, charts, maps, and video footage. Research features include searching, linking, browsing, and printing. *Newsweek InterActive* features multimedia versions of selected headline stories. Four hours of live radio interviews, articles from the *Washington Post,* and a database of stories from the past three months of print editions are included.

Teachers and students who are focusing on geography have additional resources to the atlases discussed earlier. *Geopedia* CD-ROM uses six entry pathways to explore 1,200 articles; 2,000 pictures, maps, charts, graphics, and tables; and over 20 video clips. Users can create their own graphs and charts as well. This product is designed to accommodate students with different styles of thinking and learning. LucusFilm and The National Geographic Society have partnered to produce *GTV: A Geographic Perspective on American History,* an interactive videodisc set covering American history from pre-Columbian times to present day. Presentations can be created and saved to disk. In addition to 60 short video segments, there are 1,600 still images and over 200 maps. A new version of the *HyperCard* stacks was released in 1994.

Social studies students can also gain special understanding of various cultures and subcultures using CD-ROMs that provide nuance and depth that may be missing in other resources. *The American Indian: A Multimedia Encyclopedia* includes history, geography, tribes, legends, photos, maps, drawings, sounds, documents, tribe locations, museums, and societies. Information on 150 American Indian tribes found in the United States and Canada is provided. Researchers can view rare maps, treaties, and photos from the National Archives. Students can hear the recorded sounds of authentic American Indian songs in the sound module, which includes narration and music. *The African American Experience* is an electronic textbook that chronicles African Americans from the African continent. Access is simple using key word searches. Biographical sketches, rare historical prints, documents, and photographs provide a rich context for understanding.

Simulations and Social Science

As our educational software base has matured, so has the sophistication of social science simulations and games. At this point, there is a wide range of computerized simulations from which to choose. Teachers can access updated versions of classic programs such as *Oregon Trail.* The CD-ROM version provides the classic premise but brings the trip across the Oregon trail to life. This simulation of pioneer America provides a distinct personality for each character by incorporating natural-sounding digitized speech. Pioneer music adds depth to the simulation as well as vividly detailed graphics. Screen display includes windows and icons that players can use to check the status of supplies, consult the guidebook, buy, trade, hunt, talk to people, and track progress by map.

Over the last few years, software developers have created many marvelous social science simulations. Some of the best have been created by Tom Snyder Productions. Fortunately, his products span elementary and secondary grades. The *Choices, Choices* series of simulations are aimed at younger elementary students. *Taking Responsibility* and *On the Playground* guide children through cooperative discussions, role-playing, and communication skill development opportunities centered on issues they face everyday.

The *Decisions, Decisions* series provides upper elementary and secondary students with situations that require a knowledge of history, higher-level thinking skills, and group problem-solving abilities. Urbanization, environment, prejudice, colonization, immigration, the Revolutionary War, balancing the budget, foreign policy, media ethics, and election campaigning are specific topics offered in the series. Software and print material provide scenario and background information. Problems are presented by the software. Students make decisions and interact with consequences of their decisions throughout the simulation.

The Other Side is another Tom Snyder piece that asks students to simulate building a bridge between two countries cooperatively while maintaining national security—a truly timely concern in today's changing world. This complex simulation can be successfully run using small groups of one class, two classes at the same site, or, through modem, two groups or classes located at different sites.

Educational Games

There is no greater single motivator in educational computing than the game format. One of the most successful social science game/simulation collection of programs is the *Carmen San Diego* series by Broderbund. *Where in the World?, Where in Europe?, Where in USA?, Where in Time?,* and *Where in America's Past?* are separate social studies-based games that focus on solving a crime. Students take the role of detectives who solve the mystery by successfully following clues that are uncovered by students correctly guessing specific geographic or historical facts. Resource books are included with the software such as an almanac and a comprehensive tourist guide. In practice, students will use each other, teachers, encyclopedias, and anything else they can easily access to produce correct answers.

Another successful series is the *Cross Country* series by Didatech Software. Students take the role of a truck driver who must plan trips to specific destinations, carefully monitoring expenses, mileage, and time. Students must focus on geography and economic concerns to win. Individuals or groups can compete. The series includes games featuring the United States, California, Texas, and Canada.

Specialized Software Useful in Social Science

Every year, new educational software is being developed that takes advantage of the computer's capabilities to motivate the computer user. Many teachers are using these programs to increase social science understanding. Programs that allow students to create time lines, comic strips, and specialized calendars much faster, with more flexibility, and with a professional looking outcome are capturing the attention of many students. Social studies classes are becoming dynamic places where students explore new tools of learning as well as new information. This section is devoted to a brief exploration of these offerings.

Tom Snyder is a leading producer of quality software that highlights the most effective attributes of the computer. Much of his offerings are designed for social studies curricula. One of his most flexible programs, *Timeliner,* organizes information into a time line format that can be used at almost any grade level. Primary teachers can use it along with large screen projection and student input. Upper elementary and secondary students can generate time lines based on a day, week, month, or annual format. By merging time lines, students can compare and contrast vital information. For example, students can study world cultures one culture at a time, creating time lines for each separate culture. They can then merge different time lines to get a better understanding of what was going on in the world at a given time or era. Ancillary products, *Timeliner Data Disks* and *Time Patterns Toolkit,* help teachers efficiently integrate *Timeliner* into their social science lessons.

Chronos is a multimedia multilayered time-event database. Teachers or students can produce vibrant presentations that demonstrate research findings, such as time lines that incorporate color graphics, audio and digitized sound, and pop-up comments. *Comic Strip Factory* can assist secondary students in creating political cartoons that illustrate contrasting viewpoints prevalent at a specific time and place, such as the French Revolution, the American Civil War, and so on (Vlahakis, 1988).

There are also software programs, such as *CalendarMaker,* that allow users to build daily, weekly, monthly, or annual calendars. Students can be asked to develop a calendar that would depict the major battles during the American Civil War or World War II. Any information that needs to be sequenced or seen in varying relationships can be manipulated using this type of software in a unique way, allowing students to view and draw fresh conclusions (Vlahakis, 1988).

These specialized computer programs are a sampling of the social science software available to educators today. By including them in classrooms and computer laboratories, educators can give their students an opportunity to reorganize information in new and unique ways. By juxtaposing information in new ways, students have a greater opportunity to move out of the passive learner posture into an active learner who compares, contrasts, evaluates, judges, and draws conclusions.

Summary

Technology and social science curricula are providing educators with many exciting options. Students can now write, revise, and print polished reports using word-processing and desktop publishing software. They can use database management and spreadsheet software to study and solve social science problems. Graphing, mapping, and various calendar-making software can help students present social science information effectively. Students can interact with other students or experts in other states or countries using telecommunications. They can research vast amounts of multimedia information using CD-ROM and laser disc archives. Students can experience social science problems through simulations and have the chance to experience the consequences of different solution paths. The challenge to educators is to explore the many varied options and make intelligent decisions concerning purchase and use.

Science

Many computer applications that work effectively with social science work equally well with science curricula. Information collection, information structuring, information reorganization, and information reporting are all necessary components to scientific inquiry. The computer is a tool that can assist in performing these functions quickly and accurately.

Furthermore, recent attempts to develop national standards for science instruction in the United States have focused on the interconnectedness of disciplines such as science, math, and technology. As part of New York state's overall plan for school improvement, New Compact for Learning, the committee is designing performance criteria to support the development of curriculum and assessment. Three outcome statements focus on the interconnectedness of mathematics, technology, and science— that students be able to identify themes that are common to all three disciplines; apply integrated knowledge; and solve interdisciplinary problems and develop habits that will enable them to work cooperatively with others as they solve these problems (Selvy, 1993).

This section will overview the many ways that computers can assist educators in teaching science, not only preparing students to actively interact with the inquiry approach but also motivating some for a potential career. Collection of scientific data can be achieved by microcomputer-driven data-collection devices. Data collection can be further enhanced by telecommunication and multimedia resources found in CD-ROM and laser disc formats. This same information can then be organized and reorganized using database and spreadsheet tools. Results can be professionally presented using graphics, word processing, and new multimedia reporting software. Many educators are also increasing scientific understanding through computer simulations.

Information Collection

The microcomputer has brought new avenues of data collection to elementary and secondary classrooms. With the help of computer technology, students can set up in-class experiments, monitor and record data, use telecommunications to send and receive information from other sites, and access information through multimedia resources.

Computer as Lab Instrument

Software that turns the computer into a lab instrument has met with success. Microcomputer-based laboratories (MBLs) are gaining popularity in elementary and secondary science programs. These laboratory tools combine personal computers with reasonably priced data-collecting instruments and appropriate software. Broderbund's *Science Toolkit Plus Master Module* and additional modules have given the teacher a tool that records and charts data. The kit includes a book of experiments, software that records and graphs information, as well as temperature and light probes.

Measuring and recording temperature changes of a classroom over a 24-hour period or light emitted from different surfaces are possible with these *Science Toolkit* modules. The software can store the results of the measurements for later analysis or they can be displayed on the screen in real time. The immediacy of taking raw data such as heart rate or temperature and displaying the information in dynamic graph form gives learners a motivating way of deducing scientific principles. When compared with direct expository statements, this method gives learners the real-life opportunity to draw conclusions rather than passively recalling information. For example, by moving a temperature probe from the bottom of a beaker of hot liquid to the top, students learn firsthand that heat rises. Other modules in the series are designed to assist teachers in conducting experiments involving speed and motion, earthquakes, and the human body.

Motion detectors assist teachers in teaching physics principles. *Playing with Science: Motion* is an award-winning example of programs designed to provide a hands-on approach to understanding relationships among time, distance, and velocity. Experiments involving acceleration and velocity over time can be enhanced by graphic output. By studying the movement of toy cars in controlled settings using these computerized sensors, students can graph and compare changes. A hypothesis can more easily be verified using immediate data. Temperature, light, sound, and motion probes can be integrated into biology, chemistry, earth science, physics, and technology study.

At the high school level, the *Explore Science Series* provides a comprehensive microcomputer-based laboratory in the fields of biology, chemistry, and physics. Students explore science phenomena that would be almost impossible in traditional laboratory settings. An integrated spreadsheet is included and students can present data in varied graphic formats.

Telecommunication

Telecommunication (see Chapter 9, Networks and Telecommunication) is becoming a valuable electronic tool that links students nationally or internationally, allowing them to collect and distribute local data to the rest of the participating network of students. By sharing data, each site then gains valuable up-to-the-minute information from the rest of the network, giving all participants the opportunity to analyze and evaluate immediate conditions on a greater scale than previously possible. In a shrinking world, activities such as this give students a much greater perspective and acceptance of the possibility of national and global cooperation.

Chapter 1, The Impact of Computers in Educations, discussed the National Geographic Kids Network, which allows students in grades 4 through 9 to share research data with students across the United States and 20 other countries. McGraw-Hill sponsored a telecommunication science project where students across the United States grew corn from seeds indoors, standardizing conditions and researching soil types while comparing growth patterns. Another telecommunication project involving daily reports of weather conditions throughout the United States and Canada allowed students to access all information reported. Many students were motivated to ask why temperatures in British Columbia, Canada, were much warmer than many areas in the United States located south of that location (Solomon, 1989). Projects such as these provide an immediate, real audience to share data, ideas, and hypotheses and to uncover a broader perspective than possible before using telecommunications.

High school biology classes in Middletown, Delaware, have participated in the Global Laboratory, a telecommunications project initiated by Cambridge-based TERC. Students from all parts of the globe focus on local ecological exploration and worldwide collaboration. The Middletown students have marked out a two-kilometer section of forest and are tracking differences in the number and health of lichens as a measure of air pollution. Temperature and precipitation are measured daily. Sample pond water is taken weekly for the purpose of measuring dissolved oxygen and acidity. Using Eco-Net, an international telecommunications network specializing in ecology, students share findings with students in countries such as Indonesia, Mexico, Japan, and Russia. Students are becoming computer literate and globally aware as they actively participate in this real-world research project (Weiss, 1992).

Some innovative teachers have been exploring how to use networked computers (computers that are electronically linked together) to increase student interaction during key points of the discovery process. One teacher demonstrated the beginning of an experiment and then asked students to send their hypotheses concerning the outcome through electronic mail to the teacher. The compiled printout of all hypotheses was used to begin the discussion about the lab the next day. Students were able to see their hypothesis in relation to that of their classmates, and the teacher previewed current student understanding and altered the next lesson to best meet student needs. Another strong use of E-mail is the practice of having students send questions to the teacher, which allows all students to have questions answered. Some teachers are requiring that student science logs be kept on the network. Students can summarize experiments, articulate what they have learned, present personal questions, and make observations. This information could be directed to the teacher or other students for comment (Brienne & Goldman, 1990). The use of *GROUPwriter* also allows students to participate in live, online discussions over networks.

Multimedia Tools

Students can also obtain important information through researching CD-ROM and videodisc collections of audio, visual, and textual information (see Chapter 8, Multimedia/Hypermedia). These sophisticated collections provide students with tools to quickly search video clips, pictures, slides, charts, and diagrams to obtain needed information. Compendiums that focus on specific topics are becoming more prevalent. For example, *The Dictionary of the Living World* CD-ROM provides educators and students with over 2,600 files covering 5,000 species, over 100 video clips, 100 wildlife sounds, and hundreds of full-color photographs. Users can search the collection using a wide range of buttons such as index, query, QuickTime, sound, and global map. Not only are students quickly accessing pertinent multimedia information but they are also gaining practice in using searching techniques that may be valuable for later life. Videodiscovery publishes a range of high-quality videodisc and CD-ROM science products in life science, earth science, and physical science fields.

Information Structuring and Restructuring Tools

After data are acquired, the information needs to be organized and possibly reorganized to gain understanding. Database management and spreadsheet tools (see Chapter 7, Tool Applications) provide learners with flexibility and accuracy. Innovative use of electronic mail can also provide students with additional opportunities to reevaluate information.

Database

Database management is one application that can assist students in determining relationships among discrete data. Sorting on a dinosaur database that describes physical attributes and habitat of the species can lead students to discover how physical attributes and habitat are interrelated. Students can deduce why some dinosaurs had claws and others did not, why some had armor and others did not. The act of deducing accurately produces students who gain confidence in their own thinking processes. It increases confidence and produces students who are comfortable working with unknowns—a necessary task when working as a scientist, architect, or engineer (Turner & Land, 1988).

Student-developed databases are more challenging. By focusing on a problem or body of information, students are forced to make numerous decisions that are similar to scientific inquiry. Students must have a clear focus on what information needs to be collected to approach solving stated problems. They must select the categories that determine how the information will be sorted. A trial and error approach is usually used until useful categories are found. Then students must formulate questions that can be answered using the database format, moving closer to a solution of the problem posed. Because the field of science consists of collections of qualitative and quantitative information, database management software is a valuable tool.

For example, information on planets of the solar system can be gathered, categorized, placed in a database format, sorted, searched, analyzed, and used to answer student-made questions. Plant, tree, and flower identification goals can be met by using student-made databases designed for that purpose.

Databases are also used to organize data collected from experiments using microcomputers as lab instruments. Students collect data generated from light and/or temperature effect on plant growth. Those data are then entered into a database management program and sorted to discover or verify patterns that can then be used to predict future possibilities.

Spreadsheets

Spreadsheet software helps students calculate relationships among many categorized bits of information. These programs assist students in experimenting with data by changing values and drawing conclusions based on how the changes influence the entire data collection. This makes it the perfect tool to help students predict and test their hypotheses. Once students understand what a spreadsheet is, what it can do, and how to manipulate data to answer specific questions, it becomes an exciting learning tool.

At the primary level, teachers typically manipulate the spreadsheet software using a projection system. Students help provide information, which the teacher displays on a large screen, and class or small group discussion can be used to draw conclusions.

Experiments comparing plant or mold growth in varying conditions can be enhanced using a spreadsheet. Daily or weekly growth data can be entered into the spreadsheet program. Categories could include plants grown under artificial light, in shade, or in direct sunlight. Plant height would be measured and data entered on a daily basis. Formulas inserted into the spreadsheet would automatically compute comparisons on a daily basis, leaving the students to spend time and energy drawing conclusions and making inferences.

Upper-elementary science curricula frequently includes weather. Students can record the precipitation of several major cities located in different parts of the United States over a specified period of time, drawing comparisons such as which city has the most, or least, rainfall. Students can then research previous annual rainfall figures for the locations, average the amounts, and compare them to the recently obtained figures.

The study of trends can be enhanced using spreadsheet programs. Endangered species is a timely topic. Through research, students could determine the number of animals of an endangered species existing 30 years ago, 20 years ago, 15 years ago, and so on. After entering the data into a spreadsheet, students can calculate the rate at which the species is disappearing, then use the formula to predict how many animals will exist 5 years from now, 10 years from now, and so forth. Those activities in the science curriculum that involve numerical comparisons may be best accomplished using spreadsheet software. This allows students to go beyond calculation, using important class time to compare, contrast, and test hypothesis.

Information Reporting Tools

After data have been generated, structured, and/or restructured, the information is generally reported. There are several types of software that can assist in this process.

Word Processing

Generating scientific reports is a part of science curricula. Word-processing software can enhance report writing by giving students a medium that allows them to change text easily and provide a professional-looking output. Some teachers have asked students to keep journals that require them to observe a phenomenon over time, such as a specific tree during a school year. Word-processing programs save valuable time. Students can easily add to their observations at appropriate times, then print out interim and final reports without wasting time retyping. Word-processing software could also simplify comparisons of different trees by using *merge* commands. Some teachers are also blending simulation and word processing. Students are asked to produce word-processed reports of group findings drawn from simulation experimentation.

Graphing Software

Whenever numeric information is compared, graphs are valuable tools in presenting information visually. Graphing software can be used to check student understanding of collected data. By putting information in graph formats, students have to select categories and labels and decide which graph format to use, (e.g., pie, bar, etc.). All these decisions provide valuable practice at higher-level thinking skills.

Graphs, Charts and Tables in the Sciences teaches students in grades 5 through 12 how to construct and interpret visual representations of data. In a series of three modules, students interact with various charts. *Graph Power* and *Graph Maker: Introduction to Graphs and Charts* are easy-to-use graphing programs that can be learned quickly. Spreadsheet programs such as *Microsoft Excel* or integrated packages such as *Microsoft Works* and *WordPerfect Works* provide charting options.

Research investigating use of graphs and MBL experiences has shown the value of using real-time graphing of phenomena as they occur. For example, in using a probe to measure heart rate, the student immediately sees the graph made by activities such as jumping up and down, drinking a soft drink, or relaxing. Using real-time graphing pairs events with their symbolic representations (Mokros & Tinker, 1987). The graphing aspect of *The Science Toolkit* is ideal for introducing real-time graphing to the measurement of physical phenomena such as temperature, light, force, pressure, and sound.

Multimedia Reporting Tools

MediaMax is a multimedia software tool that allows students and teachers to combine videodisc images and movie clips with computer graphics, text, sound, and animation. Users can also access CD-ROM, Photo CD, and QuickTime movies. When combined with the videodisc science databases provided by Videodiscovery, teachers can easily create custom lesson plans incorporating bar codes for class lectures. *HyperStudio* is another multimedia presentation tool that allows students to present current understanding using sound, color graphics, animation, QuickTime movies, laser disc, video, and text. *MediaText* is an enhanced word processor that allows users to link to a variety of media such as video clips, QuickTime movies, graphics, sound clips, and animation. These multimedia reporting tools provide students with an exciting, motivating option to reporting. They can incorporate media that will appeal to multiple senses and varied learning styles.

Simulation Software

Simulation and science have been partnered for many years. This computer application stretches across many scientific fields throughout the physical and life sciences. The simulations vary in levels of sophistication, ranging from a simple animated graphic model demonstrating the piston engine to multimedia experiences controlled by microcomputers simulating an expedition down the Amazon River. This category of science software is growing rapidly and, with the advent of CD-ROM and videodisc, is being enhanced with multimedia capabilities. These interactive formats allow students to build problem-solving skills, expand student background, and introduce new subject matter in motivating multimodal ways.

The Great Ocean Rescue is a laser disc simulation where students are invited to protect the sea. Students form collaborative teams to solve environmental ocean problems such as toxic waste and coral reef damage. Student teams take the roles of four ocean specialists: geologist, oceanographer, marine biologist, and environmentalist. Each role is given a pamphlet of background support material. The simulation is controlled by a computer. Students log decisions and the computer reports the consequences of those decisions. After the computer simulation, each team reports its conclusions to the entire class. The second side of the disc includes support material such as maps, still pictures, and short movies. A teacher guide and support material are provided.

The *Forces and Motion* CD-ROM focuses on exploration of concepts of force, energy, motion, and work. Students interact with great scientists of the past, such as Galileo, as they learn about scientific principles. These scientific experts tell about their lives and times. Illustrated stories include video clips, animations, maps, and photos. Scientists suggest experiments based on their discoveries. Students pick up and move objects such as pendulums, weights, and scales to explore the principles of gravity, friction, and motion. Students can write in their logs, recording ongoing information for later printout.

The Amazon Trail CD-ROM is a spinoff of *The Oregon Trail,* but this simulation is set in the Amazon jungle. Users explore the Amazon rain forest and interact with various people, plants, and animals found along the Amazon. Players can "photograph" and identify plants and places in their personal albums. They can also gather information about the geography, resources, and history of the region as well as trade for supplies and develop map reading skills as they canoe toward their final destination up the river. A teacher's manual provides background information, activities, and a selection of resources.

Summary

Many types of software are available to assist teachers in meeting their science curricular objectives. A number of these computer programs have the added benefit of being intrinsically motivating and requiring sophisticated thinking skills. The United States needs qualified scientists. Much of the technological workpool is coming from other countries. Fewer and fewer math and science majors are choosing teaching as a career, leaving students to be taught by nonexperts. This further jeopardizes the development of future scientists. It is important to motivate students in the elementary and secondary levels and even more important to not "turn off" interested students. Many of these electronic tools can be easily and independently learned by gifted students. Even though class time may be too limited to introduce all the tools a teacher may wish to use, giving students opportunities to access and experiment with available software can produce large dividends in the future.

Technology and science have been strong allies. Educators are using diverse hardware and software tools to help students collect, analyze, and report scientific information. Using the computer as a laboratory collection device and as a communication device can help prepare students for the workforce. Manipulation of data restructuring tools such as databases and spreadsheets increases student thinking skills. Reporting conclusions, findings, or understandings using electronic tools such as word processing, graphing, and multimedia reporting software increases motivation and enhances organizational and presentation capabilities.

Mathematics

Microcomputers have provided elementary and secondary teachers with numerous means to enhance and exercise mathematical thinking. In overviewing the National Council of Teachers of Mathematics (NCTM) documents, *Curriculum and Evaluation Standards for School Mathematics* (1989), and *Professional Standards for Teaching Mathematics* (1991), educators are clearly focused on reform. There is significant emphasis placed on updating teacher and student roles to reflect mathematical workplace practices in elementary and secondary schools. These documents recommend that elementary and secondary students learn to make appropriate and confident use of calculators and computer software to perform mathematical tasks (Eiser, 1993).

The demands of the workplace have moved from dependence on paper-and-pencil calculations to requiring a workforce that can effectively and appropriately use technology. Professions using mathematics need members who can set up problems and appropriate operations rather than focus on computations and manipulations. Employers need employees who can successfully interact with open-ended, complex, real problems rather than simple contrived problems. "Technology can help students think more deeply about mathematics, facilitate generalization, empower students to solve difficult problems and furnish a concrete link between geometry and algebra, algebra and statistics, and real problem situations and associated mathematical models" (Demana & Waits, 1990, p. 28).

In overviewing how technology supports mathematics curriculum, this section will present how drill-and-practice, tutorial, and simulation software can provide effective reinforcement of mathematical concepts; how tutorials can support mathematical learning; and how modeling software can provide opportunities for learners to control models of dynamic mathematical principles. The advent of electronic math manipulatives will be shown along with multimedia problem-solving programs. Finally, the integration of tool applications such as spreadsheets and graphing programs with thematic instruction involving mathematics, science, and social science will be presented.

Computer-Assisted Instruction

Over the last decade, CAI software has grown in sophistication but still provides basic tutorial/drill-and-practice products on almost all levels of mathematics education. Since computer gaming has become a big business, many developers now include gaming elements to capture student attention and more of the home and educational market.

Drill and Practice

Although the mathematics reform movement is stressing mathematical concepts, processes, applications, and critical thinking, many students never leave lower-level mathematics due to their inability to memorize basic math facts. Products such as *Math Blaster Plus* provide learners with drill and practice to master basic math facts in addition, subtraction, multiplication and division. A game similar to an arcade provides users with motivation to memorize selected math facts. This use of computers has helped students, parents, and teachers alike, often easing tensions and eliminating barriers to future confidence in mathematics. *Math Blaster: In Search of Spot* on CD-ROM provides additional access to number patterns, estimation, fractions, decimals, and percents and can be used with grades 1 through 6.

Other programs such as *Number Munchers* and *Fraction Munchers* give students a motivating arcade game format that requires students to select appropriate factors, primes, multiples, and so on while watching out for the dreaded "Troggles" that can end the game by "eating" the student's cursor icon. These drill-and-practice games help students master information to an automatic response level. It is important to remember that concepts presented in this game-based format rely on previous instruction and basic student understanding of the concepts before using the program. Although this format typically is limited to discrete sets of lower-level skills, strengths of the approach include motivation, ease of use, and assurance of correct student response and mastery.

A newer, more exploratory format is helping young children enter the world of mathematics. In *Playroom,* children are motivated to explore by clicking on objects of interest such as a clock, a radio, or a fish. Clicking on an object offers children an opportunity to explore a subject or skill such as telling time or counting. *Millie's Math House* provides young children with opportunities to interact with numbers, patterns, sizes, and shapes using animated characters, colorful graphics, animations, and digitized speech. Children explore by pointing and clicking and interacting with animated, speaking characters. These characters help students choose the correct shoe for each of them or help students recognize and create three-step patterns using animals and shapes.

Tutorial

Tutorial programs that make the computer a "teacher" can be helpful to teachers and students alike. By presenting new concepts, checking for understanding, providing explanations when appropriate, and indicating mastery of concept, tutorials can fill in instructional gaps and reinforce concept learning. The advantages of being interactive, providing immediate feedback, and emulating infinite patience make mathematic tutorials valuable. Electronic tutorials are most effective when they are properly introduced by providing context and bridging current student understanding to the tutorial content. Experts caution that when students are operating electronic tutorials in pairs, teachers should monitor the use of cooperative learning strategies closely (Clements, 1989). One disadvantage of mathematic tutorials is that the screen size frequently limits the amount of information that can be displayed at one time, forcing inappropriate segmentation of information presentations.

Mastering Mathematics: Decimals is a basic example of a math tutorial. In this program, as in other math tutorials, information is presented and the student is asked a question that tests for comprehension of the information just presented. Few math tutorials are available, most likely due to the amount of development time to produce an effective product and the amount of computer equipment and time needed to teach each basic concept (Dinkheller, Gaffney, & Vockell, 1989).

Simulations

Math simulations provide students with opportunities to discover relationships in real-life settings. Some products allow users to have real-time interaction with both the process and content of science and mathematics. *The Physics Explorer* is a collection of products that provide mathematically accurate, highly interactive models for exploring the physical sciences. *Gravity, Harmonic Motion, One Body,* and *Waves* include dynamic graphing and integrated spreadsheet tools to help students and teachers use mathematical principles to better understand the concept being studied. The software helps students learn physics by doing physics. One activity in *Gravity* gives students control over such variables as mass, initial height, and initial speed of an orbiting object. The software allows users to view the selected orbit from various vantage points, providing them with integrated pictorial, graphic, and numeric data to observe, analyze, predict, and evaluate outcomes (Kinnaman, 1990).

In the age of multimedia, math simulations are becoming engrossing, real-life, interactive programs that involve students directly in solving problems as individuals, in small groups, or as a whole class. *Math Sleuths* provides students with video clips of characters who present real-life problems to be solved. Students may choose to access resources such as graphs, maps, lab reports, periodical literature, and photos as well as interviews of expert witnesses. Ten scenarios are available to solve. One involves helping developers and conservationists to divide property for profit and protection. Another asks students to determine how far out in space a defense shield against meteoroids should be constructed. Assessment components help evaluate reasoning, calculation, collaboration, and communication. Print-support material helps students develop proofs and demonstrate their work. Solutions require logical thinking, planning, research, writing, and oral communication. Specific skills include estimation; calculation of percentages, averages, cost, and profit; exploring geometric properties; and scientific measurement.

To further explore the potential of this multimedia format, a team from Vanderbilt University has been developing and conducting research on the effectiveness of using video to furnish real-world problem-solving contexts. The results are a series of videodiscs called *The Adventures of Jasper Woodbury.* Advantages of using this format over traditional word problems are plentiful. First of all, students are motivated to interact with video-based information. Furthermore, problems can be more complex and interconnected than when presented in written form. Also, poor readers and learners of a second language are given more opportunities to participate in determining solutions.

This videodisc format provides students with aids to search information. The collaborative problem-solving format is enhanced by the fact that students must generate their own subproblems that supply information necessary for the final solution to the problem. In effect, the students must pose their own questions. Whereas many students are taught rote methods of detecting key words to solve word problems, the lack of written text places the student in a real-world context. Students must identify pertinent embedded information. Furthermore, they must be able to sustain investigation over time, simulating real-world problem solving.

The solution to the first adventure requires at least 15 interrelated calculations. Episodes involve map reading, estimating, decimals, ratios, integers, and other mathematics topics consistent with the NCTM's curriculum standards for grades 5 through 8. Research on *Jasper* materials have shown that students who are taught by using this format are better at solving one-, two-, and multiple-step word problems and more successful at formulating or generating problems to be solved. Attitudes toward mathematics were increasingly more positive as well (Cognition & Technology Group, 1993).

Computer-Based Math Manipulatives

Math manipulatives are physical objects that can be collected, picked up, turned, and rearranged. Manipulatives have been traditionally used as concrete introductions to abstract ideas. Computer software that simulates the use of manipulatives can provide a valuable link, or transition, from concrete, physical manipulatives to the abstract or symbolic representation of an idea (Perl, 1990). Chapter 1, The Impact of Computers in Education, introduced several computer-based manipulative programs and explained how they can be effectively integrated into the math classroom. This text has also shown how actual physical objects controlled by a computer, such as digital trains and *Lego TC Logo* construction sets (see Chapter 11, Computer as Tutee), can help students understand abstract concepts.

With new graphical tools, even high school students can touch, stretch, and move mathematical forms. *Calculus* provides users with the capability to drag a mouse along a curve and watch the slope-line appear at each point designated through the mouse. At the same time, the appropriate algebraic expression is displayed. Programs such as this are allowing students greater flexibility in manipulating shapes and discovering new concepts on their own. Using *Math Connections: Algebra I,* students can work with objects that display variables, functions, and graphs. Through manipulating an object, students visualize a concept and discover its algebraic properties. This is quite different from memorizing abstract ideas.

Problem Solving

Most math curricula directly or indirectly focus on the development of problem-solving skills. There has been much experimentation in this area, providing educators with many fine tools to assist in developing and practicing problem-solving skills. The current software base provides tutorials, simulations, strategy-oriented game formats, as well as problem-solving tools. Problem-solving tutorials may take the form of a traditionally based didactic approach where the software "walks" users through problem-solving steps. *Read and Solve Math Problems* uses this format to help teach students how to convert one- and two-step word problems to number problems. There are also electronic compendiums of organized word problems on disk such as *Pondering Problems: Grades 2, 3, 4, 5* where on-screen characters help make the problem-solving process simpler by guiding students through each step.

Another award-winning program, *Math Blaster Mystery,* provides a motivating way for students to learn steps needed to solve word problems. Students select options such as Follow the Steps, which provides a four-step process for solving word problems, or Weigh the Evidence, where students learn how to break problems into smaller parts. In Decipher the Code, students may make inferences and test hypotheses regarding numbers in a mystery equation, and in Search for Clues, inductional and deduction are used to look for a mystery number. The program offers four levels of difficulty.

Math simulations vary widely in sophistication. Multimedia simulations, as previously discussed, provide a real-world opportunity for students to develop problem-solving capabilities. Tom Snyder's series, *The Wonderful Problems of Fizz & Martina,* consists of math video kits that provide students with opportunities to solve problems collaboratively. These animated segments are highly motivating to upper-elementary students, giving them opportunities to improve their abilities to define problems, identify relevant details, and collaborate effectively with peers in the process. Newer versions are on videodisc and provide instant access by remote control or barcode.

MicroWorld's Math Links package extends the LogoWriter world. Students and teachers unfamiliar with basic Logo can develop exciting multimedia projects. For example, students can work with electronic tangram pieces by just clicking and dragging pieces where desired. The accompanying program, *MicroWorld's Projects,* provides "project starters" and basic tools for exploration of the topic being introduced such as map reading. Hypermedia tools such as buttons, text boxes, and painting tools are available, as well as new concepts such as *sliders,* which allow students to easily explore the concept of variables (Yoder, 1994).

Teachers who need help to motivate and provide ample opportunities for students to practice problem-solving strategies have a multifaceted assistant in the microcomputer. As long as teachers keep their objectives in mind when teaching specific problem-solving strategies, using appropriate mathematical software is effective. Software developers are marketing reasonably priced, graphics-based tools that students can use to develop their problem-solving capabilities. Problem-solving software can help students pose problems or simulate real-life problems, test hypothetical solutions, and receive immediate feedback and assistance when needed.

Tool Applications

Math educators have also started taking advantage of computerized tools typically used in the workplace—namely, spreadsheet and graphic applications. These tools are being used successfully in many elementary- and secondary-level interdisciplinary units. The advantages of using these tool applications are that more complex problems may be chosen because the computer program can assist in organization of information and calculation. With these tools, multiple solution paths are prevalent. An additional benefit is that students are gaining practice with tools used by adults in work settings (Clements, 1989).

Spreadsheets

The process of understanding how a spreadsheet operates supports several mathematical objectives such as the development of formulas to solve classes of problems, estimation, and the effects of changes of variables on other variables. Spreadsheets can help students realize the vital link between mathematics and other content areas such as science and the social sciences. Student-created spreadsheets that convert temperatures from Fahrenheit to Celsius and vice versa blend mathematical with scientific objectives. Using a student-constructed spreadsheet to calculate and compare cost of kilowatt hours expended on various electric bills merges economics and physics objectives in a meaningful way.

Spreadsheets are also effective instruments in helping students explore numerical relationships. Teachers can challenge students to deduce the hidden formula by studying the relationships between values present in various columns. For example, a teacher could define column B as A*3 and place values in column A to be 1, 2, 3, 4.... Students are then asked to look at the values present in each row and deduce what formula was used to select the values present in column B. Students can then be asked to develop other similar problems and challenge student partners. This process could be followed with the computer program *King's Rule,* which further challenges students to guess hidden rules.

The Cruncher is a talking spreadsheet application designed to help young children learn and use spreadsheets. The program incorporates sound, music, and animated graphics to help keep young minds involved. Step-by-step tutorials and motivating projects help prepare students to use spreadsheet applications. Addition, subtraction, multiplication, division, square root, sum, and average are supported. Graphing tools include bar, line, scatter, column, and pie charts.

Graphing Software

Some students grasp relationships more easily when they are represented graphically. For example, if students are shown a bar graph depicting the amount of gas used at different speeds, some will better understand the importance of reducing speed to save gas. Electronic tools such as graphing software offer students a means to explore mathematical principles without getting mired in the mechanics of producing hand-drawn graphs. Student time is expended on interpretation and clarification of data.

"Reading, interpreting and constructing tables, charts and graphs" is one of the 10 basic skills identified by the National Council of Supervisors of Mathematics. As citizens are inundated with increasingly more data presented as raw numbers, percentages, or graphs, the need for students to understand these formats has increased. Transferring information into data that can be represented has subtleties that frequently requires direct instruction.

The Graph Club is a highly motivating innovative multimedia kit that helps K–4 students learn to gather, sort, and classify information in order to produce graphs and analyze data to answer questions and make decisions. Simple menus and voice cues guide users in simplified graph alteration. Side-by-side windows make comparing graphs easy. This product can provide students and teachers with a flexible intercurricular tool that teaches graphing basics. *Zap a Graph, Interpreting Graphs,* and *Logo-Writer Graph Tools* are recommended for junior and high school environments.

Some aspects of data representation can be easily taught using an electronic graphing tool that allows data to be entered and then easily formatted and reformatted. *Data Insights* performs statistical calculations and then graphs resulting data. Line, bar, scatter, stem and leaf, histogram, box plot, and line plot are options. Documentation helps teachers integrate graphing into mathematic, science, and social science curricula.

The *Mathematics Exploration Toolkit,* developed by WICAT Systems for IBM, is a valuable tool for the introduction and exploration of mathematical concepts. The *Toolkit* provides a powerful calculator, a symbol manipulator, and a function plotter. The calculator performs the standard arithmetic operations, as well as logarithmic and trigonometric functions. It can also calculate permutations, combinations, and factorials. The symbol manipulator manipulates symbols and variables, solves equations, and factors polynomials. Expressions can be stored and manipulated. Differentiation and integration can also be performed. The function plotter can graph functions in up to three colors.

The following example, taken from the *Mathematics Exploration Toolkit* manual, shows how a teacher might use the *Toolkit* with a projection screen to demonstrate how to solve two equations in two unknowns by substitution:

Enter	*Result*	*Explanation*
$3x + 2 = y$	$3x + 2 = y$	Displays expression in expression window
store a	$3x + 2 = y$	Stores equation in variable a for later use
$-2x + 7 = y$	$-2x + 7 = y$	Displays expression in expression window
substitute $3x + 2y$	$-2x + 7 = 3x + 2$	Substitutes $3x + 2$ for y
solve for x	$x = 1$	Finds value of x
a	$3x + 2 = y$	Retrieves expression stored in variable a
substitute $1\ x$	$3 * 1 + 2 = y$	Substitutes 1 for x
simplify	$5 = y$	Simplifies the expression

The use of graphs to solve the same equations can then be demonstrated by issuing the commands:

a	$3x + 2 = y$	Retrieves expression stored in variable a
graph	$3x + 2 = y$	Draws graph of current expression $3x + 2 = y$
$-2x + 7 = y$	$-2x + 7 = y$	Displays expression in expression window
graph	$-2x + 7 = y$	Draws graph of second equation

Mathematica and *Macsyma* are similar but even more powerful tools that are being used at the university level. *Mathematica* can plot and animate functions using two- or three-dimensional graphics. It can also perform calculations to any specified level of precision.

Summary

This section overviewed how computer-assisted instruction (CAI) programs such as drill-and-practice, tutorial, and simulation software can effectively reinforce mathematical learning. The benefits of modeling software were presented where students controlled electronic models of mathematical principles for exploration and discovery. Presentation of electronic math manipulatives demonstrated how these newer programs can help students bridge from math manipulatives to more abstract problem-solving techniques. Finally, the integration of tool applications such as spreadsheets and graphing programs into thematic instruction involving mathematics, science, and social science was presented.

Exercises

Social Science

1. Discuss how your future students might use computers to store, organize, reorganize, and display social science information. Include examples of exemplary software.
2. Designate specific software programs developed to support social science curricula and indicate ways to incorporate them into social science curricula.
3. List ways that productivity software such as database management, spreadsheet, graphing, and telecommunications can help meet social science objectives.

Science

1. Describe how computers can be used for collection of science data.
2. Describe how computers can be used to structure and restructure scientific information.
3. Describe how computers can be used to report scientific information.

Math

1. How would you incorporate math CAI (drill and practice, tutorial, and simulation) into your curricula?
2. How do computerized math manipulatives relate to traditional math manipulatives?
3. How can computers be used to develop problem-solving skills?
4. How would you use tool applications to develop math skills?

References

Social Science References

African American Encyclopedia. [CD-ROM]. Minneapolis, MN: Computerized Educational Resources.

American Indian: A Multimedia Encyclopedia. [CD-ROM]. New York: Facts on File.

American Vista. [CD-ROM]. West Chester, PA: Applied Optical Media.

Brady, H. (1989, September). Interactive multimedia: The next wave. *Classroom Computer Learning*, 56–61.

Children's Writing & Publishing Center. [Computer Program]. Fremont, CA: Learning Co.

Choices, Choices. [Computer Program]. Watertown, MA: Tom Snyder Productions.

Chronos. [Computer Program]. Watertown, MA: Tom Snyder Productions.

ClarisWorks. [Computer Program]. Mountain View, CA: Claris.

Comic Strip Factory. [Computer Program]. Minneapolis, MN: Foundation Publishing.

Compton's Interactive Encyclopedia. [CD-ROM]. Carlsbad, CA: Compton's New Media.

Cross-Country Series. [Computer Program]. Burnaby, BC, Canada: Didatech Software.

Decisions, Decisions. [Computer Program Series]. Watertown, MA: Tom Snyder Productions.

Excel. [Computer Program]. Redmond, WA: Microsoft Corp.

Friendly Filer. [Computer Program]. Danbury, CT: Grolier Electronic Publishing.

Geopedia. [CD-ROM]. San Francisco, CA: Encyclopedia Britannica Educational Corp.

Getting on the electronic highway. (1994, Winter). *Teaching Exceptional Children,* 64–69.

Graph Power. [Computer Program]. Grover City, CA: Ventura Education.

Grolier' Multimedia Encyclopedia. [Computer Program]. Danbury, CT: Grolier.

GTV: A Geographic Perspective on American History. [Computer Program]. National Geographic Society.

Kadrmas, S. (1994, March/April). Teaching global studies with technology. *Media & Methods,* 24–25.

Klenow, C. (1992, October). *Instructor,* 65–66.

Langhorne, M., Donham, J., Gross, J., & Rehmke, D. (1989). *Teaching with computers: A new menu for the '90s.* Oryx Press.

Lehrer, A. (1989, September). The '88 vote: Campaign for the White House. *Classroom Computer Learning,* 18–19.

Lotus 1-2-3. [Computer Program]. Cambridge, MA: Lotus Development Corp.

Mac Globe. [Computer Program]. Novato, CA: Broderbund.

Mac USA. [Computer Program]. Novato, CA: Broderbund.

Mageau, T. (1990, March). Laser-disc technology. *Electronic Learning,* 23–28.

Marriott, C. (1993, November/December). The searchers. *Electronic Learning,* 39–39.

McCarthy, R. (1989, June). Multimedia: What the excitement's all about. *Electronic Learning,* 26–31.

Microsoft Works. [Computer Program]. Redmond, WA: Microsoft Corp.

Newsweek Interactive. [CD-ROM]. Novato, CA: Software Toolworks.

On the Playground. [Computer Program]. Watertown, MA: Tom Snyder Productions.

Oregon Trail. [CD-ROM]. St. Paul, MN: MECC.

Other Side. [Computer Program]. Watertown, MA: Tom Snyder Productions

Parham, C. (1993, May/June). Electronic atlases: The world at the click of a mouse. *Technology & Learning,* 56–67.

PC Globe. [Computer Program]. Novato, CA: Broderbund.

PC USA. [Computer Program]. Novato, CA: Broderbund.

Roberts, N., Carter, R., Friel, S., & Miller, M. (1988). *Integrating computers into the elementary and middle school.* Englewood Cliffs, NJ: Prentice Hall.

Taking Responsibility. [Computer Program]. Watertown, MA: Tom Snyder Productions.

Timeliner. [Computer Program]. Watertown, MA: Tom Snyder Productions.

Timeliner Data Disks. [Computer Program]. Watertown, MA: Tom Snyder Productions.

20th Century Video Almanac. [CD-ROM]. Novato, CA: Software Toolworks.

Vlahakis, R. (1988, November/December) The computer-infused social studies classroom. *Classroom Computer Learning,* 58–61.

Where in the . . . Is Carmen San Diego? [Computer Program Series]. Novato, CA: Broderbund.

Wood, V. (1993, October). Reflections on history. *Electronic Learning,* 34–35.

World Vista. [CD-ROM]. West Chester, PA: Applied Optical Media.

Telecommunication References

AT&T Learning Network, P.O. Box 6391, Parsippany, NJ 07054, 800-367-7225.

FrEdMail Foundation, P.O. Box 243, Bonita, CA 91908, 619-475-4852, Internet: arogers@bonita.cerf.fred.org

K12 NET, 1151 SW Vermont St., Portland, OR 97219, 503-280-5280, Internet jmurray@psg.com

Science References

Amazon Trail. [CD-ROM]. Minneapolis, MN: MECC.

Baird, W. (1989, Summer). Status of use: Microcomputers and science teaching. *Journal of Computers in Mathematics and Science Teaching,* 14–27.

Bio Sci II. [Videodisc]. Seattle, WA: Videodiscovery.

Brienne, D., & Goldman, S. (1990, September). Network news. *Science and Children,* 26–29.

Chemistry. [Videodisc]. Seattle, WA: Videodiscovery.

ClarisWorks. [Computer Program]. Cupertino, CA: Claris.

Data Insights. [Computer Program]. Pleasantville, NY: Sunburst.

Dictionary of the Living World. [CD-ROM]. Carlsbad, CA: Comptons.

Finkel, L., McManus, J., & Zeitz, L. (1990). *Hands-on Microsoft Works for the IBM PC and compatibles.* Gilroy, CA: Computer Literacy Press.

FrEdBase. [Computer Program]. Concord, CA: Softswap.

Friendly Filer. [Computer Program]. Danbury, CT: Grolier Electronic Publishing.

Getting on the Electronic Highway. (1994, Winter). *Teaching Exceptional Children,* 64–69.

Graph Maker: Introduction to Graphs and Charts. [Computer Program]. Troll.

GraphPower. [Computer Program]. Grover Beach, CA: Ventura Ed.

Graphs, Charts and Tables in the Sciences. [Computer Program]. Educational Activities.

Great Ocean Rescue. [Videodisc]. Watertown, MA: Tom Snyder Productions.

GROUPwriter. [Computer Program]. Seattle, WA: Sunburst/Wings.

Hood, B. J. (1991, Summer). An integrated approach to teaching students the use of computers in science. *Journal of Computers in Mathematics and Science Teaching,* 27–35.

HyperStudio. [Computer Program]. El Cajon, CA: Roger Wagner.

Julyan, C. (1989, October). National Geographic Kids Network: Real science in the elementary classroom. *Classroom Computer Learning,* 30–31.

Luehrmann, A., & Peckhan, H. (1987). *Hands-on AppleWorks.* Gilroy, CA: Computer Literacy Press.

MediaMAX. [Computer Program]. Seattle, WA: Videodiscovery.

MediaText. [Computer Program]. Seattle, WA: Sunburst/Wings.

Microsoft Excel. [Computer Program]. Redmond, WA: Microsoft Corp.

Microsoft Works. [Computer Program]. Redmond, WA: Microsoft Corp.

Mokros, J., & Tinker, R. (1987). The impact to microcomputer-based labs on children's ability to interpret graphs. *Journal of Research in Science Teaching, 24*(4), 369–383.

Moursand, D. (Ed.). (1989, October). *Microsoft works in education.* Eugene, OR: International Society for Technology in Education.

Nogales, P., & McAllister C. (1987). *AppleWorks for teachers.* Irvine, CA: Franklin, Beedle & Associates.

Personal Science Laboratory. [Computer Program]. Atlanta, GA: IBM Educational Systems.

Physics at Work. [Videodisc]. Seattle, WA: Videodiscovery.

Playing with Science: Motion. [Computer Program]. Pleasantville, NY: Sunburst/Wings.

Roberts, N., Carter, R., Friel, S., & Miller, M. (1988). *Integrating computers into the elementary and middle school.* Englewood Cliffs, NJ: Prentice Hall.

Science and Nature Facts. [Computer Program]. Danbury, CT: Grolier Electronic Publishing.

Science Toolkit Plus Master Module. [Computer Program]. Novato, CA: Broderbund.

Selvy, C. (1993, October). Outcomes-based education. *The Science Teacher,* 48–52.

Sneider, C., & Barber, J. (1990, October). The new probeware: Science labs in a box. *Technology & Learning,* 32–39.

Soloman, G. (1989, April). Hands-on science projects with help from online networks. *Electronic Learning,* 22–23.

Turner, S., & Land, M. (1988) *Tools for schools: Applications software for the classroom.* Belmont, CA: Wadsworth.

Universal Lab Interface. [Computer Program]. Portland, OR: Vernier Software.

Weiss, J. (1992, March). Real-world science in today's world. *Technology & Learning,* 20–24.

Wetzel, K. (1990). *Microsoft works for the Macintosh: A workbook for educators.* Eugene, OR: ISTE, University of Oregon.

WordPerfect Works. [Computer Program]. Orem, UT: WordPerfect.

Math References

Adventures of Jasper Woodbury. [Videodisc Series]. Warren, NJ: Optical Data Corporation.

Calculus. [Computer Program]. Novato, CA: Broderbund.

Clements, D. (1989). *Computers in elementary mathematics education.* Englewood Cliffs, NJ: Prentice Hall.

Cognition & Technology Group at Vanderbilt University. (1993, April). *Arithmetic Teacher,* 474–478.

Cruncher. [Computer Program]. Torrance, CA: Davidson.

Data Insights. [Computer Program]. Pleasantville, NY: Sunburst/Wings.

Demana, F., & Waits, B. (1990, January). The role of technology in teaching mathematics. *Mathematics Teacher,* 27–31.

Dinkheller, A., Gaffney, J., & Vockell, E. (1989) *The computer in the mathematics curriculum.* Santa Cruz, CA: Mitchell.

Duren, P. (1990–91, December/January). Enhancing inquiry skills using graphics software. *The Computing Teacher,* 23–25.

Eiser, L. (1993, March). Math for a reason. *Technology & Learning,* 52–59.

Fraction Munchers. [Computer Program]. St. Paul, MN: MECC.

Graph Club. (Snyder) [Multimedia Kit]. Watertown, MA: Tom Snyder Productions.

Gravity. [Computer Program]. Pleasantville, NY: Sunburst/Wings.

Harmonic Motion. [Computer Program]. Pleasantville, NY: Sunburst/Wings.

Interpreting Graphs. [Computer Program]. Pleasantville, NY: Sunburst/Wings.

King's Rule. [Computer Program]. Pleasantville, NY: Sunburst/Wings.

Kinnaman, D. (1990, September). What the future holds. *Technology & Learning.*

LogoWriter Graph Tools. [Computer Program]. Pointe Claire, Quebec, Canada: LCSI.

Mastering Mathematics: Decimals. [Computer Program]. Elizabethtown, PA: Continental Press.

Math Blaster: In Search of Spot. [CD-ROM]. Torrance, CA: Davidson.

Math Blaster Mystery. [Computer Program]. Torrance, CA: Davidson.

Math Blaster Plus. [Computer Program]. Torrance, CA: Davidson.

Math Connections: Algebra I. [Computer Program]. Pleasantville, NY: Sunburst/Wings.

Math Sleuths. [Videodisc]. Seattle, WA: Videodiscovery.

MicroWorlds Math Links. [Computer Program]. Pointe Claire, Quebec, Canada: LCSI.

Millie's Math House. [Computer Program]. Redmond, WA: Edmark.

National Council of Teachers of Mathematics, Commission on Standards for School Mathematics. (1989). *Curriculum and evaluation standards for school mathematics.* Reston, VA: The Council.

National Council of Teachers of Mathematics, Commission on Standards for School Mathematics. (1991). *Professional standards for teaching mathematics.* Reston, VA: The Council.

Number Munchers. [Computer Program]. St. Paul, MN: MECC.

Perl, T. (1990, March). Manipulatives and the computer: A powerful partnership for learners of all ages. *Classroom Computer Learning,* 20–29.

Physics Explorer. [Computer Program]. Pleasantville, NY: Sunburst/Wings.

Playroom. [Computer Program]. Novato, CA: Broderbund.

Pondering Problems: Grades 2,3,4,5. [Computer Software]. Micrograms.

Read and Solve Math Problems. [Computer Program]. Baldwin, NY: Education Activities.

Wonderful Problems of Fizz & Martina. [Video Kit]. Watertown, MA: Tom Snyder Productions.

Yoder, S. (1994, May). Math, MicroWorlds, and hypermedia. *The Computing Teacher,* 18–20.

Zap a Graph. [Computer Program]. Santa Barbara, CA: Intellimation.

Chapter *14*

Curriculum Integration
Meeting Diverse Needs

As individuals, we all learn in unique ways. This chapter will demonstrate how technology can assist *all* learners. Even though labels and categories are used, it is recognized that people—our personal learning styles as well as our capabilities—do not fit neatly into any single category. It is hoped that you will begin to see the many ways that technology can serve an individual's quest for empowerment, communication, and lifelong learning.

This chapter provides entry-level information on selected categories. First, general trends of special education technology are presented, followed with inclusion suggestions. It is recommended that all interested educators review the information on how technology supports and will support students who are hearing impaired, visually impaired, severely disabled, physically challenged, learning disabled or gifted. The chapter also discusses how technology can assist English language development and students with limited English proficiency (referred to as *ESL students*).

At its best, technology is transparent. It is a tool, much like this book or a pen. It may be used to gain or impart knowledge. We will first look at an example of how technology can be infused into a second-grade classroom where students are empowered to discover knowledge by using many tools, including technology. Students in this classroom are of diverse backgrounds, such as low socioeconomic, minority, ESL, exceptional, and in need of special servicing.

The second-grade classroom is filled with learning opportunities. Students are given ample time to explore new technologies and to choose from many learning opportunities. One learning center incorporates technology by connecting a computer to a camera that gives students the capability to digitize the effect of water as it erodes mountains built in the classroom sand box. Students are able to capture single moments of the erosion process and later compare and draw conclusions. Other students have selected to view specific slides of paintings from a laser disc featuring Van Gogh. After viewing specific examples of his technique, students are invited to paint using the same style. Other student outcomes include *HyperCard* stacks with scanned pictures of plants and animals. Students have had to make the decisions of what to scan, what to write, and how to link cards. Students even elect to create electronic books, complete with digitized voices in Spanish and English.

These particular student outcomes are more sophisticated and more advanced than most developed by other students of the same age. By giving students choices, responsibilities, and access to advanced learning tools, they may find success and take control of their learning, regardless of exceptionality or skill level (Prickett, Higgins, & Boone, 1994).

General Trends: Technology and Special Education

How is technology being used to support special education student learning? How successful has it been to date? What should we expect in the near future?

In general, *technology does and will continue to help people with disabilities to gain greater independence and integration into society.* The field of special education has moved from an emphasis on using educational technology as an instructional delivery tool to more application-oriented uses. Drill and practice is being supplanted by database manipulation, writing assistance programs, and computer-mediated text—in short, programs that support knowledge construction and development of higher-order thinking skills. Research has indicated improvement in academic achievement, motivation, and time on task. The teacher's role has become *more* rather than *less* critical, moving from central source of information to facilitator, consultant, and encourager (Okolo, Bahr, & Rieth, 1993).

Trends in hardware development are helping students with disabilities gain greater independence and integration into society. Speech recognition systems, electronic communications, personal computers, robots, and artificial intelligence are making a difference. The movement toward miniaturization, use of lighter materials, and higher-capacity information processing are making devices more *transparent.* Devices such as wristwatch computers will provide students with unobtrusive support. Peripheral devices are becoming more adaptable to multimodalities. Computers that are activated by voice and have synthesized speech are assisting students who are physically handicapped, blind, and at risk. Captions and enhanced narration of TV programs are also helping students who have physical and language disabilities. Distance education, telecommunications, expert systems, and artificial intelligence are projected to become more prevalent and especially valuable to the special education populace (Sawyer & Santal-Wiener, 1993).

Another strong trend in U.S. education is the placement of special populations into full-time regular classrooms, commonly called *inclusion.*

Inclusion and Technology

Inclusion of children who have special needs into regular classrooms can be greatly enhanced with technology. Inclusion differs from mainstreaming practices in that students in mainstreamed settings are typically in separate special education classrooms for most of the day and are moved into regular classrooms for the remainder of the day. Full inclusion requires that students remain in regular classes all day and receive support from trained personnel in that regular classroom, not on a pull-out basis.

Many experts believe that the successful inclusion of many special education students relies on technology. Technology support can range from students using spellcheckers to using augmentive communication devices to using talking word processors. Written tests may be scanned into the computer and the computer "reads" the test, using synthesized speech, to the user. Students then input answers using a braille-topped keyboard.

Inclusion classrooms become unique environments for learning. For example, students who are hearing impaired tend to write in simple noun-verb form. In one class, hearing students with hearing helped students with hearing impairments fill in missing articles and adjectives when working on cooperative word-processing projects. In another setting, a kindergarten class insisted that a classmate with communication disabilities be given the opportunity to participate fully in a class play by taking a speaking part, which was made possible by use of a Language Master communication device. In yet another class, a student with cerebral palsy was able to contribute to class storytime by operating a mouse-driven CD-ROM-based story. So, synergistic educational events can be fostered in inclusion classrooms enhanced by technology.

In another inclusion setting, a geometry teacher required that all students draw geometric figures. Rather than reducing standards, the teacher found a software program that helped a student with cerebral palsy draw by using a mouse. In yet another site, a student who was visually impaired was able to complete assignments both in braille and traditional print by use of braille-literate software and special output devices. Thus, technology solutions can help educators maintain standards in inclusion classrooms (Wall & Siegel, 1994). Inclusion classroom environments can create conditions that promote creative cooperative problem solving of individual problems. Students can work cooperatively to produce solutions that enhance learning for *all* students.

As we move towards inclusion, regular classroom teachers will need to research how technology can support students who have special needs. With this as a primary motivation, let's explore the various ways technology is supporting these students in classrooms.

A federal act, Technology-Related Assistance for Individuals with Disabilities Act (Tech Act), provides federal funds to states for the development of easily available, consumer-responsive systems of access to assistive technology, technology services, and information. The standard definition of *assistive technology* comes from this act. Assistive technology is "any tool or item that increased, maintains, or improves functional capabilities of individuals with disabilities" (Alliance for Technology Access, 1994, p. 52). When classifying assistive devices, experts frequently follow three categories: alternate input devices, processing aids, and alternate output devices. Keep in mind that there are many more products available in each of the categories presented here. Also, it is important to note that many products are used by individuals who have different disabilities.

Students with Hearing Impairments

Technology that has supported the deaf and hearing impaired is impressive and effective. Research has indicated that computer-assisted instruction (CAI) has improved language facility and word recognition skills (Askov et al., 1989) and that students who are deaf or hearing impaired learn more quickly and show better retention of material (Hart-Davis, 1985). Students report that they feel empowered by technology and feel a control over their learning. In many instances, technology provides a face-saving method of learning. Advantages include privacy, individualization with immediate feedback, flexibility of scheduling, open entry/open exit curricula, and direct experience with modern tools that are used in the workplace (Askov et al., 1989).

Hardware/software combinations are helping students who are hearing impaired learn how to talk by using products such as *SpeechViewer,* which provides visual feedback as students participate in speech therapy. Communication is supported in diverse ways. Programs such as *Micro-Interpreter* and *PC Fingers* present American Sign Language (ASL) finger spelling and signed words. Systems such as EduQuest's *Principle of the Alphabet Literacy System (PALS)* help adult students who are hearing impaired to learn to read and write (Askov et al., 1989).

Some sites are using multimedia to support learning environments where students who are hearing impaired are learning alongside students who hear. Administrators indicate that by providing a visual emphasis, they are supporting *all* students simultaneously. One school uses hallway TV monitors with open-caption viewing as their public address system. By using computerized voice recognition systems such as *VoiceType,* students who are hearing impaired can dictate reports to a computer that is trained to recognize their voices. Students who are deaf can read interactive stories mounted on laser discs that use signing and text (Multimedia for the Hearing-Impaired, 1994).

Students with Visual Impairments

Reading and writing traditionally challenge students who are visually impaired. Technology continues to minimize this challenge. These students are receiving technical support by word processors that provide large print on the screen such as *Bank Street Writer III* and *Magic Slate.* Don Johnston and Harley Courseware software vendors also provide large-print word processors.

Macintosh offers a screen-magnifying utility, *CloseView,* which is included in the Macintosh system software. Other screen enlargement programs are available through companies such as Berkeley Systems and Apple Computer. Enlargement programs focus on a a small portion of the screen at a time and enlarge it, so software that requires viewing of a large portion of the screen at one time is not supported with these products.

Braille embossers and translators are electronic tools that help braille users create and read documents. A braille printer transfers computer-generated text into embossed braille output. Braille translator programs take normal electronic text and create a braille version. Embossers are very expensive—thousands of dollars—whereas translators are generally several hundred dollars.

Speech synthesizers receive information going to the screen in the form of letters, numbers, and punctuation marks, and "speak" it aloud. They usually take the form of an external device that plugs into the computer or as a card that is placed into a slot in the computer. Most speech synthesizers work with software that converts text to speech. They are valuable tools, allowing students to hear what they have written. When coupled with a scanner, a speech synthesizer can read aloud newspaper or magazine articles that have been scanned into the computer. This provides students who previously were limited to braille products, audiotapes, or human readers with an additional option. Don Johnston, Hartley, and IntelliTools publish talking word processors.

A *screen reader* is a software program that works in conjunction with a speech synthesizer. It "speaks" everything presented on the screen, including menus, text, and punctuation. These readers vary drastically in price and functions. Some screen readers can utilize built-in speech synthesis capability such as that found in Macintosh computers and do not require a speech synthesizer to function. Vendors include Berkeley Systems and Telesensory.

Reading machines transform printed material into electronic data that are read by a speech synthesizer. Also, standard computers can be modified to act like dedicated reading machines by adding a scanner and reading system software. Upgrading a standard machine can cost between $1,500 to $4,000, whereas stand-alone versions average around $5,000. Telesensory and Arkenstone both market reading machine products.

Keyboard Kits for visually impaired students offer keyboard caps that fit snugly on keyboard keys. Thus, large-print and braille equivalents may be mounted on each key to assist students who are visually impaired.

Students with Severe Disabilities and Physical Challenges

Many students with severe disabilities and physical challenges who previously had no way to communicate their needs, wishes, and thoughts are now able to impact their environments using assistive devices. One empowering assistive device is the switch. *Switches* are input devices that allow computer users to indicate choices, keyboard functions, or commands. Switches come in many different styles and sizes, as shown in Figure 14–1. Frequently, interface devices are used to connect switches to computers. Most standard software can be operated by a switch with the aid of additional devices. Typically, switches allow users to select choices that are sequentially highlighted on a computer screen.

In addition to helping users operate software, switches can give students more control over their environments. By connecting switches to various electrical and electronic devices—such as tape players, TVs, or page turners—students who are severely disabled and physically challenged can control devices that provide information. Furthermore, young children can use switches to explore concepts such as cause and effect. By using a simple switch, a child can cause a connected toy to move—an important act for a child who has little motoric capacity. There are more than 400 special switches on the market that can be modified to meet specific needs (Cooper, 1993).

FIGURE 14–1   Switches

Other input devices that can assist students to access computers are electronic pointing devices and nonelectronic pointing and typing aids. All use an on-screen keyboard. *Electronic pointing devices* allow users to operate the cursor on the screen using ultrasound or an infrared beam. Some of these devices require the ability to activate a switch, others allow users to "dwell" on a key to select it, and still others allow cursor control by head motion. *Nonelectronic pointing and typing aids* are typically in the form of a wand or stick that is used to strike keys on the keyboard. These devices can be worn on the head, held in the mouth, strapped to the chin, or held in the hand.

Many students who are physically challenged are accessing computers by using specialized *alternative keyboards.* These keyboards provide users with a greater variety of options, such as size, layout, and complexity. Many are programmable, so letters, numbers, words, or phrases can be entered when appropriate keys are activated. Intellikeys (see Figure 14–2) is a large programmable keyboard that uses plastic overlays. It can be daisy-chained to a traditional keyboard so that both keyboards can be used simultaneously.

The keyboard comes with seven plastic overlays that provide alternative input formats. By using the *Overlay Maker* software program, individualized overlays may be easily produced to meet specific needs. Set-up control options allow alteration of such things as response rate of key-press and mouse-pointer speed.

Communication boards and language boards have opened many doors for students who are severely and physically challenged. Communication boards such as *Voice Output Communication Aids (VOCAs)* allow students to use picture overlays and words that

FIGURE 14–2   Intellikeys

students can touch to activate electronic voice equivalents (Gelman, 1993). By using simple overlays, students can make choices, such as what kind of treat they want, how they are feeling, as well as holding complex conversations with teachers and students.

Another valuable input device for students who benefit from a more direct and simplified way of accessing computer software is the touch screen. *Touch screens* are attached to the computer monitor (or built into it) and allow direct selection or activation of the computer by a touch on the screen. Touch screens typically move a cursor, imitate the mouse, or make a selection. Usually, the mouse and keyboard are still active input devices along with the touch screen.

Most of the input devices discussed require an interface device to interact with the computer and software. An interface device provides access to the keyboard functions and (sometimes) mouse controls by assistive input devices such as switches and alternate keyboards. These interface devices become the "translators" between the alternative input device, the computer, and the software. Interface devices vary in complexity. They may act as an interface between one input device and the computer or many different input devices and the computer. The *Adaptive Firmware Card (AFC),* a popular interface device, plugs into the computer and increases the kinds of input devices that can be used.

This card, plus the Ke:nx for the Macintosh, provides access to different methods of interacting with software such as scanning software where the cursor sequentially rotates through screen options, waiting for the user to select an option. Users may also choose Morse code to signal the computer which letters or numbers the user wants entered (Male, 1994). Truly, technology is providing a highly flexible set of alternatives to assist students in communicating and controlling their environment.

Students with Learning Disabilities

Technology support for students with learning disabilities can take many forms. Word processing and spell-checkers help students to share their thoughts on paper. Resistance to proofing and editing is diminished. Gone is the embarrassment of having to turn in a paper full of erasures or cross-outs. One teacher reported that a student's work consisted of words so strung together that a reader could not tell one word from the next. After using a word processor, the student was able to more clearly present himself and his personal creativity (Holzberg, 1994). Another valuable technology support are talking word processors. Students can hear what they have just written as immediate feedback to help them eliminate errors.

Demonstrating understanding has traditionally challenged many students who are learning disabled. Using multimedia tools for demonstration of understanding has been highly successful in many settings. *HyperCard* stacks and videotapes have become empowering methods, showing conceptual understanding to others. One second-grade group prepared an interactive activity where users could view and classify pictures of animals that live around the Rio Grande River. Several stack authors had learning disabilities (Prickett, 1992).

Marion School District in Marion, Arkansas, has used videodisc technology to help support junior high school students who have mild disabilities. Students who needed more contact with presented material could check out videotape copies of particular videodisc lessons to review at home. Other videodiscs—consisting of slide collections, video segments, and text material—were used by teachers as powerful visual aids that augmented, clarified, and presented new information in alternative ways. Grades and test scores of average and below-average students rose significantly in classes where videodisc technology was used. Before using videodiscs, 40 percent of all students in the earth science classes were getting Ds and Fs. With videodisc technology, the failure rate was reduced to 10 percent. Teachers noted that the attentiveness and involvement of students, as well as the self-esteem of low-achieving students, increased.

Enumclaw School District in Enumclaw, Washington, researched how multimedia could support special education classes for students who are developmentally delayed and mentally retarded. Success was reported using a thematic approach coupled with multimedia instruction. Students used laser discs to obtain information on the animal of choice. Video cameras were used to capture footage of the animal viewed on field trips or brought into the classroom. Final products included videotapes that provided specific facts students had learned about each animal.

A school in Kentucky, consisting of students who have above-average intelligence but specific learning disabilities such as dyslexia or difficulty with auditory processing, used technology to support real-life science research. Students at the site took on the challenge of measuring the extent of water contamination in local groundwater. Each of the nine student teams conducted a separate research task. Some teams charted physical features of the area, others counted garbage and recorded types of trash, some collected water and soil samples and tested pollutant and bacteria levels, and still others shot live-action videos of research in progress. Students created databases, conducted statistical analysis, and produced *hyperCard*-based research reports complete with scanned photos and hypertext links to live-action video sequences (Holzberg, 1993).

Use of electronic resources, such as electronic encyclopedias, by students who have learning disabilities is being studied. Teachers are developing units that introduce searching skills, note-taking skills, and instruction on the perils of plagiarism (Heyn, 1992). Researchers are recommending that teachers of these students provide direct instruction of electronic searching skills. When left to use intuitive searching skills, a majority of the students with disabilities who were studied were unsuccessful in using an electronic searching interface (Edyburn, 1991).

Students with Gifts and Talents

Although most schools and school districts recognize the existence of students who are gifted and talented, as a group, these students have traditionally been neglected in U.S. schools. Although many programs exist, they typically are underfunded and thus are supported by parents who are eager to provide their children with additional resources and experiences. A typical elementary-level technology program for the gifted and talented is one that is after school and often off site, requiring parents to arrange for special transportation. The overwhelming response to this population has been, "Don't worry; they can take care of themselves."

When support *is* provided to the gifted and talented, special tracks of classes are usually provided at the secondary level or special magnet schools are created. One such school is the Central Virginia Governor's School for Science and Technology. Here, eleventh- and twelfth-graders attend math, science, research, and technology courses in the morning and return to their regular schools in the afternoon for the rest of their coursework needs. The use of technology infusion at this site has three aims: increase personal productivity, expose students to emerging technologies, and use techniques that enhance the instructional environment in general.

The students are asked to assume more responsibility for their own learning, develop problem solving, and exercise critical thinking, analysis, synthesis, and design skills. Furthermore, the curricula place emphasis on developing skills for obtaining and organizing information, strategies for discerning relevancy, skills in formulating and making connections between theory and practice, and skills in examining trade-offs and risks. In short, students are being asked to use technology to practice skills necessary for the next generation of leaders.

In research and physics classes, students must complete all assignments using technology, thus demonstrating proficiency in tool use as well as concept understanding. Students submit word-processed research papers, which include tables and graphs developed by using database, spreadsheet, statistical, and graphics software. They use CD-ROM and telecommunications to research and develop computer multimedia presentations. The school has found that accessing Internet has provided students with remote computers, databases, and the ability to communicate with other experts and students around the world. The use of E-mail has given students additional opportunities to query teachers and has provided teachers with extra opportunities to give individual support and encouragement.

Students choose from nine technology laboratories that range from fields such as analytical chemistry to robotics. They have six weeks to complete a laboratory—the first three weeks to explore the technology and the last three weeks to develop a product that demonstrates understanding (Morgan, 1993).

Whether educators are working with students who are learning disabled or gifted, there are conditions that promote successful programs that integrate technology into content curricula. Students are given choice and time to explore technological tools and are asked to interact and problem solve with other students as they employ these tools. Technological tools are used to save time and to help students focus their attention on concepts to be learned. Students are involved in active learning that allow them to construct their own knowledge and understanding.

English as a Second Language (ESL) or English Language Development (ELD)

Educators are beginning to explore the potential of technology and how it can strengthen current second-language acquisition practices. Early uses of technology to support second-language learning have been positive. "Technology is becoming a bigger part of both in-class and home study, as the traditional use of audio and films is supplemented by computer-assisted instruction and interactive media technologies" (Willetts, 1992, p. 3). U.S. educators who teach second languages to English speakers have been using technology such as CAI, CD-ROM, videodisc, local area networks (LANs), telecommunication networks, and satellite broadcasting from foreign countries to supplement teaching practices. English language development (ELD) teachers can also develop similar practices for their field. In fact, software developers are beginning to market software that can greatly assist ELD teachers and students.

Let's view one scenario that depicts how technology is supporting a seventh-grade student, recently immigrated from China, who is learning English with the help of an unusual aid. She is using a CD-ROM-based product that provides text and synchronized pronunciation of words in Cantonese and English. The student is reading *The Tale of Benjamin Bunny* by Beatrix Potter. She can elect to have the tale read to her aloud as the text is displayed on the screen in either English or Cantonese. She may also have unfamiliar words and illustrations defined in either language. Even though she is new to U.S. schools and has little understanding of the language, with the help of technology, she has control over her own learning experience (Lalas & Wilson, 1993).

Word Processing and English Language Development

Learning a new language is supported by meaningful input, social interaction, risk taking, and purpose. Technology such as word processing can provide an environment that allows pairs or groups to communicate as they experiment, make predictions, and take a risk in their use of the new language. Teachers are developing lessons that require students to use technology to ask for information, give directions, and express emotions. By using technological resources that offer the students' acquired language as well as the new target language, students are motivated to foster more reading, writing, and thinking in both languages (Lalas & Wilson, 1993).

One ELD teacher who works with beginning-level adults successfully uses a computer to create cooperatively developed products. The products are then used in subsequent class activities. Students are divided into groups of three and cycled to the computer on a rotation basis. The first cooperatively developed product is a simple list of students' names and phone numbers. Next, they create a class restaurant menu. Students, working in threes, are asked to enter the name of one dish and its price listed under one of four categories provided by the teacher. Then students develop grocery lists organized under categories such as produce, dairy, meat, and so on. Finally, they create commercial advertisements for food, clothing, and household goods. After completion, the products are used for role-playing activities such as ordering at a restaurant or shopping at a grocery store (Payne, 1993).

Word-processing programs placed on a computer network are fostering collaborative writing. One ELD class meets two to six hours weekly in such a computer laboratory. The networking system allows students to work on the same document using their own computers. They can read each other's papers, make revisions, and work in teams. The students are given the task of creating a play. Working in pairs, they write the dialogue for one character. Students must determine plot, characterization, setting, motivations, and a final resolution. Communication and negotiation are special outcomes of the completion of the project (Smoke, 1993).

Another educator who teaches ELD students describes her experience working in a computer-assisted writing laboratory at the University of Texas at Austin. The focus of student interactions is a specific writing assignment, such as a student essay, poem, or whatever. Each student's typed responses are transmitted to all the other students' computer screens, simulating a conversation with many participants. So, students and teachers can interact on the form and substance of the student work currently being studied. The networked computer lab provides a forum for social interaction, collaboration, negotiation of meaning, and dissention.

Analysis of student interactions on this system indicated that instructor remarks were in a distinct minority when compared to student responses. This is in opposition with analysis of most research dealing with student/teacher classroom interaction. Other studies have attributed 65 to 75 percent of classroom conversation time to teachers—leaving students with minimal classroom interaction time. By changing the physical environment of the classroom to include networked computers, the student/teacher interaction pattern was significantly modified. It is postulated that working with a computer screen and keyboard was less threatening than having to speak outloud in front of peers and instructors. By interacting on networked computers, students were more apt to communicate and more able to gain practice in negotiating meaning and improving problem-solving skills (Sullivan, 1993).

Fortunately, more multilingual writing tools are being marketed than ever before. *The ESL Writer* combines features of a basic word processor with a grammar- and speller-checker programmed to anticipate and respond to errors typically made by ELD students from a variety of linguistic backgrounds. Humanities Software provides titles for first-language Spanish students, such as *Word Weaver,* that is an inexpensive word processor with menus in English and Spanish, a bilingual thesaurus, and spell-checker. This same product has "frozen text" features for teachers to develop personalized electronic writing opportunities as well as the ability to design Big Books and cloze (fill in the blanks) formatted activities. Some instructors working with advanced English-speaking LEP students are using *Writer's Helper* to promote prewriting and revision skills (Davis-Wiley, 1994). *KidWorks 2* is also being used to motivate reticent writers and to provide instant feedback to students through its read-aloud feature. Students may have the machine orally read what they have just typed.

Multimedia and ELD Students

Multimedia products are also providing educators with effective tools for developing second-language skills. Davidson's *Story Club* is a comprehensive interactive package that engages ELD/LEP students through the whole language approach, which provides opportunities for listening, speaking, writing, and reading in English. The system includes CD-ROM, videodiscs, audiotapes that house 42 thematic units with 15 read-aloud stories, and extensive print-support materials. Positive, affirming, well-drawn characters from diverse cultures are highlighted. Videodiscs are designed to assist teachers in introducing the folktales to students. The folktales have been selected from the traditions of Jamaica, France, Russia, Africa, and South America and are portrayed through high-quality colorful cartoons and photos and a blend of real voices. Words, language structures, and concepts are reinforced by activities designed for individual, small group, or whole group configurations and can be completed on or off the computer. The CD-ROM provides three sections that students can use to "play" with the language they are learning. Students can explore the folktales by clicking on interactive screens to reinforce vocabulary and listening skills. Activities include writing, illustrating, and recording their own versions of the stories. Vocabulary work is supported by true multimedia enhancements such as photographs and speech and sound effects. The CD-ROM also houses a full-featured talking word processor that helps motivate students to use their new language. This package also includes eight hours of staff development training (Lopez & McLester, 1994).

Designed to help fourth- through twelfth-grade ELD students, *Steps to English Language Development* by Josten's provides a comprehensive, networked multimedia CD-ROM interactive environment. The system takes users through an on-screen community, Cornerstone, where they can interact with inhabitants in authentic, high-interest conversations and activities. Eight thematic units integrate listening, speaking, writing, and reading skill practice. Early-level activities involve locating, moving, classifying, and sorting objects. Students follow directions, make decisions, and participate in simulations. The program allows them to record their own voices at any time during the lessons to provide instant self-checking and feedback opportunities. The second level of the program is designed for middle and high school students. Five thematic units require students to plan, prioritize, gather, and evaluate material. Activities include development of a handbook for new ELD students, researching citizenship and the U.S. Constitution, debating global issues, and career exploration. Sophisticated software tools are provided such as *First Connections: The Golden Book Encyclopedia* (a multimedia beginning-level program), *Microsoft Works,* and *The Writing Center* from Learning Company. Again, this product requires major financial commitment from purchasers (Lopez & McLester, 1994).

Many CD-ROM storybooks are suitable for ELD classrooms. Both *Discus Books* and *Living Books* provide alternative sound tracks in one or more languages. This allows users to toggle back and forth from one language to another to fulfill individual student needs. *Sitting on the Farm* tells this marvelous story in three languages: English, French, and Spanish. Children can explore this highly motivating environment in several ways. They are encouraged to create products using the provided word processor or record their own voices as they sing along to the words. *Story Time* is a CD-ROM series with text and narration in Spanish and English, a bilingual multimedia dictionary, and a writing tool.

More companies are now incorporating second-language support into their product line. *Windows on Science* and *Living Textbook Series* offer second soundtracks with Spanish narration. On-line student materials are also available in Cantonese, Tagalog, and Vietnamese. *Progressive Science Instruction* was designed as a course for students whose first language is Spanish. The program can be set to be only in Spanish, Spanish with English subtitles, or English with Spanish translations.

As well as multimedia, traditional computer programs are also becoming more available to ELD populations. Other developers are reissuing popular programs in Spanish versions, such as Broderbund's *Donde Esta Carmen San Diego?* MECC has released *USA GeoGraph* in Spanish and is working on other titles. Mindplay, Scholastic, Software Toolworks, and Tom Snyder are software producers currently offering and developing second-language editions (Lopez & McLester, 1994).

ELD teachers may also benefit from overviewing software designed to teach English to foreign-language speakers. Programs that use a bilingual approach where students can toggle back and forth from one language to another may be especially valuable to ELD populations. Recommended software developers are Applied Optical Media, Fairfield Language Technologies, Gessler Educational Software, Nordic Software, Penton Oversees, and Syracuse Language Systems (Lopez & McLester, 1994). Consult Chapter 16 for addresses.

Telecommunications and ELD Students

Foreign-language teachers are using telecommunication and the Internet (review Chapter 9, Networks and Telecommunication) to increase student contact with foreign language and culture. ELD teachers may also find value in reviewing ongoing collaborations between language educators throughout the world. Orillas: An Intercultural Distance Teach Teaching Network has used electronic mail and computer-based conferencing to plan and implement joint educational projects between classes located in different parts of the world. After the formal cultural exchange, teachers publish the collaboratively developed products electronically. Orillas can be contacted by its Internet address Orillas@NYC.nyued.fred.org or by phone at 212-998-5485.

Other foreign-language teachers are turning their classrooms into virtual communities of language learners. By using E-mail exchanges and collaborative on-line projects, students are writing for real audiences and getting feedback from their peers in other settings. AT&T Learning Network helped one foreign-language teacher connect with a school in France. The student information exchange provided both classes with a teen perspective as opposed to an adult textbook perspective. This same teacher has found classes for her Spanish students to collaborate with in New Mexico and Argentina (Kanarek & Moeller, 1994).

If ELD teachers seek to understand and value the cultures of the students they serve, connecting ELD students with other cultures may provide motivating and authentic language and cultural exchanges. All students, whether ELD or not, can benefit from on-line global interactions. By connecting with an ELD student's home country, that student may become a valuable resource and become motivated to take a proactive stance in the learning exchange. Synergistic outcomes may be uncovered.

Exercises

1. Discuss general technology trends in special education.
2. Discuss how teachers can enhance inclusion classrooms by using technology.
3. How can technology support students who are sight or hearing impaired in classrooms?
4. How can students who are learning disabled support their own learning by using technology?
5. How would you use word processing to help English language learners increase their literacy skills?
6. How would you use multimedia with English language learners?
7. In what ways are educators using technology to support all students as they learn?

References

Alliance for Technology Access. (1994). *Computer resources for people with disabilities.* Alameda, CA: Hunter House.

Askov, E., et al. (1989). *Adult literacy, computer technology and the hearing impaired.* Literacy & Hearing Impaired Conference Proceedings. ERIC: ED 353 733.

Bank Street Writer III. [Computer Program]. New York: Scholastic.

Bilingual Writing Center. [Computer Program]. Fremont, CA: Learning Company.

Cooper, R. (1993, August/September). Simple switch technology for students with disabilities. *The Computing Teacher,* 34, 35, 55.

Davis-Wiley, P. (1994, May/June). Software for bilingual computing projects. *Media & Methods,* 8.

Discus Books. [CD-ROM]. Toronto, Ontario, Canada: Discus.

Donde esta Carmen San Diego? [Computer Program]. Novato, CA: Broderbund.

Edyburn, D. (1991, Fall). Fact retrieval by students with and without learning handicaps using print and electronic encylopedias. *Journal of Special Education Technology,* 74–88.

Enumclaw School District. (1992). Success with technology. ERIC: ED 357 551.

ESL Writer. [Computer Program]. New York: Scholastic.

Gelman, S. (1993, November). Innovative technology for students with disabilities. *Principal,* 52–54.

Hart-Davis, S. (1985). The classroom computer as a partner in teaching basic skills to hearing impaired children. *American Annals of the Deaf, 130*(5), 410–414.

Heyn, M. (1992). Using a hypermedia encyclopedia with third graders. *1992 TAM Topical Guide,* 39–44.

Holzberg, C. (1993, January). Special education success stories. *Technology & Learning,* 53–56.

Holzberg, C. (1994, April). Technology in special education. *Technology & Learning,* 18–20.

Hunt, N. (1993, Autumn). A view of advanced technologies for L2 learning. *TESOL Journal,* 8–9.

Intellikeys. [Keyboard]. Richmond, CA: Intellitools.

Kanarek, K., & Moeller, B. (1994, March). Foreign exchange. *Electronic Learning,* 22.

Ke:nx. [Hardware]. Wauconda, IL: Johnston.

Keyboard Kits. [Keyboard Caps]. Cottonwood, AR: Hooleon.

Kid Works 2. [Computer Program]. Torrance, CA: Davidson.

Lalas, J., & Wilson, T. (1993, March/April). Focus on multicultural schools: New technologies for ESL Students. *Media & Methods,* 18–21.

Living Books. [CD-ROM]. Novato, CA: Broderbund.

Lopez, D., & McLester, S. (1994, April). Smart choices for the ESL classroom. *Technology & Learning,* 22–26.

Magic Slate. [Computer Program]. Pleasantville, NY: Sunburst/Wings.

Male, M. (1994). *Technology for inclusion.* Boston: Allyn and Bacon.

Marion School District. *Success with technology.* ERIC: ED 357551.

MIcro-Interpreter. [Hardware]. Exton, PA: EduQuest.

Morgan, T. (1993). Technology: An essential tool for gifted and talented education. *Journal for the Education of the Gifted, 16*(4), 358–371.

Multimedia for the Hearing-Impaired. (1994). EduQuest Promotional Material, IBM, p. 4.

Oddone, A. (1993, Fall). Inclusive classroom applications. *Teaching Exceptional Children,* 74.

Okolo, C., Bahr, C., & Rieth, H. (1993, Spring). Retrospective view of computer-based instruction. *Journal of Special Education Technology,* 1–27.

Overlay Maker. [Computer Program]. Wauconda, IL: Johnston.

Payne, J. (1993, Autumn). Shared computer projects for beginners. *TESOL Journal,* 38–39.

PC-Fingers. [Computer Program]. Exton, PA: EduQuest.

PhoneCommunicator. [Computer Program]. Exton, PA: EduQuest.

Prickett, E. (1992). The multimedia classroom. *TAM Topical Guide,* 56–65.

Prickett, E., Higgins, K., & Boone, R. (1994, Summer). Technology for learning . . . Not learning about technology. *Teaching Exceptional Children,* 56–58.

Reading Edge. [Computer Program]. Peabody, MA: Xerox Imaging Systems.

Sawyer, R., & Santal-Wiener, K. (1993, Fall). Emerging trends in technology for students with disabilities. *Teaching Exceptional Children,* 70–75.

Sitting on the Farm. [CD-ROM]. San Mateo, CA: Sanctuary Woods.

Smoke, T. (1993, Autumn). The last entry was love: Writing a play on a network. *TESOL Journal,* 40.

SpeechViewer. [Computer Program]. Exton, PA: EduQuest.

Steps to English Language Development. [Computer Program]. San Diego, CA: Jostens Learning Corporation.

Story Club. [Computer Program]. Torrance, CA: Davidson.

Story Time. [Computer Program]. Dallas, TX: Houghton Mifflin.

Sullivan, N. (1993, Autumn). Teaching writing on a computer network. *TESOL Journal,* 34–35.

Tale of Benjamin Bunny. [CD-ROM]. Toronto, Ontario, Canada: Discus.

USA GeoGraph. [Computer Program]. Minneapolis, MN: MECC

VoiceType. [Computer Program]. Exton, PA: EduQuest.

Wall, T., & Siegel, J. (1994, March). All included. *Electronic Learning,* 24–34.

Willetts, K. (1992). Technology and second language learning. ERIC: ED 350 883.

Windows on Science and Living Textbook Series. [Computer Program]. Warren, NJ: Optical Data.

Word Weaver. [Computer Program]. Hood River, OR: Humanities.

Writer's Helper. [Computer Program]. Iowa City, IA: Conduit.

Assistive Equipment Manufacturers

Ablenet Inc., 1081 Tenth Ave. SE, Minneapolis, MN 55414-1312.

B.E.S.T. Switch Interface (BSI, serial port), 63 Forest St., Chestnut Hill, MA 02167.

Creative Switch Industries, PO Box 5256, Des Moines, IA 50306.

Don Johnston Developmental Equipment, Inc., PO Box 639, Wauconda, IL 60084.

Enabling Devices, 385 Warburton Ave., Hastings-on-Hudson, NY 10706.

NHATEC, PO Box 370, Laconia, NH 03247.

PC-Pedal (parallel), Brown & Co., PO Box 861, Georgetown, MA 01833.

Pointer Systems, Inc., 1 Mill St., Burlington, VT 05401.

Prentke Romich Co., 1022 Heyl Rd., Wooster, OH 44691.

Regenesis Development Corp., 1046 Deep Cove Rd., N. Vancouver, British Columbia, Canada V7G 1S3.

TASH, 70 Gibson Dr., Unit #12, Markham, Ontario, Canada L3R 4C2.

TASH, 91 Station St., Unit #1, Ajax, Ontario, Canada, L1S 3H2.

Toys for Special Children, 385 Warburton Ave., Hastings-on-Hudson, NY 10706.

Zygo Industries, Inc., PO Box 1008, Portland, OR 97207.

Augmentative Communication Manufacturers

ADAMLAB, 33500 Van Born Rd., Wayne, MI 48184.

American Printing House for the Blind, PO Box 6085, Louisville, KY 40206.

Consultants for Communication Technology, 508 Bellevue Terr., Pittsburgh, PA 15202.

Detroit Institute for Children, 5447 Woodward Ave., Detroit, MI 48202.

Don Johnson Developmental Equipment, 1000 N. Rand Bldg. 115, Wauconda, IL 60084.

EKEG Electronics Co, Ltd., PO Box 46199, Station G, Vancouver, British Columbia, Canada V6R 4G5.

Enabling Technologies Co., 3102 SE Jay St., Stuart, FL 34997.

Innocomp, 33195 Wagon Wheel Dr., Solon, OH 44139.

Prentke Romich Co., 1022 Heyl Rd., Wooster, OH 44691.

Royal Data Systems, Route 14, Box 230, Morganton, NC 28655.

Sentient Systems Technology, 5001 Baum Blvd., Pittsburgh, PA 15213.

Speller Teller Communications, 3234 S. Villa Cir., West Allis, WI 53227.

Tiger Communication System, 155 E. Broad St., #325, Rochester, NY 14604.

Voice Connection, 17835 Skypark Cir., Suite C, Irvine, CA 92714.

Zygo Industries, Inc., PO Box 1008, Portland, OR 97207.

Chapter *15*

Issues in
Educational Computing

As technology has played a greater part in our lives, we have been slow to recognize the subtle social and ethical changes placed on us. The swift pace of technological advancements has further complicated our efforts to keep pace with these changes.

The focus of this chapter is to produce greater awareness of ethical, legal, and cultural issues surrounding educational computing. It is hoped that by heightening awareness of frequently overlooked areas, educators can help train individuals who are better prepared to solve present and future computing problems.

First, we will look at ethical issues such as equitable distribution of computer access and training. Gender and minority concerns will be overviewed. Second, computer crime, including software piracy and computer viruses, will be discussed. Cultural issues of computer use will then be addressed, including impact on work, home, and leisure and how hidden cultural biases can be transferred using technology. The final section will focus on the future, providing information to help educators make informed decisions about educational computing in the future.

Ethical Issues

Now that hardware development has become a highly competitive field and is being driven at breakneck speed by its developers, computer users are constantly being faced with decisions. Software developers and researchers find themselves running behind, frequently spending too much time trying to generate possible applications without taking the time to look at other less pressing issues. Fortunately, representatives of special-interest groups such as the disabled, special education, minorities, and women have voiced concerns of ethical computer use.

Equal Access

As long as educators have software and hardware shortages, the issue of equal access remains a concern. Whenever shortages exist, priorities and compromises become strong realities. Many questions emerge concerning who determines criteria and who makes the ultimate decisions regarding computer usage.

Who should have access to computers when computer resources are insufficient to meet student needs? In most cases, if every student is given equal computer time, little effect will be realized. Use of the computer may be restricted to once a month for a short session. What criteria should be used to determine who accesses computers? Should those students who stand to make the greatest gain have priority? Should the computer be primarily used for remedial purposes? Students who have special needs can be powerfully served by computers. Yet, gifted children can profit from the intellectual challenge and have a strong chance of being primary computer users as adults. What about the majority of students who are neither remedial nor gifted?

Another topic that keeps surfacing is gender—namely, ensuring that girls have equitable access to technology in schools. When microcomputers were first introduced into school settings, stereotypical thinking affected some teachers' attitudes and decisions when determining access.

Although research supports that males and females equally access technology in the early grades, as they approach early adolescence the girls fall behind. In order to counterbalance this trend, some high schools are experimenting with separate classes for girls, particularly in the fields of math, science, and computers. Teachers of mixed-gender classes are being cautioned to be aware of who controls the keyboard, who does the analysis, and who takes notes.

In order to assure equity of access for both males and females, some experts recommend that computers be a required part of specific curricula. Others suggest that half the computers in a lab be devoted to areas of interest to females, such as graphics, word processing, and creative programs. Other sites are hosting after-school clubs or small group projects for girls only to provide environments free of competition (McAdoo, 1994).

In terms of equitable computer use, minority students form another at-risk group. Minority students are more likely to be in poorer school districts where computer equipment is limited. As educators offer more computer-assisted instruction and computer tool usage in classrooms, students who do not have access are losing not only valuable computer literacy experience but also valuable instructional time. If educational decision makers are giving priority access to students who are talented and gifted, that means minority children are also underrepresented. The equity issue of home access to technology remains a concern. According to the Computer in American Schools study, 82 percent of high-income eleventh-graders, 48 percent of middle-income eleventh-graders, and 14 percent of low-income eleventh-graders have home computers. Computer clubs, after-school computer programs at libraries, YWCAs, and other community organizations are attempting to create more equitable access (McAdoo, 1994).

Research reviewers on computer equity indicated that computer use during the 1980s further exaggerated the distance between groups of students. Minorities, the poor, females, and low-achievers were likely to be further behind after the introduction of computers into schools (Kirby, 1990; Nelson & Watson, 1990–91; Johnson & Maddux, 1991).

Experts argue that the real changes in education will come from intervention programs, not from hardware. It is recommended that rather than purchasing more hardware to solve equity problems, educators identify effective programs that have made a difference. For example, the Kentucky Educational Reform Act of 1990 included a plan that provided an equitable hardware base throughout the state. The act also required that every school in the state name a technology coordinator who receives summer workshop training and refresher courses (McAdoo, 1994).

Sharon Bell, director of educational technology, New Orleans School District, believes that equity requires strong teacher preparation that links teachers to technology, pedagogy, and curriculum. Suburban and wealthier urban schools tend to use computers for more independent and creative functions such as problem solving, science simulations, and drawing conclusions based on evidence than inner-city sites. Bell has argued that equity of "level access" focuses on *all* students using computers for higher-level thinking (Bell, 1994).

Legal Issues

As the computer continues to pervade our society, people need to be educated as to the ethics and legalities of computer use. Paradoxically, one of the great assets of the computer—its versatility—has become one of its greatest liabilities. The versatility of the computer has made it a valuable tool for criminal purposes.

Computer crime is relatively new. Educating computer users, young and old alike, to recognize and prevent computer crime is another ethical consideration for school systems. Educators may help prevent computer misuse by becoming knowledgeable and by teaching computer ethics. A brief overview of computer crime may help readers take the first step toward active involvement in computer crime prevention. Active instruction on computer ethics will achieve the vital second step to increase ethical computer use.

Computer Crime

Computer crime includes all activities in which a computer is used in a criminal act. Such crimes include information destruction, theft of service, theft of information, physical destruction, alteration of data, theft of money, and software piracy.

An information destruction crime is the erasing of information housed on a computer. Several information destruction incidents involving disgruntled ex-employees have been reported. A theft of service may be accomplished by an intruder who uses a company computer for private purposes. Theft of information may be committed by competitors interested in confidential trade information. TRW Information Service, the largest credit bureau in the United States, reported that an intruder had accessed confidential information that could be used in credit card fraud. Physical destruction of information involves destruction of computer files. The Red Brigade, an Italian terrorist group, reportedly destroyed vital computer files of several large Italian corporations, universities, and government agencies. An example of alteration of information is when a student uses a home computer and modem to access a school database to alter undesirable grades (Perry & Wallich, 1984).

As the number of people who use computers increases, the probability of computers being used for criminal purposes increases. As far as can be determined, computer crime is relatively limited, although experts indicate that reported computer crime represents only a small percentage of total computer crime (Parker, 1983). Even though perpetrators are generally authorized insiders who take advantage of the system, unauthorized individuals gaining entrance to computer systems (hackers) have also created damage.

Hackers

Hackers are individuals who are fascinated with computer systems and have made a hobby of studying how they work. Some hackers make a game of breaking into computer systems illegally. One of the most famous examples of computer hackers who went too far is a group of Milwaukee Explorer Scouts who, in 1983, were caught after gaining illegal entry into over 60 government and business computers in Canada and the United States (Rothman & Mosmann, 1985). Hackers can cause havoc with computer systems and can benefit from computer information. They provide another reason for computer ethic information being included in all computer education curricula at all levels of education.

Software Piracy

Software sales worldwide have grown from $250 million in 1980 to $2 billion in 1984 to $8 billion by 1989 (Forester, 1990). Ironically, software losses for 1992 alone were $9.7 billion, demonstrating not only the high growth pattern of the industry but also the severity of software piracy. Software piracy, the illegal duplication of software, remains a severe and chronic international problem.

Although losses due to software piracy totaled only $7.4 billion worldwide in 1993, down from $9.7 billion in 1992, the Software Publishers Association noted that the reduction was attributed to lower software prices. The number of software products copied and illegally sold rose about 1.5 percent (Techwatch, 1994). Organizations such as the Business Software Alliance are working to slow the growth of illegal software duplication. The alliance, representing about two dozen of the largest software companies in the United States, settled cases against companies totaling $3.6 million and expects to settle many more (*Science Update,* 1994).

Software piracy extends from students making illegal copies of computer programs to large corporations (primarily located in Taiwan, Singapore, and Hong Kong) that market "bootlegged" copies of programs such as *Lotus 1-2-3* for as little as $10 (Forester, 1990). Although major software publishing firms are making progress in halting large-scale software piracy in key foreign countries by pressuring them to adopt strong copyright acts, business and individual illegal copying of software still remains a chronic problem.

Software piracy has been further complicated by the practice of abandoning protection codes (used to reduce illegal copying). This is stemming from the need to remain competitive in business markets, placing the burden back on individuals making ethical decisions. There is no doubt that ethical training concerning software piracy has a place in all computer education curricula. The International Council for Computers in Education (ICCE) has addressed this concern by publishing a policy statement aimed at solving the problems inherent in providing and securing educational software. The stated need is to assure that educators can access quality software for reasonable prices and that hardware and software developers and vendors can maintain a fair return on their investment.

Ethical practices of educators include (1) implementing district-approved written policy statements asserting that copyright laws and publisher license agreements will be observed, (2) preventing unauthorized copying of programs on school equipment, (3) designating a school-level representative to be responsible for enforcement, and (4) instructing students on legal and ethical issues of computer use.

Software developer ethical practices include (1) providing a backup copy of all purchases, (2) allowing on-approval purchases to provide adequate preview, (3) assisting in development of regional centers for software demonstration, (4) helping to design a process that encourages flexibility yet discourages theft, and (5) providing multiple-copy pricing for educational institutions (ICCE, 1983).

In the last few years, software publishers have been experimenting with a variety of permissible copying standards. Site licensing agreements are becoming more prevalent, as are lab packs that allow owners to make a certain number of legal copies and network pricing. As the educational software market continues to grow, software publishers are making greater strides in assisting educators to meet student needs with limited budgets. It is up to the educational community to help reduce illegal software duplication through modeling appropriate computer ethics as well as providing appropriate training. For specific help, educators may obtain a booklet entitled *Ethical Use of Information Technologies in Education* (Silvin & Bialo, 1992) and/or request the Ethics Kit from EDUCOM, which includes brochures and handouts focusing on ethical computer use.

Computer Viruses

In 1986 and 1987, two Pakistani brothers had the distinction of becoming the first individuals to unleash a computer virus on the world. A *computer virus* "is a program that infects other programs by modifying them to include a version of itself. And like real viruses, these carry a genetic code which is recorded in machine language. The code tells a 'host' system to place the virus into its main logic, usually on a hard disk" (Palmore, 1989). Once the virus infects a computer system, it lays dormant and infects any other program it can reach. Disks initialized on that computer or programs that are sent over telecommunication lines will carry the virus to other computers.

Many viral strains have been discovered and new ones are expected. Presently, the viruses act in different ways and are typically placed into several categories. The *Brain* or *Scores* virus attacks the operating system and affects other programs on the disk; the *Trojan Horse* virus disguises itself and damages the user's data; the *Worm* generally eats away files as the disks are used; and *Time Bombs* wait until a particular date and leave a message or destroy a disk (Palmore, 1989).

Viruses have been used as pranks and as weapons of destruction. Examples include a West German computer club called Chaos that introduced a virus into the NASA computer network, which reportedly did not influence data critical to operations. A message for international peace was implanted on thousands of unopened Macintosh software programs. IBM computers have also had their share of viruses. "Viruses have been reported by a major aerospace company, an air traffic control system, a newspaper and several government agencies" (Palmore, 1989, p. 27).

High-profile cases have helped publicize software viruses and the price that may be paid. A Cornell computer science graduate student, Robert T. Morris, Jr., was the first to test the 1986 U.S. Federal Computer Fraud and Abuse Act. He was found guilty of releasing a worm (virus), fined $10,000, placed on probation for three years, and ordered to perform 400 hours of community service (Johnson, 1994).

In addition to legal action, software developers and users are waging war against computer viruses with "vaccines." There are a growing number of programs for sale or free through users' groups. Most programs range from $10 to $250 and are effective with only some viruses.

When discussing computer viruses, recommendations range from, "Don't worry about it. It will never happen to you" to "Routinely use a variety of antiviral programs to check out all your disks, being careful of downloading programs from electronic bulletin boards and not using a disk until you have checked it out." In some cases, recovering from a virus infection may require that you erase your infected floppies and hard disk by reinitializing them and then reload your viral-free programs.

Cultural Issues

Cultural attitudes are frequently accepted unconsciously by individuals. Most of us are surprised when someone points out a cultural influence. Often, we feel a cultural influence but do not actively recognize that it is alterable. Educators are socializing agents who need to be aware of the many ways they disseminate cultural attitudes and biases.

As computing has permeated our culture in the last 15 years, many people have not stopped to look at the impact computers have made in the workplace, at home, and on our leisure activities. This section will provide general information to heighten awareness of how technology is creating a rapidly changing culture. Also, a word of caution is given regarding how cultural bias can be transmitted through technology.

Influence of Computers in the Workplace

A brief overview of any text that focuses on computer use provides a lengthy list of computer applications influencing almost all aspects of the workplace. Topics range from using computers to assist in forecasting weather, analyzing seismic activity, studying economic models, solving engineering problems, transferring funds, assisting in product distribution and keeping track of inventories, assisting in marketing decisions, increasing communication, billing, keeping track of multistep tasks, designing parts for manufacturing, and so on. The list is endless (Rothman & Mosmann, 1985).

As computer and related technology permeate the workplace, conditions have changed dramatically and will continue to do so. Experts are quick to present the advantages and disadvantages of the increasing use of technology in the workplace. For example, computers in the form of robots are working in hazardous conditions by handling toxic waste and moving goods in deep-freeze warehouses (Carlton, 1988). Manufacturing robots are being used to process faster, provide greater degree of accuracy, reduce cost per unit, and increase uniformity (Stern & Stern, 1983).

Communication capabilities have grown so much that the *global village* concept is getting closer to reality. Computers are being used by phone companies, airlines, and businesses to increase communication and boost sales. Communication satellite systems have made international communication immediate and accessible. Fax machines now provide individual access to text and graphic transfer over telephone lines.

Businesses are now relying on computer assistance at all levels. Payroll, inventory, purchasing, billing, communication, financial planning, project management, even transfer of funds are being orchestrated with computer assistance. Some experts are concerned that this reliance on computers will result in workers neither being in control over their work nor understanding it (Carlton, 1988). The concern is what to do when the computer breaks down.

A greater concern is how technology is affecting the number of jobs available for humans. As computers take over more jobs and perform with greater competence, people are becoming displaced. Draftspersons are being replaced by computer-assisted design systems, telephone technicians by multilink transmission systems, and production line welders and tomato pickers by robots (Carlton, 1988). The number of tomato pickers used in California dropped from 40,000 in the 1970s to 8,000 in the 1980s due to the use of tomato-picking robots.

Kalman A. Toth, founder of Silico-Magnetic Intelligence Corporation, believes that our reliance on computer technology, particularly "intelligent" machinery such as robots equipped with artificial intelligence, is inevitable. He postulates that we will become a workless society. "In the twenty-first century, intelligent machines will replace almost all workers and people will get paid for doing nothing" (Toth, 1990, p. 33). Computer programmers, engineers, truckers, and pilots will be replaced by intelligent robots. Ultimately, a multipurpose robot could take over the operation of family life by not only overseeing the kitchen but also the family doctor role. As computerized systems assume more human responsibilities, humans will be left with the important task of "reexamining the meaning of our human endeavor and separate human dignity from our quickly disappearing jobs" (Toth, 1990, p. 37). This is one reason why industry, business, and local communities are becoming proactive in restructuring our educational system. As machines take more human responsibilities, social issues emerge as well as educational concerns.

Influence of Computers at Home and at Leisure

If the futurists are correct about Americans gaining more leisure time, computer use at home and at leisure activities will no doubt increase. Microcomputers in the home are being used in many ways. Frequently, children use home computers for educational and leisure purposes. Educational games and general computer games are available for almost all brands of microcomputers. Parents who have opted to teach their children in their homes have many educational programs to assist them in meeting learning objectives.

Financial management has also caught the attention of many home computer users. Tax preparation, stock market analysis, and bookkeeping software are readily available at most software stores. Checkbook balancing and banking through modems are also possible.

Record-keeping options such as inventorying possessions for insurance purposes and keeping track of recipes, car maintenance history, geneological records, and such have been popular. Some people are even beginning to buy consumer goods through television access.

A variety of home security products are available where computers assist in providing a security response. Computerized home control options such as monitoring lights, temperature, music, and so on have also been marketed.

The computer has not yet influenced the home and leisure activities to the extent that it has influenced the workplace. However, as we spend more time at home and at leisure rather than at work, the computer will undoubtedly grow in importance in these arenas.

Hidden Cultural Bias

Another aspect of educational computing that is not readily apparent is the hidden cultural biases that are presented by the computer programmer. Most educators are still in the beginning stages of understanding the computer and are not aware of potentially hidden biases. Some experts feel that the computer mirrors our twentieth-century technocratic mindset. These experts warn that we all need to think of the computer as a mediator of culture as we bring computing into the classroom. We are further asked to keep in mind that the individual and cultural biases of the programmer are reflected in his or her work. Gender, racial, and technological biases will be transmitted in a seemingly neutral setting.

C. A. Bowers has asked us to remember that just as a stick reduces a sense of touch and the telephone reduces communication by eliminating physical context and body language, "the microcomputer selects out and reduces aspects of experience from the transmission-of-knowledge process that characterizes the educational setting" (1988, p. 33). Bowers has further indicated that technology amplifies a sense of objectivity and reduces awareness of the perspective adapted by the person who collects and organizes the presented information.

Teachers must be reflective practitioners who point out the mindset of the programmer to students as well as the cultural forces present in the classroom that are influenced by the computer, technology, and the selected software. Third World educators are also urged to consider the biases that are present in software developed in other cultures. Cultural biases of the software such as the materialistic view of success, separation of culture and nature, and the notion of the autonomous individual can be transmitted unknowingly. Representatives of host cultures may not want these messages transmitted and need to be vigilant in their awareness. In short, educators need to understand that technology is not necessarily neutral and that computer programs carry the biases of their authors (Bowers, 1988).

Future Issues

Again, due to the fast pace of computer development in this country, our mechanisms for looking into the future must change. As competition forces business and other institutions to keep pace with innovative advancements in technology, people who have a perspective of the future become more valuable. Trend study and extrapolation have become important in our economic system.

Educational institutions are also paying greater attention to the future, particularly when it involves purchasing expensive computer or related equipment and software. Purchasing equipment that quickly becomes obsolete due to lack of software or manufacturing support is a costly mistake. Reliance on consulting experts who are studying computing trends is becoming a more prevalent practice in education (Putka, 1990).

Internet and the Changes It Brings

Probably the most influential change in educational technology in the last few years has been the advancement of the Internet (see Chapter 9, Networks and Telecommunication). To many people, it remains the single-most powerful communication breakthrough since the invention of the telephone.

The Internet is a collection of networks that exists free from local, state, national, or international regulation. It allows people to communicate globally, inexpensively, and in an environment that is free from outside control. The concept of one person placing a request onto the "Net," waking the next morning to find seven answers to the question, three of them from people in other nations, brings new life to the concept of *global communication.* One teacher reported her struggles to help an 8-year-old, Quechua-speaking, Inca Indian to learn English. Exhausting traditional methods of securing linguistic assistance, she placed a message on *MacPost* and *Linguist* on the Internet and within 24 hours received messages from professors at Princeton and Cornell Universities as well as a linguist whose aunt spoke Quechua (Clovis, 1994).

Children are communicating with children across vast distances in new ways. Students in Europe and the United States talk directly to Israeli children about what SCUD attacks are really like. Students from Japan and the United States discuss the price of rice in Japan and other countries. The results are a discovery of the principles of protectionist trade policies (Rogers, 1994).

Over 20 million people connect to each other on the Internet in a continuously evolving nature. With the population on the Net doubling annually, this form of communication is and will continue to have a major impact on social interaction and culture. A new on-line culture is evolving, complete with its own rules and practices. New newsgroups are created by one person making a request and calling for a vote showing a two-thirds majority in favor of the new group. *Newsgroup hosts* are volunteers who guide conversations, making sure arguments are not repeated, and moderating exchanges, including harsh personal attacks ("flames") on individuals. Conversations among participants are controlled only by the participants. A sense of community that is developed has been likened to a corner cafe with regular customers.

Two institutions that many experts are predicting will be impacted by the information exchange promoted by the Internet are libraries and higher education. There is much debate regarding how these pillars of education will react and be altered by widespread inexpensive telecommunications.

Learning, Higher Education, Libraries, and Internet

There is no doubt that we will soon be forced to break down artificial barriers that we currently hold sacred. The Internet is creating new forms of information exchanges that have never before been possible. Whereas the twentieth century created an infinite division of labor to perform tasks and solve problems, advanced information technology of the twenty-first century offers the possibility of removing boundaries and combining activities in new ways (Ward, 1994). How will networks impact higher education and its primary missions of research, teaching and learning, and community service? With present networking capabilities, learning environments can "have the information density of the Library of Congress, the pedagogical skill of Socrates and the excitement and holding power of a video game" (Peters, 1994, p. 63).

Libraries are being transformed into portals through which learners may instantly access information resources of the world. "Within the library community, discussions about the long-term impacts of electronic networking tend to spark debates about whether certain facilities (such as libraries), functions (such as cataloging) and artifacts (such as books and periodicals) will continue to exist in the age of networks" (Peters, 1994, p. 62). Both higher education and the community of libraries are faced with new options. Libraries are already allowing the linkages through telecommunications that are changing our current concept of *library* to a gateway to information access and exchange.

Responses to potential changes affecting higher education, libraries, education, communication, and information exchange may best be made by those remembering that technology is a tool and not a goal and that our goal is to find the right place for our continuously evolving facilities, functions, and artifacts (Peters, 1994).

Internet Concerns

Easy access to the Internet brings concern over uncontrolled access to erotic material—particularly by children and adolescents. Three of the five most widely read newsgroups are devoted to erotic material. Currently, there are no methods to block user access of downloading material. Experts anticipate a mechanism similar to 900 telephone number blocks where unauthorized persons would be prevented from accessing certain portions of the Net.

Other concerns revolve around the type and quality of interactions on Internet. Anonymity allows some people to ask questions they would not normally ask; it also allows others to send inflammatory or harassing messages without fear of reprisals. Attempts to control inappropriate messaging have been ineffectual. Just as people learn to drive automobiles, they will need to learn how to communicate using socially accepted methods.

The quality of discussions have been criticized by some. One popular explanation for the limited quality of on-line debates is the lack of social and nonverbal cues afforded by body language that help guide conversation. Others have offered that the quickness in offering the message, with little cost and knowing that it will last only a few weeks, offers little incentive to spend much time in deep thought. "Usenet encourages participants to be helpful but discourages eloquence. It fosters . . . honest discussion but also allows for harassment without retribution" (Steinburg, 1994, p. 25).

Another new form of communication is real-time multiparty exchanges. The real-time communication offered by multi-user dimensions (MUDs) and Internet relay chats (IRCs) bring a new form of communication. Messages arrive on users' screens in a matter of seconds but only to those who are currently listening; messages are not saved. Conversations are more like talking on CB radio than to an E-mail exchange. IRCs are chats among 2 to 40 participants. Anyone can join, and over 60 countries are represented.

MUDs are also communicating in real time but each provides a theme and the illusion of a virtual world. Each MUD provides its own geography and theme, from alien worlds to medieval Europe. Interactions such as these destroy the notion that identity is rooted in the body. People can take on roles, communicate in ways they have never been able to, be cooperatively creative, and develop close communal ties with fellow participants. This provides an interactive, more personalized form of entertainment, communication, and community building than watching TV, viewing a video, or reading a book. It also reemphasizes the power of written text (Steinberg, 1994).

Virtual Realities

One of the most exciting fields of computer research is virtual reality technology. Just as microscopes and telescopes were invented to extend our vision to view things too small or too far away, we are viewing the nonexistent by creating alternate realities using computerized technology.

After 20 years of development, we are beginning to see commercial applications of virtual reality technology. One of the most prominent examples of virtual reality (VR) is in the field of architecture. Architects can design buildings using VR and then take clients for tours of the "virtual" building. Users experience the virtual world as if it is real. Both architect and client wear a set of goggles that place two miniature computer screens directly in front of the users' eyes. This gives the users the illusion that they are surrounded by the computerized conditions generated by software. No matter what direction users look, the software adjusts so that the users are seeing what they would normally see if the virtual reality was not artificial. To provide further feeling of control, users can move through the virtual reality by using a sensor-lined glove to open doors and windows (Branwyn, 1990).

NASA is looking into VR to support its concept of sending robots into space to repair space equipment by connecting the robots to humans on earth that are experiencing a virtual reality of the robot's reality. So, a human's actions would directly control the robot's actions. NASA is also looking into the prospect of developing virtual realities using data collected from other worlds. Scientists can enter and explore other worlds without leaving this one.

In the summer of 1991, five groups of students, aged 9 to 15 took part in a virtual reality experiment at Seattle's Pacific Science Center. The students created their own virtual worlds. Children found VR compelling and intuitive. They indirectly learned programming, networking, and design. Students learned by doing and experiencing concepts and phenomena directly. Students outside Newcastle, England, developed virtual cities where students shop in virtually real French and German streets, and calculate and pay in virtual francs or marks. Students have also successfully built a virtual factory for a health and safety education project (Sherman, 1992). Educators are just beginning to explore the potentials of virtual reality in K–12 settings.

Potential Impact of Technology on U.S. Education

Other professionals, outside the traditional realm of education, have taken an interest in educational computing issues. In some communities, business/school alliances have produced new educational structures that have a technological component. For example, the Chiron Middle School in Minneapolis placed 300 fifth- through eighth-grade students into a unique program. Students attended nine-week sessions at a series of learning centers in various locations in the community. Government, communications, manufacturing, environment, health, retailing, and information processing were the focus of these sessions. Multiage teams worked in real-life settings using real-life technology.

Experimental educational programs are striving to connect schools to the workplace and the technological tools that are already in existence. They are demanding active student participation, no longer allowing passive participation. Educators are experimenting with more worklike practices that require students to create and produce as they will need to when they reach the workforce.

Fred D'Ignazio, noted media specialist, further supports this educational computing issue. He has stated that the twenty-first century will boast electronic highways consisting of communication satellites, fiber optic lines, cable TV, microwave transmissions, cellular phones, computer modems, fax machines, broadcast television, and radio. The question is whether educators will elect to travel these electronic roads or further isolate themselves by creating deadend electronic dirt roads of their own.

Each educator has choices. How far each is willing to extend the potential of educational computing is dependent on the vision of the possible. New paradigms of educational computing can include new avenues of information access that can "turn the classroom into a *vehicle* that teachers *and* students can use to travel the *real* electronic highways in order to experience new knowledge for themselves" (D'Ignazio,

1990, p. 21). If the computer is perceived as a vehicle rather than as a standstill stand-alone machine, we drastically change our perspective on the possibilities.

Restructuring U.S. Learning

Technology continues to be a catalyst for school reform. New organizational systems are finding their way into U.S. schools with surprising results. Initially, the computer was predicted to create isolation in classrooms. A restructuring of Ralph Bunche School in Harlem has demonstrated just the opposite. By creating a schoolwide LAN (local area network) with a fileserver, students can access their work, no matter where in the school they are working. So, all data, no matter what form, can be accessed in classroom, computer lab, library, and home, at any time. This flexible system has spawned a new learning community—a community where students and teachers take greater initiative by gathering before and after school to edit a school newspaper or complete routine record-keeping tasks. One class voluntarily stayed after school every day for additional math instruction. A collaborative project-based approach is motivating students and teachers alike. Development of collaborative "workplace" electronic folders, where groups of students can store information, has created a new and stronger focus for learning. The technology has even led students and teachers to the development of multiyear projects (Newman & Reese, in press).

Other schools are planning for the future by targeting full access of teachers and students to information via voice, video, and computer data, any time, any place (Van Dam, 1994). Others are encouraging paradigm changes by considering moving from organizing schools from the outmoded industrial model to a service-industry model. Technology may help us better address the learning needs of all students. Swanton High School, a 1993 winner of GTE's Pioneering Partners program, developed teams of teachers who, along with students, parents, and administrators, shared responsibility for student learning. Teams met for three to four hours daily, and the use of Flex Passes allowed them to alter the amount of time they spent at certain locations. Technology support included assessment by computer-based program, satellite-delivered learning using one-way video and two-way audio transmissions, videodiscs, hypermedia, Internet access, and videotaped lectures available for checkout (Holden, 1994).

Restructuring educational systems may take many forms. Some school systems are restructuring to help prepare students interested in pursuing careers involving technology. One technology plan incorporated professional and technical programs around job fields such as telecommunications. Students were introduced to professional information on occupations such as electronic mail specialist, fiber optics systems specialist, and satellite systems engineer. The telecommunication technical occupation list included data network technician, fiber optics technician, and network control technician. By reorganizing high schools to help students better understand the positions available to them and to provide them with entry-level skills, we are better preparing our students to join the workforce of tomorrow.

What's Next?

Which of the new technologies may influence education? Who knows? Here are some technology bites—tidbits—describing potential educational technologies.

Pen computing is writing on an LCD screen with an electronic pen. This input device attaches to a computer much like a mouse or keyboard. IBM's *ThinkPad* and most personal digital assistants (PDAs), such as Apple's *Newton,* have pen capabilities built in. Although the technology is still young, and problems with personal handwriting characteristics are limiting use in K–12 instruction, experts are predicting that pen computing will become state of the art soon. Developers predict that teachers will use wireless computers to send messages to students' computers by simply pointing an infrared pen at the students' PDAs (Salvador, 1994). Current educational uses of PDAs include collecting observations as teachers move through classrooms then uploading notes to a cumulative file on a computer network, as well as students electronically recording notes during field trips.

Wireless networks, or portable radio modems for laptops, are coming. Low-price wireless E-mail service is being developed now. Students and teachers will be able to access their personal files from any location at school or home.

Voice recognition is advancing to a manageable level. People with physical disabilities may use voice recognition software to activate program commands by speech. Children will be able to ask computers questions using natural speech and the program will be able to provide immediate response. Dragon Systems is projecting that it will be marketing educational programs that students can control and navigate by voice in the near future (What's New in Voice Recognition?, 1994).

Text-to-speech software is capitalizing on the computer translating text and converting it into speech. Immediate beneficiaries are students who speak English as a second language and students who are visually impaired.

Broadband networks will allow the delivery of high-quality, interactive instructional programming. Real-time interactive exchanges delivered by cable or satellite will add new meaning to distance learning.

Groupware products will allow teachers and students to jointly author, share, and disseminate electronic documents. Organizations are already improving writing skills using groupware and process writing techniques. Furthermore, this technology increases motivation by incorporating video clips, graphic images, and sound.

Knowbots, short for knowledge robots, are automated systems for collecting, screening, and organizing data. Users define what kind of information they want. The knowbot then searches incoming data—such as that received on an Internet mailing list, databases, and data from a local area networks—and then selects and organizes the information based on predetermined criteria (Hancock & Betts, 1994).

Summary

Educators are faced with many concerns in this rapidly changing world. Technology continues to increase the pace of change, bringing new perspectives as well as new opportunities. Access to educational computing remains a primary concern. Who is accessing and who is not accessing computers and related technology in classrooms? Hopefully, educators will continue to ask this question often and make the appropriate and frequent adjustments necessary to keep striving for equitable access.

The legal aspects of computing are complex and multilayered. Teachers can help society by practicing ethical computer use, avoiding software piracy, and providing direct instruction on ethical computing practices.

Educators can address cultural computing issues in several ways. First, educators need to become more aware of how cultural perspectives influence students. Second, they can prepare students for a continually changing workplace. Next, they can help students adjust to living lives that include a greater emphasis on home and leisure. And last, they can increase general awareness of how hidden biases can be transmitted using technology.

Cultural issues can best be addressed by teachers becoming more aware of cultural computing issues, preparing students for a highly fluid workplace and the possibilities of living a life with more leisure and home-based activities. Warning educators and students of the possibility of hidden cultural biases transferred through computer software gains importance as our world continues to get smaller through advanced communication systems.

With respect to future issues, teachers need to find a way of continually updating themselves on educational computing issues. Resources cited in Chapter 16 of this text may help. Keeping flexible and responsive to hardware and software changes will also make a valuable contribution to educational decision making. It is hoped that education will effectively partner with the worlds of business, industry, and community to produce increasingly viable educational environments needed to prepare students for their ever-changing futures.

Exercises

1. Which steps can be taken to assure computer equity in your school?
2. How can you inform your students about computer crime?
3. What is a computer virus? What impact can it have on a computer? What preventive steps should be taken?
4. How can future computer issues affect your students?
5. Select a cultural issue and discuss how you can address it in your classroom.

References

Bell, S. (1994, April). Teach your teachers well. *Electronic Learning,* 34.

Bowers, C. (1988) *The cultural dimensions of educational computing.* New York: Teachers College Press.

Branwyn, G. (1990, May/June). Virtual reality. *The Futurist,* 45.

Carlton, R. (1988, January/February). The role of computers in the automated workplace. *Computers and People,* 12–17.

Clovis, D. (1994, April). The Quechua connection. *Educational Leadership, 73.*

Computer Literacy Survey. (1983). *Computer literacy.* Berkeley, CA.

Conally, F. (1992 July/August). The ethics kit. *EDUCOM Review,* 14–15.

D'Ignazio, F. (1990, May). Electronic highways and the classroom of the future. *The Computing Teacher,* 20–24.

EDUCOM. 1112 16th St. N.W. Suite 600, Washington, DC 200036.

Forester, T. (1990, March). Software theft and the problem of intellectual property rights. *Computers & Society,* 2–11.

Hancock, V., & Betts, F. (1994, April). From the lagging to the leading edge. *Educational Leadership,* 24–29.

Holden, D. (1994, March). Restructuring schools on a service-industry model. *T.H.E. Journal,* 70–71.

ICCE. (1983, September). ICCE policy statement on network and multiple-machine software. *The Computing Teacher,* 18–22.

Johnson, D. (1994). *Computer ethics* (2nd ed.). Englewood Cliffs, NJ: Prentice Hall.

Johnson, D., & Maddux, C. (1991). The birth and nurturing of a new discipline. *Computers in the Schools,* 5–13.

Kirby, P. (1990). Computers in schools: A new source of inequity. *Computer Education, 14*(6), 537–541.

McAdoo, M. (1994, April). Equity. *Electronic Learning,* 24–33.

Nelson, C., & Watson, J. (1990–91). The computer gender gap: Children's attitudes, performance and socialization. *Journal of Educational Technology Systems, 19*(4), 345–353.

Newman, D., & Reese, P. (in press). The Ralph Bunche Computer Mini-School: A design for individual and community work. In J. Hawkins & A. Collins (Eds.), *Design experiments: Restructuring through technology.* Cambridge: Cambridge University Press.

Palmore, T. (1989, March/April). Computer bytes, viruses and vaccines. *Tech Trends,* 26–28.

Parker, D. (1983). *Fighting computer crime.* New York: Scribners.

Perry, T., & Wallich, P. (1984, May). Can computer crime be stopped? *IEEE Spectrum,* 34–49.

Peters, P. (1994, January/February). Is the library a "place" in the age of networks? *EDUCOM Review,* 62–63.

Putka, G. (1990, July 25). Helping schools learn how to teach. *Wall Street Journal,* pp. B1–B6.

Rogers, A. (1994, May/June). Living the global village. *Electronic Learning,* 28–29.

Rothman, S., & Mosmann, C. (1985). *Computer uses and issues.* Chicago: Science Research Associates.

Salvador, R. (1994, September). What's new in pen computing? *Electronic Learning,* 14.

Science Update (1994, July 28). *Salt Lake City Tribune.*

Sherman, B. (1992). *Glimpses of heaven, visions of hell, virtual reality and its implications.* Suffolk, Great Britain: Hodder & Stoughton.

Silvin, J., & Bialo, E. (1992). *Ethical use of information technologies in education.* Washington, DC: United States Department of Justice/Department of Education.

Steinberg, S. (1994, July). Travels on the Net. *Technology Review,* 20–31.

Stern, N., & Stern, R. (1983). *Computers in society.* Englewood Cliffs, NJ: Prentice Hall.

Talab, R. (1994, March). Copyright, legal, and ethical issues in the Internet environment. *Tech Trends,* 11–14.

Techwatch (1994, January/February). *EDUCOM Review.*

Toth, K. (1990, May/June). The workless society. *The Futurist,* 33–37.

Van Dam, J. (1994, January). Redesigning schools for 21st century technologies: A middle school with the power to improve. *Technology and Learning,* 55–61.

Ward, D. (1994, January/February). Technology and the changing boundaries of higher education. *EDUCOM Review,* 23–27.

What's New in Voice Recognition? (1994, February). *Electronic Learning,* 10.

Chapter *16*

Resources for Further Study

This chapter provides you with an organized set of references and additional resources for further study. The first section describes support organizations for local user groups. The next four sections list associations for educators interested in technology, databases and networks of interest to educators, educational computing periodicals, and major publishers of educational software, respectively.

User Groups

User groups are organizations or clubs where local residents interested in personal computing meet on a regular basis. These clubs facilitate grass-roots networking, which allows interested individuals to access each other. General computer information, assistance, and computer programs are exchanged. A local user group may have a subgroup of educators. User groups can usually be located through local microcomputer dealers.

Associations for Educators Interested in Technology

American Educational Research Association (AERA), 1230 17th Street NW, Washington, DC 20036.

Association for Computers in Mathematics and Science Teaching, PO Box 4455, Austin, TX 78765.

Association for Educational Communications and Technology (AECT), 1126 Sixteenth Street NW, Washington DC 20036.

Computers, Reading and Language Arts (CRLA). PO Box 13039, Oakland, CA 94661.

International Society for Technology in Education (ISTE), University of Oregon, 1787 Agate St., Eugene, OR 97403.

Minnesota Educational Computing Consortium (MECC), 2520 Broadway Dr., St Paul, MN 55113.

National Council of Teachers of Mathematics (NCTM), 1906 Association Dr., Reston, VA 22091.

National Science Teachers Association (NSTA), 1742 Connecticut Ave. NW, Washington DC 20009.

Databases and Networks

America Online, 8619 Westwood Center Dr., Vienna, VA (800-227-6364).

AppleLink, Apple Computer, Inc., 20525 Mariani Ave., Cupertino, CA 95014.

AT&T Learning Network, PO Box 6391, Parsippany, NJ 07054.

California Online Resources for Education (CORE), Keith Vogt, California Technology Project, Box 3842, Seal Beach, CA 90740-7842.

Compuserve, PO Box 20212, Columbus, OH 43220.

CompuServe Information Service, 5000 Arlington Center Blvd., PO Box 20212, Columbus, OH 43220.

CoSN, PO Box 65193, Washington, DC 20035-5193.

Delphi Internet Services, 1030 Massachusetts Ave., Cambridge, MA 02138.

Dialog Information Services, 3460 Hillview Ave., Palo Alto, CA 94304.

EcoNet, PeaceNet and Conflictnet, 18 De Boom St., San Francisco, CA 94107.

ERIC, Educational Resources Center, National Institute of Education, Washington, DC 20208.

Florida Information Resource Network (FIRN), Florida Education Center, Room B114, 325 West Gaines St., Tallahassee, FL 32399.

FrEdMail or Global School Net, PO Box 243, Bonita CA 91908.

GEnie, 401 N. Washington St., Rockville, MD 20850.

Global SchoolNet (*See* FrEdMail)

GTE Educational Services, Irving, TX (800-927-3000).

K12NET, Janet Murray, 1151 SW Vermont St., Portland, OR 97219.

Learning Link/IntroLink, 1400 E. Touhy Ave., Suite 260, Des Plaines, IL.

NASA Spacelink, Huntsville, AL (205-544-6360).

National Geographic Kids Network, National Geographic Society, Educational Services, 17th and M Streets, NW, Washington DC, 20036.

New York State Education and Research Network (NYSERNet), 200 Elwood Davis Rd., Liverpool, NY 13088-6147.

Northwest Regional Educational Laboratory (NWREL), 101 Southwest Main St., Suite 500, Portland, OR 97204.

PBS Learning Link, 1320 Boaddock Pl., Alexandria, VA 22314.

PeaceNet, IGC Networks, Institute for Global Communications, 3228 Sacramento St., San Francisco, CA 94115.

Prodigy, 445 Hamilton Ave., White Plains, NY 10615.

Scholastic Network, Jefferson City, MO (800-246-2986).

SouthEastern Regional Vision for Education (SERVE), 41 Manetta St. NW, Suite 1000, Atlanta, GA 30303.

SpecialNet, GTE Educational Network Services, 5525 MacArthur Blvd., Suite 320, Irving, TX 75038.

TERC's Global Lab and LabNet, 2067 Massachusetts Ave., Cambridge, MA 02140.

Periodicals

AEDS Journal and AEDS Monitor, 1201 16th St. NW, Washington, DC 20036.

Arithmetic Teacher, NCTM, 1906 Association Dr., Reston, VA 22091.

Classroom Computer Learning (*See* Technology and Learning)

Computing Teacher, International Society for Technology in Education, University of Oregon, 1787 Agate St., Eugene, OR 97403.

Educational Technology Pub., 720 Palisade Ave., Englewood Cliffs, NJ 07632.

Electronic Learning, Scholastic Inc., 730 Broadway, New York, NY 10003.

Journal of Computers in Mathematics and Science Teaching, PO Box 2966, Charlottesville, VA 22902

Media and Methods, 1429 Walnut St., Philadelphia, PA 19102.

School Library Journal, PO Box 1878, Marion, OH 43305.

Science Teacher, 1742 Connecticut Ave., NW, Washington DC, 20009.

Technology and Learning, 2451 E. River Rd., Dayton, OH 45439.

T.H.E. Journal, 150 El Camino Real, Suite 112, Tustin, CA 92680.

Educational Software Publishers

ABC News Interactive (*See* Optical Data Corporation)

Active Learning Systems, 5365-J Avenida Encinas, Carlsbad, CA 92008.

Addison-Wesley Publishing Co., Innovative Division, 2725 Sand Hill Rd., Menlo Park, CA 94025.

Advanced Ideas, 2902 San Pablo Ave., Berkeley, CA 94702.

Aldus Corporation, 411 First Ave, South, Seattle, WA 98104-2171.

Apple Computer, Inc., 20525 Mariani Ave., Cupertino, CA 95014.

Applied Optical Media, 1450 Bood Rd., Bldg. 400, West Chester, PA 19380.

Arandu, Inc., 330 West Campbell Ave., Roanoke, VA 24016.

Ashton-Tate, 20101 Hamilton Ave., Torrance, CA 90502.

Autodesk, Inc., 2320 Marinship Way, Sausalito, CA 94965.

Beagle Brothers, Inc., 6215 Ferris Square, Suite 100, San Diego, CA 92121.

Britannica Software Inc., 345 Fourth St., San Francisco, CA 94107.

Broderbund Software, Inc., 500 Redwood Blvd., PO Box 6121, Novato, CA 94948-6121.

Claris Corporation, 5201 Patrick Henry Dr., Santa Clara, CA 95052-8168.

Conduit, University of Iowa, 100 Oakdale Campus, Iowa City, IA 52242.

Continental Press, Inc., 520 E. Bainbridge St., Elizabethtown, PA 17022.

Creative Publications, Suite 101, 1101 San Antonio Rd., Mountain View, CA 94043.

Creative Pursuits, 12151 La Casa La., Los Angeles, CA 90049

CyberEdge Journal, 1 Gate Six Rd., Suite G, New York, NY 10027.

Davidson and Associates, Inc., 19840 Pioneer Ave., Torrance, CA 90503.

DCH (D. C. Heath & Co), 125 Spring St., Lexington, MA 02173.

Didatech Software Ltd., 720 Olive Way, Suite 930, Seattle, WA 98101-7874.

Discis Books, 45 Shepard Ave., E., Suite 410, Toronto, Ontario, Canada M2N 5W9.

DLM, Teaching Resources, One DLM Park, Allen, TX 75002.

Don Johnston Developmental Equipment, Inc., PO Box 639 (1000 N. Rand Rd., Bldg. 115), Wauconda, IL 60084.

Educational Activities, Inc., 1937 Grand Ave., Baldwin, NY 11510.

Educational Publishing Concepts, Rte. 1, Box 286C, Wala Wala, WA 99362.

EduQuest, 4111 Northside Pkwy., Atlanta, GA 30327.

Encyclopedia Britannica, 310 S. Michigan Ave., Chicago, IL 60604.

Fairfield Language Technologies, 122 S. Main St., Harrisonburg, VA 22801.

Gamco Education Materials, Box 1911, Big Spring, TX 79721-1911.

Gessler Education Software, 55 West 13 St., New York, NY 10011-7958.

Great Wave Software, 5353 Scotts Valley Dr., Scotts Valley, CA 95066.

Hartley Courseware, 3001 Coolidge Rd., Suite 400, East Lansing, MI 48823.

Hoffman Educational Systems, 1863 Business Center Dr., Duarte, CA 91010.

HyperGlot Software, 505 Forest Hills Blvd., Knoxville, TN 37919.

IBM Corporation EduQuest Division, PO Box 2150, Atlanta, GA 30055.

Intechnica International, Inc., PO Box 30877, Midwest City, OK 73140.

Intellimation, 130 Cremona Dr., Santa Barbara, CA 93116.

IntelliTools, 5221 Central Ave., Suite 205, Richmond, CA 94804.

InterLex, PO Box 252, Ithaca, NY 14851.

International Software, PO Box 486, Westerville, OH 43081.

Jostens Learning Corporation, 6170 Cornerstone Ct. E., San Diego, CA 92121.

K–12 Micro Media, 6 Arrow Rd., Ramsey, NJ 07446.

Krell Software, 1320 Stony Brook Rd., Stony Brook, NY 10803.

Laureate Learning Systems Inc., 110 E. Spring St., Winooski, VT 05404-1837.

Learning Company, 6493 Kaiser Dr., Fremont, CA 94555.

Logo Computer Systems, Inc., 3300 Cote Vertu Rd., #210, Montreal, Quebec, Canada H4R 2B7.

Lotus Development Corporation, Educational Telemarketing, 55 Cambridge Pkwy., Cambridge, MA 02142.

MacroMind/Paracomp, 600 Townsend, Suite 310, San Franciso, CA 94102.

McGraw-Hill Educational Resources, 11 W. 19th St., New York, NY 10011.

MECC, 6160 Summit Dr. North, Minneapolis, MN 55430-4003.

Media Learning Systems, 1492 W. Colorado Blvd., Pasadena, CA 91105.

Micro Power & Light Co., 8814 Sanshire Ave., Dallas, TX 75231.

Microsoft Corporation, One Microsoft Way, Bldg. 13, Redmond, WA 98052-6399.

Milliken Publishing Co., 1100 Research Blvd., St. Louis, MO 63122.

Mindplay, 3130 North Dodge Blvd., Tucson, AZ 85716.

Mindscape, Inc., 3444 Dundee Rd., Northbrook, IL 60062.

National Geographic Society, Educational Services Division, 1145 17th St. NW, Washington, DC 20036.

Optical Data Corporation, 30 Technology Dr., Warren, NJ 07059.

Optimum Resource, 10 Station Pl., Norfolk, CT 06058.

Perma-Bound, East Vandalia Rd., Jacksonville IL 62650.

Prentke Romich Company, 1022 Heyl Rd., Wooster, OH 44691.

Random House School Division, 400 Hahn Rd., Westminster, MD 21157.

Scholastic Software, 730 Broadway, New York, NY 10003.

Sensible Software, 335 East Big Beaver, Suite 204, Troy, MI 48084.

Simon & Schuster, Gulf & Western Bldg., 1 Gulf & Western Plaza, New York, NY 10023.

Software Publishing Corporation, 1901 Landings Dr., Mountain View, CA 94043.

Spinnaker Software Corporation, 201 Broadway, Cambridge, MA 02139.

Sunburst/Wings Communications, 39 Washington Ave., PO Box 40, Pleasantville, NY 10570.

Syracuse Language Systems, 719 E. Genesee St., Syracuse, NY 13210.

Teacher Support Software Inc., 1035 NW 57th St., Gainesville, FL 32605.

Terrapin Software Inc., 400 Riverside St., Portland, ME 04103.

Texas Caviar, 3933 Steck Ave., #B115, Austin, TX 78759.

Tom Snyder Productions, 800 Coolidge Hill Rd., Watertown, MA 02172.

Ventura Educational Systems, 910 Ramona Ave., Suite E, Grover City, CA 93433.

Videodiscovery, Inc., 1700 Westlake Ave. N., Suite 600, Seattle, WA 98109-3012.

Virtual Reality Development System (VREAM), 2568 N. Clark St., #250, Chicago, IL 60614.

Voyager Company, 1 Bridge St., Irvington, NY 10533.

VPL Research, Inc., 656 Bair Island Rd., Third Floor, Redwood City, CA 94063.

Weekly Reader (*See* Optimum Resource)

Westcliff Software, Inc., 200 Washington St., Suite 207, Santa Cruz, CA 95060.

Glossary

Accumulator   A special-purpose storage location or register found in the CPU that handles almost all data that are processed by the computer.

Acoustic Coupler   A modem with cups to fit over a standard telephone receiver.

Active Simulation   A simulation that allows students to participate and actively manipulate artificial experiences.

Alphanumeric Expression   (*See* String value)

Analog Recording   A representation of information, such as sound or video, that is similar to or analogous to the original sound or video waves.

Analog Transmission   Wavelike transmission, such as that used by phone lines and other communication channels.

Application Server   A network server that enables several client computers connected via a network to access application programs, such as word processors, spreadsheets, and so on stored on a common hard-disk drive.

Artificial Intelligence   Computer-based systems that furnish intellectual decisions comparable to those of intelligent human beings.

ASCII Code (American Standard Code for Information Interchange)   A numeric code or representation for the characters used by a computer, including the letters of the alphabet, numerals 0 through 9, and punctuation symbols.

Assembly Language   A low-level language which uses mnemonic commands, rather than the binary commands of machine language.

Audiovisual Mock-Up System   An audiovisual form of presentation system used in a simulation.

Authoring System   An integrated set of tools designed to simplify the programming process that allows nonprofessional programmers to develop computer-based, multimedia programs.

Automaticity   A level of learning at which students are able to quickly produce the appropriate response when given a stimulus. This level of learning is frequently achieved through the use of drill-and-practice techniques.

Auxiliary Storage   Secondary- or external-information storage, used to supplement internal or primary storage.

Barcode Reader   An electronic device that reads information encoded into a set of printed lines (barcodes). Barcodes are used to encode videodisc player commands.

BASIC (Beginners All-purpose Symbolic Instruction Code).   The computer language built into most microcomputers.

Batch Processing   Computer programs are fed into the computer and executed in batches, with little or no interaction between the computer and the user.

Binary   Refers to two items or events. A binary decision involves two possible alternatives, such as true and false. Binary numbers only have two digits: 1 and 0. All information stored in a computer is represented in binary by two different voltage levels or magnetic states.

Bit   A binary digit, either 1 or 0. The smallest unit of information stored or processed by a computer.

Block Copy   Word-processor function whereby a section or block of text is copied from one location in a document and pasted at another location without deleting the original.

Block Move   Word-processor function whereby a section or block of text may be moved from one part of a document to another.

Boot   When a microcomputer power switch is turned on, a short program in ROM is executed that loads and starts the execution of a larger program, such as the disk-operating system.

Branching   The selection of a certain branch, or segment, within a program; selection can be based on one or more responses of the student.

Bulletin Boards   Computer data files that store announcements and messages that may be accessed by registered participants through the use of computer telecommunications.

Business Graphics Programs   Computer programs that convert numeric data into graphs and charts.

Byte   Memory space required to store one character of information. Usually made up of eight binary digits or bits.

Categories of Learning Outcomes   Five domains of learned capabilities proposed by Gagné: (1) intellectual skills, (2) cognitive strategies, (3) verbal information, (4) motor skills, and (5) attitudes.

CAV (Constant Angular Velocity)   Videodisc format that records one video frame per circular track, thus allowing random access to individual frames.

CD-I (Compact Disk Interactive)   A combination of CD-ROM and computer technology designed for interactive presentations of multimedia information

CD-ROM (Compact Disk-Read Only Memory)   An optical disk designed to store information for use with a computer.

Central Processing Unit (CPU)   The "brains" of the computer; composed of the control unit and the arithmetic-logic unit.

Chip   A small flat piece of silicon onto which electronic circuits are etched.

Clip Art Computer-based pictures, drawings, and other graphics created by professional artists that may be purchased and incorporated into one's own documents.

CLV (Constant Linear Velocity) Videodisc format that records more than one video frame per track, thus doubling the number of frames that can be placed on one side of the disc.

Colossus An electronic digital computer designed by the British during World War II for the purpose of breaking German secret codes. Claimed by some to have been the world's first electronic digital computer.

Command Term usually used interchangeably with *instruction* in referring to a statement or element of a computer program.

Communication Server A network server that facilitates communication between servers and client computers across local and remote networks.

Communications Transfer of information from one computer to another, usually over telephone lines or direct-cable connections.

Compiled Language A high-level language in which commands are translated to machine language prior to the execution of the program.

Computer An electronic device that processes information according to specified instructions or commands.

Computer Conferences The use of computer-telecommunications and data files to conduct discussions on specific topics.

Computer Crime An illegal act involving a computer.

Computer Database (*See* Database)

Computer Gradebook A special-purpose database-management program used to keep track of student assignment and test scores. It can also be used to calculate final grades and generate various progress reports.

Computer Integration (*See* Curriculum Integration)

Computer Laboratory A centralized location within a school where several microcomputers are housed, along with associated peripherals, such as disk drives and printers. The computers are often connected together into a network with a network server. The laboratory is generally used by students from several different classes.

Computer Language A set of commands that can be used to instruct the computer to perform specific tasks.

Computer Literacy General skills and perceptions needed to function effectively in a society or segment of society that is dependent on computer and information technology. Being able to make the computer do what one wants or needs it to do.

Computer Program A set of commands written in a computer language to instruct the computer to perform a task.

Computer System What most people think of as a computer. It includes four major hardware components: (1) central processing unit (CPU); (2) internal memory; (3) input devices; and (4) output devices.

Computer Test Generation A computer-managed instruction application used to generate tests by randomly selecting items from a large computer database. This application facilitates the implementation of individualized mastery instruction.

Computer Test Scoring   A computer-managed instruction application used to score tests. Test item responses are entered into the computer via a mark-sensing or optical-scanning device. The computer analyzes the responses and outputs the total number correct for each student, as well as summarizes information about individual test items and the total test.

Computer Virus   (*See* Virus)

Computer-Assisted Instruction (CAI)   The use of the computer to assist in instructional activities. Commonly used to refer to tutor applications, such as drill and practice, tutorials, simulations, and games.

Computer-Based Education (CBE)   The use of the computer in support of the educational process; synonymous with *computer-assisted instruction.*

Computer-Based Manipulatives   Computer software that simulates on a computer screen physical objects that are used to help children move from concrete to abstract ideas.

Computer-Controlled Adaptive Strategy   An instructional procedure used by a computer program that determines the number, type, and sequence of instructional events to be presented to learners according to a set of sophisticated decision rules based on instructional theory.

Computer-Managed Instruction   The use of the computer to manage the instructional process, including maintaining student records, controlling the availability and timing of instructional events, and providing progress reports to instructors, students, parents, and administrators.

Copying Response   A response elicited by an instructional system that requires the student to copy, verbatim, some information presented in the same frame.

Courseware   Computer materials designed for classroom use, including software and accompanying printed materials.

Coursewriter   A computer language designed by IBM for developing instructional modules.

CPU   (*See* Central Processing Unit)

Curriculum Integration   The coordinated combination of computer technology and traditional teaching procedures to produce student learning.

Cursor   A marker on the video display that indicates where the next character to be typed will be located.

Daisy-Wheel Printer   An impact printer that prints preformed characters that are located on a removable print wheel.

Data   Basic elements of information that can be processed or produced by a computer.

Databank   (*See* Database)

Database   A collection of information stored in computer files, usually on some external storage device.

Database Management System (DBMS)   A computer program that allows a user to enter, update, organize, and retrieve information in a computer database.

Default Problem-Solving Software   Software not specifically designed to teach and reinforce problem-solving skills but that teachers use successfully to do so anyway.

Delete   Removing a character, word, line, paragraph, or other specified amount of text from a document.

Desktop Presentation   Computer tool application for the preparation and presentation of electronic displays, slides, or transparencies.

Desktop Publishing   Computer application that provides an electronic pasteboard for laying out text and graphics elements to produce professional-quality documents such as fliers, brochures, newsletters, magazines, and books.

Digital Trains   An electric train with accessory devices controlled by commands in the form of numbers or digits sent by a computer or controller device.

Digital Video   The representation and storage of video information by numbers or digits. Compression techniques are usually required to minimize storage requirements.

Digitized Sound   The representation of sound, including music and human voice, using numbers or digits. The digital representations may be stored on compact discs or hard drives and manipulated by computer programs.

Disk   (*See* Diskette)

Disk Drive   A device used for external information storage. It saves information to, and reads information from, a diskette.

Disk File   (*See* File)

Diskette   An electromagnetic disk on which information can be stored.

Domain   A group to which a computer belongs. The domain label specifies a type of organization or institution. Domains and subdomains are used in Internet addresses to identify a particular computer.

Dot-Matrix Printer   An impact printer that prints characters composed of dots formed by a wire matrix print head.

Drill and Practice   Computer programs that provide repetitive opportunities for students to pair stimuli with appropriate responses.

DVI (Digital Video Interactive)   Hardware and compression algorithms that enable full-motion digital video on a computer.

Electronic Bulletin Board   (*See* Bulletin Boards)

Electronic Chalkboard   Use of the computer to display information on a large screen in front of a classroom.

Electronic Gradebook   (*See* Computer Gradebook)

Electronic Mail (E-mail)   Use of computer telecommunication to transmit messages.

Electronic Spreadsheet   Computer programs that allow the user to enter rows and columns of numbers similar to those entered on accountants' pads. Mathematical formulas may be entered in any cell of the spreadsheet to automatically compute values based on data in other sections of the spreadsheet.

ENIAC (Electronic Numerical Integrator and Calculator)   A large digital computer developed at the University of Pennsylvania during World War II and put to full use in 1945. Claimed by some to have been the world's first electronic digital computer.

Ergonomics   The study of the physiological interaction between humans and machines. Ergonomic factors are taken into account to minimize discomfort, error, and fatigue resulting from the use of computers.

Events of Instruction   Those activities included in any instructional system designed to aid students in achieving specified objectives. The following nine events have been identified: gaining attention, presenting objectives, recalling prerequisite learning, presenting stimuli, providing guidance, eliciting performance, providing feedback, assessing performance, and enhancing retention.

Execution   The actual processing of a program.

Expert Systems   A computer-based system capable of solving complex problems (in a limited domain) at the competency level of a human expert.

Fidelity   The amount of realism in an artificial environment such as simulations.

Field   A single piece of information within a record.

File   A group of records stored together under a common label. A database consists of a group of related files.

File Management Systems   Database management programs that use only one file at a time and store information in clearly defined records and fields.

File Server   A network server that enables several client computers connected via a network to access files on a common hard-disk drive.

File Transfer Protocol (FTP)   A standard method for transferring files over the Internet.

Find and Replace   (*See* Search and Replace)

Flat-File Manager   (*See* File Management Systems)

Font   Type style; many printers are capable of using a variety of fonts.

Free-Format Database Programs   Database-management programs that do not require that the data be entered in a preset format.

Full-Scale Mock-Up System   A simulation in which everything appears to be exactly the same as reality.

Futurists   Experts who study trends and extrapolate from them to predict future events and conditions.

General-Purpose Database Programs   Computer programs designed for a wide variety of database applications.

General-Purpose Language   Any computer language designed to be flexible enough for use in a variety of applications.

Global Search and Replace   A function of a word processor that locates all occurrences of a particular word or phrase in a document and automatically replaces them with another word or phrase.

Gopher   A set of servers that provide an intuitive hierarchical menu system for accessing information over the Internet.

Gradebook   (*See* Computer Gradebook)

Grammar-Checker   A computer program that checks a text file or document for errors in punctuation, format, grammar, usage, and style and offers suggestions for correcting the errors.

Graphics Tablet   A device that can be used to transfer movement from a hand-operated "pencil" to the screen in creating graphic images on the computer monitor.

Hacker   A person who gains unauthorized entry into a computer system.

Hard Disk   A high-cost, high-density, rigid plastic or metal magnetic disk that has a storage capacity much greater than that of a floppy disk.

Hardware   The tangible, physical components of a computer or computer system.

HDTV (High-Definition Television) A proposed new standard for higher-resolution television.

Headers and Footers Special information, such as the title of the paper, the author's name, and so on, that can be automatically placed by a word processor at the top or bottom of each page of a document, at the option of the user.

Hertz (Hz) The unit of measurement of frequency of sound vibration. One hertz refers to one vibration or cycle per second.

High-Level Language A computer-programming language that uses commands that are similar to words found in a spoken language, such as English.

Home-Based Learning An organized educational program that is based in the home rather than in the school.

HyperCard One of the first microcomputer programs that implemented many features of hypertext and hypermedia.

Hypermedia A computer-based system that allows the user to quickly and easily access and navigate through information from a variety of media formats, including text, graphics, video, and sound.

Hypertext A computer-based system that allows the user to quickly and easily jump from one document to another, or to another section in the same document.

Impact Printer A printer with elements such as wires (dot-matrix) or preformed characters (daisy-wheel) that strike against a ribbon and paper to make impressions.

Initialize To prepare a blank disk for use as an information-storage medium.

Ink-Jet Printer A nonimpact printer that uses a stream of charged ink to form a character.

Input Information that is submitted to the computer for processing.

Input Device A device used to enter information into a computer.

Integrated Learning Systems (ILS) A computer-managed instructional system that provides a large set of interrelated computer-based instruction programs that are stored on a file server and are accessible from networked microcomputers.

Integrated Tools Software packages that integrate several computer tools—such as spreadsheets, database management, graphics, and word processing—into one comprehensive program. Such programs generally are able to easily transfer data from one application to another.

Intelligent Authoring Tools Computer programs that help users organize curricula and develop instructional packages consistent with best practice and research findings.

Intelligent Computer-Assisted Instruction (ICAI) (*See* Intelligent Tutoring Systems)

Intelligent Tutoring Systems A computer program that attempts to facilitate student learning through the use of sophisticated tutoring strategies that take into account the student's current knowledge and skill level and the knowledge base of an expert.

Interactive Fiction Software that places users in fictional settings where they become active characters who must make choices to advance story plot lines.

Interactive Language A language that allows user input while a program is executing.

Internal Memory A section of the computer where information can be stored permanently (ROM) or temporarily (RAM).

Internet A global network that connects thousands of local area and wide area networks from across the world.

Interpreted Language   A high-level language that is translated to machine language during execution of a program.

Joystick   An input device used to control a cursor or object on a computer monitor.

JPEG (Joint Photographic Experts Group)   Standard specification for picture compression.

Justification   Vertical alignment of the print at the left margin, right margin, both margins, or center of the page for left, right, full, or center justification, respectively.

K   A symbol that represents 1,000 (actually 1,024) storage locations or units.

Laptop/Palmtop Computer   A very lightweight computer that can be stored in a briefcase or easily carried.

Laser   An electronic device that generates a high-intensity narrow beam of light; Used to record and read information to and from optical discs, such as videodiscs and compact discs.

Laser Disc   (*See* Videodisc)

Laser Printer   A nonimpact printer that uses a laser to make high-quality impressions.

Learner-Control Strategy   An instructional procedure that allows students to make decisions about what lessons to study next, which instructional activities to engage in, and when to take tests.

Learning Outcomes   Goals or accomplishments students are expected to achieve as a result of a given learning effort.

Light Pen   A pen-shaped object that uses a photoelectric cell on its tip to draw images on a video screen.

Local Area Network (LAN)   A set of computers, usually located at a single site, such as a computer laboratory or school, connected together into a network with shared peripherals, such as a printer and network server.

Loop   A sequence of operations repeated two or more times.

Low-Level Language   A language that uses symbolic commands dissimilar to those that might be used in a spoken language, such as English. Assembly and machine languages are examples of low-level languages.

Machine Language   The native language of the computer; uses binary commands.

Mainframe Computer   The largest of the general-purpose computers, a mainframe typically supports a large institution with many people using the same computer at once.

Manipulatives   Physical objects that can be touched, felt, picked up, and arranged in different patterns as an aid to help children move from concrete to abstract ideas.

Mark-Sensing Device   A machine used to read special answer sheets on which students have marked their responses to test items. The device is often interfaced with a computer that analyzes the response data.

MECC   (*See* Minnesota Educational Computing Consortium)

Microcomputer   A computer designed for a single individual; Also called a *personal computer* or *home computer.*

MIDI (Musical Instrument Digital Interface)   A specification or standard agreed upon by music synthesizer manufacturers that makes it possible for electronic musical instruments and associated devices to communicate with one another using a common music language and hardware interface.

Minicomputer   A computer designed for multiple users—typically a small to medi-um-size department or work group.

Minnesota Educational Computing Consortium   A Minnesota-based organization es-tablished to facilitate and coordinate the educational use of computers throughout the state of Minnesota. Now a major source of educational software nationwide.

Modem   A device that modulates and demodulates information transmitted from one computer to another over telephone lines.

Monitor   A video display unit that is often used as an output device for a computer system.

Mosaic   A cross-platform program that provides a graphical-user interface for brows-ing the World Wide Web over the Internet.

Mouse   A small hand-held input device with a rotating ball underneath. A computer screen cursor or pointer may be controlled by moving the mouse on a desktop.

MPEG (Motion Picture Experts Group)   A standard specification for motion-video compression.

Multimedia   The integration of several types of media such as text, graphics, sound, animation, and motion video into a single computer application.

Multimedia Authoring System   (*See* Authoring System)

Network Operating System (NOS)   A computer program that manages files on a net-work server and controls the transmission of information across the network.

Network Server   A computer with associated peripherals, such as a large hard-disk drive, that are shared by several client computers connected together into a net-work. Network operating system software is often installed on the server to control the operation of the network. The server may provide print, file, applications, or communication services.

Networks   Several stand-alone or independent computers connected together by ca-bles or telephone lines. In a school computer laboratory, a network usually consists of several microcomputers connected together with a shared network server and printer. The local network may also be connected to remote networks such as the Internet.

Operand   A bit string indicating the memory location or data being operated upon by an operation in machine language.

Operation Code (Op Code)   A bit string code used to indicate the operation or process to be performed in machine language.

Optical Disk   A storage medium that holds large amounts of information. The infor-mation is read from the disk using an optical laser.

Optical Mark Reader   A machine capable of reading the location of small dots from paper, typically used to record test or survey information.

Optical Scanner   A machine capable of transferring information from the printed page to the computer through light-sensitive recognition devices.

Optical Videodisc Player   (*See* Videodisc Player)

Outliner   A computer program or feature of a word processor that allows for the cre-ation of an outline showing the various levels of document headings using corre-sponding levels of indention.

Output   Information that is received from the computer.

Output Device   A device that allows the user to receive information from a computer. Printers and monitors are common output devices.

Page Scrolling   Shifting the screen display forward or backward through the pages of a document.

Page Turners   Computer programs that present page after page of information without requiring meaningful response from the learner.

Pagination   Pages are numbered automatically by a word processor. If text is rearranged, pages are automatically renumbered.

Partial Mock-Up System   A simulation in which only part of the replicated task closely resembles reality.

Passive Simulation   A simulation in which the student merely spectates, having no interaction with the simulation medium.

Password   A secret word or number that must be typed on a keyboard in order to access a computer program or computerized account, thus limiting access to authorized persons.

Peripherals   Any device that is connected to and controlled by the computer.

Personal Computer   A computer designed for a single individual, sometimes referred to as a *microcomputer.*

Personal Workstation   A computer designed for a single individual that has exceptional capabilities, such as high resolution graphics.

Photo CD   A compact disc format developed by Eastman Kodak Company and Philips that provides for the storage and playback of consumer photographs.

Piracy   (*See* Software Piracy)

Pitch   Refers to the number of characters/inch output by a printer.

Pixel   A single dot or element on a video screen.

PLATO   A computer system developed at the University of Illinois for delivering computer-assisted instruction.

Plotter   An output device that uses pens to create high-resolution graphic images on paper.

Portable Computer   A computer designed for use by a single individual and light enough to be portable.

Presentation System   A component of a simulation that simulates the senses to give the illusion of the actual experience.

Print Server   A network server that enables several client computers connected via a network to share a common printer.

Printer   An output device that prints characters on paper.

Problem Solving   Those skills in critical thinking and/or logic that allow one to arrive at a previously unattained personal solution.

Program   (*See* Computer Program)

Projection LCD Plate   A liquid crystal plate that can be laid on top of an overhead projector to project a computer's visual output.

Proportional Spacing   The display or printing of text such that the amount of space occupied by each character varies according to the actual size of the character.

Public Information Services   Commercial businesses that provide telecommunication access, by the general public, to a wide variety of information stored on large computers.

Quantization Error   The difference between the actual amplitude of the sound or video wave curve for a given sample and the digital value used to represent the amplitude.

QuickTime   A trademark of Apple Computer to refer to a whole set of components that make it possible to manipulate, by computer, dynamic data that change over time such as digital video, sound, or animations.

RAM (Random-Access Memory)   Internal memory space designed for temporary storage of programs or data. Information in RAM can be easily changed but is volatile (lost when the computer is turned off).

RAM Disk   An area of random access memory that emulates a diskette or hard disk.

Random Frame Access   The capability of searching for and finding a specified single picture on a videodisc within a matter of seconds and without having to sequentially read through all previous frames on the disc.

Record   A set of data or information about a single item that is treated as a unit. Several records make up a file.

Relational-Database Programs   Database management programs that allow users to manipulate several related databases simultaneously.

Review Pool   A set of drill-and-practice items that have been previously learned but that need to be reviewed at spaced intervals. In sophisticated programs, each item may have a review date associated with it.

Rights   Different types of privileges to access various files on a network server. *Read-only* rights allow a user to only read or view a file; *read-write* rights allow a user to read, change, and/or write to a file.

ROM (Read-Only Memory)   Memory space that includes programs or data that may be read by the computer but that may not be erased or altered. Usually includes programs to boot the computer and a computer language, such as BASIC. The contents of ROM are not lost when the power is turned off.

Sampling   Part of the process of digitizing sound or video by representing the amplitude of a sound or video wave at discrete points in time as binary digits.

Search and Replace   A function of a word processor designed to automatically find a word or phrase and replace in with another.

Sequential Access Storage   Auxiliary storage that contains information arranged in a linear fashion, such as on a cassette tape.

Simulation   An experience designed to give the illusion of reality.

Skill-Centered Problem-Solving Software   Software specifically designed to teach and provide practice in problem-solving skills not in any particular subject area.

Software   Programs used to instruct a computer.

Software Piracy   Illegal copying of software.

Special-Purpose Database Programs   Computer programs tailored to meet the needs of specific database applications.

Special-Purpose Language   A language designed to serve a specific purpose, such as business applications, computer-assisted instruction, and so on.

Spell-Checker   A program or word-processing feature that compares the words in a document with an electronic dictionary to determine if the words are spelled correctly.

Still Frame   A picture from a film or video recording that contains no motion. With motion pictures, this is achieved by a series of identical frames. However, on an optical videodisc, a still frame may be only a single frame that is played over and over again.

String Value   Any combination of letters, numerals, or other symbols treated as a unit in a computer program.

Structured Language   A computer language that emphasizes modularity and minimizes the use of GOTO statements.

Subject-Centered Problem-Solving Software   Software specifically designed to teach and provide practice in problem-solving skills in a subject area.

Supercomputer   The fastest computer available, supercomputers are typically used to process extremely large amounts of data.

Syntax   Rules for writing program statements that can be recognized and executed by the computer.

Synthesized Sound   Use of computer program instructions to generate and play sounds, including music and human speech.

System Controls   In a simulation, anything that the student controls.

System Manager   In a simulation, either a person or a computer with decision-making capabilities. The system manager keeps track of what has happened and regulates the simulation accordingly.

Telecommunication   Use of electronic communication lines such as cables, telephone lines, or wireless connections (infrared, microwave, or satellite) to transfer information from one computer to another.

Teleconferencing   A method of holding conferences through the use of computers connected by telephone lines.

Terminal Emulation   The use of a microcomputer and communications software to simulate a computer terminal.

Terminal-Based CMI   A computer-managed instruction application that uses a microcomputer or terminal to administer test items directly to students. The computer selects the test items, scores and analyzes student responses, stores the results on diskette, and generates progress reports.

Test Generation   (*See* Computer Test Generation)

Test Scoring   (*See* Computer Test Scoring)

Text-Retrieval Program   A computer program that provides for sophisticated search strategies to rapidly locate words or phrases in large, free-format text files.

Thesaurus   A word-processing feature that displays a list of synonyms and antonyms for a selected word.

TICCIT (Time-shared, Interactive, Computer-Controlled Information Television)   An educational computer system developed by the MITRE Corporation, University of Texas, and Brigham Young University.

Time-Sharing System   Several computer terminals connected to a large central computer. The terminals usually have minimal processing capability since most processing functions are handled by the central computer.

Tool Applications   The computer assists the user in accomplishing a task.

Tutee Applications   The computer becomes the tutee and the user becomes the tutor. The user teaches the computer how to perform a task by writing and executing computer programs.

Tutor Applications   Computer programs that carry the burden of instruction by providing most of the necessary instructional events.

USENET   A popular electronic bulletin board information service, available over the Internet, covering a wide range of topics.

Variable   An alphanumeric name assigned to a value stored in a computer's memory. The value assigned to the variable may be changed.

Verbal Description Mock-Up System   A simulation in which only verbal descriptions are used to simulate the senses in an effort to represent reality.

Veronica   A service that provides keyword searches of menus of Gopher servers on the Internet.

Videodisc   A 12-inch platter, very similar in appearance to a 78 rpm phonograph record, that contains prerecorded video material.

Videodisc Player   An electronic player that reads prerecorded video material from a videodisc and displays it on an attached television screen. Optical videodisc players read the information with a laser beam and can display the video in normal motion, slow motion, or as a still frame. The individual video frames are randomly accessible. Most players can be interfaced to, and controlled by, a microcomputer.

Virtual Reality   Hardware and software configuration that simulates alternate realities.

Virus   A program that infects other programs by modifying them to include a version of itself. It often will infect any program it can reach.

Voice Generation   (*See* Synthesized Sound)

Voice Recognition   The ability for a machine to recognize (not just record) a sound.

Wide Area Network (WAN)   A set of computers and shared peripherals connected together in a network. The computers are usually located at several different sites connected by commercial transmission lines.

Word Processing   The use of electronic equipment to create, modify, and print written material.

Word Processor   The system or combination of hardware and software used to do word processing.

Word Wrap   When a word is too long to fit on the end of the line being typed, the entire word is automatically placed on the next line.

Working Pool   A subset of drill-and-practice items being studied.

World Wide Web (WWW)   A set of servers that provide hypertext links to access information over the Internet.

WORM Drive   An optical data storage device designed to write once and read data many times.

Index of Names
and Subjects

Index of Computer Software, Videodisc, and CD-ROM Titles